HAKE'S GUIDE TO TV COLLECTIBLES

AN ILLUSTRATED PRICE GUIDE

TED HAKE

WALLACE-HOMESTEAD BOOK COMPANY
RADNOR, PENNSYLVANIA

NOTICE

Values for items pictured in this book are based on the author's experience as well as actual prices realized for specific items sold through the catalogues of Hake's Americana & Collectibles Mail & Phone Bid Auctions. The prices are offered in this book for information purposes only. Many factors, including condition and rarity of the item, geographic location, and the knowledge and opinions of both buyers and sellers influence prices asked and prices paid. As the prices in this book are approximations, neither the author nor the publisher shall be held responsible for any losses that may occur through the use of this book in the purchase or sale of items.

MERCHANDISE COPYRIGHTS

For each illustrated item, we have acknowledged and identified the copyright holder and/or licensee wherever possible. We regret any omissions caused by error or the absence of identifying information on the item.

Copyright © 1990 by Ted Hake
All Rights Reserved
Published in Radnor, Pennsylvania 19089, by Wallace-Homestead,
a division of Chilton Book Company

No part of this book may be reproduced, transmitted, or stored
in any form or by any means, electronic or mechanical,
without prior written permission from the publisher

Color photography by Jim Conroy
Front cover photos: see the appropriate TV show title sections for listings of these items.
Back cover photos:
    Hopalong Cassidy Roto-Vue Lamp by Econolite, circa 1950; $300.
    Porcelain figure, 9" tall, by Beswick of England, in the likeness of Roy Rogers and
    Trigger, circa 1950s; $350.

Library of Congress Cataloging-in-Publication Data
Hake, Theodore L.
    Hake's guide to TV collectibles: an illustrated price guide/ by
  Ted Hake.
        p.   cm.
    Includes bibliographical references and index.
    ISBN 0-87069-571-1 (pbk.)
    1. Television broadcasting–Collectibles–Catalogs.   I. Title.
  II. Title: Guide to TV collectibles.
  PN1992.8.C64H35   1990
  791.45'75–dc20   90-70399
                                          CIP

Manufactured in the United States of America

2 3 4 5 6 7 8 9 0   9 8 7 6 5 4 3 2 1

CONTENTS

SHOW TITLES

APPENDIX

COLOR PAGES

Premiums and Pinback Buttons
Boxed Games
Lamps
Coloring Books
Dolls
Lunch Boxes
Figures
Model Kits

To Ted J. Hake, my son,
with the hope he finds a vocation as pleasurable as my own.

ACKNOWLEDGMENTS

For many years, I have wanted to present selected television collectibles and information from my auction catalogues in the format of a reference book for collectors.

My thanks go to Harry Rinker for providing the impetus to get the project underway. Ron Hoxter, Edna Jones, Tony Jacobson, Jim Conroy and the entire Wallace-Homestead staff provided all the support and cooperation so essential to an author.

Much appreciated is my staff for their many and varied contributions to the book: Deak Stagemyer, Betty Burkins, Joan Carbaugh, Alex Winter and Vonnie Burkins. Special thanks are due Russ King for photography, research and descriptions. Ellen Ehlenbeck provided the typesetting and recommendations on design.

As always, my wife Jonell and son Ted offered their support and understanding as the hours required to bring this book into being ticked away.

Ted Hake
July, 1990

INTRODUCTION

Television as a mass medium in the United States is only about 40 years old, a relatively young age to become the subject of today's widespread collectible interest.

Television existed in experimental or demonstrative form since the 1920s and, by 1938, New York City boasted better than 20,000 sets in service – the nation's only television location in any significant sense. World War II abruptly stopped the growth of television, and radio continued to be the country's mass medium throughout the war years. With the war's conclusion in 1945, the stage was set for television's re-birth.

Regular network service began in 1946 when NBC's New York City station, WNBT, started feeding a few programs to faraway Schenectady, N.Y., and Philadelphia, Pa. Other networks quickly formed and the television boom was on. By 1949, television sets were being purchased nationally at a rate of 100,000 units a week; by 1955 over a third of U.S. households owned a set; by 1985 nearly 100 percent of American homes had one or more sets.

TV's early era – tiny viewing screens, black-and-white picture only, limited broadcast hours – is quaint by today's standards. Despite these characteristics, the infancy and growing years created a devoted fandom: today's collectors of television memorabilia.

Potential television collectibles also emerged in the late 1940s in the form of locally issued viewing schedule guides and objects related to a few select children's shows, such as The Howdy Doody Show which began in 1947 and Hopalong Cassidy in 1949. As television popularity and programming expanded in the 1950s, so did the quantity of items destined to become collectibles. To many collectors, the two decades of the 1950s and 60s were the "golden" era of television's creativity and charm.

Virtually every U.S. citizen born since 1950 has been directly exposed to television, a unique characteristic which explains in large part the soaring interest in television collectibles. Over the years, many television shows, personalities, and characters captured the affections of large segments of the viewing public, making the objects related to these favorites true artifacts of American popular culture.

The scope of "popular culture" items necessarily has a broad definition. Generally speaking, such items are generated originally by mass appeal of one individual, specific products, eras or social movements. General utilitarian or household items – furniture, furnishings, etc. – are different, although valid, collecting specialities.

My own involvement with television collectibles began in the late 1960s. A few years earlier, while a graduate student at the New York University Film School, I began issuing sales lists devoted to presidential campaign items, primarily pin-back buttons. Often when buying political buttons, "non-political" buttons of all sorts came along with the group. I found these to be generally more colorful and interesting from a graphic viewpoint than the politicals, although collector interest was very limited.

A change in my educational plans took me to Philadelphia and the University of Pennsylvania's Annenberg School of Communication in 1967. My collectibles dealings also underwent a transformation: I established an auction catalogue format so customers could bid on the illustrated items by mail and telephone.

In addition to political collectibles, buttons related to product advertising, transportation, sports, expositions, wars and entertainment were now offered and eagerly purchased by collectors riding the crest of the nostalgia and collecting wave sweeping America in the late 60s. Objects other than buttons were soon included in the catalogue and Hake's Americana & Collectibles became the first collectibles business in the United States – perhaps in the world – specializing in the sale of popular culture collectibles through a mail and phone bid auction catalogue.

Our original handful of TV collectibles in each auction has now expanded to approximately 400 television-related items among the 3,000 total collectibles offered in each bi-monthly catalogue. During the past 20 years, winning bids for television collectibles have risen sharply. The number of bidders in this category has also increased steadily and collector enthusiasm shows every sign of continued escalation for both "oldtime" and new TV collectibles.

USING THIS BOOK

Collectibles related to over 200 television shows are pictured, described and evaluated in this book. The time period represented ranges from the late 1940s into the early 1980s and over 1,600 collectibles are included. The entry for each show is organized as follows:

SHOW LISTINGS: The book is arranged alphabetically by the first letter of the show's full title. The Contents lists all the shows by title and the index lists the names of people and characters.

DATES: Each show's network and the original first and last date of telecast is specified. Shows designated "Syndicated" were sold to local stations regardless of network affiliation. Live-action shows later produced as an animated cartoon series are noted. As there are other references devoted to television broadcast history, this book does not provide complete information about the history of each show. Many shows switched networks, underwent title changes, or went into syndication in the years following the original first-run telecasts.

COLLECTIBLES PICTURED: All collectibles shown in this book appeared in the mail and phone bid auction catalogues of Hake's Americana & Collectibles from 1982 to 1990. For the most part, collectibles pictured in this book were issued during the years that the show was being televised. For example, Buck Rogers collectibles can date back to the 1930s but those selected for this book are from the 1950 and 1979 television program depictions of the character.

DESCRIPTION: Quotation marks indicate words actually appearing on the item described. Information is provided about types of material used to make the item, sizes, parts to help determine completeness, and date of issue. Copyright notices and manufacturers are specified if known.

NUMBERING SYSTEM: Each television show covered in this guide is assigned a three-letter code abbreviated from the show's title. Each item is also numbered. Therefore any item in the book can be referenced by specifying the code and number that appear under the photo or at the beginning of each description. This numbering system is intended to facilitate communication about the items. Collectors or dealers are welcome to use these "Hake" numbers provided that advertisements, sales lists or auction catalogues acknowledge the title of this book, author and publisher.

PRICES: While the collectibles shown in this book were all offered in Hake's Americana & Collectibles mail and phone bid auction catalogues, the prices indicated are not auction "prices realized" for several reasons. Some items in every auction go unsold while some are subject to intense bidding by two or three bidders. In addition, auction prices for many of the items are outdated since they apply to items sold as long as eight years ago. The price estimates in this book are based on a combination of factors, including the author's experience, auction prices realized, sales lists and typical prices at collectibles shows. Prices assume the item is in excellent, complete condition without damage or significant wear. If an item is illustrated with a box or other packaging, the price reflects this fact. The same item, even in excellent condition, may have a value 25%-50% less if the box or packaging is missing. IMPORTANT: Prices specified are retail prices. Dealers have business expenses and need to make a profit on their sales to stay in business. Most dealers will pay 50%, or a bit more, of an item's retail value, depending upon their own circumstances and the ease with which an item can be sold.

TYPES OF TELEVISION COLLECTIBLES

TV collectibles are generally issued by either (1) a licensed manufacturer for retail sales or (2) as a premium by a sponsor of a particular program. Both are almost always directed to the youthful, rather than adult, viewer. Among the general collectibles – usually retailed originally – are board games, figural playsets, replica toys, lunch boxes, clothing and costumes, model kits, drinking glasses, jigsaw puzzles, storybooks, coloring books, punch-out books, and dolls including puppets, marionettes, and the popular vinyl "action" figures.

Premiums, usually from cereal companies or other food makers, are offered as part of the product packaging or by mail order with proof of purchase. As a result, premiums are often smaller sized items such as decoders, buttons or badges, toy rings, cards, booklets and the like. Premiums, to a lesser extent, have also been offered by fast-food franchises, as well as department stores and other non-food retailers.

Also popular among collectors are TV-related publications, not associated with a particular program, such as TV schedule guides and TV fan magazines.

Featured in this book are examples of the most frequently sought TV collectibles. Any types of items not included may certainly have collectible value but are likely to exist in insufficient variations to form a substantial collection. There are, of course, many known items for certain shows that are not pictured due to space limitations. Extremely popular shows and characters can generate hundreds of items. For this type show, we have selected items that are of interest due to factors such as rarity or their popularity with collectors.

When deciding what to collect, most people attempt to define their interests. It takes deep pockets, full time pursuit, and a huge warehouse to collect "all" TV collectibles. Some people prefer to concentrate on a single type of item (example, lunch boxes) regardless of the TV show or character depicted. Others prefer to collect any type of item as long as it relates to a particular show, personality or character. Others collect over a category of show types (examples: western, situation comedies, police and spy, or children's shows).

By any approach, the popularity of the show will be a reasonable gauge to the popularity (but not necessarily the value) of the collectible. In the case of an extremely popular show with few known collectibles, values will normally increase even further.

Collectibles are not limited to actual shows or show characters. In some instances, a character or creature from a TV commercial (examples: Speedy Alka-Seltzer, Tony The Tiger, Charlie The Tuna) have surfaced as collectibles. Overall, prime time programs and Saturday morning children's shows are responsible for the bulk of collectibles, although a few board games are based on popular daytime quiz or audience participation shows of the 1950s. Very few collectibles have resulted otherwise from daytime programming; there are, for instance, practically none from the "soaps."

AVAILABILITY

Many TV collectibles may still be found at flea markets or possibly even yard and garage sales. The true collector knows the enjoyment of a reasonably priced "find" at these sources, although extraordinary good luck is needed to locate items in complete and/or desirable condition from sources such as garage sales. Better possibilities exist at toy shows or scattered radio, film and television specialty shows, if travel to such shows is convenient. General antiques shops or co-ops are also a possibility but obviously the likelihood of finding desirable items will increase in geographic areas where actual TV broadcasting saturation and population density is heavier. Items produced specifically in distant countries, but based on American TV shows, are a bit limited in quantity but do appear in marketplaces in this country.

Beginning collectors usually concentrate attention on their local area but these resources can be quickly exhausted. Over the past 20 years, a number of publications and an even larger number of clubs have developed as collectors sharing similar interests discovered each other across the country. While some of the publications are very broad in scope and some of the clubs very specific in their interests, quite a few names and addresses that may serve as sources for information and collectibles are listed on pages 174-176 of this book. A good first step is to write (including a self-addressed stamped envelope) to inquire if a sample of the organization's publication is available. We also encourage written inquiries to Hake's Americana & Collectibles. Address your comments, questions or corrections to P.O. Box 1444Z, York, PA 17405.

CONDITION

As with any collectible, the better the condition the better the value. Collectors can reasonably expect that items will have been used, particularly if from the earlier years. Most collectors will accept normal minor wear of an item if otherwise in complete condition. Obvious heavy wear, defacement, permanent soiling, missing parts or accessories, all quickly reduce the value of an item. Original packaging, if it was provided, is equally important to the majority of collectors. Packaging includes boxes or cartons for larger toys, dolls or similar figures. The packaging frequently has copyright date, name of maker and other information that may not appear on the item itself. The value of a mail premium is enhanced greatly if the original mailing container and enclosure leaflets are intact. Repairs or cleaning of items may increase an item's value if done with care, caution and expertise. Crude repairs or harsh cleaning can just as easily decrease normal value.

The following terms and definitions are used to describe items in Hake's Americana & Collectibles auctions. These definitions are fairly standard throughout the collectibles hobby, although some dealers, who do not describe each item in detail, have adopted a shorthand system wherein the letter "C" for "Condition" and a number from 1 to 10 is used to designate condition. In this system "C10" equals "mint," "C9" equals "near mint" and so on. The system used at Hake's Americana is:

Mint	Flawless condition. Usually applied to items made of metal or items that are boxed or otherwise packaged. MIB stands for mint in box.
Near Mint (NM)	Just the slightest detectable wear but appearance is still like new.
Excellent (Exc.)	Only the slightest detectable wear, if any at all. Usually applied to buttons, paper and other non-metallic items. Also used for metallic items that just miss the near mint or mint level.
Very Fine (VF)	Bright clean condition. An item that has seen little use and was well cared for with only very minor wear or aging.
Fine	An item in nice condition with some general wear but no serious defects.
Very Good (VG)	Shows use but no serious defect and still nice for display. Metal items may have luster or paint wear. Paper items may have some small tears or creases.
Good	May have some obvious overall wear and/or some specific defect but still with some collectible value.
Fair	Obvious damage to some extent.
Poor	Extensive damage or wear.

At Hake's we grade our items conservatively; less than 1% of the 20,000 items we sell annually are returned due to an error in describing the item's condition. However, in the collectibles business much wishful thinking occurs regarding condition, particularly by less experienced dealers and among the general public attempting to sell off items found around the house. When purchasing items through the mail, it is best to have a clear understanding with the seller that the item can be returned for a refund if the item has more wear or damage than the seller specified.

VALUE

TV collectibles have sold well in Hake's auctions beginning with the first catalogues in the late 1960s. A sampling of some popular types of TV collectibles offered in our auctions between 1970 and 1990 show a significant upward trend in prices paid by bidders.

	Buttons	Games	Lunch Boxes	Dolls/Figures	Premiums
1970	$ 3	$ 10	$ 8	$ 15	$ 12
1975	9	12	14	15	15
1980	20	37	17	30	29
1985	31	41	60	83	71
1990	55	78	122	132	113

Average prices paid for "scarce" items in these categories over 20 years.

Remember, these typical increases apply to "scarce" collectibles in excellent condition – not to commonly available items.

Many factors come into play to determine the value of a TV collectible. Supply and demand is the bottom line influenced by:

1. CONDITION – wear and damage obviously detract from an item's value. Many price guides admonish collectors to accept only "mint" items and the resulting competition for the relatively few items that truly meet this criteria results in premium prices for "mint" items. Original boxes, particularly for toys, can often add 50% or more over the price for a comparable unboxed example. The collector who can emotionally live with less than "mint" items has a powerful bargaining chip and can often acquire items that are visually perfect for a fraction of the cost for items truly "mint."

2. COMPLETENESS – this factor applies to items with many parts or accessories. Typical items are playsets and figures. If the item was played with, there is a good chance small pieces were lost. In the absence of a box or instruction sheet, it is difficult to determine if in fact the item is complete so it is best to have an understanding with the seller if the item is being sold as complete or as is.

3. DESIGN FEATURES – aesthetics play a role in determining value. Items made with quality materials, excellent graphics, or some special unique feature will set themselves apart from similar but less appealing objects and command a higher price.

4. CROSSOVER INTEREST – quite a few items appeal to more than one group of collectors. For example, a "Cheyenne" boxed board game could be of interest to game collectors, western collectors and fans of Clint Walker. Each type of collector probably has his or her own opinion of the item's value, but this sort of multiple interest can create higher asking prices and/or spirited auction bidding.

5. RARITY – competition for rare items related to popular shows or characters stimulates high prices, but rarity alone does not force prices up. There are many rare items available at reasonable prices for those shows not among the ranks of the most popular. Likewise, if little merchandise was produced for a show, the item may be exceedingly rare but not sought after because there is not enough variety to inspire the attempt to build a collection.

6. DISTRIBUTION – sometimes items were not distributed evenly throughout the country. Small manufacturers did not get their products into as many stores and often more expensive items were

offered by a limited number of stores, usually in metropolitan areas. The offer of premiums was also frequently limited to certain geographical areas.

7.   LOCATION – prices do tend to be higher on the east and west coasts. Along with denser populations are larger concentrations of collectors looking for similar items.

8.   EMOTIONS – both dealers and collectors of TV collectibles have a fond appreciation for the objects, which accounts for the excitement and satisfaction derived from the quest to obtain them. These emotions also come into play in the pricing of items and the decision whether or not to make a purchase. Balancing the factors just discussed, as well as becoming aware of the state of the market through show attendance, review of sales list prices and auction results, and communication with other collectors and dealers, will all contribute to making the correct decision when faced with the crucial question – should I or shouldn't I pay this much?

Remember, the price estimates in this book assume excellent, complete condition without damage or any significant wear. These prices are based on the author's experience, auction prices realized, sales lists and typical show prices. There are no absolutely correct prices regarding collectibles. The goal is to enjoy the search and continued satisfaction with the objects once purchased.

REPRODUCTIONS

As items become valuable and original examples dwindle, TV collectible reproductions can be expected as in other collectible areas. Fortunately, manufacturing costs for many types of items are prohibitive and, therefore, reproductions are not a serious problem with a few exceptions.

Stretching the definition of a TV collectible to include Elvis and the Beatles, it should be noted that extra care is needed in these areas. While there are reproductions of some items, there are even more "fantasy" items. Fantasy items are those things that were not licensed and did not even exist during the time period that produced other original collectibles. Fantasy collectibles are produced later on and intended to appeal to (or defraud) collectors who are unaware that the items are newly made, never licensed, and not from the time period of the personality's or character's original popularity.

One other area where reproductions and fantasy items exist is western hero collectibles. A few pin-back buttons depicting Roy Rogers, Hopalong Cassidy and Gene Autry exist as reproductions. There is also a recently issued fabric scarf with an image of Hoppy riding Topper printed in thick black ink.

By and large, reproductions and fantasy items are not a serious problem for TV collectors. Still, an attempt should be made to acquaint oneself with the minute variations that may exist in a chosen specialty of collecting. Purchases preferably should be made from a reputable dealer who guarantees authenticity, completeness, and condition.

THE FUTURE

Television memorabilia is firmly established as a desirable Americana collectible. There is every reason to believe that games, toys, figures, etc., issued in the 1980s and 1990s will become tomorrow's collectibles to yet another generation.

Generally speaking, a collector of today's items for the future should keep in mind several factors. Figural (dimensional) items are more desirable to more people than paper items. Original complete packing, commonly referred to as MIB (Mint in Box) will greatly enhance value as the item evolves from face value to collectible value. Complex playsets appear to have a very strong future, if complete and in choice condition. Premiums, particularly if limited in distribution, also hold potential.

While new shows will continue to generate new collectibles, equally important to sustained collectible value is the fact that new generations are exposed to classic favorites of the past through syndicated re-runs and videos. Some portion of this constantly evolving audience will most likely join the ranks of TV collectors to sustain and renew the interest in the broad spectrum of TV collectibles. As "American" television programming becomes available globally, collectors from distant lands are also emerging. TV collectibles, and other popular culture items, are indeed gaining international interest.

THE ADDAMS FAMILY

ABC: September 18, 1964 – September 2, 1966

Prime time macabre comedy based on the cartoons of Charles F. Addams; a Saturday morning animated version followed on NBC September 8, 1973 – August 30, 1975. Items from the 1964-1966 series normally have copyright by Filmways TV Productions Inc. Items from the 1973-1975 series normally have copyright by Hanna-Barbera Studios. Main characters: Gomez (John Astin), Morticia (Carolyn Jones), Uncle Fester (Jackie Coogan), Lurch (Ted Cassidy), Grandmama (Blossom Rock), Pugsley (Ken Weatherwax), Wednesday (Lisa Loring).

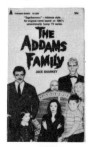 

ADF-1   ADF-2

ADF-1. "THE ADDAMS FAMILY" 1965 PAPERBACK LIBRARY Edition novel with 176 pages. **$5.**

ADF-2. "THE ADDAMS FAMILY" 1965 SAALFIELD COLORING BOOK #4595, 8.5x11". **$25.**

ADF-3   ADF-4

ADF-3. "TV GUIDE" weekly issue for October 30, 1965 with Addams Family cover article. **$20.**

ADF-4. "THE ADDAMS FAMILY" 1965 COLORFORMS TOY "Cartoon Kit" of thin vinyl adhering character body parts and insert scene board in 8x12" box. **$50.**

ADF-5

ADF-5. "THE ADDAMS FAMILY GAME" 1964 boxed game by Ideal Toy Co., consisting of playing board, spinner and character cards in 10x19.5" box. **$50.**

ADF-6

ADF-6. "THE THING FROM THE ADDAMS FAMILY" circa 1964-1966 mechanical plastic bank featuring a hand which snaps outward to snatch coin inserted in slot. Pictured are two panels from 3.5x4.5x4.5" box plus bank in vertical position. **$50.**

ADF-7   ADF-8

ADF-7. "UNCLE FESTER'S MYSTERY LIGHT BULB FROM THE ADDAMS FAMILY" a 4" glass bulb designed to light when pressed against an AA battery, in 5x7" box circa 1964-1966. **$50.**

ADF-8. UNCLE FESTER 1964 CHARACTER FIGURE by Remco Plastics with hard plastic body, movable soft vinyl head, and total height of 4.5". A simulated frog is held in the hand. **$150.**

ADF-9   ADF-10

ADF-9. "MORTICIA" HAND PUPPET © 1964 Ideal Toys. Soft vinyl head with fabric hand cover body printed with her name and clothing design. Total height is 10.5". **$75.**

ADF-10. "THE ADDAMS FAMILY" 45-RPM PROMOTIONAL RECORD circa 1964 on RCA Victor label, featuring the show's "Main Theme" music on Side A. Both sides are performed by Vic Mizzy and Side B is theme for the "Kentucky Jones" show. **$20.**

ADF-11

ADF-12

ADF-11. "THE ADDAMS FAMILY GAME" 1973 BOXED GAME by Milton Bradley based on the 1973-1975 animated cartoon series. Box is 8.5x16.5". **$25.**

ADF-12. "THE ADDAMS FAMILY" STEEL LUNCH BOX by King-Seeley Co. ©1974; based on the 1973-1975 animated cartoon series. **$40.**

THE ADVENTURES OF CHAMPION

CBS: September 30, 1955 – February 3, 1956

Live action western series produced by Gene Autry featuring his Wonder Horse Champion, and German shepherd dog, "Rebel," plus juvenile star Barry Curtis as Ricky North and Jim Bannon as his Uncle Sandy. Items are normally copyrighted Flying A Productions.

ACH-1   ACH-2

ACH-1. "GENE AUTRY AND CHAMPION" 6.5x8" Little Golden Book with 24 pages and 1956 ©by Simon & Schuster. **$10.**

ACH-2. "CHAMPION THE WONDER HORSE" 8.5x11" English-published book with 124 pages and 1958 Gene Autry © **$15.**

ACH-3   ACH-4

ACH-3. "CHAMPION THE WONDER HORSE" 8.25x11" English-published book with 124 pages and 1957 Gene Autry © **$15.**

ACH-4. "CHAMPION THE WONDER HORSE" 8.25x11" English-published book with 124 pages and 1958 Gene Autry © **$15.**

THE ADVENTURES OF JIM BOWIE

ABC: September 7, 1956 – August 29, 1958

Western starring Scott Forbes as Bowie, a 19th century knife-wielding American adventurer. Items are normally copyrighted Jim Bowie Enterprises.

AJB-1   AJB-2   AJB-3

AJB-1. "THE ADVENTURES OF JIM BOWIE" WHITMAN BIG LITTLE BOOK #1648 from "TV Series" ©1958 in 4.5x5.75" size with 276 pages. **$10.**

AJB-2. JIM BOWIE HARTLAND FIGURE. Plastic figures of Bowie and his horse Blaze from "Western And Historical Horsemen" series by Hartland Plastics, Inc. circa late 1950s. Complete figure includes saddle, hat, rifle and miniature Bowie knife. Bowie is depicted in simulated dark brown buckskin jacket and tan buckskin trousers. **$200.**

AJB-3. "JIM BOWIE" RCA VICTOR 45-RPM RECORD with theme song of the show. **$15.**

THE ADVENTURES OF KIT CARSON

Syndicated 1951 – 1955 (104 Episodes)

Western adventure series starring Bill Williams as Kit Carson and also featuring Don Diamond as El Toro. Items are normally copyrighted MCA Television.

AKC-1

AKC-1. "KIT CARSON" KERCHIEF KIT early 1950s premium from Coca-Cola in 7x9" mailing envelope that also includes 4-page folder. Kerchief is 21x23" with red/green/white design. **$50.**

| AKC-2 | AKC-3 | AKC-4 |

AKC-2. "KIT CARSON KERCHIEF" POSTER. A 16x24" paper poster by Coca-Cola with 1953 ©. Carson is pictured wearing the kerchief and design colors are red/green/white. **$50.**

AKC-3. "KIT CARSON COLOR KIT" 10x12" cardboard folder containing coloring pictures, crayons and magic slate with pencil. 1957 © by Lowe Co. **$25.**

AKC-4. "COWBOYS" TRU-VUE FILM CARD SET with full color photos for stereo viewing. Three cards feature Bill Williams as Kit Carson, Gail Davis as Annie Oakley, and Rex Allen. Card numbers are T-7, T-8, T-10. Mid-1950s. **$20.**

THE ADVENTURES OF OZZIE AND HARRIET

ABC: October 3, 1952 – September 3, 1966

One of TV's longest running situation comedies starring the Nelson family as themselves including sons Ricky and David.

| AOH-1 | AOH-2 |

AOH-1. "THE NELSON FAMILY" 3.5x5.5" exhibit card showing the family around an ABC microphone with facsimile signature of each. Card is circa early 1950s as radio version of show was concurrent with television version through 1954. **$12.**

AOH-2. "OZZIE AND HARRIET – DAVID AND RICKY COLORING BOOK" 11x14" undated but early 1950s Saalfield book. **$35.**

| AOH-3 | AOH-4 |

AOH-3. "TV GUIDE" weekly issue for May 15, 1953 with cover article "The Nelson Knack: Bringing Up Ricky" although both Ricky and brother David are pictured in cover photo. **$10.**

AOH-4. "THE ADVENTURES OF OZZIE AND HARRIET" 3x6x11" retail box which contained "Peter Paul Almond Joy" candy bars. Lid inscription also includes titles of other sponsored shows, "Maverick" and "Roaring 20s." Circa late 1950s. **$60.**

THE ADVENTURES OF RIN TIN TIN

ABC: October 15, 1954 – August 28, 1959

Half-hour western series featuring German shepherd kept by members of the 101st Cavalry, also known as "The Fighting Blue Devils." Items normally will have copyright of Screen Gems Inc. Main characters: Rusty (Lee Aaker), Lt. Ripley "Rip" Masters (Jim L. Brown), Sgt. Biff O'Hara (Joe Sawyer), Cpl. Boone (Rand Brooks).

| ART-1 | ART-2 |

ART-1. "RIN-TIN-TIN" DOLL with original tag picturing him and Rusty plus plastic collar inscribed with Rin-Tin-Tin name. Toy is about 4x7x11" with rubber head stitched to plush stuffed body. 1959 © by Smile Novelty Toy Co. **$60.**

ART-2. "RIN TIN TIN DOG SUPPLY CENTER" 7x20" red/white/blue lithographed tin sign from a store rack display. © 1956. **$50.**

ART-3

ART-5

ART-4

ART-3. "RIN-TIN-TIN" FIGURE 2x6.5x9" painted hard plastic with original tag on cord around neck. Tag is printed on each side with photo of him plus his name and that of "Fighting Blue Devils." Realistically molded and colored. Late 1950s. **$75.**

ART-4. "RIN-TIN-TIN" ONE-PIECE FABRIC COSTUME in brown/tan/black circa 1956. Costume came originally with face mask. **$35.**

ART-5. "RIN-TIN-TIN MAGIC ERASABLE PICTURES" set by Transogram ©1956. Kit consists of 12 different erasable pictures plus crayons and sharpener. Our photo shows 8x17" box lid plus contents. **$25.**

ART-6   ART-7

ART-6. "T-VUE TIME" circa 1960 weekly issue of television guide from the Baltimore Sunday American newspaper with full color photo of Lee Aakers as Rusty on front cover. Year not indicated but issue is for week of June 30. **$10.**

ART-7. "RIN TIN TIN FORT APACHE" playset #3627 by Marx Toys circa late 1950s. Set is in 5x11x22" cardboard box with tin and plastic pieces and scaled figures to form a play fort with blockhouses, cabin, cavalry men, Indians, horses and figures of Rusty, Rin-Tin-Tin, Lt. Masters. **$350.**

ART-8

ART-10

ART-9

ART-8. "RIN-TIN-TIN AND RUSTY" 3" yellow plastic mug with picture in black/blue. Nabisco premium from the 1954-1956 years of its sponsorship. Inscription above picture is "Yo, Ho! Rinty!" **$30.**

ART-9. "THE ADVENTURES OF RIN TIN TIN – THE FIGHTING BLUE DEVILS – 101st CAVALRY OUTFIT" consisting of black leather holster, belt and cartridge clip with three wooden bullets on 10x13" store display card. A fourth item may originally have been held on card. By Empire Novelty Co. ©1955. **$75.**

ART-10. "RIN-TIN-TIN AND RUSTY" CHILD'S NECKTIE showing them with facsimile signature of Rusty and facsimile paw print of Rinty. Circa 1956. **$20.**

ART-11   ART-12

ART-11. "RIN-TIN-TIN AND RUSTY – FIGHTING BLUE DEVILS" BLACK FELT HAT with blue/white/yellow picture patch on front edge of upturned brim. Crown of hat is trimmed with band of yellow braid. Nabisco premium from 1954-1956 years of sponsorship. **$35.**

ART-12. "SEE RIN-TIN-TIN ON ABC-TV FOR 'P.F.' CANVAS SHOES" 7x12" paper pennant with photo of Rinty holding a peace pipe while seated between two Indians. Pennant was store display for sneakers made by B.F.Goodrich. Late 1950s. **$30.**

THE ADVENTURES OF ROBIN HOOD
CBS: September 26, 1955 - September 22, 1958

British import series starring Richard Greene in the title role. Items are normally copyrighted Sapphire Films Ltd. or Official Film Corp.

ARH-1   ARH-2

ARH-1. "ROBIN HOOD" METAL LUNCH BOX by Aladdin Industries ©1957. **$50.**

ARH-2. "ROBIN HOOD" 11x13" frame tray jigsaw puzzle with color photo portrait. By Built-Rite ©1955 Official Film Corp. **$20.**

ARH-3   ARH-4

ARH-3. "THE ADVENTURES OF ROBIN HOOD" GAME by Bettye-Bye Products circa 1955-1958. Game is in 14.5x20.25" box with playing pieces featuring a molded thin three-dimensional plastic game board formed in replica of Sherwood Forest terrain. Other game parts are cardboard chips representing horses, chests of gold, shields and armor, bows and arrows. ©by Official Films Corp. **$40.**

ARH-4. "ROBIN HOOD SHIELDS" on 10.5x11" cardboard store display. Card holds 12 silvered metal badges, each with his name and raised portrait plus decorative red cut glass stone. Card has Official Film Corp. © circa 1955-1958. **FULL CARD $75. EACH BADGE $5.**

THE ADVENTURES OF SUPERMAN

Syndicated July 1951 - November 1957
(104 Episodes)

Live action series starring George Reeves as Superman and his alter-ego Clark Kent, offered in syndication but telecast mostly by ABC. Animated cartoon versions for Saturday morning viewers appeared on CBS September 10, 1966 through September, 1970 under various titles including Superman, New Adventures Of Superman, Superman-Aquaman Hour, Batman-Superman Hour. In 1973 an animated Superman was part of the Superfriends cartoon series. Items will normally have copyright by National Comics Publication Inc., or National Periodical Publication Inc. Main characters: Lois Lane (Phyllis Coates 1951-1953, Noel Neill 1953-1957), Perry White (John Hamilton), Jimmy Olsen (Jack Larson), Inspector William Henderson (Robert Shayne).

ASM-1   ASM-2

ASM-1. GEORGE REEVES AS SUPERMAN PHOTO CARD 5x7" black-and-white picture post card with facsimile signature "Best Wishes, George Reeves." Reverse has advertising and pictures of three covers of comic books from National Comics Publications. Early 1950s. **$40.**

ASM-2. SUPERMAN 3-D KELLOGG'S CUT-OUT PICTURE 4.5x6.5" full color assembled cardboard cut-out from the back of Kellogg's cereal box circa 1953-1957. Superman portrait is mounted in front of background for slightly dimensional image. Inscription across bottom of simulated frame is "Best Wishes From Your Friend Superman." **$75.**

ASM-3

ASM-4

ASM-3. "CALLING SUPERMAN – A GAME OF NEWS REPORTING" 1954 Transogram boxed game including playing board, two spinners, playing cards, plastic playing pieces plus two die-cut cardboard figures of Superman with wood bases. Our photo shows lid plus detail of sticker label from game board. **$60.**

ASM-4. "SUPERMAN OFFICIAL 2-PIECE KIDDIE SET" boxed set of rubber swim fins and a pair of underwater goggles, each printed with Superman picture or "S" symbol. Mid-1950s in 3x5x8" box. **$75.**

ASM-5

ASM-5. "SUPERMAN OFFICIAL 8-PIECE JUNIOR QUOIT SET" boxed indoor-outdoor game holding four quoits and two bases, all made of rubber plus two wood pegs, instruction booklet and membership card for the "Superman Official Sports Club." Box is 5.5x12". **$75.**

ASM-6   ASM-7

ASM-6. "SUPERMAN KRYPTON ROCKET" boxed 1956 propulsion toy featuring a Krypton Generating Pump, Reserve Fuel Tank, and Krypton Rocket Missile. Propulsion fuel is water. Box is 2x9x9.5". **$300.**

ASM-7. SUPERMAN BELT. Red plastic belt with large aluminum buckle with "S" symbol in bright red and yellow. Belt is 28" long and buckle is 2x2.75". Early 1950s Kellogg's premium. **$150.**

ASM-8   ASM-9

ASM-8. SUPERMAN OUTFIT. Fabric costume of red pants and cape, blue shirt with red/blue/yellow Superman logo on the chest plus yellow belt. Inscription on shirt bottom is "Remember – This Suit Won't Make You Fly – Only Superman Can Fly." 1950s. **$75.**

ASM-9. "SUPERMAN SPACE SATELLITE LAUNCHER SET" 1950s Kellogg's premium consisting of plastic gun and satellite wheel which is fired from it. Set comes with instruction sheet and original mailing box from Kellogg's. **$125.**

ASM-10   ASM-11   ASM-12

ASM-10. "OFFICIAL MEMBER SUPERMAN CLUB" 3.5" full color button from 1966 with thin clear acetate film over image. **$15.**

ASM-11. "SUPERMAN PAINT BY NUMBER BOOK" 11x13.5" Whitman book from 1966 with "forty authorized pictures" plus color chart on back cover as coloring guide. **$20.**

ASM-12. "SUPERMAN" THERMOS 6.5" metal thermos with red plastic cap. By King-Seeley Co. ©1967. Thermos came originally in item ASM-13. **$40.**

ASM-13   ASM-14

ASM-13. "SUPERMAN" STEEL LUNCH BOX By King-Seeley Co. ©1967. **$75.**

ASM-14. "SUPERMAN PLASTIC ASSEMBLY KIT" ©1963 by Aurora Plastics in 2.5x5x13" box. **$150.**

ASM-15   ASM-16   ASM-17

ASM-15. "SUPERMAN" RECORD AND CLUB MEMBERSHIP KIT from 1966 consisting of 33 1/3 LP record, Superman Club card, shoulder patch and 1" lithographed tin club button. Record reads the story from the original comic magazine story. Box is 12.5" square. **$40.**

ASM-16. "SUPERMAN SUPERWATCH" 6x9" store card holding plastic toy watch with movable hands. Watch is centered in plastic replica of "S" chest symbol. By Toy House ©1967. **$30.**

ASM-17. "SUPERMAN AND SUPERGIRL PUSH BUTTON PUP-PETS" boxed 1968 set © by Kohner containing pair of mechanical figure puppets which move when plunger in bottom of base is depressed. Box is 2x6x7" with cellophane display window. **$75.**

ASM-18. "SUPERMAN MOVIE VIEWER" on 5.5x7.5" store display card. 1965 plastic hand viewer with two boxes of film. **$20.**

ASM-19. "SUPERMAN" FULL COLOR LINEN-LIKE CLOTH PICTURE with rod inserted through top edge for hanging. Printed depictions are of Superman against a city skyline, smashing a rock, and flying in space near planets. 16x25" with ©1966. **$150.**

ASM-20. "SUPERMAN" VINYL WALLPAPER SECTION ©1966 from original 20.5" wide wall covering roll. Action picture elements are repeated and include Superman crashing through a wall, fighting a dragon, lifting an automobile and deflecting a cannon shot. Scenes repeat every 25 inches. Complete 25" section. **$25.**

ASM-21   ASM-22

ASM-23

ASM-21. SUPERMAN "BOONTONWARE CHILDREN'S SET" 3x8x16" store display box holding 7" plate, 5.5" bowl, 3.5" cup, all white plastic with Superman printed image. By Boontonware Molding Company ©1966. **$75.**

ASM-22. "SUPERMAN" WHITE GLASS MUG with picture image in red and blue. Reverse picture is Superman breaking a chain. 1966. **$20.**

ASM-23. SUPERMAN "AVON" BOTTLE 9.5" tall vinyl figural that held bubble bath liquid. Superman is depicted towering over city skyscrapers. ©1978. **$10.**

ASM-24

ASM-24. "SUPERMAN CARDS" 1966 Topps Gum store display box holding original 24 gum packages, each with black/white picture cards with scenes from the television series. Display box is 2x4x8". **EACH PACK $10. COMPLETE BOX $300.**

ASM-18   ASM-19   ASM-20

THE ADVENTURES OF WILD BILL HICKOCK

Syndicated 1951 – 1958 (113 Episodes)

Western adventure series starring Guy Madison as Marshal James Butler (Wild Bill) Hickock and Andy Devine as his sidekick Jingles B. Jones. Although syndicated, the series was seen regularly in later years of syndication on both CBS and ABC, in addition to a concurrent radio version on Mutual from 1951-1956. Items will normally have a Desilu Corporation copyright.

ABH-1

ABH-1. "WILD BILL HICKOCK AND JINGLES" FRAME TRAY INLAY JIGSAW PUZZLES by Built-Rite circa 1950s. Each is 11x13.5" with full color photo scene from the series. **EACH $20.**

ABH-2   **ABH-3**

ABH-2. "PONY EXPRESS GAME" by Built-Rite Co. ©1956. Box is 7.5x14" with playing board and small cardboard markers which also may be used for playing conventional game of checkers on reverse side of playing board. **$25.**

ABH-3. "FAMOUS TV STARS" BOXED JIGSAW PUZZLE from series © 1956 by Built-Rite. Puzzle picture is full color photo of 100 large pieces in 6.5x8" box. **$15.**

ABH-4   **ABH-5**

ABH-4. "WILD BILL HICKOCK AND JINGLES" LUNCH BOX AND THERMOS. Steel box and metal thermos with plastic cap, issued as set by Aladdin ©1955. **LUNCH BOX $75. THERMOS $40.**

ABH-5. "WILD BILL HICKOCK AND JINGLES 1957 SAALFIELD COLORING BOOK with cover art on glossy paper. **$35.**

ABH-6

ABH-6. "WILD BILL HICKOCK AND JINGLES OFFICIAL COWBOY OUTFIT" by M. H. Henry Ltd. Dundas, Ont. Can. ©1955. Display box holds leather double holster set with 9" metal cap guns plus "Marshal" metal clip badge. Box is 11.5x11.5x2". **$150.**

ABH-7   **ABH-8**

ABH-7. "KELLOGG'S SUGAR POPS" complete 2x7.5x9.5" cereal box picturing Devine as Jingles on front panel. Front and back panel have picture ad for "Exploding Battleship" premium. Circa 1960. **$50.**

ABH-8. "KELLOGG'S SUGAR CORN POPS" complete 2x7.5x9.5" cereal box with picture of Devine as Jingles on front panel. Back panel has picture ad for Wild Bill Hickock Treasure Map premium. 1952-1954. **$50.**

ALL IN THE FAMILY

CBS: January 12, 1971 – September 21, 1983

One of the classic family situation comedies which attained highest popularity rating for five consecutive years during original format era. The format and supporting cast characters changed in the fall of 1979 as show became Archie Bunker's Place, based on his bar rather than domestic life. Featured was Carroll O'Connor as Archie Bunker with cast members in the original version of Edith Bunker (Jean Stapleton), Gloria Bunker (Sally Struthers), and Mike Stivic (Rob Reiner). Items will normally have copyright of Tandem Productions Inc.

AIF-1   **AIF-2**

AIF-1. "ALL IN THE FAMILY CARD GAME" © 1972 Milton Bradley in 6x10" box. Cards have full color photos of cast members and other playing pieces are "Ding Bat Tally" score cards. **$8.**

AIF-2. "ALL IN THE FAMILY GAME" ©1972 Milton Bradley in 7x11" box. Game parts include a question book plus paper sheets for recording answers to questions. **$10.**

AIF-3   AIF-4

AIF-3. "ARCHIE BUNKER FOR PRESIDENT" 5" glazed white ceramic beer mug with Bunker portrait and lettering in red and blue © 1976. **$8.**

AIF-4. EDITH BUNKER/GLORIA CAMPAIGN GLASSES. Pair of 5" clear drinking glasses for Archie Bunker's 1972 'campaign' for the presidency. Each glass has red/white illustration with Edith touted for "Foist Lady" and Gloria for "Consumer Affairs." Campaign slogans for Archie are on reverse side of each glass. **EACH $6.**

THE ALVIN SHOW

CBS: October 4, 1961 – September 5, 1962

Prime time animated cartoon series featuring the trio of singing "Chipmunks" and their songwriter-manager David Seville, a name used by actual creator Ross Bagdasarian. Alvin, Simon and Theodore were the Chipmunk names. The series continued after its prime time run, on Saturday mornings by both CBS and NBC. Items may have copyright of either Bagdasarian or Monarch Music Company.

ALV-1   ALV-2   ALV-3

ALV-1. ALVIN THE CHIPMUNK STUFFED CLOTH DOLL with original cloth tag by Knickerbocker Toys ©1963. Cloth body 13.5" tall with vinyl head. **$25.**

ALV-2. THE CHIPMUNKS SOAKY CONTAINERS. Set of 3 "Soaky" bubble soap containers depicting Alvin, Theodore and Simon. Each is 10" tall with hard plastic head and soft vinyl body. Circa mid-1960s. **EACH $8.**

ALV-3. "CHIPMUNKS" WHITE VINYL PLASTIC WALLET with 3x3.5" closed size. 1959 ©from song record era prior to TV series. **$15.**

ALV-4

ALV-4. "THE THREE CHIPMUNKS 'BIG RECORD' NEW SURPRISE GAME" 1960 board game by Hassenfeld Bros. Inc. (Hasbro) in 8.5x16.5" box. Playing board has design of large 45-rpm record in center. From song era prior to TV series. **$25.**

AMERICAN BANDSTAND

ABC: August 5, 1957 - August 30, 1963

One of television's longest-running musical series, originally the first network series devoted solely to rock-and-roll music, with continuation under different titles and formats into the late 1970s. The series was an offshoot of a Philadelphia local show of the early 1950s. In its 1957 format, the series went into an ABC prime time slot from October 7, 1957 through December 30th of that year. The original series, and other versions to follow under different titles, were hosted by Dick Clark. Items are normally copyrighted American Broadcasting Co.

AMB-1   AMB-2

AMB-1. "DICK CLARK OFFICIAL AMERICAN BANDSTAND YEARBOOK" undated but circa 1959 magazine with 40 pages of photos of guest stars and scenes from the American Bandstand show. Contents include poll selection of Elvis Presley as favorite male vocalist and Annette Funicello most promising female vocalist. 9x12". **$35.**

AMB-2. "DICK CLARK" DOLL 25" tall with stuffed cloth body, rubber head and hands, and fabric clothing outfit consisting of jacket with facsimile signature, vest and necktie, trousers, saddle shoes. Doll is by Juro circa late 1950s. **$200.**

AMB-3   AMB-4

AMB-3. "TV GUIDE" weekly issue for October 4, 1958 with cover photo plus 3-page article on Clark and his American Bandstand. **$15.**

AMB-4. "DICK CLARK/AMERICAN BANDSTAND/SECRET DIARY" vinyl-covered diary ledger with metal fastener and closed size of 4x5.5". Late 1950s. **$40.**

THE ANDY GRIFFITH SHOW

CBS: October 3, 1960 – September 16, 1968

Rural situation comedy starring Griffith as Sheriff Andy Taylor in community of Mayberry, North Carolina. The show was later syndicated as "Andy of Mayberry" and a spin-off series "Mayberry, R.F.D." continued from 1968 into 1971 although minus Griffith as Sheriff Taylor. Main characters: Deputy Barney Fife (Don Knotts), son Opie (Ronnie Howard), Aunt Bee Taylor (Frances Bavier), Gomer Pyle (Jim Nabors). Items are normally copyrighted Mayberry Productions.

ANG-1   ANG-2

ANG-1. "TV GUIDE" for week of January 28, 1961 with cover photo of Griffith and Howard plus 3-page article about them and the series. **$20.**

ANG-2. AUTOGRAPHED 'ANDY GRIFFITH SHOW' PHOTO 7x9" glossy bw photo from early 1960s with inked signatures of both Griffith as Sheriff Andy Taylor and Howard as son Opie. **$40.**

ANG-3

ANG-4

ANG-3. "RONNY HOWARD OF THE ANDY GRIFFITH SHOW" 1962 Saalfield coloring book #5644. 8x11". **$125.**

ANG-4. ANDY GRIFFITH SHOW RE-RUN PROMOTION FOLDER from 1970s or later syndicated version of original show. Closed size is 8.5x11", and inside panel has silvered plastic "Deputy Sheriff" badge pin. **$20.**

ANNIE OAKLEY

Syndicated 1952-1956 (81 episodes)

Gene Autry Flying A Productions copyrighted western series set in the town of Diablo starring Gail Davis (a frequent co-star in earlier Autry movies) in the title role with other main cast members of Sheriff Lofty Craig (Brad Johnson) and Tagg, Annie's kid brother (Jimmy Hawkins). The show was later re-run by ABC in 1959-1960 and 1964-1965. The series is believed to be the first TV western to star a woman.

AOK-1   AOK-2

AOK-1. GAIL DAVIS AUTOGRAPHED PHOTO 8x10" glossy black/white photo with personal signature. **$40.**

AOK-2. "ANNIE OAKLEY GAME" by Game Gems ©1965. Box is 9.5x18.5" with game parts including playing board with design of western territory plus card deck and miniature plastic stand-up figures representing cowboys and Indians. **$25.**

AOK-3

AOK-3. "ANNIE OAKLEY" BOXED PLAY SUIT mid-1950s cowgirl outfit of blouse, vest and skirt plus neckerchief band. Skirt and vest are fabric with fringe trim, and each has a pair of fabric picture patches of Gail Davis as Oakley. Set is by Pla-Master Play Suits in 10.5x12.5" box that has © of Annie Oakley Enterprises. **$35.**

AOK-4   AOK-5

AOK-4. "ANNIE OAKLEY CUT-OUT DOLLS" 1954 Whitman book in 10.5x13" size with punch-out figures on front and back cover of Annie, Lofty and Tagg plus 8 pages of western clothing outfits. **$40.**

AOK-5. ANNIE OAKLEY HARTLAND FIGURE of her and horse from late 1950s – early 1960s series by Hartland Plastics Inc. Figure comes with hat and gun. **$100.**

AOK-6

AOK-6. "ANNIE OAKLEY SPARKLE PICTURE CRAFT" set by Gabriel Toys © 1955 in 12x17" box. Contents are craft materials for forming two wall pictures of Oakley. **$25.**

AOK-7   AOK-8

AOK-7. "ANNIE OAKLEY AND TAGG" LUNCH BOX AND THERMOS. Steel box and metal thermos with plastic lid, issued by Aladdin © 1955. **LUNCH BOX $175. THERMOS $75.**

AOK-8. "ANNIE OAKLEY MAGIC ERASABLE PICTURES" 1959 set by Transogram with 12 stiff cardboard pages of pictures to be used with erasable crayons and erasing cloth included as part of kit. 9x10". **$25.**

THE ARCHIE SHOW

CBS: September 14, 1968 – September 6, 1969

Animated cartoon series by Filmation Studios based on "Archie" comic strip by Bob Montana featuring perennial students Archie Andrews, Jughead Jones, Betty Cooper, Veronica Lodge, Reggie Mantle and Sabrina, all of Riverdale High School. The show later continued over CBS or NBC under about seven different titles from September 13, 1969 until January 28, 1978. Items will normally have copyright of Archie Comic Publications Inc.

ARC-1   ARC-2

ARC-1. "ARCHIE" BUTTONS .875" lithographed tin buttons in various bright colors, each with either a picture of Archie character or an Archie phrase. Each button rim has © 1978. **EACH $1.50.**

ARC-2. "THE ARCHIES" LUNCH BOX. Steel box by Aladdin © 1969. **$25.**

ARC-3   ARC-4

ARC-3. "THE ARCHIES" THERMOS 6.5" plastic thermos by Aladdin © 1969. Issued originally with item **ARC-2. $15.**

ARC-4. "ARCHIE" VEHICLE 5x7" retail package holding 2.5" long, die-cast metal replica of hot rod jalopy. By LJN Toys © 1975. **$12.**

ARTHUR GODFREY SHOW

CBS: January 12, 1949 – April 28, 1959

One of the most popular personalities and shows of 1950s television with original show title "Arthur Godfrey And His Friends." Other titles and formats during the 1950s, all on CBS, were "Arthur Godfrey's Talent Scouts" and "Arthur Godfrey And His Ukelele." The "Arthur Godfrey Show" title began September 23, 1958 for duration of the series.

AGD-1   AGD-2

AGD-1. "GODFREY THE GREAT" 1951 biography hardcover book by Jack O'Brian with 64 pages including 57 of "life-story pictures." 8.5x11". **$25.**

AGD-2. "ARTHUR GODFREY'S TV CALENDAR SONGS" 1953 song folio. 9x12" album with 44 pages including songs for each month by Godfrey and "all the little Godfreys." Text includes claim that contents are from "First Musical Revue Score Written For Television." **$20.**

AGD-3

AGD-4

ANT-4

AGD-3. ARTHUR GODFREY "STORIES I LIKE TO TELL" 1952 Simon & Schuster 160 page book of "306 Of The Best Jokes And Anecdotes I Have Heard In Twenty Years Of Radio And TV." 5.5x8". **$12.**

AGD-4. "TV GUIDE" for week of March 7, 1952 with cover photo of Godfrey plus article titled "My Best Stories." **$15.**

THE ATOM ANT SHOW

NBC: October 2, 1965 – September 2, 1967

Animated cartoon series by Hanna-Barbera Studios which continued September 9, 1967-September 7, 1968 as the Atom Ant & Secret Squirrel Show, combining the two shows which had started separately. Among the featured characters on the Atom Ant Show were Precious Pup, Granny Sweet and the "Rugg" family – Paw, Maw, Flora, Shag. Secret Squirrel characters include Squiddly Diddly, Winsome Witch and Morocco Mole. Items will normally have a Hanna-Barbera copyright.

ANT-1

ANT-2   ANT-3

ANT-1. "ATOM ANT PLAY FUN" 1966 Whitman punch-out set in 9x12" box containing cardboard parts for assembly of Atom Ant community on a large printed landscape paper sheet. Our photo shows lid and example character pieces. **$40.**

ANT-2. "ATOM ANT SAVES THE DAY" 1966 boxed board game by Transogram in 8x15" box. **$35.**

ANT-3. "ATOM ANT KITE" toy in 7x38" display package. Toy is by Roalex Company and comes in display package covered with printed clear plastic protective cover. **$35.**

ANT-4. "ATOM ANT/SECRET SQUIRREL AND MOROCCO MOLE" LUNCH BOX. Steel box and thermos, each picturing characters from the combined show version. By King-Seeley Thermos Co. © 1966. **LUNCH BOX $65. THERMOS $35.**

ANT-5   ANT-6   ANT-7

ANT-5. "WINSOME WITCH BUBBLE CLUB" SOAP CONTAINER 10.5" hard plastic figural soap container from series issued by Purex Corp. in late 1960s. Figure is 10.5" tall with coloring mostly in blue/black/pink. **$30.**

ANT-6. "MOROCCO MOLE BUBBLE CLUB" SOAP CONTAINER 7" hard plastic figural soap container from late 1960s series by Purex Corp. Figure is a variation in the series as it has a visible removable cap on top rather than a removable threaded head. Colors are mostly brown and tan. **$30.**

ANT-7. "SQUIDDLY DIDDLY BUBBLE CLUB" 10.5" hard plastic figural soap bottle from series of late 1960s by Purex Corp. Colors are mostly purple and pink. **$30.**

AUGIE DOGGIE AND DOGGIE DADDY

See Quick Draw McDraw

THE AVENGERS

ABC: March 28, 1966 – September 15, 1969

Spy drama based on British television series of early 1960s, starring Patrick Macnee as Jonathan Steed and Diana Rigg as Emma Peel. Items are normally copyrighted ABC Television.

BAT MASTERSON

NBC: October 8, 1959 – September 21, 1961

Western adventure series starring Gene Barry in the title role as a lawyer and professional gambler in addition to fashionable dresser characterized by black derby plus swaggerstick cane. Items will normally have copyright of ZIV Television Programs Inc.

AVG-1   AVG-2

BTM-2

AVG-3

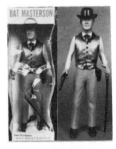

BTM-1   BTM-3

AVG-1. "THE AVENGERS" 8x11" English-published hardcover annual book with 80 pages of stories and photos. 1969 © by ABC Television Films. **$25.**

AVG-2. "THE AVENGERS" FIRST ISSUE of 68-page black/white English comic book with story "The Mohocks." ©1966. **$12.**

AVG-3. "MEET THE AVENGERS" BRITISH-PUBLISHED MAGAZINE with photo and text about "ABC's Top TV Show" although featured is English version starring Cathy Gale as Honor Blackman in the female role rather than U.S. version of Emma Peel. 7x9.5" with 40 pages. **$25.**

BTM-1. "BAT MASTERSON PLAY SUIT" boxed costume for child with fabric white shirt and black trousers, thin plastic derby flocked in black plus fabric vest. Accessories include a vinyl belt plus a cardboard extension cane operated by a rubber band. Costume is by Ben Cooper in 11x13x2" box circa 1960. **$60.**

BTM-2. "BAT MASTERSON HOLSTER SET WITH CANE AND VEST" consisting of two-part wooden cane, leather belt with play bullets, decorated vest, and black leather holster with Masterson name and silhouette. Holster holds metal cap gun. By Carnell Company, Brooklyn in 13x18" box circa 1960. **$100.**

BTM-3. "BAT MASTERSON" BOXED HARTLAND FIGURE 7.5" tall hard plastic figure from early 1960s "Gunfighter" series by Hartland Plastics Inc. Box is 2x3.25x9.25" with clear cellophane display window. Figure comes with hat, cane and gun. **$200.**

AVG-4

AVG-4. "THE NEW AVENGERS" ENGLISH BOXED BOARD GAME by Denys Fisher Toys © 1977. Game is based on renewal verision of series in England. Game parts include unusual plastic spinner which is a replica black derby with umbrella through the middle. Box is 9.5x18". Our photo shows lid and playing board detail. **$30.**

BTM-4   BTM-5

BTM-4. "TV GUIDE" with Bat Masterson cover article. Weekly issue for May 21, 1960 with color cover photo plus article. **$15.**

BTM-5. "BAT MASTERSON" 5.5X8" Whitman 1960 hardcover book. **$10.**

BTM-6

BTM-6. "BAT MASTERSON" GAME 1958 by Lowell Toys featuring a three-dimensional cardboard row of western main street business places, small punch-out western figures representing Masterson and six outlaws, plus playing cards, dice and dice shaker cup. The village buildings are placed on a playing board nearly 20x20". Box is 2.5x10x20". Our photo shows box lid and example buildings. **$40.**

BATMAN

ABC: January 12, 1966 – March 14, 1968

Popular crimefighter fantasy adventure series based on characters created originally by Bob Kane in 1939. The show was telecast twice weekly during the first year, and then once weekly beginning the 1967 season. Although duration of original series was relatively brief, a wealth of merchandise items resulted from it. Items from the 1966-1968 era will normally have a copyright by National Periodical Publications, Inc. Later items may have copyright of DC Comics. Adam West starred as Batman and his alter-ego Bruce Wayne with Burt Ward as Robin and his alter-ego Dick Grayson. Animated cartoon versions followed in 1968-1970 on CBS under title "Batman-Superman Hour" plus reruns of original show were telecast on Sunday mornings in 1969-1970 under the title "The Adventures of Batman." Later animated versions were seen under titles Batman-Tarzan Adventure Hour, Tarzan And The Super 7, and Superfriends. Main characters of original cast: Batgirl (Barbara Gordon, Yvonne Craig), Penguin (Burgess Meredith), The Joker (Cesar Romero), Catwoman (Julie Newmar, Lee Ann Meriwether, Eartha Kitt).

BAT-1

BAT-1. EARLY "BATMAN" PREMIUM MASK 5x8.5" die-cut black/white thin cardboard mask with illustrations and text on reverse for introduction of the Batman and Robin comic strip in daily and Sunday editions of Philadelphia newspaper circa early 1940s. Earlier than the television era, but an example of the few Batman collectible items prior to 1966. **$200.**

BAT-2 BAT-3

BAT-2. BATMAN-ROBIN FACE MASK 8x11" full color thin cardboard sheet die-cut in image of Batman on one side and Robin on the reverse. Premium mask by "General Electric Television" © 1966. **$10.**

BAT-3. "BATMAN" BRASS BADGE with black/white image of Batman. Our shown example has engraved personal name and date in 1970. 2.5" with metal clasp on reverse. **$20.**

BAT-4 BAT-5 BAT-6

BAT-4. "BATMAN WITH ROBIN THE BOY WONDER" 1966 Whitman 8.5x11" "Sticker Fun" book containing pages of colorful stickers to be pasted on pictures throughout the book. **$30.**

BAT-5. "BATMAN COLORING BOOK" 1967 Whitman book #1140. 8x11". **$20.**

BAT-6. "BATMAN COLORING BOOK" 1966 Whitman book #1140 with different cover than **BAT-5.** 8x11". **$20.**

BAT-7 BAT-8 BAT-9

BAT-7. "BATMAN COLORING BOOK" 1966 Whitman book #1140 but different cover design than either **BAT-5** or **BAT-6.** 8x11". **$20.**

BAT-8. "3-D BATMAN ADVENTURES" 1966 National Periodical Publications. 8.5x11" comic book with pictures printed for use with enclosed 3-D paper glasses. **$35.**

BAT-9. "BATMAN MAGIC SLATE" 1966 Whitman display card holding film plastic slate and stylus wood marker. 8.5x14". **$35.**

BAT-10   **BAT-11**

BAT-10. "BATMAN FOLLOW THE COLOR/MAGIC RUB-OFF" 1966 kit by Whitman in 1.5x9x12" box. Contents include 8 printed pictures to be colored by enclosed crayons and then wiped off by enclosed tissues. **$35.**

BAT-11. "BATMAN COINS" 1966 Transogram set of 25 colorful plastic coins depicting Batman and other characters in gold portraits. Set is on 9x12" card under shrinkwrap seal. Card subtitle is "Authentically Engraved Trade N Play Coins." **$35.**

BAT-12   **BAT-13**   **BAT-14**

BAT-12. "BATMAN" VINYL WALLPAPER. Full color section from 20.5" wide roll of wallcovering paper. Sheet has repeated designs of Batman in action poses plus Robin, Batmobile and Bat Plane. Scene repeats every 25 inches. Complete 25" section. **$25.**

BAT-13. "THE PENGUIN VS. BATMAN" 16x27" full color linen-like cloth wall hanging with wooden rod inserted through top edge. Each end of rod is tied to hanging cord. ©1966. **$75.**

BAT-14. "THE JOKER VS. BATMAN" 16x28" full color linen-like cloth wall hanging with wood rod inserted through top edge. Each end of rod is attached to hanging cord. ©1966. **$75.**

BAT-15   **BAT-16**

BAT-15. "BATMAN AND ROBIN" LUNCHBOX AND THERMOS. Steel box and 6.5" metal thermos set by Aladdin ©1966. Large picture panels on lid and bottom are lightly embossed. **LUNCH BOX $100. THERMOS $50.**

BAT-16. "ROBIN THE BOY WONDER" plastic figure assembly kit by Aurora Plastics ©1966 in 2x4x13" box. **$75.**

BAT-17

BAT-17. "BATMAN-ROBIN" BOXED TIN RIFLE. Japanese-made 18" lithographed tin rifle in original box. Batman-Robin name on box lid is in English with rest of inscriptions on lid and gun in Japanese language characters. The rifle clicks loudly and flashes some sparks under red plastic cover on barrel when trigger is pulled. Toy was made in Japan and not intended for distribution in the United States. **$150.**

BAT-18

BAT-18. "BATMAN PICTURE PISTOL" by Marx Toys in 2.5x8x16" original box ©1966. Set features a 15" red/black plastic pistol which runs on 3 batteries and comes with Batman film plus 3 extras involving super hero characters. Gun and films are used to project images on wall or screen. **$300.**

BAT-19

BAT-19. "BATMAN PLAY SET" sold by Sears, Roebuck & Co. ©1966. Original 8x10.5x11" cardboard box has title stenciled on one side. Play set parts are brightly colored three-dimensional plastic and include figures of Batman and Robin plus other characters such as Joker, Kaltor, Mouse Man, Brain Storm, Thunderbolt. Other parts include plastic buildings, control panels, background scenery and a cave entrance with the word "Sanctuary" over the entrance. **$750.**

BAT-20

BAT-20. "SWITCH 'N GO BATMAN BATMOBILE SET" by Mattel ©1966 in original 4x14x20" colorful box with lid illustration of assembled set. Batmobile is 2.5x3x9" and runs by battery on elaborate track including Batcave, bridge, crossovers and other features. Set also includes six small target figures depicting Batman villains. **$300.**

BAT-21

BAT-21. "BATMAN ROAD RACING SET" from 1976 © DC Comics and Azrak-Hamway in 2x11x13" box. Set includes small replica of Batmobile and Jokermobile plus sections of racing track, fence sections, battery box, paper cut-outs. **$100.**

BAT-22

BAT-22. "BATMOBILE" BATTERY-OPERATED CAR circa early 1970s by Cien Ge Toys in 4x4x12" box. Car is colorfully lithographed metal with small Batman and Robin figures mounted in seats. **$150.**

BAT-23

BAT-23. "TALKING BATMOBILE BY PALITOY" with 1977 DC Comics ©. Batmobile is in 3.5x4x10" box and is solid black with dark blue canopy, both plastic. Battery is required to cause a series of typical Batman phrases to be voiced although car itself is not driven by a battery but rather is pushed manually. **$125.**

BAT-24

BAT-24. "BATMOBILE" CAR by Mego Toys ©1974 in 3.5x6x13" box. Car is black/red hard plastic and is designed for Mego's 8" action figure. **$80.**

BAT-25   **BAT-26**

BAT-25. "BATMAN'S BATCYCLE" by Mego Toys ©1974. Hard plastic 5x6x10" motorcycle with sidecar is designed for use with Mego 8" action figures. **$80.**

BAT-26. "BATMOBILE" MODEL assembly kit by Aurora Plastics containing parts in 1.5x5.25x13" box. Assembled replica would be about 6.5" long. Kit #486-98 ©1966. **$250.**

BAT-27   **BAT-28**

BAT-27. "BATCOPTER" REPLICA HELICOPTER by Corgi Toys in 2.5x3x8" box ©1976. **$35.**

BAT-28. BATMAN AND ROBIN "ROLYKINS" miniature 1" tall figures by Marx Toys ©1966. An English issue with small roller bearing inserted in bottom of base. Both are in 1x1x1.25" box. **EACH $80.**

BAT-29   BAT-30   BAT-31

BAT-35. "BATMAN" ACTION FIGURE by Mego Toys with 1976 DC Comics © and 2x10x14" retail display box. Figure is 12.5" tall of hard plastic with soft vinyl head plus fabric costume. **$80.**

BAT-36. "BATMAN" ACTION FIGURE DOLL by Mego Toys © 1972. Figure is 8" tall with hard plastic body and soft vinyl head plus fabric outfit with vinyl gloves and boots. Outfit has small Batman sticker on the chest. **$40.**

BAT-37. "ROBIN" ACTION FIGURE DOLL by Mego Toys © 1979 with original 7x10" blister package. Figure is 8" tall with hard plastic body and soft vinyl head plus fabric outfit with vinyl boots, gloves and belt. **$70.**

BAT-29. "BATMAN" GLAZED CHINA FIGURAL BANK 6.75" tall. Coin slot is in back and bottom of base has trap. Maker is not identified but © 1966. **$60.**

BAT-30. ROBIN GLAZED CHINA FIGURAL BANK, companion bank to **BAT-29**. Maker is not identified but © 1966. **$60.**

BAT-31. BATMAN NIGHT LIGHT. 3.5x3.5x11" realistically molded and colored vinyl figure light that operates electrically with small interior bulb. © 1966. **$85.**

BATTLESTAR GALACTICA

ABC: September 17, 1978 – August 4, 1979

Expensive science-fiction series patterned along the lines of earlier Star Wars starring Lorne Greene as Commander Adama of the spaceship Galactica and its crew in outer space battles against the evil Cylons. Items will normally have copyright by Universal City Studios Inc.

BAT-32   BAT-33   BAT-34

BAT-32. BATMAN DOLL. Stuffed plush and felt fabric 17" doll colored mostly in traditional outfit colors of blue and gray with yellow belt and chest symbol. Cape is removable by a snap at the neck. Maker and copyright date not indicated although circa 1966. **$75.**

BAT-33. BATMAN "SOAKY" 10" hard plastic figural bottle from series of character bubble bath soap containers. Figure is painted in purple/blue/yellow/fleshtint colors. © 1966. **$60.**

BAT-34. ROBIN "SOAKY" 9.5" hard plastic companion soap bottle to **BAT-33** with painted coloring of black/red/fleshtint. © 1966. **$60.**

BSG-1

BSG-1. "BATTLESTAR GALACTICA SPACE STATION KIT" premium by General Mills in original 12x15" mailing envelope. Kit includes 20x28" colorful poster plus control center replica pieces of headset, activator card, space mission cards, squadron patch, iron-on transfers. © 1978. **$50.**

BAT-35   BAT-36   BAT-37   BSG-2   BSG-3   BSG-4

BSG-2. "BATTLESTAR GALACTICA" PHOTO NECKLACE in original 1x2.5x3" display box. Necklace is thin chain of gold-colored metal with pendant that holds cameo portrait photo of Greene as Commander Adama. ©1978. **$10.**

BSG-3. "BATTLESTAR GALACTICA COLONIAL WARRIOR" 11.5" action figure in 3x7.5x14" display box. Figure is hard plastic with soft vinyl head plus outfit of fabric and plastic. Accessories include a laser pistol operated by two penlight batteries. Figure is by Mattel © 1978. **$35.**

BSG-4. 'CYLON' BATTLESTAR GALACTICA 12.5" hard plastic figure of enemy Cylon Centurion. Figure uses batteries to light up left or right eye by switch at back of head, as well as a light in the chest and tip of gun. Figure is by Mattel ©1978. **$40.**

BSG-5   BSG-6

BSG-5. "IMPERIOUS LEADER" ACTION FIGURE on 6x9" retail card from 1978 series by Mattel. Plastic figure is 4.5" with purple hair/lavender body/maroon fabric gown. **$5.**

BSG-6. "BATTLESTAR GALACTICA COLONIAL STELLAR PROBE" spaceship in 2x9x9" display box. By Mattel ©1978. **$15.**

BSG-7

BSG-8

BSG-7. "BATTLESTAR GALACTICA" LUNCH BOX. Steel box with lightly embossed large panels. By Aladdin ©1978. **$20.**

BSG-8. "BATTLESTAR GALACTICA" BOARD GAME by Parker Brothers ©1978. Game is in 9x18" box with contents including game board, spinner and 4 colonial viper die-cut cardboard spaceships. **$10.**

THE BEANY & CECIL SHOW

ABC: January 6, 1962 – September 3, 1967

Animated cartoon series featuring characters created by Bob Clampett. The title characters were actually from the 1950s and both originally appeared nationally in 1960-1962 series titled Matty's Funday Funnies sponsored by Mattel Toys. Starting in 1962 the show title was Matty's Funnies with Beany and Cecil although this title was shortened early in 1962 to The Beany and Cecil show. ABC continued to offer the show in syndication from 1968 into 1976. Principal characters are Beany, Cecil, Captain Horatio K. Huffenpuff, Dishonest John. Most items were issued by Mattel and normally all will have Clampett copyright.

BAC-1   BAC-2

BAC-1. MATTEL "BEANY" TALKING DOLL. 18" stuffed cloth doll with soft vinyl plastic head, hands and shoes. Back of head has molded vinyl cap with small plastic propeller that actually turns. Doll has pullstring on one leg which activates internal voice box to utter several phrases. Mattel tag on other leg has 1949 Clampett © although doll is from early 1960s. **$150.**

BAC-2. MATTEL "CECIL" TALKING DOLL. Early 1960s stuffed plush toy formed in permanent curled seated position with 16" height. Body is mostly green plush accented by felt pieces on tail, neck and eyelashes plus white plastic eye disks that have movable eyeballs. Pullstring operates internal voice box to utter several phrases. Attached Mattel tag ©1950. **$150.**

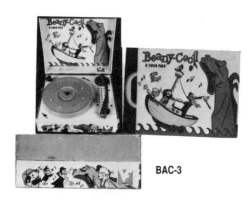

BAC-3

BAC-3. "BEANY-CECIL & THEIR PALS" RECORD PLAYER. Electrically-powered record player by Vanity Fair ©1961. Player case is 5.5x10.5x12.5" of thick cardboard with litho paper design. Player is adaptable for either 45 or 78-rpm records. Our photo shows case lid, example side panel and opened record player. **$50.**

BAC-4

BAC-8. "BEANY-CECIL MATCH-IT" GAME by Mattel ©1961. Playing surface is 14x18" heavy cardboard for use with perforated cardboard tiles to be removed from original packaging and used as playing pieces. Our photo section shows entire board and detail of single tile. **$20.**

BAC-9. "BEANY-CECIL" ANIMATED CLOCK. 1x3.5x4" wood clock case on 1.5x4" wood base. Clock runs by spring winding mechanism and features a small die-cut figure of Beany mounted on dial face to rock back and forth as the clock runs. Maker is not identified. **$175.**

BAC-10   **BAC-11**

BAC-4. "BEANY & CECIL LUNCH KIT" AND THERMOS. Vinyl-covered stiff cardboard box and 8.25" metal thermos with plastic lid. Illustrations are on lid and each side. By King-Seeley ©1961. **LUNCH BOX $500. THERMOS $100.**

BAC-10. "BEANY-COPTER" Mattel toy on 10x17" retail card © 1961. Card holds red plastic beanie designed to fire plastic "copter" disks by pulling chin string. Each disk has small secret message compartment. Our photo shows complete card and detail from the beanie. **$90.**

BAC-11. "BOB CLAMPETT'S BEANY COLORING BOOK" 8.5x11" Whitman book #2034:25 with 1953 © although issued early 1960s. **$40.**

BAC-5   **BAC-6**   **BAC-7**

BAC-5. "BEANY & CECIL" CARRYING CASE of stiff cardboard covered by red vinyl with colorful group picture printed on lid. Case has design of small hat box with 9" diameter and 3" depth plus matching red carrying strap. **$20.**

BAC-6. "CECIL & BEANY'S LEAKIN' LENA" 7x15.5x18" cardboard packaging holding propeller-driven plastic replica boat which actually floats and rolls in water. By Irwin Corp. ©1962. **$150.**

BAC-7. "BEANY & CECIL" GAMEBOARD 13.5x13.5" lithographed metal gameboard with 5 small circular drilled holes which are assigned point values. Playing board only from original game which was played either with marbles or pegs. **$30.**

BAC-12

BAC-13

BAC-12. "LEAKIN' LENA POUND 'N' PULL" WOOD TOY by Pressman Toys from early 1960s. Toy is pulled by a string and has off-center cam front wheel which causes it to raise up and down when pulled. Toy comes with 5 pegs and wood hammer. **$30.**

BAC-13. "JUMPING DJ SURPRISE ACTION GAME" 1962 Mattel game featuring vinyl and cardboard pneumatic figure of Dishonest John which is pressed downward and then jumps up at unknown time to determine course of game. Other game parts are a metal scoreboard plus card deck. Game is in 3x9x11" display box. **$50.**

BAC-8   **BAC-9**

THE BEATLES

ABC: September 25, 1965 – September 7, 1968

Animated cartoon version by King Features based on real life rock group which dominated the later 1960s. The actual Beatles appeared only a few times in live concert on television following their initial February 9, 1964 guest appearance on U.S. television during the Ed Sullivan Show. Few, if any, Beatle items are directly related to the cartoon series although following is a selection of mid-1960s scarcer Beatle memorabilia. Items are normally copyrighted NEMS Enterprises Ltd. or SELTAEB.

BTL-5

BTL-5. BEATLES RUG 21x36" woven fabric with portraits mostly in brown/black/fleshtints with variety of background colors. Rug is fringed on each end. **$350.**

BTL-1   BTL-2

BTL-6

BTL-1. BEATLES BOBBING HEAD SET of 4 composition figures, each about 8" tall from 1964 Car Mascot series. Each Beatle's name is a decal on front edge of gold colored base **SET OF FOUR $300.**

BTL-2. "THE BEATLES DISK-GO-CASE" 7.5" diameter by 7" tall hard plastic case for carrying 45-rpm records. Lid has plastic carrying handle that twists to lock or unlock. Case comes with informational tag that pictures the group. Versions are known in seven different color combinations. By Charter Industries © 1966. **$150.**

BTL-7   BTL-8

BTL-6. "THE BEATLES" SHOULDER BAG 9.5x11" vinyl tote with carrying cord. Various known color combinations. **$175.**

BTL-7. "THE BEATLES" PENCIL CASE 3.5x7" zippered vinyl with repeated portrait illustrations over entire surface. **$200.**

BTL-8. "BEATLES NEW BEAT GUITAR" 31" tall hard plastic made by Selcol of United Kingdom with group picture sticker and facsimile autographs on guitar face. Coloring is mostly red, maroon and orange. Guitar comes in cardboard box that also has full color portrait sticker. **$700.**

BTL-3   BTL-4

BTL-3. BEATLES FIGURE SET of four figures by Remco Plastics, each about 4.5" tall with hard plastic body, soft vinyl head and rooted artificial lifelike hair. Each figure holds a removable die-cut plastic instrument which has his name in facsimile signature in gold. Back of each has "The Beatles" name with © 1964. **SET OF FOUR $280.**

BTL-4. "THE BEATLES" BEACH TOWEL 34x56" terrycloth with large group illustration of Beatles in swimsuits. © 1965. **$150.**

BTL-9

BTL-9. BEATLES "FLIP YOUR WIG" GAME. 1964 Milton Bradley board game in 9.5x19" box. Game parts are playing board which opens to 16x18.5" with color group photo, 48 cards, 4 small portrait player pieces, a die. **$125.**

BTL-10

BTL-10. "THE BEATLES" LUNCH BOX. Large panels each have lightly embossed group portraits and other panels have different illustrations except surface under handle which has facsimile signatures. By Aladdin Industries ©1965. **$200.**

BTL-11

BTL-11. "YELLOW SUBMARINE" LUNCH BOX. Steel box with full color scenes from Beatles animated movie on all surfaces. Box is by King-Seeley ©1968 King Features and Subafilms Ltd. **$200.**

BTL-12

BTL-12. BEATLES "YELLOW SUBMARINE" TOY 2x5x3" diecast metal replica from 1968 Beatles animated film. By Corgi Toys with extremely fine detail and realistic coloring plus several mechanical moving features. In 2.5x3.5x6.5" display box that has back panel that extends upward an additional 3.5". English-made by Corgi ©1968 King Features and Subafilms Ltd. **$250.**

BEN CASEY

ABC: October 2, 1961 – March 21, 1966

Medical drama starring Vince Edwards as Dr. Ben Casey, a neurosurgeon at County General Hospital. Items are normally copyrighted Bing Crosby Productions.

BCA-1   BCA-2

BCA-1. "DR. BEN CASEY M.D." BOBBING HEAD FIGURE. 6.5" composition figure with spring-mounted head. Figure comes in 3x3x7" box. **$75.**

BCA-2. "BEN CASEY M.D. GAME" 1961 Transogram boxed board game. **$20.**

BCA-3   BCA-4

BCA-3. "BEN CASEY M.D. PLAY HOSPITAL SET" 1962 Transogram set in 4x15.5x18" box. Contents include plastic medicine chest with medicinal supplies, plastic instruments, medical bag and certificate, hospital charts, doctor's cap. **$40.**

BCA-4. "BEN CASEY M.D." PLAYSUIT. Boxed child's white medical costume with embroidered "Ben Casey M.D." above the lapel pocket. The playsuit comes with long rubber and silvered plastic stethoscope in 1.5x10.5x13" box. **$40.**

BCA-5

BCA-5. "BEN CASEY" VINYL OVERNIGHT CASE with colorful photo portrait on lid. Case is about 12" diameter by 5" deep with vinyl carrying strap. Bing Crosby Productions ©1962. **$40.**

THE BEVERLY HILLBILLIES

CBS: September 26, 1962 – September 7, 1971

One of the most popular situation comedies about a backwoods family with sudden wealth, causing a move to Beverly Hills. Main characters: Jed Clampett (Buddy Ebsen), Granny, otherwise known as Daisy Moses, Jed's mother-in-law (Irene Ryan), Elly Mae Clampett (Donna Douglas), Jethro Bodine (Max Baer Jr.). Items will normally have copyright by Filmways TV Productions.

BEV-1   BEV-2

BEV-1. "BEVERLY HILLBILLIES CAR" 1963 Ideal Toys 8x10x22" replica soft plastic car with spring-wound motor and original box. The car comes with five hard plastic removable character figures, each about 8" tall. Accessories include a bench, table, chairs, barrel, and various tool replica pieces. **$500.**

BEV-2. "THE BEVERLY HILLBILLIES ANNUAL" English-published 7.5x10.5" hardcover book with 96 pages of full color comic book-style stories. **$20.**

BEV-3   BEV-4   BEV-5

BEV-3. "THE BEVERLY HILLBILLIES ANNUAL" English-published 7.5x10.5" hardcover book ©1965 with contents including 9 full color cartoon strip-style stories. **$25.**

BEV-4. "THE BEVERLY HILLBILLIES PUNCH-OUT" BOOK. 1964 Whitman book #1949 in 10x14" size with punch-out pages including principal characters and their dog Duke plus jalopy car and their mansion. **$25.**

BEV-5. "THE BEVERLY HILLBILLIES PICTURE PUZZLE" by Jaymar 1963 with assembled 10x14" size. Box is 2x7x10". **$20.**

BEV-6   BEV-7

BEV-6. "THE BEVERLY HILLBILLIES" LUNCH BOX AND THERMOS. Steel box with embossed picture scenes plus 6.5" metal thermos. By Aladdin Industries circa 1963-1965. **LUNCH BOX $45. THERMOS $25.**

BEV-7. "THE BEVERLY HILLBILLIES GAME" 1963 boxed board game by Standard Toykraft consisting of gameboard, 4 different decks of cards. Game is in 9x18" box. **$30.**

BEV-8

BEV-8. "THE BEVERLY HILLBILLIES" COLORFORMS "CARTOON KIT" 1963 set illustrating the front room of their mansion. Box is 8x12". **$100.**

BEWITCHED

ABC: September 17, 1964 – July 1, 1972

Situation comedy about a suburban married couple of Samantha Stephens, a winsome witch with supernatural powers activated by a wriggle of her upper lip, played by Elizabeth Montgomery, and husband Darrin plus her mother Endora. Montgomery also played the role of Samantha's twin cousin Serena. Items will normally have copyright by Screen Gems, Inc. Main characters: Darrin Stephens (Dick York 1964-1969, Dick Sargent 1969-1972), Endora (Agnes Moorehead), daughter Tabatha (Erin and Diane Murphy).

BEW-1   BEW-2

BEW-1. "BEWITCHED-SAMANTHA" PAPERDOLL KIT ©1965 by Magic Wand in 9.5x15" box. Die-cut stiff cardboard stand-up doll is 14.5" tall with two sheets of clothing designed to be applied by a small plastic wand which is included. **$60.**

BEW-2. "BEWITCHED" 8x11" Grosset & Dunlap 48-page storybook ©1965. **$15.**

BEW-3   BEW-4

BEW-3. "BEWITCHED/FUN AND ACTIVITY BOOK" by Treasure Books ©1965, 8x11" with 64 pages of stories, puzzles and games. **$15.**

BEW-4. "BEWITCHED" SHEET MUSIC 8.5x11" ©1964 with two pages of words and music for theme song for the series. **$35.**

BEW-5   BEW-6

BEW-5. "STYMIE CARD GAME INSPIRED BY THE BEWITCHED TV SERIES" 1964 ©Milton Bradley game with thin vinyl gameboard and card deck in 6x10" box. **$25.**

BEW-6. "THE SAMANTHA & ENDORA GAME/BEWITCHED" 1965 ©boxed game by T. Cohn Inc. Game parts are playing board, spinner and die-cut cardboard character playing pieces. **$40.**

THE BIONIC WOMAN

ABC: January 14, 1976 – May 1977
NBC: May 1977 – September 2, 1978

A spinoff from "The Six Million Dollar Man" series starring Lindsay Wagner as Jaime Somers, an intelligence agent outfitted with bionic legs, right arm and right ear following a skydiving injury. Items will normally have copyright of Universal City Studios.

BIO-1   BIO-2

BIO-1. "THE BIONIC WOMAN" LUNCH BOX AND THERMOS. Steel box with embossed scenes plus all-plastic 6.5" thermos by Aladdin Industries with no copyright date indicated but circa 1977. **LUNCH BOX $20. THERMOS $10.**

BIO-2. "THE BIONIC WOMAN" GAME ©1976 by Parker Brothers in 9x18" box. Game parts include 18x18" playing board plus card deck. **$15.**

BIO-3   BIO-4

BIO-3. "THE BIONIC WOMAN REPAIR KIT" snap-together plastic assembly model kit by MTC ©1976 in 3.5x6.5x9" box. Kit parts include figures of Jaime Somers, Oscar Goldman, background display, operating table, overhead high intensity light. **$20.**

BIO-4. "THE BIONIC WOMAN" 12" hard plastic action figure doll plus accessories. Doll is ©1977 by Kenner Toys and has lifelike blonde hair, a simulated bionic hearing mechanism, removable arms, legs and modules for her arms and legs. Accessories are a map case, billfold, make-up case, decoder, and cosmetic items. **$80.**

BONANZA

NBC: September 12, 1959 – January 16, 1973

Second longest-running television western series about the Cartwright family of the Ponderosa Ranch near Virginia City, Nevada. Main characters: Ben Cartwright (Lorne Greene), sons Adam (Pernell Roberts, left the series at end of 1964-1965 season), Hoss (Dan Blocker), Little Joe (Michael Landon). Items may have copyright of National Broadcasting Co.

BNZ-1   BNZ-2

BNZ-1. "TV GUIDE" weekly issue for May 13, 1961 with cover photo plus four-page article about Greene as Ben Cartwright. **$15.**

BNZ-2. "BEN CARTWRIGHT" CHEVROLET PROMOTION RECORD in 6.5x6.5" mailing envelope. Record is 33 1/3-rpm with musical message by him plus "Bill And Glenn" for promotion of a demonstration drive in a new 1964 Chevrolet, a sponsor of the television series. Record is printed on 6x6" cardboard sheet. **$25.**

BNZ-3

BNZ-9   BNZ-10

BNZ-3. "BONANZA" DOUBLE GUN AND HOLSTER SET by Halpern Company (HALCO) circa 1965. Belt and attached holsters are in light tan color with character portraits printed in black. Matched pair of cap guns are each 9.5" long of silvered white metal with green plastic grips. Each gun has "Bonanza" name on left side. Back center of belt has leather cartridge clip strap which is missing in our photo example. **$125.**

BNZ-4   BNZ-5   BNZ-6

BNZ-4. "BONANZA HOLSTER SET" by Halpern-Nichols circa 1965. Set is in 8x12" display box with clear cellophane window. Holster is a dark brown simulated leather with black leather belt. The holster cover has large decorative tin die-cut pattern centered by a simulated large glass gemstone. Cap pistol is 9.5" long of white metal with plastic grips. **$75.**

BNZ-5. "BONANZA COLORING BOOK" 8.25x11" Saalfield book #4535 ©1965. **$15.**

BNZ-6. "BONANZA" 8.25x11" Saalfield coloring book #1617 © 1965. **$15.**

BNZ-7   BNZ-8

BNZ-7. "PONDEROSA RANCH" SILVERED TIN SOUVENIR CUP with full color lithographed photo design of Cartwright family plus actual ranch residence used in the series as site of the Ponderosa. No maker and undated but circa 1964 or earlier. Cup is 3.5" in diameter by 2.75" tall. **$20.**

BNZ-8. "BEN AND HIS HORSE" FIGURE KIT © 1966 by American Character consisting of 8" hard plastic action figure of Ben Cartwright plus his horse in 3x10x18" display box designed like a stable. Accessory parts are a six-gun, gun belt and holster, hat, canteen, lariat, rifle holster, rifle, spurs and straps, vest and bandanna, saddle, saddlebags, bedroll, bridle, bit and reins. The horse figure has small ball bearings mounted in bottom of hooves. **$200.**

BNZ-9. "HOSS AND HIS HORSE" FIGURE KIT © 1966 and similar to **BNZ-8** except set is issued by Palitoy of England. Set has 8" hard plastic action figure of Hoss Cartwright with different colored horse but otherwise same accessories as number **BNZ-8.** Display box is 3x10x18" with design of stable which is different from **BNZ-8.** Our photo shows complete display box plus enclosed package of accessories for Hoss. **$150.**

BNZ-10. "BONANZA" MODEL KIT by Revell Plastics © 1966. Box is 3x10x10" with plastic parts for assembly of character figures of Ben Cartwright, Hoss and Little Joe. Plastic figures each have a front and back section which snap together to form a 9" tall completed figure with realistic likeness to each character. **$125.**

BNZ-11   BNZ-12

BNZ-11. "BONANZA MOVIE VIEWER" on 5.5x7.5" display blister card that also holds two "Bonanza" films for the viewer. From "K-Kids" series ©1961. **$45.**

BNZ-12. "BONANZA" TRU-VUE "MAGIC EYES" SET on 8.5x11" sealed retail card holding three Tru-Vue stereo picture cards. Set is by GAF ©1964. **$25.**

BNZ-13   BNZ-14

BNZ-13. "BONANZA" STEEL LUNCH BOX with embossed picture panels. By Aladdin Industries circa 1965-1966. **$75.**

BNZ-14. "BONANZA" STEEL THERMOS by Aladdin Industries circa 1965-1966. Thermos came with item **BNZ-13.** **$40.**

BOZO THE CLOWN

Syndicated 1956 – 1960s

Live action program also known as "Bozo's Big Top" featuring Bozo, a trademark figure of Capitol Records children's series. In 1956 Larry Harmon purchased the television rights for the character and franchised the idea of a live Bozo character to host a cartoon show. Each local station provided their own Bozo. Items are normally copyrighted Larry Harmon Pictures Corp.

BZO-1

BZO-2

BZO-1. "BOZO HAS A PARTY" Capitol record album © 1952 with two 78-rpm records plus 20-page full color section illustrating the story. Album is 10.5x12". **$15.**

BZO-2. "BOZO THE CLOWN" LUNCH BOX AND THERMOS. Steel box and 6.5" steel thermos. Box is domed variety with design of circus wagon. By Aladdin Industries © 1963. **LUNCH BOX $100. THERMOS $35.**

BZO-3   BZO-4

BZO-3. "LARRY HARMON'S TV BOZO" TALKING HAND PUPPET by Mattel © 1963. Puppet is in 4.5x7x11.5" display carton with clear cellophane cover. Figure has fabric handcover body and soft vinyl head accented by orange yarn hair. Puppet has voice box operated by pull string plus head is designed so that mouth may be moved by the fingers as string is pulled. By Mattel Toys with additional copyrights for Bozo the Capitol Clown and Capitol Records. **$50.**

BZO-4. "LARRY HARMON'S BOZO'S POCKET WATCH" in unopened 4x6" plastic display bag with header card. Contents are a 3.5" diameter die-cut cardboard display backing formed like a pocket watch which holds a small plastic toy watch picturing Bozo. The toy watch has movable metal hands and stem that turns. Undated and no maker indicated other than "Japan." **$10.**

THE BRADY BUNCH

ABC: September 26, 1969 – August 30, 1974

A situation comedy about a widower with three sons who married a widow with three daughters, which proved to be a popular show although few collectibles were licensed for it. Main characters: Mike Brady (Robert Reed), wife Carol (Florence Henderson), children Marcia (Maureen McCormick), Jan (Eve Plumb), Cindy (Susan Olsen), Greg (Barry Williams), Peter (Christopher Knight), Bobby (Mike Lookinland) and housekeeper Alice Nelson (Ann Davis). An animated cartoon spinoff series titled "The Brady Kids" followed on ABC beginning September 16, 1972 through August 31, 1974 with voices used of the six live action characters. Later spinoff series were "The Brady Bunch Hour" with the same live action cast as original series which was run by ABC from January 23 – May 25, 1977; and a three-episode series by NBC, "The Brady Brides" from February 6 – April 17, 1981. Items are normally copyrighted Paramount TV Inc.

BRB-1   BRB-2

BRB-1. "THE BRADY BUNCH" 11.5x14.5" frame tray inlay jigsaw puzzle by Whitman ©1972. **$15.**

BRB-2. "THE BRADY BUNCH FISHIN' FUN SET" 6.25x11" retail card with clear plastic holding ten plastic parts die-cut in shape of fishes. These parts may be used with two enclosed plastic fishing poles, each with string and small hook, or fish parts can also be used as a puzzle. Paramount Pictures ©1973. **$15.**

BRAVE EAGLE

CBS: September 28, 1955 – June 6, 1956

Western adventure series from the Indian viewpoint starring Keith Larsen in the title role. Items are normally copyrighted Frontiers, Inc.

BVE-1   BVE-2   BVE-3

BVE-1. "BRAVE EAGLE COLORING BOOK" 8.5x11" Whitman #1314 ©1955 by Roy Rogers Enterprises. **$12.**

BVE-2. "BRAVE EAGLE" 6.5x8" Little Golden Book by Simon & Schuster ©1957. **$6.**

BVE-3. "BRAVE EAGLE" LUNCH BOX AND THERMOS. Steel box and thermos with plastic cup by American Thermos Bottle Co., undated but circa 1955-1956. **LUNCH BOX $125. THERMOS $40.**

BREEZLY AND SNEEZLY

See The Peter Potamus Show

BROKEN ARROW

ABC: September 25, 1956 – September 18, 1960

Western adventure drama co-starring John Lupton as Tom Jeffords, an Indian agent, and Michael Ansara as Cochise an Apache chief. Items will normally have copyright of 20th Century-Fox Television. The series was later syndicated for daytime use.

BKA-1   BKA-2

BKA-1. "BROKEN ARROW" 45-RPM RECORD on RCA Victor label in cover jacket. Record is music theme from the series. **$20.**

BKA-2. "BROKEN ARROW" 11x13.5" frame tray inlay jigsaw puzzle by Built-Rite circa 1956 or later. **$10.**

BKA-3   BKA-4

BKA-3. "BROKEN ARROW" 11x13.5" frame tray inlay jigsaw puzzle by Built-Rite circa 1956 or later. **$10.**

BKA-4. "COCHISE" HARTLAND FIGURE WITH BOX. Realistically detailed plastic figure from early 1960s series by Hartland Plastics based on television western characters. Figure is in 3.25x8.5x9.25" box. Cochise is depicted in yellow jacket, tan trousers, orange boots. The horse is a black/white pinto. Accessory parts are a pistol and rifle. **BOXED FIGURE $150. UNBOXED $75.**

BKA-5   BKA-6

BKA-5. TOM JEFFORDS HARTLAND FIGURE from same series as **BKA-4.** Jeffords figure is depicted in blue shirt, orange trousers and white hat. The horse is a blend of gray and white. Accessories are a rifle and knife. **$100.**

BKA-6. "JOHN LUPTON AS TOM JEFFORDS" 8x10" pencil tablet with full color photo cover. **$8.**

BUCK ROGERS IN THE 25TH CENTURY

NBC: September 20, 1979 – April 16, 1981

The most recent television version which resulted in quite a few items compared to the original ABC version which aired from April 15, 1950 – January 30, 1951. NBC major characters: Buck Rogers (Gil Gerard), Wilma Deering (Erin Gray), Twiki, Buck's favorite robot (Felix Silla), Dr. Elias Huer (Tim O'Connor). Other characters were introduced in the show's second season. Items from the 1979-1981 era will normally have copyrights of Robert C. Dille and Universal City Studios. There are many older items available from the 1930s when the character enjoyed great radio and newspaper comic strip popularity.

BRG-1

BRG-2

BRG-1. "BUCK ROGERS SPACE RANGER KIT" 1952 premium from Sylvania "Halo-Light" TV dealers in original 11x15" envelope. Kit has six punch-out sheets with richly colored parts for forming exotic space equipment or objects. **$75.**

BRG-2. "BUCK ROGERS SUPER-SCOPE" WITH BOX telescope toy by Norton-Honer Co. Chicago with 1953 patent application date. Telescope is 9" long in green/yellow/red plastic. Small gear wheels are at the rear for adjusting focus. Box is 2x6x12". **$75.**

BRG-3   BRG-4   BRG-8   BRG-9

BRG-3. "BUCK ROGERS SONIC RAY" futuristic gun that lights and makes buzzing sound. Gun is in original box and comes with International Morse Code and Buck Rogers Secret Interplanetary Code charts. By Commonwealth Utilities Co., Chicago, circa early 1950s. **$90.**

BRG-4. "BUCK ROGERS IN THE 25TH CENTURY" frame tray inlay jigsaw puzzle by Milton Bradley © 1952. Puzzle is 10.25x14.5" and comes with same sized paper cover sleeve that has identical picture scene as puzzle itself. **$20.**

BRG-8. "BUCK ROGERS STARFIGHTER" rocketship popularized in television series. Replica is about 6" long and formed from metal and plastic. Accessory pieces are small figures of Buck Rogers and robot Twiki. By Corgi in 3.5x4.5x7" display box. **$50.**

BRG-9. "BUCK ROGERS MARAUDER" boxed model kit by Monogram © 1969. Box is 3x9x11" and contains assembly parts for detailed replica of very futuristic spaceship. **$15.**

BRG-5

BRG-5. "BUCK ROGERS COLORFORMS ADVENTURE SET" in 8x12.5" box. Set consists of thin die-cut vinyl parts for assembling character figures on a scene board. Circa 1979. **$20.**

BUFFALO BILL, JR.

Syndicated 1955

Series produced by Gene Autry Flying A Productions starring Dick Jones in the title role, Nancy Gilbert as Calamity, his younger sister; and Harry Cheshire as Judge Ben Wiley, their guardian.

BRG-6   BRG-7

BBJ-1   BBJ-2

BRG-6. "BUCK ROGERS IN THE 25TH CENTURY" 12" hard plastic action figure doll in 9x13.5" display box. Doll is by Mego Toys © 1979 from a series based on the television series. The figure is clad in a white stretch fabric outfit with black pistol belt. **$70.**

BRG-7. "BUCK ROGERS IN THE 25TH CENTURY" LUNCH BOX AND THERMOS. Steel box with embossed illustrations plus 6.5" tall plastic thermos. Set is by Aladdin Industries © 1979. **LUNCH BOX $20. THERMOS $10.**

BBJ-1. "BUFFALO BILL JR." pair of 11x13.5" cardboard frame tray inlay jigsaw puzzles by Built-Rite © 1956. **EACH $10.**

BBJ-2. "BUFFALO BILL JR." CHILD'S WESTERN OUTFIT. Two-part cowboy outfit of long-sleeved brown flannel shirt and tan twill fabric chaps. Shirt is trimmed in yellow with tan plastic fringe across the back. Shirt front has removable flannel panel which has Buffalo Bill Jr. name plus western design. The front waist of the chaps has vinyl design of simulated animal fur. Maker and date are unknown although circa 1955-1956. **$75.**

BBJ-3   BBJ-4

BBJ-3. "BUFFALO BILL JR'S CATTLE ROUND-UP GAME" by Built-Rite ©1956 featuring 14x14" playing board with generic western scene. Game is played with small cardboard picture disks. Reverse of playing board is printed with another game based on horse racing. Box is 7.5x14". **$20.**

BBJ-4. "BUFFALO BILL, JR." 100-piece jigsaw puzzle from Built-Rite "Famous TV Stars" puzzle series ©1956. Puzzle box has full color lid photo. **$15.**

THE BUGS BUNNY SHOW

ABC: October 11, 1960 – September 25, 1962

After the initial 1960-1962 prime time run, Bugs and his friends appeared on both ABC and CBS throughout the 1960s and 1970s. In the hour-long format the show was called "The Bugs Bunny/Road Runner Hour." Items related to the show and its characters will normally have copyright of Warner Bros. Pictures.

BGB-1

BGB-1. "BUGS BUNNY ADVENTURE GAME" by Milton Bradley ©1961. Box is 9.5x19" and game features a 16x18.5" playing board depicting many other characters in addition to Bugs including Speedy Gonzales, Yosemite Sam, Wile E. Coyote, Foghorn Leghorn, Tweety, Porky Pig, Road Runner, Elmer Fudd, Daffy Duck, Sheep Dog, Sylvester, Pepe LePew. The same characters are depicted on small stand-up playing figures. **$30.**

BGB-2   BGB-3

BGB-2. BUGS BUNNY/TWEETY BOXED COSTUME by Collegeville Costumes circa mid-1960s. Set consists of a thin plastic mask plus one-piece synthetic fabric costume. The Bugs mask is in safety 'glow' colors of white and blue with red nose and orange inner ears. The costume has chest area design of Bugs plus Tweety in colors mostly of red/white/light blue. Box is 3x8.5x11" with clear cellophane display window. **$15.**

BGB-3. "YOSEMITE SAM" BOBBING HEAD FIGURE 6.25" painted composition figure with spring-mounted head. Figure is depicted in brightly colored outfit with a soft artificial lifelike mustache. Molded base is round and finished in solid green. Bottom of base has undated Warner Bros. ©but circa 1960s. **$85.**

BGB-4   BGB-5   BGB-6

BGB-4. "WILE E. COYOTE" 18" stuffed plush and fabric doll. Head and body parts are tan and soft brown. Clothing is mostly in shades of blue accented by orange and white. Original tag is attached for maker, Mighty Star Limited, Montreal ©1971. **$20.**

BGB-5. "ROAD RUNNER" 13" stuffed doll figure with attached tag for maker, Mighty Star Limited, Montreal circa 1971. Body colors are gray/purple with red legs and yellow beak tipped by red tongue. **$20.**

BGB-6. TAZMANIAN DEVIL 13" stuffed plush figure with original tag by maker, Mighty Star Limited, Montreal ©1971. Body colors are mostly brown with gray chest area and small black and red accent colors on horns and ears. **$20.**

THE BULLWINKLE SHOW

NBC: September 24, 1961 – September 16, 1962

Rocky The Flying Squirrel and Bullwinkle originally appeared in the 1959-1960 weekday show on ABC titled "Rocky And His Friends." In 1963-1964 The Bullwinkle Show was an NBC weekend feature but returned to ABC and ran from September 20, 1964 – September 2, 1973. The show included the spies Boris and Natasha plus segments featuring Mr. Peabody and Sherman or the noble mounty Dudley Do-Right and the evil Snidely Whiplash. Items will normally have copyright of P.A.T.-Ward Productions.

BWK-1   BWK-2   BWK-3

BWK-1. "ROCKY & HIS FRIENDS TOOTH PASTE/TOOTH BRUSH" HOLDER 1.5x4x6" glazed china holder depicting Rocky, Mr. Peabody and Bullwinkle. Coloring is in soft shades of blue/gray/white/pink/tan/yellow/green. Unmarked circa late 1950s-early 1960s. **$200.**

BWK-2. "ROCKY & HIS FRIENDS BANK" very colorful 2x5x5.5" glazed china bank depicting Rocky, Sherman, Mr. Peabody and Bullwinkle. ©1960. Reverse side is blank. **$150.**

BWK-3. "BULLWINKLE BANK" 3x4x6" colorful glazed china bank with coin slot in back. Circa late 1950s – 1960s. **$150.**

| BWK-4 | BWK-5 | BWK-6 |

BWK-4. ROCKY 2x3.5x4.5" glazed china figural bank depicting him with exaggerated large tail that has coin slot at top. Figure is mostly glossy gray with the aviator cap in light blue. Late 1950s - 1960s. **$150.**

BWK-5. "ROCKY" 4.75" tall hollow glazed china figure finished in soft gray body colors accented by crisp black/white face markings and light blue aviator cap. Base is light green with his name in black. ©1960 and "Made In Japan" sticker are on bottom of base. **$150.**

BWK-6. "MR. PEABODY BANK" 6" tall glazed china bank with figure depicted in white accented by red and yellow on eyeglasses, muzzle and bow tie. The base is light green with his name in black. Circa early 1960s. **$200.**

BWK-7

BWK-7. "ROCKY & BULLWINKLE 'PRESTO-SPARKLE' PAINT-ING SET" by Kenner Toys ©1962. Box is 2x11x15.5" and contains packet of six cartoon pictures, each 6.5x10", plus two 10x19.5" comic strip panels. Pictures are to be painted with enclosed water colors before application of glittery sparkle finish which also is included. **$60.**

| BWK-8 | BWK-9 | BWK-10 |

BWK-8. "ROCKY/BULLWINKLE/TELSTAR" 8" metal thermos with plastic cup. Continuous scene is of Rocky seated on a Sputnik-like space ball and Bullwinkle seated on a space module which has "USA" on the side. Between them is a "Telstar" space transmitter with TV screen and Bullwinkle is pictured in the center of it. Thermos is ©1963 by King-Seeley and came with a vinyl box picturing Bullwinkle and Boris on the moon (not shown). **LUNCH BOX $400. THERMOS $100.**

BWK-9. "BULLWINKLE HIDE 'N SEEK GAME" by Milton Bradley ©1962. Original box is 8.5x16". **$75.**

BWK-10. "BULLWINKLE MAGNETIC TRAVEL GAME" by Larami Corp. ©1971. Game is a magnetic playing board designed like "Grand Prix" auto race course. Game is held in plastic blister on 7x10" retail card. **$35.**

| BWK-11 | BWK-12 |

BWK-11. "BULLWINKLE AND ROCKY" LUNCH BOX in flat steel with blue background ©1962 by Universal. Box came with a matching steel thermos with a white cup (not shown). **LUNCH BOX $200. THERMOS $75.**

BWK-12. "BULLWINKLE TRAVEL ADVENTURE GAME" by Transogram ©1970. Box is 8x15" and contains 15x15" gameboard plus 36 cardboard counters, each picturing Rocky. A spinner dial is also included. **$50.**

| BWK-13 | BWK-14 |

BWK-13. "ROCKY AND HIS FRIENDS GAME" by Milton Bradley ©1960. Box is 9.5x19" and contains 16x19" gameboard and 32 character cards. Game object is to fill 8 desks in a school room with proper character cards. **$50.**

BWK-14. "ROCKY AND HIS FRIENDS" Little Golden Book © 1960. **$15.**

BWK-15

BWK-15. "TV RADIO MIRROR" MAGAZINE from January 1962 with cover illustration and inside article about the Rocky and Bullwinkle Show with full page illustration of the entire cast. 8.5x11". **$20.**

| BWK-16 | BWK-17 | BWK-18 |

BWK-16. "ROCKY AND BULLWINKLE COLORING BOOK" by Watkins-Strathmore © 1962. Book is 8x11" with 24 coloring pages. **$35.**

BWK-17. "ROCKY THE FLYING SQUIRREL COLORING BOOK" by Whitman #1037 ©1960. 8x11". **$35.**

BWK-18. "BULLWINKLE THE MOOSE – PAINTLESS PAINT BOOK" by Whitman #1421 © 1960. Book is 8.5x11.5" with pages designed to be colored by simply using a moist brush. **$35.**

BWK-19   BWK-20

BWK-19. "BULLWINKLE & ROCKY" WASTE CAN 11.5" tall by 11" rounded oval lithographed metal waste basket picturing Bullwinkle, Rocky, Dudley Do-Right, Inspector Fenwick, Aesop's Son, Gidney & Lloyd (the moonmen), Sherman, Mr. Peabody, Natasha, Boris and Snidely Whiplash who carries away Nell Fenwick. ©1961. **$75.**

BWK-20. BULLWINKLE-ROCKY CLOCK BANK 6.25x9" retail card with plastic blister holding 4.5" diameter by 1.5" plastic mechanical clock bank. A plastic button on back of bank is turned to open the coin slot on top, and also to move Bullwinkle's arms to "Learn To Tell Time." Top of clock dial has die-cut opening around picture of Rocky which apparently moves as other operations take place. By Larami Corp. ©1969. **$65.**

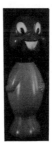 

BWK-21   BWK-22

BWK-21. ROCKY SOAKY BOTTLE 9" hard plastic figure with painted gray body and green aviator cap. Bottle originally held liquid bubble soap and is from circa 1966 series of cartoon character bottles. **$30.**

BWK-22. BULLWINKLE SOAKY BOTTLE 10.5" hard plastic soap container with paint finish mostly in red/yellow. ©1966. **$30.**

BWK-23   BWK-24

BWK-23. BULLWINKLE BOXED FIGURE from "Dakin's T.V. Cartoon Theater" series ©1976. Figure is 7.5" tall with jointed hard plastic body and soft vinyl head. Body parts are mostly brown with depiction of green cheerleader sweater which has red "B" on the chest. Figure holds a simulated megaphone inscribed "What's-A-Matta U." Box is 2x3.5x8" with diecut design to resemble a theater stage. **$35.**

BWK-24. ROCKY BOXED FIGURE from same Dakin series as **BWK-23.** Figure is 6.5" with jointed hard plastic body plus movable vinyl head. Body is gray with blue aviator's cap. Display box is 2x3.5x8" with same design as **BWK-23** but with different coloring. ©1976. **$35.**

BWK-25

BWK-26

CAPTAIN GALLANT OF THE FOREIGN LEGION

NBC: February 13, 1955 – December 7, 1957

Adventure series for children starring Buster Crabbe as Captain Michael Gallant, commander of the North African headquarters of the French Foreign Legion. Also featured was his real life son, Cullen Crabbe, as Cuffy Sanders, a Legion orphan. After its initial run, the series was syndicated under the title "Foreign Legionnaires." Items are normally copyrighted Frantel Inc.

CGL-1

BWK-25. MR. PEABODY AND SHERMAN FLEXIBLE CHAR-ACTER FIGURES from 1972 series © Wham-O Co. Each figure is about 4" tall of soft flexible material over wire support rods. Figures originally came packaged by maker. **EACH $10.**

BWK-26. "DUDLEY DORIGHT" FLEXIBLE FIGURE under plastic blister on 6.5x9.5" retail card. Figure is 5" tall and made of soft flexible material over wire rods. From 1972 series ©Wham-O Co. **$20.**

CGL-1. "CAPTAIN GALLANT ADVENTURE GAME" by Transogram ©1955. Game is in 9x17.5" box. Parts include 17x17" gameboard and small plastic Legionnaires and tribesmen. Our photo shows box lid and center detail of playing board. **$25.**

BWK-27

CGL-2   CGL-3

CGL-2. "CAPTAIN GALLANT OF THE FOREIGN LEGION" BOXED HOLSTER SET by Halco Toys circa 1955-1957. Box is 2x14.5x15" and holds set consisting of black simulated leather belt and flap holster, "Army 45" cap pistol, binoculars, magnetic compass, canteen, wallet, swagger stick. The holster has a foil picture sticker on one side, and the wallet pictures him on the cover. The cap pistol is silvered metal with white plastic grips, made by Hubley. Box lid is die-cut to resemble television screen that has clear plastic display window insert. **$100.**

CGL-3. "SEE CAPTAIN GALLANT ON ABC-TV FOR P.F. CANVAS SHOES" 8x13" paper pennant in bright yellow with red type plus blue/white picture of Cuffy on his horse. Pennant was issued by B.F. Goodrich, makers of the shoes, and is probably from the late 1950s syndication era of the show. **$15.**

BWK-28   BWK-29

BWK-27. "SNIDELY" FLEXIBLE FIGURE under plastic blister on 6.5x9.5" retail card. Figure is 5" tall and made of soft flexible material over wire rods. From 1972 series ©Wham-O Co. **$20.**

BWK-28. "BULLWINKLE'S CIRCUS TIME" TOY on 5.5x9" retail card. Plastic blister holds a mechanical balance toy depicting Bullwinkle seated on an elephant. ©1969. **$20.**

BWK-29. "BULLWINKLE'S CIRCUS TIME" TOY on 5.5x9" card from same series as **BWK-28** except enclosed mechanical balance toy depicts Rocky on a circus horse. ©1969. **$20.**

CGL-4

CGL-4. "OFFICIAL CAPTAIN GALLANT OF THE FOREIGN LEGION" MARX PLAYSET #4730 circa 1955-1957 in 3.5x15x20" illustrated carton. Contents include a main building, walls and towers plus accessories including figures of Foreign Legion soldiers, sheiks, horses, camel, and character figures of Captain Gallant and Cuffy. **$600.**

CGL-5   CGL-6

CGL-5. "CAPTAIN GALLANT OF THE FOREIGN LEGION" FAN MEMBERSHIP KIT in original 7.5x10.5" mailing envelope. Kit consists of full color comic book, a "Junior Legionnaires" membership certificate and two 5x7" sepia photos of Captain Gallant and Cuffy, each with facsimile signature. 1955. **$65.**

CGL-6. "CUFFY AND CAPTAIN GALLANT" COLORING BOOK #2521 by Samuel Lowe Co. ©1956 in 8x11" format. **$15.**

CAPTAIN KANGAROO

CBS: October 3, 1955 – September 19, 1964

Award-winning children's educational series, generally considered television's longest-running network children's series which continued at various time slots into the 1980s following its original weekday morning format. The series starred Bob Keeshan, formerly Clarabell of the Howdy Doody show, as Captain Kangaroo who hosted the show from his Treasure House with regular assistance of Mr. Greenjeans (Hugh "Lumpy" Brannum) and an assortment of human and puppet characters. Among the regular features in the late 1950s were Terrytoons episodes of Tom Terrific, a cartoon boy who could turn himself into anything, and his canine sidekick, Mighty Manfred the Wonder Dog. Items will normally have copyright of CBS Television Enterprises.

CTK-1   CTK-2

CTK-1. "THE GAME OF CAPTAIN KANGAROO" by Milton Bradley ©1956. Game is in 9.5x19" box with 18.5x18.5" gameboard that has movable cardboard disk dial, small die-cut character pieces mounted on wood bases, Bunny Rabbit cards and "Dot" cards. **$20.**

CTK-2. "CAPTAIN KANGAROO'S FINGER PAINT SET" by Hasbro © 1956. Box is 8x12" and contains paper sheets, wooden spoons, 4 jars of finger paint, and instructions. **$20.**

CTK-3   CTK-4

CTK-3. "CAPTAIN KANGAROO" STEEL THERMOS by King-Seeley ©1964. 6.5" tall. **$25.**

CTK-4. "CAPTAIN KANGAROO – LET'S BUILD A HOUSE" GAME with Gardner Games ©1956 that also has © of Keeshan-Miller Enterprises Corp. Box is 14.5x16.5" and game parts include puzzle pieces to make a house, plus bag of small hard plastic tools such as saw, hammer, wrench. **$15.**

CTK-5   CTK-6

CTK-5. "CAPTAIN KANGAROO VIEW-MASTER REEL SET" 4.5x4.5" cover packet holding set of three 3-D picture reels titled "Bunny Rabbit Hunt, Bunny Rabbit Paints A Picture, The Pie Machine." ©1957. **$15.**

CTK-6. "TOM TERRIFIC! WITH MIGHTY MANFRED THE WONDER DOG" 6.5x8" Wonder Book ©1958. **$15.**

CAPTAIN MIDNIGHT

CBS: September 4, 1954 – May 12, 1956

A long-running radio show that offered many premiums under the sponsorship of Ovaltine. The brief television run, starring Richard Webb, produced very few premiums.

CTM-1   CTM-2   CTM-3

CTM-1. AUTOGRAPHED CAPTAIN MIDNIGHT PHOTOGRAPH, 8x10" bw photo on low gloss paper of portrayer Webb in Captain Midnight uniform circa 1954-1956. Uniform has "SQ" insignias on jacket and helmet. Our example is signed in red ink "To Mildred – Captain Midnight." **$35.**

CTM-2. CAPTAIN MIDNIGHT "SQ" PATCH. 2.25" Secret Squadron cloth emblem patch issued as Ovaltine premium circa 1955-1956. Colors are intense red plus black/white. Back has original peel-off film. **$30.**

CTM-3. CAPTAIN MIDNIGHT "SQ" PATCH. 2.25" Secret Squadron emblem paper peel-off patch issued for 15th anniversary of Ovaltine sponsorship in late 1956-1957. Patch is red/white/blue with initials "SQ" and "XV" (Roman Numerals for 15) in gold. Sealed in original clear cellophane packet. **$40.**

CTM-4

CTM-5

CTM-4. CAPTAIN MIDNIGHT "THE SECRET SQUADRON" CLUB MEMBERSHIP CARD. 2.5x3.25" red/white/blue stiff paper with printed Secret Squadron emblem and individual serial number. Issued for 1957 member. Reverse is blank. **$40.**

CTM-5. "CAPTAIN MIDNIGHT" OVALTINE PREMIUM MUG 3.25" tall of red plastic with full color decal. Circa 1953. **$40.**

CTM-6

CTM-6. "CAPTAIN MIDNIGHT" SHAKE-UP MUG with papers. Ovaltine premium circa fifteenth anniversary celebration in 1957 consisting of 4.75" red plastic mug with full color decal plus blue plastic cap. Paper items are a folder sheet depicting him using the mug, a four-page sheet to mothers promoting Ovaltine, and a single small sheet with washing instructions for the mug. Premium came in a mailing box. **MUG $65. WITH PAPERS $100.**

CAPTAIN VIDEO AND HIS VIDEO RANGERS

Dumont Network: June 27, 1949 – April 1, 1955

Television's earliest space serial and one of the most popular children's programs of the early 1950s. The character of Captain Video was played during 1949-1950 by Richard Coogan and from 1951-1955 by Al Hodge, formerly the voice of radio's "Green Hornet." The show was noted, among other features, for the elaborate crime-fighting weapons used against villains of both earthly and extraterrestrial nature.

CTV-1   CTV-2

CTV-1. "TV GUIDE" with Captain Video cover, Volume 6 Number 12, August 31 – September 6, 1951 weekly issue with black/white cover photo of Captain Video holding his "Cosmic Ray Vibrator." Issue has no further reference to him. **$25.**

CTV-2. "VIDEO RANGER" CLUB MEMBERSHIP CARD 2.25x4" with portrait illustration on front and Video Ranger Oath on reverse. Probably a Post Cereal premium of early 1950s. **$40.**

CTV-3

CTV-3. "CAPTAIN VIDEO" BOXED SPACE GAME by Milton Bradley from early 1950s. Box is 9.5x19" with game parts including a full color 18.5x18.5" playing board and a fold-out cardboard section forming a 3-D simulated spaceship instrument panel. **$75.**

CTV-4   CTV-5

CTV-4. "CAPTAIN VIDEO" 10.5x14.5" inlaid frame tray jigsaw puzzle with original cover wrapper which duplicates puzzle scene. By Milton Bradley. Early 1950s. Back of wrapper has duplicate picture for framing. $30.

CTV-5. "CAPTAIN VIDEO AND HIS VIDEO RANGERS" 6 IN 1 RECORD ALBUM by RCA Victor containing two 78-rpm records plus materials for story reading keyed to the records, pictures to color, punch-out finger puppets and a small punch-out puppet stage, plus invitation to join "Little Nipper" record club of RCA Victor. Album is 7.5x7.5" paper booklet. Inside back cover lists other albums including another Captain Video title, "Captives of Saturn." Records are by original cast of the show. Undated except for September 1, 1953 expiration date for joining Little Nipper Club. $35.

CTV-6

CTV-6. "CAPTAIN VIDEO SECRET RAY GUN" early 1950s premium by Power House candy bar consisting of 3.5" battery-operated flashlight gun, 3x4" "Luma-Glo" card for writing secret messages, four-page instruction and order coupon leaflet, all in original but unmarked 1x4x6" box. $35.

CAR 54, WHERE ARE YOU?

NBC: September 17, 1961 – September 8, 1963

The first situation comedy about police officers starring Joe E. Ross as Officer Gunther Toody and Fred Gwynne as Officer Francis Muldoon, a noisy and somber pair who patrolled New York City's 53rd Precinct in their "Car 54." Items will normally have copyright of Eupolis Productions, Inc.

| CAR-1 | CAR-2 | CAR-3 |

CAR-1. "CAR 54, WHERE ARE YOU" COMIC BOOK #1257 by Dell Publishing Co. for March-May 1962. $20.

CAR-2. "CAR 54, WHERE ARE YOU" COLORING BOOK #1157 by Whitman ©1962. 128 pages in 8x11" format. $40.

CAR-3. "CAR 54" SPONSOR'S CONTEST SHEET. 6.75x8.25" entry sheet for cash contest sponsored by Procter & Gamble ©1962. Contest object was to help Toody and Muldoon find the shortest round trip route to visit all 33 locations shown on U.S. map. $35.

| CAR-4 | CAR-5 |

CAR-4. "OFFICIAL CAR 54 POLICE CARS" TOY SIGN. Full color 6.5x18" die-cut cardboard retail display card for toy police cars (see CAR-5) based on "Car 54" series. $40.

CAR-5. CAR 54 FRICTION TOY. 2.5x3x7" lithographed metal friction siren car with rubber tires. The car is green/white and has black inscriptions including "54" on both doors and the hood. "High Way Patrol" is on each rear fender and a gold "N.Y.C." badge is depicted on trunk lid. Circa 1961-1963. $75.

| CAR-6 | CAR-7 |

CAR-6. "CAR 54, WHERE ARE YOU?" GAME by Allison Toys ©1961. Box is 10x22" and game parts are a playing board, 13 miniature plastic cars, a police radio control device of cardboard, 30 car location cards, 15 dispatch cards, and 4 location cards for up to four players. $90.

CAR-7. "CAR 54, WHERE ARE YOU?" SINGLE 33 1/3-RPM RECORD in 12x12" cardboard album sleeve. Record has three "Toody Tales" fairy tale-type stories told by Joe E. Ross. ©1963. $30.

CASPER, THE FRIENDLY GHOST

ABC: October 5, 1963 – December 27, 1969

Animated cartoon series about an innocent child-like ghost who preferred to help people rather than frighten them. The character of Casper originally appeared in Paramount cartoons as early as the 1940s and a Casper series was syndicated for television in 1953. ABC ran the series between 1963-1967 under the title "The New Casper Cartoon Show" and items from this era will normally have copyright by Harvey Famous Cartoons. A later spinoff cartoon series by Hanna-Barbera Studios was aired on NBC September 22, 1979 – May 3, 1980.

| CAS-1 | CAS-2 |

CAS-1. "CASPER THE FRIENDLY GHOST GAME" by Milton Bradley ©1959. Game is in 8x15.5" box and features a 15.25x15.25" playing board with spooky illustrations. **$12.**

CAS-2. "CASPER" 8" TALL HAND PUPPET with white cloth body and hard plastic head that has recessed eyes and tongue which bounce around internally on a spring. Circa 1950s-1960s. **$35.**

| CAS-3 | CAS-4 |

CAS-3. "I'M CASPER THE TALKING GHOST!" DOLL WITH BOX. 15" doll by Mattel ©1961 with hard plastic head and stuffed white terrycloth body which extends to a hood over back part of head. Doll has original tag looped over one arm. Neck has pullstring to activate internal voice box mechanism designed to say 11 different typical Casper phrases. Box is 5.5x7.5x16" with design of haunted house that has front display window for the doll. **$100.**

CAS-4. CASPER LITHOGRAPHED TIN WIND-UP TOY by Line Mar circa 1950s. When wound, the figure hops around as his head, mounted on a thin piece of spring steel, bounces up and down. **$175.**

CHAMPION
See The Adventures Of Champion

CHARLIE BROWN AND SNOOPY SHOW

CBS: September 17, 1983 – August 23, 1986

This was a Saturday morning version featuring Charles Schulz's "Peanuts" characters although many earlier prime-time specials were aired since 1965. A huge number of "Peanuts" collectibles exist. A few earlier items are shown. Items are normally copyrighted Charles M. Schulz and/or United Features Syndicate Inc.

| CBN-1 | CBN-2 | CBN-3 |

CBN-1. "CHARLIE BROWN" BOBBING HEAD FIGURE. 5.5" painted composition figure with head mounted on a neck spring. Figure is on a 2.5x2.5" black base which has his name on front edge. Bottom of base has a Lego (Japan) ©sticker circa mid-1960s. **$40.**

CBN-2. "SNOOPY" BOBBING HEAD FIGURE. 5.5" painted composition figure with head mounted on a neck spring. Figure is on a 2.5x2.5" black base which has a Lego(Japan) ©sticker circa mid-1960s. **$40.**

CBN-3. "LUCY" BOBBING HEAD FIGURE. 5.5" painted composition figure with head mounted on a neck spring. Figure is on a 2.5x2.5" black base which has a Lego(Japan) ©sticker circa mid-1960s. **$40.**

| CBN-4 | CBN-5 |

CBN-4. "PEANUTS" CHARACTER FIGURES. Two figures from a ©1958 early set of at least 7 vinyl dolls, each about 9" tall or shorter but all to the same scale. Figures are all colorfully painted with very realistic likeness of each character. **EACH $40.**

CBN-5. "SNOOPY IN THE MUSIC BOX" MUSICAL TOY by Mattel ©1966. Litho steel box is 5x5x5.5" with crank handle which is turned to produce short tune before vinyl and cloth figure of Snoopy pops out of the box. **$30.**

| CBN-6 | CBN-7 |

CBN-6. "PEANUTS" LUNCH BOX of vinyl-covered stiff cardboard with plastic handle. Copyright date is 1965 but possibly issued later. **$40.**

CBN-7. "SNOOPY" STEEL DOME LUNCH BOX with pictorial scene titled "Have Lunch With Snoopy" and other side has different pictorial scene titled "Go To School With Snoopy" by American Thermos ©1968. **$25.**

| CBN-8 |

CBN-8. "PEANUTS" GAME by Selchow & Righter ©1959. Game is in 9.5x19" box containing cardboard tiles with character depictions of Charlie, Lucy, Linus, Patty, Pig-Pen, Snoopy, Shermy, Violet and Schroeder plus playing board and other game parts. **$35.**

CHARLIE'S ANGELS

ABC: September 22, 1976 – August 19, 1981

Hour-long crime show featuring three glamorous young women, all police academy graduates employed by the Charles Townsend Private Detective Agency. Items will normally have copyright of Spelling-Goldberg Productions. Main characters: Sabrina Duncan (Kate Jackson), Jill Munroe (Farrah Fawcett), Kelly Garrett (Jaclyn Smith), David Doyle (John Bosley) with the voice of Charlie Townsend who always communicated only by telephone by John Forsythe. During the series, both Fawcett-Majors and Jackson left the show and were replaced by characters Kris Munroe (Cheryl Ladd) and Tiffany Welles (Shelly Hack).

CHEYENNE

ABC: September 20, 1955 – September 13, 1963

Hour-long western series starring Clint Walker as Cheyenne Bodie. The series was one of the first produced for television by Warner Bros. and items will normally have copyright by that studio. During the 1957-1958 season, the Cheyenne show was alternated by Warner Bros. with two other westerns, "Sugarfoot" and "Bronco." In 1958 Walker left the series although it continued under the title "Cheyenne" but starring Ty Hardin as Bronco Layne. This programming change was reflected in the design of a few collectibles produced for the series between Walker's departure and his return to the series in mid-1959.

CHA-1   CHA-2

CHY-1   CHY-2   CHY-3

CHA-1. "CHARLIE'S ANGELS GAME" by Milton Bradley © 1977. Box is 9.5x19" and game parts include playing board, small punch-out character figures for each Angel plus message cards and dice. Pictured on lid and playing board are original three Angel characters. **$10.**

CHA-2. "CHARLIE'S ANGELS" EMBOSSED STEEL LUNCH BOX by Aladdin Industries © 1978. **$25.**

CHY-1. WARNER BROS. TV WESTERNS/ACME BOOTS STORE SIGN. 21x33" die-cut stiff cardboard easel sign for line of cowboy boots endorsed by seven stars of Warner Bros. television shows. The upper part of sign is devoted to large die-cut image of cowboy representing "Cheyenne" star although portrait is illustration without direct reference to either Clint Walker or Ty Hardin. The lower part has identified photos of Will Hutchins of "Sugarfoot"; Jack Kelly and James Garner of "Maverick"; Wayde Preston of "Colt .45"; Peter Brown and John Russell of "Lawman." Undated but circa 1957-1960. **$250.**

CHY-2. CHEYENNE HARTLAND FIGURE. Realistically detailed hard plastic figure from series of TV cowboy stars circa late 1950s-1960s by Hartland Plastics. Cheyenne figure is depicted in white hat, tan jacket, yellow shirt, dark blue trousers. Small accessory pieces are six-shooter and knife. **$125.**

CHY-3. "WARNER BROS. CHEYENNE" 6.5x8" Little Golden Book by Simon & Schuster © 1958. **$10.**

CHA-3   CHA-4

CHA-3. "CHARLIE'S ANGELS" ACTION FIGURE DOLL in 8x12" retail blister card with 1977 © by Hasbro. Action figure doll is 8.5" tall and represents "Sabrina" played by Kate Jackson in the series. Doll is clothed in fabric jumpsuit and scarf plus plastic boots. The head has rooted lifelike hair. **$20.**

CHA-4. "CHARLIE'S ANGELS 'JILL' PAPER DOLL" KIT by Toy Factory circa 1977 or earlier as depicted doll is Jill Munroe played by Farrah Fawcett-Majors of the original cast. Box is 7.25x15.25" and contains 13.5" stiff cardboard stand-up doll and base plus three sheets of paper clothing printed with adhesive backing which can be applied and removed from the doll at will. **$20.**

CHY-4   CHY-5

CHY-4. "CHEYENNE GAME" by Milton Bradley © 1958 in 9.5x19" box. Game parts include 15.5x18.5" playing board and cardboard character figures. **$35.**

CHY-5. "CHEYENNE GAME" by Milton Bradley © 1958 in 10x19" box. **$25.**

CHY-6

CHY-6. "CHEYENNE" 3-PUZZLE SET in 9.5x12.5" box by Milton Bradley ©1957. Each jigsaw puzzle has assembled size of 9x12" and one is color photo of Clint Walker as Cheyenne. The second puzzle scene is color illustration of him with life-like image and this is repeated on box lid. The third puzzle scene is a generic "Cowboy Roundup" cattle drive. **$70.**

CHY-7

CHY-7. "CHEYENNE" COSTUME. Child's colorful western outfit made mostly from drill fabric with vinyl accents. The chaps are red at the pelvis area with the flared lower legs in black. Each leg has "Cheyenne" name in silvery gray lettering. Accent colors are mostly yellow. The vest front is red and black vinyl trimmed in yellow. Each front side of vest has plastic clip for three toy bullets. Circa late 1950s. **$60.**

CHY-8

CHY-8. "CHEYENNE TARGET GAME" in 2.5x17x24" cardboard display carton. Set is English-made by Mettoy ©1962. Set consists of 16.5x24" beautiful full color lithograph metal target board with photo of Clint Walker, plus 26.5" long black plastic rifle and pair of plastic darts with rubber cup ends. Darts are spring-loaded into barrel and then fired by pulling the trigger. Back of target board has cardboard easel. **$300.**

CIRCUS BOY

NBC: September 23, 1956 – September 8, 1957
ABC: September 19, 1957 – September 11, 1958

Children's adventure series starring Mickey Braddock as Corky, a youthful orphan working the circus at the turn of the century. Braddock's real name is Mickey Dolenz, later to become one of the Monkees rock music group. Series was by Screen Gems Productions.

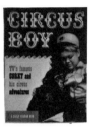

CSB-1

CSB-2

CSB-3

CSB-1. "CIRCUS BOY" 8.25x11" hardcover 1958 Daily Mirror Book (England) with 128 pages with story and art based on the series. **$15.**

CSB-2. "CIRCUS BOY UNDER THE BIG TOP" 5.5x8" hardcover Whitman book #1549:49 ©1957 with 284-page story. **$12.**

CSB-3. "CIRCUS BOY/WAR ON WHEELS" 5.5x8" hardcover Whitman book #1578 ©1958 with 284-page story. **$12.**

CSB-4

CSB-4. "CIRCUS BOY" GAME by H.G. Toys ©1956 in 12.5x13.5" box. Game features a recessed insert gameboard that has a small three-dimensional cardboard tent in center mounted at the peak with a plastic spinner. Game is played with small disks. **$50.**

THE CISCO KID

Syndicated by Ziv TV 1950 – 1956 (156 Episodes)

Popular early western series based on character which began on radio in addition to even earlier appearances in movie and book versions. The television version starred Duncan Renaldo as Cisco and Leo Carillo as his chubby, jovial sidekick Pancho. The series had extended popularity in syndication as all episodes were filmed in color for later use, although stations showed them in black and white throughout the 1950s. Items are normally copyrighted Ziv TV.

CSK-5

CSK-5. "LISTEN TO CISCO KID" PREMIUM MASK 10.5x12.5" die-cut stiff paper mask with inscription on reverse for Cisco Kid Cookies and Cisco Kid Sweet Buns baked by Schofer's Bakery ©1949. Reverse also has publicity for radio show over station WRAW (Reading, Pa). Mask image is fleshtone face accented by brown and black with sombrero in dark brown. **$20.**

| CSK-1 | CSK-2 | CSK-3 |

CSK-1. "DON'T MISS CISCO ON TV!" PREMIUM PICTURE. 8x10" stiff glossy paper sheet with black/white photo of Cisco on his horse Diablo. Picture has facsimile signature and bottom margin has advertising text for Weber's Bread plus broadcast times for four television stations in the Southern California area. Early 1950s and probably used in other geographic areas with changed imprint across bottom margin. **$25.**

CSK-2. "CISCO KID AND PANCHO COLORING BOOK" 11x14" Saalfield book #4567 ©1951. A thick book with 80 coloring pages. **$20.**

CSK-3. "CISCO KID" CARD WITH "SHERIFF" BADGE. 3x4.25" full color retail card depicting Cisco with inscription "Robin Hood Of The Range." Attached by keychain to the card is a 1.75" brass star accented by green paint. Card is marked "By Prevue" and also has © Doubleday & Co. Undated but early 1950s. **$25.**

CSK-6

CSK-7

CSK-6. "LISTEN TO CISCO KID" PREMIUM MASK. Companion mask to **CSK-5** with same size, color and back inscriptions although Pancho is depicted on mask image. **$20.**

CSK-7. "CISCO KID AND PANCHO" WHITE GLASS CEREAL BOWL with inscriptions and picture scene in black. Bowl is 5" diameter by 2.5" tall. Undated early 1950s. **$35.**

CSK-4

CSK-4. "CISCO KID AND PANCHO" PREMIUM JIGSAW PUZZLE with 7.5x8.5" paper envelope. Both puzzle and envelope have name of sponsor Tip-Top Bread ©1953. Assembled puzzle is 7.25x8.25" with full color illustration picture. **$50.**

CSK-8

CSK-8. "THE CISCO KID AND PANCHO" 3" tall white glass mug with inscription and scene printed in red. Undated early 1950s. **$25.**

COLT .45

ABC: October 18, 1957 – September 20, 1960

One of several western television adventure shows produced by Warner Bros. Wayde Preston starred as Christopher Colt, a government agent and son of the inventor of the Colt revolver.

CLT-1   CLT-2

CLT-1. CHRIS COLT HARTLAND FIGURE. 7.5" hard plastic standing figure by Hartland Plastics circa late 1950s – 1960 from their "Gunfighter" series based on television western stars. Figure has movable arms plus pair of pistols. The hat and jacket are light blue with trousers depicted in dark blue. **$150.**

CLT-2. "COLT .45" COLORING BOOK. 8x10.5" Saalfield book #4541 ©1959. **$20.**

COMBAT!

ABC: October 2, 1962 – August 29, 1967

The longest-running World War II drama of the 1960s starring Rick Jason as Lt. Gil Hanley and Vic Morrow as Sgt. Chip Saunders. Items are normally copyrighted Selmur Productions Inc.

COM-1   COM-2

COM-1. "VIC MORROW" 3.5x5.5" black/white exhibit card circa mid-1960s with facsimile signature. **$5.**

COM-2. "COMBAT" GUM WRAPPER. 5x6" waxed paper wrapper from bubblegum package issued by Donruss ©1964. Wrapper is the variety with "Lt. Hanley and Sgt. Saunders." **$15.**

COM-3   COM-4

COM-3. "COMBAT!" 8.5x11" Saalfield coloring book #9586 © 1963. **$20.**

COM-4. "COMBAT!" CARD GAME by Milton Bradley ©1964 in 1x6x7.5" box. Cards are oversized 3.5x5" and picture World War II era airplanes. **$20.**

COM-5   COM-6

COM-5. "COMBAT! THE FIGHTING INFANTRY GAME" by Ideal Toys ©1963 in 10x19.5" box. **$25.**

COM-6. "COMBAT! OFFICIAL PLAY SET BASED ON THE ABC-TV NETWORK SHOW" by Superior Toys (T. Cohn) ©1963. Box is 3x15x30" and holds six tanks, four trucks, two jeep and trailer units, eight various types of guns, two personnel carriers and forty-eight soldiers. **$150.**

COWBOY GUN & HOLSTER SETS

Selected gun sets for shows that otherwise produced few collectibles

CGS-1   CGS-2

CGS-1. "THE ADVENTURES OF JOHNNY RINGO" GUN AND HOLSTER SET by Esquire Novelty Corp. ©1960. Set is based on the CBS October 1, 1959 – September 29, 1960 half-hour western starring Don Durant as Ringo, a former gunslinger who became the sheriff of Velardi, Arizona. Ringo's gun in the series was a double-barreled LeMat Special which fired both .45 bullets and shotgun shells. Box is 3x12x15" with lid picture of Durant. The double holster set is black leather accented by gold tooling. Each holster is marked "Johnny Ringo." Each gun is silvered white metal with black/gold plastic grips plus extra long barrel for 12" overall length. Back of belt has clip for six bullets. **$150.**

CGS-2. "THE LANYARD PULL ACTION OFFICIAL JOHNNY RINGO FAST DRAW GUN AND HOLSTER" by Marx Toys ©1960 on 12x16" display card. Set is based on same series as **CGS-1** and consists of 10.5" black metal gun and brown plastic holster. Card description is "The Strangest, Fastest Gun In The West" with depiction of Durant as Ringo. Holster has name "Johnny Ringo" and is designed with a pair of rigid braces rather than holster cover for quick-drawing. **$85.**

CGS-3   CGS-4

CGS-3. "LAW AND ORDER" DOUBLE GUN AND HOLSTER SET by Daisy Mfg. Co. circa 1960s. Insert card in 2x10x10.5" display box is marked "TV Holsters Of The West" with no reference to a specific television show. The belt and holsters are finished brown leather with a silvered metal decorative piece added to each holster, each centered by a simulated turquoise stone. Each gun is an 8" silvered metal with simulated pearl grips of plastic. Each gun is inscribed "Big Buck." **$100.**

CGS-4. "MACKENZIES RAIDERS" PACKAGED GUN AND HOLSTER/CANEEN SET based on the syndicated series by Ziv TV Productions which began and ended in 1958. The show starred Richard Carlson as Colonel Ranald Mackenzie, a U.S. cavalry officer on the Mexican Border in the 1870s. Carlson is pictured on the package header card. Display card is 8x13" with cellophane bagging. Contents are a plastic canteen plus plastic belt with silvered metal buckle, dark red vinyl holster with 8.5" silvery gray plastic pistol. Attached to the holster is a silver-colored "U.S. Marshal/Sheriff" badge. **$50.**

CGS-5

CGS-5. "WYATT EARP/FRONTIER MARSHAL" DOUBLE GUN AND HOLSTER SET circa 1960s although not a licensed item for the ABC 1955-1961 series starring Hugh O'Brian. Box is 2.5x11.5x14" and holds black leather holster set detailed in bright silver. The belt has Earp name and three plastic bullets in clip on back. The guns are silver plated with metal grips finished in black. Each gun is marked "Coyote" and are by Hubley. **$150.**

COWBOY IN AFRICA

CBS: September 11, 1967 – September 16, 1968

Adventure series starring Chuck Connors as Jim Sinclair, an American rodeo star working on a wildlife project in Kenya, Africa. Items are normally copyrighted Ivan Tors Productions.

CIA-1

CIA-1. "CHUCK CONNORS/COWBOY IN AFRICA" STEEL LUNCH BOX by King-Seeley ©1968. **$60.**

CIA-2   CIA-3

CIA-2. "CHUCK CONNORS/COWBOY IN AFRICA" STEEL THERMOS 6.5" tall by King-Seeley ©1968. Thermos came with item **CIA-1. $30.**

CIA-3. "CHUCK CONNORS/COWBOY IN AFRICA" BOXED "FANNER-50" GUN by Mattel Toys ©1967. Cap gun is black metal with white plastic grips and comes with box of Mattel "Greenies" caps. Box is 8x11" with lid design and photo scene based on the series. **$90.**

CRUSADER RABBIT

Syndicated 1949 – 1958

One of the earliest animated cartoons made especially for television by Jay Ward and Alexander Anderson in the late 1940s. The first series was offered to NBC in 1949 although declined. A second set of cartoons was developed in 1956 and syndicated a year later by Creston Studios. Ward was then the creator of another series, "Rocky And His Friends." Crusader Rabbit was a small but heroic figure assisted by his sidekick Rags The Tiger who was not noted for his intelligence. Items are normally copyrighted T.A.P. Inc.

CRR-1   CRR-2   CRR-3

44

CRR-1. "CRUSADER RABBIT" 6.5x8" stiff-covered 20-page Wonder Book ©1958. **$25.**

CRR-2. "CRUSADER RABBIT TRACE AND COLOR" 8.5x11" Whitman book ©1959. **$35.**

CRR-3. "CRUSADER RABBIT IN BUBBLE TROUBLE" 6.5x7.5" hardcover Whitman storybook from Top Top Tales series ©1960. **$25.**

CRR-4   CRR-5

CRR-4. "CRUSADER RABBIT" COMIC BOOK #735 by Dell Publishing Co. ©1976. **$40.**

CRR-5. "CRUSADER RABBIT PAINT SET" circa 1957-1958 in 13x19.5" box. Lid has colorful depiction of him and Rags although contents of crayon and watercolor materials have no further reference to them. **$50.**

THE DAFFY DUCK SHOW

NBC: November 4, 1978 – September 11, 1982

Warner Bros. half-hour Saturday morning cartoon show which added Speedy Gonzales, a Mexican mouse, as co-star in 1981 under new show title "The Daffy-Speedy Show." Also appearing were Pepe LePew and Foghorn Leghorn. In 1982 the show moved to CBS as part of the "Sylvester & Tweety" show.

DAF-1   DAF-2

DAF-1. DAFFY DUCK CEL original animation painted art on 10.5x12.5" clear acetate sheet. Actual art size is 2x3" in handpainted full color. Circa late 1970s. **$75.**

DAF-2. FOGHORN LEGHORN 9" HAND PUPPET with fabric handcover body and vinyl molded head which has inset plastic eyes that move. Puppet depicts talkative, southern-accented rooster character originally introduced in mid-1940s by Merry Melodies although puppet is circa 1960s. **$25.**

DAF-3   DAF-4

DAF-3. SPEEDY GONZALES 5.5" hand-painted hollow china figure made in Italy with Warner Bros. © stamped on bottom. Circa early 1980s. **$25.**

DAF-4. SPEEDY GONZALES 7.5" vinyl figure with tag on fabric shirt by maker Dakin & Co. ©1970. Body has movable head, arms, and legs. Clothing is a thin vinyl yellow sombrero, green fabric shirt, red shoulder sash, and white trousers. The head has small black whiskers and reverse has a long black rubber tail. **$30.**

DAKTARI

CBS: January 11, 1966 – January 15, 1969

African adventure series deriving its name from native word for "Doctor" starring Marshall Thompson as Dr. Marsh Tracy and Cheryl Miller as his daughter Paula. Items will normally have copyright of Ivan Tors Films.

DAK-1   DAK-2

DAK-1. "DAKTARI" VIEW-MASTER REEL SET. 4.5x4.5" sealed packet with complete set of three stereo photo reels and 16-page story booklet from the series. By GAF ©1968. **$15.**

DAK-2. "DAKTARI" CORGI "GIFT SET 7" by Mettoy Co. Ltd. of England ©1973, probably generated by popularity of series in United Kingdom. Display box is 1.5x3x7" and contains realistically detailed diecast scale model jeep with hard plastic figures of Dr. Tracy, Paula, Judy the chimp, Clarence the lion, plus a tiger. Jeep has small front sticker "Wameru Sub District." **$75.**

DAK-3

DAK-3. "DAKTARI PLAY SET" by Marx Toys ©1967. Original carton with printed lid design is 4x16x27.5". Set consists of a lithographed tin jungle trading post plus native huts, trees, ferns, boulders, hand-painted native and jungle animal figures, printed play sheet and other accessories. **$400.**

DANGER MAN

See Secret Agent

DANIEL BOONE

NBC: September 24, 1964 – August 27, 1970

Adventure series based on the life of pioneer Boone in Kentucky Territory in the 1770s starring Fess Parker who ten years earlier portrayed Davy Crockett on the "Disneyland" series. Items are normally copyrighted 20th Century-Fox TV.

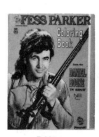

DAN-1 **DAN-2**

DAN-1. "THE FESS PARKER/DANIEL BOONE" 8.5x11" Saalfield coloring book #9596 ©1964. **$30.**

DAN-2. "FESS PARKER LUNCH KIT FROM THE DANIEL BOONE T.V. SHOW" AND THERMOS. Steel box by King-Seeley © 1965 with original 7" metal thermos. **LUNCH BOX $50. THERMOS $30.**

DAN-3 **DAN-4**

DAN-3. "DANIEL BOONE FRONTIER PLAY SET" by Marx Toys circa mid-1960s. Display box has printed lid picture and is 4x13x24". Playset parts are covered wagon and horses with driver, six frontiersmen and six Indian figures, each 6" tall, plus accessories. **$200.**

DAN-4. FESS PARKER/DANIEL BOONE "TRAIL BLAZERS GAME" by Milton Bradley ©1964. Box is 9.5x19" and contains playing board, insert board with spinner, card deck, small plastic markers, and membership application to NBC for the Trail Blazers Club. **$25.**

DARK SHADOWS

ABC: June 27, 1966 – April 2, 1971

Late afternoon suspense drama series including ghosts, vampires, werewolves and other terrors in continuing story about the Collins family in Collinsport, Maine. Among the major characters were Barnabas Collins, a 200-year-old vampire (Jonathan Frid) and Quentin Collins (David Selby). Items will normally have copyright of creator Dan Curtis.

DKS-1 **DKS-2**

DKS-1. "BARNABAS COLLINS/DARK SHADOWS GAME" by Milton Bradley ©1969. Box is 2.5x9.5x19" and comes in two slightly different design versions on lid end panels. One version has cardboard game coffin with hard plastic lid inscribed with Barnabas Collins' name. The other version has similar coffin with unmarked soft plastic lid. Both versions come with small mouthpiece fangs which glow in the dark to be worn by a player. Each also has plastic assembly pieces for a skeleton, and cardboard pieces for forming a scaffold on which the skeleton is to be assembled as part of the game. **$35.**

DKS-2. "DARK SHADOWS GAME" by Whitman ©1968 with 10.5x18" box. Large 30x30" heavy paper playing board is nicely designed with depictions of tombstones, buzzard, black cat, bats, mummy in coffin and bloody hand. Game also includes 4 cardboard stand-up playing pieces depicting other ghoulish motifs. Card deck has 52 cards plus instruction card and a wallet card that has photo of Barnabas Collins. **$45.**

DKS-3 **DKS-4** **DKS-5**

DKS-3. "DARK SHADOWS" ORIGINAL MUSIC 33 1/3-rpm record on Philips label © 1969. Record is in 12.25x12.25" album. Record has 16 original music themes from the show. Included in album is black/white photo poster with opened size of 11x22" featuring photos of Barnabas and Quentin. **RECORD ALBUM $10. WITH POSTER $25.**

DKS-4. DARK SHADOWS COMPLETE SET of twelve full color photo 5x7" post cards ©1969. **SET $50.**

DKS-5. "DARK SHADOWS" GUM CARD SET. Second version set of 66 cards issued by Philly Gum ©1969. Each card has green border with picture scene from the series. Backs of each are a puzzle piece to form large poster picture when placed together. **SET $80.**

DKS-6   DKS-7

DKS-6. "BARNABAS VAMPIRE VAN" MODEL ASSEMBLY KIT by MPC ©1969. Box is 3.5x6.5x9" and contains unpainted plastic parts for assembly of 1/25 scale model replica of sporty hearse vehicle. **$100.**

DKS-7. "DARK SHADOWS" VIEW-MASTER REEL SET in 4.5x4.5" packet envelope also including 16-page story booklet. Reels have a total of 21 color stereo pictures from the series. By GAF circa late 1960s. **$75.**

DENNIS THE MENACE

CBS: October 4, 1959 – September 22, 1963

Live action, prime time series based on the Hank Ketcham comic strip of the same name. The series starred Jay North as Dennis. Items will normally have copyright of Screen Gems Inc.

DTM-1   DTM-2

DTM-1. "DENNIS THE MENACE STORYBOOK" 8.25x11.25" hardcover Random House 68-page book © 1960. Book cover and frontispiece have photo of Jay North, and story art is by Hank Ketcham. **$15.**

DTM-2. "THE MISADVENTURES OF DENNIS THE MENACE" TV SOUNDTRACK 33 1/3-rpm record on Colpix label circa early 1960s. Each side has single adventure from series soundtrack. Album is 12.5x12.5". **$25.**

DTM-3   DTM-4

DTM-3. "DENNIS THE MENACE" 11.5x14.5 frame tray inlay jigsaw puzzle by Whitman ©1960. Puzzle scene is an illustration based on the television series although art is not by Ketcham. **$12.**

DTM-4. "DENNIS THE MENACE BACK-YARD PICNIC" SET-UP KIT by Whitman ©1960. Kit is in 9x12" cardboard album holding punch-out and cut-out sheets for 7 dolls, 29 costumes plus accessories including a lemonade stand, clubhouse, patio table and other items for a festive picnic scene. **$25.**

THE DEPUTY

NBC: September 12, 1959 – September 16, 1961

Western adventure series starring Henry Fonda as Marshal Simon Fry in Silver City, Arizona Territory during the early 1880s. Items are normally copyrighted MCA Enterprises or 20th Century Varieties Inc.

DEP-1   DEP-2

DEP-1. "THE DEPUTY GAME" by Milton Bradley ©1960. Box is 9.5x19" and game parts include a metal "Deputy Marshal" badge to be earned by player capturing the most outlaws. **$25.**

DEP-2. "THE DEPUTY" WHITE METAL BADGE on original 3x4" display card by Top Gun Co. ©1959. Card design is yellow/black/white and includes inscription "Henry Fonda As Marshal Simon Fry." **$15.**

DEPUTY DAWG

Syndicated: 1961
NBC: September 11, 1971 – September 2, 1972

Animated series with character who originally appeared in Terrytoons theatrical cartoons. Cast of characters included Gandy Goose and Sourpuss the Cat.

DPD-1   DPD-2

DPD-1. "DEPUTY DAWG" GAME by Milton Bradley ©1960 in 9.5x19" box. Game consists of three decks of small cards, plastic and wood game pieces, and 16x18.5" playing board. **$30.**

DPD-2. "DEPUTY DAWG" BAGGED FIGURE by R. Dakin Co. © 1977. Display bag is 6x10.5" and figure has hard plastic body and soft vinyl head. Head, arms and legs are movable. **$30.**

 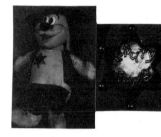

DPD-3   DPD-4

DPD-3. "DEPUTY DAWG" 9.5" hard plastic bath soap container issued in "Soaky" series ©1966. Figure is mostly in brown with yellow accent on face, arms, chest and feet plus glossy white muzzle. **$20.**

DPD-4. "DEPUTY DAWG" STUFFED CLOTH DOLL 14" tall with plush arms and feet plus soft vinyl head. His outfit is a black thin plastic hat with drawstring, plus clothing depicted in yellow, blue and red. Pinned to the chest is a 1.5" silvered metal "Deputy Dawg" badge. Doll has original tag by Ideal Toy circa 1960s. **$50.**

DICK TRACY

ABC: September 11, 1950 – February 12, 1951

Prime time live action series based on comic strip by Chester Gould. The television series starred Ralph Byrd as Tracy re-creating his role from several movies of the late 1930s and 1940s. Byrd's death in 1952 ended the live production although an animated version followed in 1961. In 1971 the animated Tracy also appeared on "The Archie Show." Most items will have copyright of Chicago Tribune.

DTY-1   DTY-2

DTY-1. DICK TRACY HAND PUPPET 10.5" with fabric handcover body and soft vinyl head. Fabric cover has printed design of him in black suit with striped necktie plus wrist radio. ©1961. **$40.**

DTY-2. "DICK TRACY FLASHLIGHT" WITH BOX, by Bantam-Lite circa late 1940s. Flashlight is palm-sized .5x1x3.25" metal with small end cover which flips open to expose beam of light. Box is .75x1x3.5". **$40.**

DTY-3

DTY-3. "DICK TRACY TWO-WAY ELECTRONIC WRIST RADIOS" BOXED SET by Remco Industries circa early 1950s. Box is 3x9x13" and contains pair of black plastic radio units, each with elastic wrist strap, with both units joined by length of wire. Each unit is designed with gold foil sticker to resemble a radio screen. The set requires batteries for operation. **$125.**

DTY-4   DTY-5   DTY-6

DTY-4. "TESS TRUEHEART" 5" frosted white heavy drinking glass with depiction and name in green of Tracy's sweetheart. By unknown maker or sponsor, circa 1940s or later. **$40.**

DTY-5. "SNOWFLAKE" 5" frosted white heavy drinking glass from same series as **DTY-4.** Title and picture are in blue. **$40.**

DTY-6. "BREATHLESS MAHONEY" 5" frosted white heavy drinking glass from same series as **DTY-4.** Title and picture are in green. **$40.**

DTY-7   DTY-8

DTY-7. "DICK TRACY'S SECRET DETECTIVE SCRAPBOOK" 3.5x5.5" paper premium manual with 16 pages, sponsored circa 1952 by Amm-i-dent Toothpaste. Back cover pictures the "Dick Tracy TV Club Coding Machine" which was membership card with special built-in decoder. Other pages have illustrated crime-solving tips. **$45.**

DTY-8. DICK TRACY "GREEN DECODER" 3.5x6.75" card issued circa 1950 by various Post's cereals. The card has green color and also came in red color with corresponding "Crime Stoppers" messages for each color card printed on box packages. **$25.**

DTY-9   DTY-10

DTY-9. "DICK TRACY" EMBOSSED STEEL LUNCH BOX by Aladdin Industries ©1967. **$250.**

DTY-10. "DICK TRACY" METAL THERMOS 6.5" by Aladdin Industries ©1967. Thermos came with item **DTY-9. $40.**

DTY-11   DTY-12   DTY-13

DTY-11. DICK TRACY 10.25" "Soaky" hard plastic bath soap container ©1965. Figure is depicted in yellow outfit with black accent colors. **$20.**

DTY-12. "DICK TRACY" PLASTIC MODEL KIT by Aurora Plastics ©1968 in 1.5x5x13" sealed box. **$250.**

DTY-13. "DICK TRACY SPACE COUPE" MODEL KIT #819-100 by Aurora Plastics ©1968 in 1.5x5.25x13.25" box. **$100.**

DTY-14   DTY-15

DTY-14. "DICK TRACY CRIME STOPPER" BATTERY GAME by Ideal Toys © 1963. Box is 5x13.5x19" and contains a 3x12x17" control panel with spinner board and eight push buttons, each with the name of an individual villain. Other game parts are a "Clue Decoder" paper roll which is turned manually in the control panel plus 20 clue cards. **$50.**

DTY-15. "DICK TRACY CARTOON KIT" by Colorforms ©1962 in 1x8x13" box. Kit has thin vinyl character pieces to be applied to background scene that includes bank and jewelry store. **$25.**

DTY-16   DTY-17

DTY-16. "DICK TRACY COPMOBILE" boxed battery vehicle by Ideal Toys ©1963. Plastic car is large 9x10x24" size with a roof siren plus antennas on the hood and trunk. When activated by batteries, the car is designed to make announcements through the siren/bullhorn by a wireless hand microphone, also used to sound the siren. The car's movement is started and stopped by tapping the trunk antenna with a long wooden rod. Original carton is 9x12x27" with picture lid. **$200.**

DTY-17. "DICK TRACY PICTURE PUZZLE" by Jaymar circa early 1960s in 2x7x10" box. Completed puzzle is 10x14" with "The Line-Up" scene which is shown on box lid. **$20.**

DTY-18

DTY-18. "DICK TRACY 2-WAY WRIST RADIO" boxed battery-operated set by American Doll & Toy Corp. circa 1961-1963. Wrist radios are black plastic with adjustable wrist straps. Radios are joined by wires and set includes a "Power Pak" unit for each radio. Set is designed to transmit and receive messages as well as pick up certain Citizens Band channels. Warranty expiration date of set is March 31, 1963. Box is 2.5x8x8". **$100.**

DTY-19   DTY-20   DTY-21

DTY-19. DICK TRACY WRIST RADIO CHRISTMAS CARD. 5.25x7" black/white/red stiff paper card picturing Tracy in a tropical setting while receiving Christmas wishes on his wrist radio. Card art is by Chester Gould and has facsimile signature. The back is blank. Circa 1950s. **$35.**

DTY-20. "DICK TRACY JUNIOR DETECTIVE KIT" 7.5x13" Golden Press stiff paper punch-out book ©1962 with six pages of full color crime detection items to be punched to form complete detective kit. **$35.**

DTY-21. "DICK TRACY PUPPETS" boxed 10" hand puppet figure of his animated television sidekick Joe Jitsu. Puppet has fabric body and soft vinyl head. Box is 3x5.5x11.5" with a vinyl 33 1/3-rpm record for play-acting with the puppet and others issued in the series. By Ideal Toys, ©1961. **$60.**

DING DONG SCHOOL

NBC: December 22, 1951 – December 28, 1956
Syndicated in 1959

One of the first educational shows for young children, hosted by "Miss Frances," Dr. Frances Horwich, head of the education department at Roosevelt College in Chicago. Items are normally copyrighted Frances R. Horwich or National Broadcasting Co.

| DDS-1 | DDS-2 | DDS-3 |

DDS-1. "MISS FRANCES/DING DONG SCHOOL" 3" red plastic mug with colorful decal by sponsor, instant Ovaltine. **$25.**

DDS-2. "MISS FRANCES' ALL-DAY-LONG BOOK" 8x10.5" "Ding Dong School Book" authored by Dr. Frances Horwich and Reinald Werrenwrath © 1954. Book has illustrated instructions for doing 46 different things of child interest. **$10.**

DDS-3. "DING DONG SCHOOL STICKER FUN" 10.5x12" Whitman book #2167 © 1955 with punch-out sticker pages, mostly designed for forming basic pictures by children on stiff paper worksheets which are also bound into the book. **$15.**

DINKY DUCK

See The Heckle & Jeckle Cartoon Show

DISNEYLAND

ABC: October 27, 1954 – September 17, 1961

Television was a perfect medium for Disney and this show was one of the most successful in broadcasting history. The program allowed Disney to promote the amusement park, preview upcoming movies and utilize cartoons and features previously completed. The most successful new dramatic shows were the five Davy Crockett segments starring Fess Parker. In 1958 the show was renamed "Walt Disney Presents" and in 1961 Disney moved to NBC (see "Walt Disney's Wonderful World Of Color"). Items are normally copyrighted Walt Disney Productions.

| DLD-1 | DLD-2 |

DLD-1. "WALT DISNEY'S DISNEYLAND GAME" by Transogram circa 1954-1955 in 9x17" box. Gameboard is in four quadrants devoted to Adventureland, Fantasyland, Tomorrowland, Frontierland, centered by illustration of the Disneyland Civic Center. Game also has sixteen playing pieces plus travel cards. Game is based on "The New Disneyland Park As Seen On TV And In The Movies." **$50.**

DLD-2. "WALT DISNEY'S TOMORROWLAND-ROCKET TO THE MOON GAME" by Parker Brothers circa 1955 in 8x16" box. **$35.**

| DLD-3 | DLD-4 |

DLD-3. "WALT DISNEY'S ADVENTURELAND GAME" by Parker Brothers circa 1957 in 12x16" box. Set includes playing board, 24 cards, a spinner and 4 small metal boats. **$25.**

DLD-4. "WALT DISNEY'S FANTASYLAND GAME" by Parker Brothers circa 1955 in 8x16" box. The playing board shows Disneyland attractions such as Mr. Toad's Wild Ride, Mad Tea Party Ride, Casey Jr. Train Ride, Flying Dumbo Ride, King Arthur's Carousel. **$35.**

| DLD-5 | DLD-6 |

DLD-5. "WALT DISNEY'S FRONTIERLAND GAME" by Parker Brothers circa 1957 in 8x16" box. Game parts include playing board, 36 cardboard disks, 4 metal cowboys on horses. **$25.**

DLD-6. "DAVY CROCKETT RESCUE RACE" GAME by Gabriel ©1955 in 10x19.5" box. Game parts include 4 plastic figures, compass, cardboard tiles, play money. **$40.**

| DLD-7 | DLD-8 | DLD-9 |

DLD-7. "DAVY CROCKETT-KING OF THE WILD FRONTIER" Little Golden Book by Simon & Schuster ©1955. **$10.**

DLD-8. "DAVY CROCKETT-KING OF THE WILD FRONTIER SONG ALBUM" by Walt Disney and Wonderland Music companies © 1955, 9x12", 16 pages. **$30.**

DLD-9. "WALT DISNEY'S DAVY CROCKETT" 10x15" Whitman punch-out book #1943 © 1955. Book has eight pages of punch-out parts to form Davy's Frontier Cabin with figures of him, Buddy Ebsen as Russel, and Indians. **$40.**

DLD-10

DLD-10. "WALT DISNEY'S OFFICIAL DAVY CROCKETT WESTERN PRAIRIE WAGON" red lithographed steel 7x8x14" wagon with full color western scenes around the edge including two pictures of Fess Parker as Crockett. The wagon comes with handle plus two wire hoops and a red/white vinyl cover to turn it into a covered wagon. The cover is inscribed "Official Walt Disney's Dry Gulch Western Prairie Wagon" and also has a Mouseketeer symbol on the side. By Adco-Liberty Corp. circa 1958-1960. **$200.**

DLD-11   DLD-12

DLD-11. "WALT DISNEY'S OFFICIAL DAVY CROCKETT AT THE ALAMO" MARX PLAYSET circa 1958-1960 in 3x11x23" picture carton. Set has lithographed tin and plastic parts including Alamo building, wall sections, archway and gates, shell-shooting cannon, cavalry and Indian figures, horses, Davy Crockett figure and other accessories. **$600.**

DLD-12. "WALT DISNEY'S SWAMP FOX" GAME by Parker Brothers circa 1959-1961 in 10x19" box. Game is based on the Disney series starring Leslie Nielsen as General Francis Marion, a Revolutionary War hero. **$25.**

DLD-13   DLD-14   DLD-15

DLD-13. "THE SWAMP FOX COLORING BOOK" 8.5x11" Whitman book © 1961 based on the same series as **DLD-12. $12.**

DLD-14. "WALT DISNEY'S ANDY BURNETT COLORING BOOK" 8.5x11" Whitman #1185 © 1958, based on series "The Saga Of Andy Burnett" starring Jerome Courtland in the title role as a pioneer who traveled from Pennsylvnia to the Rockies. **$15.**

DLD-15. BABES IN TOYLAND 6" lithographed tin windup toy by Line Mar circa late 1950s. **$200.**

DOBIE GILLIS
See The Many Loves Of Dobie Gillis

DR. KILDARE
NBC: September 28, 1961 – August 30, 1966

Medical drama starring Richard Chamberlain as Dr. James Kildare, an intern at Blair General Hospital. Items will normally have a character copyright by Metro-Goldwyn-Mayer.

DRK-1   DRK-2

DRK-1. "DR. KILDARE MEDICAL GAME FOR THE YOUNG" by Ideal Toys © 1962. Game parts include playing board designed like a hospital ward, four tokens, spinner and analyzer, diagnosis cards, doctor cards. **$20.**

DRK-2. "DR. KILDARE'S THUMPY-THE HEARTBEAT STETHO-SCOPE" medical toy on sealed 6x18" cardboard display panel by Amson Industries circa early 1960s. **$30.**

DRK-3   DRK-4

DRK-3. "DR. KILDARE" 7" composition bobbing head figure on round base circa early 1960s. **$75.**

DRK-4. "DR. KILDARE AND NURSE SUSAN" English-published paper punch-out book by Collins © 1965 with three dolls and clothing pages. **$30.**

DOCTOR WHO

Syndicated 1975

Live action science-fiction adventure series shown in England by British Broadcasting Corporation since 1963, distributed in the United States by Time-Life Films. Various actors have played the title role of a 750-year-old alien from planet Gallifrey who assumes human form. Items will normally have copyright of British Broadcasting Corporation or BBC-TV.

DRW-6   DRW-7

DRW-6. "DOCTOR WHO – TALKING K-9" 3.5x6x8" plastic robot dog battery-operated toy by Palitoy © 1978. When the button is pressed on back of toy, the tail rises and several different short phrases are voiced. Toy comes in colorful box. **$150.**

DRW-7. "DOCTOR WHO" ENGLISH-PRODUCED GAME by Denys Fisher Toys Ltd. © 1975 in 10x19.5" box. Playing board is 18.5x19.5" with science-fiction fantasy scene of four huge planets inhabited by different types of beasts. Other game parts include a miniature plastic telephone booth, deck of cards and small stand-up cardboard figure of Doctor Who. **$75.**

DRW-1   DRW-2   DRW-3

DRW-1. "THE DR. WHO ANNUAL" 7.5x10.5" English-published hardcover adventure storybook © 1965. Possibly the earliest of an annual series published for the show. **$35.**

DRW-2. AUTOGRAPHED DOCTOR WHO PHOTO CARD 4.25x6" English-published post card with color portrait photo of Patrick Troughton, one of several actors to play the title role. Autograph in blue marker ink is "Best Wishes Patrick Troughton." Circa late 1960s-early 1970s. **$35.**

DRW-3. "THE DR. WHO ANNUAL 1979" 8x11" English-published hardcover 64-page book © 1979 with actor Tom Baker pictured on cover. **$15.**

THE DONNA REED SHOW

ABC: September 24, 1958 – September 3, 1966

Wholesome American family situation comedy starring Reed as Donna Stone, the mother and Carl Betz as her husband, Alex Stone. A popular show although it appears to have generated only a paperdoll set and a few TV Guide issues as collectibles. Items are normally copyrighted Screen Gems Inc.

DRS-1   DRS-2

DRW-4   DRW-5

DRW-4. "DOCTOR WHO – TARDIS TUNER" RADIO in 3x6x8" retail box © 1978. Radio is 2.5x5x7" in science-fiction styling including flashing light bars and control button for "Morse Warp" and "Laser Beep" sound effects. Radio is battery-operated and designed for AM use. **$50.**

DRW-5. "BBC TALKING DALEK" 4x5.25x6.5" battery-operated plastic robot toy by Palitoy © 1975. The toy rotates when a button is pressed on the top while producing four sentences of commands. Toy has three plastic attachment pieces and comes in colorful box. **$150.**

DRS-1. "DONNA REED" PAPERDOLL KIT by Merry Mfg. Co. © 1964 in 1.5x5.25x19" display box. The single doll is 15" figure of die-cut thick cardboard with sheets of "Rub 'N Stay" clothing designed to cling in place by rubbing. Included is a fashion chart for mixing or matching her clothing. **$75.**

DRS-2. "TV GUIDE" weekly issue for June 29, 1963 with cover photo of co-stars Reed and Betz plus three-page article mostly about him. **$20.**

DRAGNET

NBC: January 3, 1952 – September 10, 1970

One of the most successful and longest-running police series starring Jack Webb as Sgt. Joe Friday of the Los Angeles Police Department. Later reruns were issued under title "Badge 714." Items will normally have copyright of Sherry TV Inc.

DGT-1   DGT-2

DGT-1. "JACK WEBB'S SAFETY SQUAD COLORING BOOK" by Samuel Lowe Co. with 64 pages ©1956. **$20.**

DGT-2. DRAGNET "TALKING POLICE CAR" by Ideal Toys © 1954 in 5.5x6x14.5" box. Car is 5x6x14" of black/white plastic with domed canopy that holds removable battery-operated light which can also be used as a flashlight. The trunk lid has a crank handle to activate a mechanical voice box with a single police message. Car is nicely detailed with several moving interior features including swivel seat and table. Accessories include a tommy gun, riot gun, two extra rifles, two pistols, camera with flash attachment, binoculars, telephone. **$125.**

DGT-3

DGT-4

DGT-3. "THE GAME OF DRAGNET" by Transogram ©1955 in 10x19.5" box. Game parts include playing board, six miniature plastic police squad cars, crime cards, evidence cards, score pad, single die and shaker, small plastic pieces representing suspects. **$30.**

DGT-4. "DRAGNET/BADGE 714" CAP GUN on 1.5x5.5x8" die-cut cardboard retail display package by Knickerbocker ©1955. Gun is 6.5" black plastic with red plastic grips and is designed like the "Detective Special Repeating Revolver" used by Sgt. Friday. Back of display card has a Jack Webb safety message and Dragnet identity card to be cut out. **$40.**

DGT-5   DGT-6

DGT-5. "DRAGNET BADGE 714" REPLICA in .5x2.25x4" retail box ©1955. Badge is 2.25" bright brass inscribed "Sergeant," "Dragnet," and "714." Bottom of box has Dragnet identity card to be clipped. **$30.**

DGT-6. "DRAGNET TRIPLE-FIRE COMBINATION TARGET GAME" ©1955 in 12x18" box. Set has 11x13" lithographed tin target board with design including four tip-over criminal figures on an axle rod across the front. Set also includes two Dragnet dart guns with corks, plastic whistle and Dragnet brass badge. Box design includes a Dragnet identification card to be clipped. **$75.**

DGT-7

DGT-7. "DRAGNET CRIME LAB" KIT by Transogram ©1955 in 2.5x9x12" cardboard container designed like attache case with brass carrying handle and clasp. Contents are a small plastic pistol requiring battery and bulb to be used a flashlight signal gun, badge, plastic handcuffs, microscope, magnifying glass, test tube with invisible ink, fingerprint kit, detective's wallet with Dragnet I.D. card and a "Case Closed" stamp. **$75.**

DROOP-A-LONG COYOTE

See The Magilla Gorilla Show

THE DUDLEY DO-RIGHT SHOW

See The Bullwinkle Show

THE ED SULLIVAN SHOW

CBS: June 10, 1948 – June 6, 1971

Immensely popular long-running Sunday evening variety show hosted by Sullivan who was also a syndicated newspaper columnist. The show was officially titled "The Toast Of The Town" for the first five years and introduced many performers to the American public. Among those making their TV debut on his show were Bob Hope, Walt Disney and The Beatles. Elvis Presley was signed in the summer of 1956 for three appearances but actually made his first TV appearance in January 1956 on Tommy and Jimmy Dorsey's "Stage Show." Topo Gigio, a mechanical Italian mouse, was a regular feature.

| EDS-1 | EDS-2 | EDS-3 |

EDS-1. "TV WORLD" magazine for April, 1956 with Sullivan cover photo plus short item about the show. **$10.**

EDS-2. "TV GUIDE" weekly issue for June 19, 1953 with Sullivan cover article. **$15.**

EDS-3. ED SULLIVAN autographed 7x9" bw glossy photo. **$50.**

EDS-4

EDS-5

EDS-4. "TOPO GIGIO" 5.5" ceramic bobbing head figure in 2.5x4x5" box. Head is mounted at the neck by a spring and has metal eyes and hard plastic whisker hairs. Circa late 1950s. **$45.**

EDS-5. "TOPO GIGIO" BOBBING HEAD ASHTRAY in original 3x4.5x5" box. Ashtray itself is a 4x4" ceramic replica of an upturned seashell. The figure is removable from the tray and has spring-mounted head which bobs about. The figure is mostly composition with soft flocking accents. Eyes are inset plastic and head also has wisp of lifelike hair and a small beret. Circa late 1950s. **$45.**

ELVIS PRESLEY

Elvis never had a continuing TV program but his appearance on The Ed Sullivan Show in the fall of 1956 was an epic event which helped generate considerable popularity for Elvis collectibles from the 1956 era. Authorized items are usually copyright Elvis Presley Enterprises (or E.P.E.) 1956.

EVP-1

EVP-1. "TV GUIDE" three-part article from the emergence era of Elvis as a national and international entertainment star. Issues are from 1956 for weeks of September 8-14, 22-28, 29-October 9. The entire three-part article is titled "The Plain Truth About Elvis Presley" and installment articles are "The People Who Know Say He <u>Does</u> Have Talent," "The Folks He Left Behind Him," and "What Folks Back Home Say About Presley." **SET $125.**

| EVP-2 | EVP-3 |

EVP-2. "1957 ELVIS PRESLEY ENTERPRISES" DOLL with copyright marking on back of neck. The doll is 18" tall and has a thin rubber-like soft "magic skin" covering which becomes fragile with age. The head is of heavier vinyl and original clothing includes a plaid shirt, blue pants, black belt and a pair of simulated blue suede shoes. Rarely found complete and undamaged. **$1,200.**

EVP-3. "ELVIS PRESLEY GUITAR" AND CASE by Emenee Musical Toys ©1956. Very nice quality hard plastic guitar with depth of 3", width of 11" at the widest part and length of 31". Guitar front is white with black neck and head. The entire back side is a marbled plastic in shades of soft orange, brown and tan. The guitar face has two colorful labels, one picturing Elvis with inscription "Love Me Tender" and the other picturing a sad-eyed floppy-eared beagle with caption "You Ain't Nothin' But A Hound Dog." Guitar comes with twined shoulder cord and the tuning keys, strings and bridge are all metal. The carrying case is stiff corrugated cardboard in a trapezoid shape with brass lid hinges and plastic carrying handle. The case has Elvis designs on top and bottom. **$1,000.**

EVP-4   EVP-5

EVP-4. "ELVIS PRESLEY GUITAR" a 31" English-made hard plastic guitar circa mid-1950s with carrying case. Front coloring is combination of brown and white with some silver accent color. Reverse is a maroon marbled pattern. A color picture of Elvis is on the tuning head and this is repeated on a sticker on the carrying case. **$700.**

EVP-5. "ELVIS PRESLEY" GUM CARD SET of 66 issued by Topps Gum Co. under name "Bubbles Inc." © 1956. Each card is 2.5x3.5" and pictures either a scene from studio, concert or movie "Love Me Tender." **SET $500.**

EVP-6   EVP-7   EVP-8

EVP-6. "ELVIS PRESLEY ENTERPRISES" OVERNIGHT TRAVEL CASE. Vinyl-covered rigid cardboard case 7x9x12" with repeated design of Elvis portrait and facsimile signature in brown/white. Case is trimmed with brass corner pieces, hinges and front snap. ©1956. **$600.**

EVP-7. "LOVE ME TENDER" PILLOW with original stitched tag. 10x10" white cotton stuffed pillow with blue printed picture of Elvis, song title and facsimile signature plus edge trim also in blue. Tag is stitched at edge with name of Personality Products Co. plus ©1956 Elvis Presley Enterprises. **$400.**

EVP-8. "ELVIS PRESLEY'S TEDDY BEAR" PERFUME. 1.25x1.25x4" clear glass perfume bottle with white plastic cap. Bottle label pictures Elvis in black/white and rest of label design is yellow with black lettering. Label includes facsimile signature and 1957 © Elvis Presley Enterprises. Original amber-colored perfume is by Teen-Age Perfumes Inc. which is printed on reverse side of label. **$100.**

EVP-9   EVP-10   EVP-11

EVP-9. "ELVIS PRESLEY RECORD CASE" 8x8x2.5" case for holding 45-rpm records. Exterior is pinkish-tan background with lid picture in black and white. 1956 ©Elvis Presley Enterprises. **$400.**

EVP-10. "ELVIS PRESLEY AUTOGRAPH BOOK" 4.5x5.5" pinkish-tan padded covers with black/white illustrations on front. 1956 ©E.P.E. **$300.**

EVP-11. "SINCERELY ELVIS PRESLEY" 5.5" clear drinking glass ©1957 E.P.E. Design of Elvis, music notes, records and record titles are in black and gold. **$200.**

EVP-12

EVP-13

EVP-12. "ELVIS PRESLEY ROCK 'N ROLL" BEIGE VINYL WALLET with black/white paper photo under clear plastic on cover. Elvis illustrations are in pink and white. 1956 ©Elvis Presley Enterprises. **$350.**

EVP-13. "ELVIS PRESLEY" VINYL WALLET with snap overlay fastener holding key-chain that suspends a 1.5" brass fob frame with black/white photo under plastic. Wallet cover is aqua plastic with gold accent coloring. Cover design includes three song titles. 1956 ©Elvis Presley Enterprises. **$350.**

EVP-14

EVP-15

EVP-14. "ELVIS PRESLEY ROCK 'N ROLL" TAN VINYL WAL-LET with picture and text design in pink, blue, brown, fleshtone, black/white. 1956 ©Elvis Presley Enterprises. **$350.**

EVP-15. "ELVIS PRESLEY" CARRYALL HANDBAG. 5x11" turquoise vinyl bag with three full color depictions of Elvis on cover flap. Design also includes song titles "Heartbreak Hotel", "Hound Dog", "I Want You – I Need You." 1956 ©Elvis Presley Enterprises. **$750.**

EMERGENCY!

NBC: January 22, 1972 – March 9, 1977

Adventure series of a Paramedics team assigned to Squad 51 of the Los Angeles County Fire Department. Items will normally have copyright of Emergency Productions.

EMG-1   EMG-2

EMG-1. "EMERGENCY!" EMBOSSED STEEL LUNCH BOX with matching plastic thermos by Aladdin Industries ©1973. **LUNCH BOX $35. THERMOS $20.**

EMG-2. "THE EMERGENCY! GAME" by Milton Bradley ©1974. Box is 9.5x19" and game parts include playing board designed like a city layout, hospital cards, assignment cards, spinner, and miniature plastic emergency vehicles. **$20.**

EMG-3

EMG-3. "EMERGENCY! PARAMEDIC TRUCK" in 2x5x9" box by Dinky Toys ©1978. Replica truck is 1.5x2x4.5" long with red body and small decal on each door and rear, "Emergency 51 Rescue Squad." Miniature oxygen tanks are mounted in the cargo area. **$35.**

F TROOP

ABC: September 14, 1965 – August 31, 1967

Slapstick western comedy about an inept cavalry unit and equally inept Indians. Items will normally have copyright of Warner Bros. Pictures. Main characters: Capt. Wilson Parmenter (Ken Berry), Sgt. Morgan O'Rourke (Forrest Tucker), Cpl. Randolph Agarn (Larry Storch), Wrangler Jane (Melody Patterson).

FTP-1   FTP-2

FTP-1. "F TROOP" 8.5x11" Saalfield coloring book #9560 © 1966. **$15.**

FTP-2. "F TROOP MINI-BOARD CARD GAME" by Ideal Toy © 1965 in 1.5x6.5x10" box. Lid is over styrofoam base which serves as card tray with attached thin cardboard playing surface. Game comes with deck of 45 cards. **$15.**

FTP-3

FTP-4

FTP-3. "F TROOP" DELL COMIC BOOK No. 6 from June 1967. **$8.**

FTP-4. F TROOP "TV GUIDE" weekly issues for December 11, 1965 and August 13, 1966, both with color photo cover plus short article about the show or its characters. **EACH $8.**

FAMILY AFFAIR

CBS: September 12, 1966 – September 9, 1971

Family situation comedy about a bachelor father with three ward children and a manservant. Main characters: Bill Davis (Brian Keith), Buffy (Anissa Jones), Jody (Johnnie Whitaker), Cissy (Kathy Garver), Mr. Jiles French (Sebastian Cabot). Items will usually have copyright of Family Affair Company.

FAM-1

FAM-1. "FAMILY AFFAIR" STEEL LUNCH BOX with 6.5" metal thermos by King-Seeley ©1969. **LUNCH BOX $30. THERMOS $20.**

FAM-2   FAM-3

FAM-2. "BUFFY AND MRS. BEASLEY" BOXED DOLL by Mattel ©1967. Buffy doll is 6" tall and holds a 3.5" replica doll of Mrs. Beasley. Dolls are vinyl with lifelike hair and fabric outfits. Box is 2x4x8" with clear cellophane cover. **$60.**

FAM-3. "THE FAMILY AFFAIR GAME" by Whitman ©1971 in 8x15.5" box. **$25.**

FAM-4   FAM-5

FAM-4. "BUFFY AND JODY COLORING BOOK" 8x11" by Western Publishing Co. ©1969. **$8.**

FAM-5. "BUFFY PAPERDOLL" 10x13" Whitman cardboard album ©1968. Album has 11.5" tall cardboard stand-up figure doll plus six pages of punch-out clothing. Another page has parts to form a cradle for Mrs. Beasley, her doll. **$20.**

THE FAMOUS ADVENTURES OF MR. MAGOO

NBC: September 19, 1964 – August 7, 1965

Prime time cartoon series with Jim Backus as the "voice" of Mr. Magoo, who portrayed real and fictional historical persons in the series. Mr. Magoo was a theater cartoon personality since 1949, and a later TV series was started in 1977 by CBS under title "What's New, Mr. Magoo?" Items are normally copyrighted UPA Pictures, Inc.

FMM-1   FMM-2   FMM-3

FMM-1. "MAGOO" 10" vinyl/hard plastic "Soaky" soap container bottle circa mid-1960s. Bottle comes accented in either red or blue colors on his outfit. **$20.**

FMM-2. "MR. MAGOO" 5.5" clear heavy drinking glass with inscription band in blue around lower center plus two cartoon pictures in tan. ©1962. **$30.**

FMM-3. MR. MAGOO TISSUE HOLDER. 2.25x5.5x10.5" plastic box holder for standard size facial tissue carton. Lid design is red/white/blue with UPA Pictures © probably circa 1976. **$20.**

FMM-4   FMM-5

FMM-4. "MR. MAGOO" FIGURAL PIN on 3x4" advertising card by General Electric for promotion of light bulb sales. Pin is a 1.5" painted metal die-cut figure of him holding a light bulb. Pin is very colorfully painted. Circa 1950s. **$15.**

FMM-5. MAGOO 5x8x9" battery-operated toy vehicle with lithographed tin and plastic body and vinyl/fabric appointments. When activated with battery, the car moves forward with a jerking motion. Marked on the bottom is "1961 UPA Pictures by Hubley" but back of car is marked "Japan." **$200.**

THE FANTASTIC FOUR

NBC: September 9, 1967 – August 30, 1970

Animated series, based on comic book characters, which premiered in 1967 as a Hanna-Barbera production. The title group was composed of Mr. Fantastic, Invisible Girl, Human Torch, The Thing. The series returned to NBC in September of 1978. Items will usually have copyright of Marvel Comics Group.

FTF-1   FTF-2

FTF-1. "THE FANTASTIC FOUR IN THE HOUSE OF HORRORS" Whitman Big Little Book #5775-1 ©1968 in 3.5X5" size. **$10.**

FTF-2. "FANTASTIC FOUR JIGSAW PUZZLE" by Whitman © 1969 in 1.5x5x6.5" box. Assembled puzzle is 10x13" with puzzle scene taken from Whitman's Big Little Book #2706. **$10.**

FTF-3   FTF-4

FLX-4   FLX-5   FLX-6

FTF-3. "THE FANTASTIC FOUR" 8x11" cardboard frame tray inlay jigsaw puzzle by Whitman ©1977. **$10.**

FTF-4. "FANTASTIC FOUR" 5.5" tall clear drinking glass from series issued by 7-11 convenience store chain ©1977. **$8.**

FLX-4. FELIX SQUEAKER TOY. 6" soft rubber black/white/red squeaker toy, undated and unmarked but circa 1950s – 1960s. **$30.**

FLX-5. FELIX 10" hard plastic "Soaky" liquid soap bottle from comic character series circa 1960s. Body is red with blue name on chest plus black/white facial color. A yellow polka dot bag is depicted in one hand. Figure also comes with blue body or black body. **$35.**

FLX-6. "FELIX THE CAT" FLASHLIGHT WITH WHISTLE. .5x1x3.25" plastic flashlight designed so that Felix's eyeballs light up when flashlight is operating by battery. Attached by brass key chain is small plastic whistle. Circa 1950s– 1960s. **$15.**

FARFEL

See The Milton Berle Show

FELIX THE CAT

Syndicated 1960 (260 Episodes)

Animated cartoon episodes starring Pat Sullivan character that was most popular prior to World War II although still generating a nice selection of 1950s – 1960s collectibles. Items may also have copyright by Felix The Cat Productions or King Features Syndicate.

FLASH GORDON

Syndicated 1953 – 1954 (39 Episodes)

Live action series based on popular 1930s-1940s science-fiction space character created by Alex Raymond for King Features Syndicate and collectibles normally will have this copyright. The live action TV version starred Steve Holland in the title role and Irene Champlin as Dale Arden. An animated cartoon version by Filmation titled "The New Adventures Of Flash Gordon" began September 8, 1979 and continued until January 5, 1980 on NBC.

FLX-1   FLX-2   FLX-3

FLX-1. FELIX CARTOON LAMP SHADE. Stiff paper shade 6" tall with 8" bottom diameter. Printed around side in black, red and blue on white are Felix and other characters from early 1960s cartoon series of Professor Kiddie Flub, Marty Martian, Gen. Clang Poindexter, Rock Bottom, Inky. Inside of shade has wire supports and spring clip for bulb. **$50.**

FLX-2. "FELIX THE CAT SIP-A-DRINK CUP" 5" pink plastic cup with black design on one side plus handle design to serve as a sipping straw. Circa 1960s. **$30.**

FLX-3. FELIX WRIST WATCH. 1.25" watch in gold-colored metal case with black/white/yellow dial face illustration without inscription. Circa 1960s. **$100.**

FGN-1   FGN-2

FGN-1. "FLASH GORDON" HAND PUPPET with fabric hand cover body and painted rubber head. The printed uniform is green/red/ yellow on gray background. Circa early 1950s. **$25.**

FGN-2. "FLASH GORDON" WALLET with zipper around three sides. Simulated leather picture on each side in red/blue/yellow/ black/ fleshtone on tan background with ©1949. **$25.**

PREMIUMS AND PINBACK BUTTONS *(left to right, top to bottom)*

Tom Corbett "Space Cadet" member's button. Kellogg's cereals, circa mid-1950s; **$50.** Capt. Midnight 1955–56 Ovaltine plastic Secret Squadron decoder; **$125.** Hopalong Cassidy compass ring with removable hat, circa 1950; **$200.** "Howdy Doody" Sunday comics newspaper advertising button, circa mid-1950s; **$40.** Space Patrol Hydrogen Ray Gun Ring, circa early 1950s; **$90.** "Milton Berle Make-Up Club" member's button, circa early 1950s; **$50.** "Roy Rogers Riders" movie theatre club member's button, circa 1950s; **$40.** "Roy Rogers Deputy Sheriff" Quaker Cereals premium, 1950; **$50.** "Elvis Presley National Fan Club" member's button, circa 1956; **$100.** "Boo-Boo" button from a set issued in 1960; **$15.** "Miss Case/The Green Hornet's Secretary" button from a set issued in 1966; **$10.** "I'm A Batman Crimefighter" button from 1966; **$10.** "The Lone Ranger" button, circa 1950s; **$10.** "Hey There/It's Yogi Bear" button, circa early 1960s; **$20.** "Supermen of America" club member's button from National Periodical Publications, 1961; **$30.**

BOXED GAMES *(left to right, top to bottom)*

"The Flintstones Brake Ball" by Whitman, 1962; **$40.**   "Mission Impossible" by Ideal, 1966; **$35.**   "The Addams Family" by Milton Bradley, 1965; **$25.**   "Howdy Doody's Adventure Game" by Milton Bradley, circa early 1950s; **$60.**   "Bonanza/Michigan Rummy Game" by Parker Brothers, 1964; **$25.**   "Davy Crockett Indian Scouting Game" by Whitman, 1955; **$40.**   "The Beverly Hillbillies" by Milton Bradley, 1963; **$20.**

LAMPS *(left to right, top to bottom)*

Batman 11″ vinyl figure with fabric cape, circa 1966; **$85.**   "Dick Tracy" plaster lamp by Plasto Mfg. Co., circa 1950. **$300.**
"Soupy Sales" 13.5″ plastic lamp with metal base, 1965; **$100.**   The Lone Ranger and Tonto 12″-long lamp made from Arizona
cactus by Whitmer Lamp, circa 1950; **$300.**   "Mickey Mouse Club" 14″ litho tin designed like a drum by Econolite, circa late 1950s;
$100.   "Roy Rogers" 15″ plaster lamp by Plasto Mfg. Co., circa early 1950s; **$250.**   Popeye 8″ vinyl by Alan Jay, 1959; **$75.**
Howdy Doody 14″ molded plastic wall light by Royal Electric, circa early 1950s; **$125.**   "Davy Crockett" 18″ plaster lamp by Premco
Mfg. Co., circa mid-1950s; **$75.**

COLORING BOOKS *(clockwise from top)*

"The Andy Griffith Show," published by Artcraft, circa mid-1960s; **$75.** "Lone Ranger Ranch Fun Book," Cheerios premium, 1956; **$60.** "Have Gun Will Travel," published by Lowe, 1960; **$25.** "The Flintstones," published by Whitman, 1962; **$25.** "The Beatles," published by Saalfield, 1964; **$30.** "Walt Disney's Mickey Mouse Club," published by Dell, 1955; **$20.** "Peanuts," published by Saalfield, 1960; **$20.** "Felix The Cat," published by Saalfield, 1959; **$20.** "Dudley Do-Right," published by Whitman, 1972; **$15.**

FGN-3

FGN-7　　　　FGN-8　　　　FGN-9

FGN-3. "FLASH GORDON" 12x15" lithographed full color tin target by unidentified maker ©1952. Different target scene is printed on each side. Target comes with original box. **$75.**

FGN-4

FGN-4. "FLASH GORDON WATER PISTOL" 7.5" blue plastic water gun that has whistle mouthpiece at rear tip of the grip. By Marx Toys circa early 1950s in colorful 2x4.5x8.5" box. **$125.**

FGN-5　　　　　　　　FGN-6

FGN-5. "FLASH GORDON PLAYSET" in 10.5x13x15.5" carrying case with handle. Set is by Mego Corp. ©1977 and is designed for use with 9" action figures, **FGN-6** through **FGN-9,** which were sold separately. The opened playset features areas representing Ming's Throne Room and Dr. Zarkov's Secret Laboratory, both centered by a simulated computer console. Set includes a sticker sheet with insignias for throne or computer and three cardboard cards to be inserted in slot of simulated computer for viewing. Very colorful and detailed design. **$50.**

FGN-6. "FLASH GORDON" ACTION FIGURE by Mego Corp. on 8.5x13" retail blister pack ©1976. Figure is 9" tall and designed for use with playset **FGN-5.** Figure is hard plastic with movable body parts and colorful fabric outfit. Accessories are two plastic space helmets, sword and shield, knife, gun and holster. **$60.**

FGN-7. "DALE ARDEN" ACTION FIGURE on display card from same series as **FGN-6.** Accessories are sword and scabbard, knife, gun and holster, space cap. **$60.**

FGN-8. "DR. ZARKOV" ACTION FIGURE on retail card from same series as **FGN-6.** Accessories are a plastic sword and scabbard, shield, knife, gun and holster, two space helmets. **$60.**

FGN-9. "MING THE MERCILESS" ACTION FIGURE on retail card from same series as **FGN-6.** Accessories are two plastic space helmets, gun and holster, sword and scabbard, small sticker sheet for embellishing his shoulder belt. **$60.**

THE FLINTSTONES

ABC: September 30, 1960 – September 2, 1966

The longest-running animated cartoon series in prime time history, featuring the cave-age comedy exploits of Fred and Wilma Flintstone, neighbors Barney and Betty Rubble, and pet dinosaur Dino in community of Bedrock. Many Flintstone shows with various titles followed the initial run including the 1971 spinoff series of Pebbles and Bamm-Bamm, the offsprings of the two families. The show was created by Hanna-Barbera Productions and will normally have this copyright.

FTS-1　　　　　　　　FTS-2

FTS-1. "TV GUIDE" for week of June 13, 1964 with cover picture of Fred and 3.5-page article about his creators, Bill Hanna and Joe Barbera with photo of them. Article involves Flintstones, Yogi Bear and other characters. **$15.**

FTS-2. FLINTSTONES "GREAT BIG PUNCHOUT" oversized 11x22" Whitman book ©1961. Front cover has a 17.5" tall, full color unpunched figure of Fred and back cover has 16" figure of Barney. Pages include punch-out figures of Wilma and Betty to same scale plus clothing pages for each character, all printed on thin stiff cardboard. **$35.**

FTS-3   FTS-4

FTS-8   FTS-9

FTS-3. "FRED FLINTSTONE-DINO THE DINOSAUR" LARGE MARX BATTERY TOY, 12" tall by 18" long, ©1962. When activated, Dino's head moves left and right while the neck moves up and down, causing the figure of Fred to rock forward and backward in his howdah. **$350.**

FTS-4. FRED FLINTSTONE AND DINO LITHOGRAPHED TIN WIND-UP by Marx Toys © 1962. Toy is 8.5" long with very colorful lithography. When wound, Dino ambles as Fred rides. **$250.**

FTS-8. "ROCKY" unauthorized 3" diameter by 4" tall lithographed metal toy made in Japan by unidentified maker circa 1960s. Toy requires a single battery to cause it to move about in a small circle with jerky motion. Toy is in 3x3.75x4.25" box. **$250.**

FTS-9. "FRED FLINTSTONE" LITHOGRAPHED METAL WIND-UP TOY by Marx circa early 1960s. The figure has a simulated name tag around the neck and is about 3.5" tall with very colorful lithography. When wound, the toy hops up and down in a circular motion. **$200.**

FTS-5   FTS-6

FTS-5. "FRED FLINTSTONE'S BEDROCK BAND" 4x7x9" lithographed tin/plush/vinyl plastic battery-operated toy by Alps ©1962 with original box. When operating, both of Fred's feet move, with one holding a spring with rubber plunger that hits the drum while the other moves a turtle cymbal up and down. Both of the plastic hammers in his hand strike the two top snare drums and cymbal to produce considerable noise. **$400.**

FTS-6. "THE FLINTSTONES PLAY SET" by Marx Toys circa early 1960s in 5x15x24" box with complete instructions, plastic layout sheet, and figures for Fred, Wilma, Barney, Betty, Dino, plus cars, houses and many accessories. **$600.**

FTS-10   FTS-11   FTS-12

FTS-10. "BARNEY RUBBLE" LITHOGRAPHED METAL WIND-UP TOY from same series by Marx as **FTS-9.** Figure is also about 3.5" tall and performs same movements when wound. **$200.**

FTS-11. "DINO" LITHOGRAPHED METAL WIND-UP TOY from same series by Marx as **FTS-9.** Figure is also about 3.5" tall and performs same movements when wound. **$200.**

FTS-12. "WILMA" 2x3.5x4" lithographed metal friction car by Marx Toys ©1962. Wilma's head is soft vinyl mounted on her metal body. **$125.**

FTS-7

FTS-7. "THE FLINTSTONES BEDROCK EXPRESS" large and colorful wind-up toy set by Marx ©1962. Set has a 21.5x25.5" three-dimensional plastic Bedrock community layout including running track for the wind-up hand car. The car is plastic and metal and features Fred and Barney figures which rock back and forth as if operating the car. The layout course includes four molded plastic Bedrock homes which rise about 1.5" above the surface plus other rock and boulder features in very high relief. Accessories include assorted plastic rocks plus palm trees for further landscaping. The hand car itself is about 2x3.5x5.5". **$300.**

FTS-13

FTS-14

FTS-13. "THE FLINTSTONES STONEAGE GAME" by Transogram ©1961 in 9x17.5" box. **$35.**

FTS-14. "DINO THE DINOSAUR GAME" by Transogram ©1961 in 8x15" box. Scenes on playing board are of rides and amusements at a Bedrock carnival, with game parts including spinner board, 4 plastic markers and 16 play coins. **$25.**

FTS-15   FTS-16

FTS-19   FTS-20

FTS-19. "BABY PEBBLES FLINTSTONE" DOLL AND BOX by Ideal Toys ©1963. Doll is 15" tall with vinyl body, artificial hair held in place by a small white plastic bone, plus fabric diaper and flannel robe that has simulated animal fur design. Also included is a flannel blanket, also trimmed in matching simulated fur. Box is 4.5x9x16". **$125.**

FTS-20. "BAMM-BAMM " DOLL matching **FTS-19** by Ideal Toys ©1962. Doll is in vinyl with movable head, arms and legs plus artificial hair held in topknot by white plastic bone. Outfit is a fabric sleeveless shirt with printed animal spots. **$75.**

FTS-15. "THE FLINTSTONES" LAMP. 1961 © electrical lamp with 9.5" hollow plastic figure of Fred serving as the lamp column. The shade is heavy stiff paper and 8.5" diameter by 8.5" tall. Pictured around the shade are Fred, Wilma, Betty, Barney, Dino and Baby Puss. **$150.**

FTS-16. "DINO" 1961 © china bank about 4.5x4.5x8.25" tall. Figure is in soft blended glazed colors and Dino is depicted carrying a golf bag. **$125.**

FTS-17

FTS-17. "FRED LOVES WILMA" 5x6x8" ceramic bank glazed in rich soft colors of pink, blue, yellow and white accented by dark brown and black. Unmarked except for "USA" on bottom, circa 1960s. **$150.**

FTS-21

FTS-22

FTS-18

FTS-18. "FLINTSTONES AND DINO" EMBOSSED STEEL LUNCH BOX with 6.5" metal thermos by Aladdin Industries © 1962. **LUNCH BOX $80. THERMOS $40.**

FTS-21. "PEBBLES AND BAMM-BAMM" VINYL LUNCH BOX by Aladdin Industries © 1971, based on TV cartoon series featuring them as teenagers rather than toddlers. **$125.**

FTS-22. FLINTSTONES "BABY PUSS" VINYL FIGURE DOLL plus box by Knickerbocker Toys ©1961. Figure is a 10" hollow soft vinyl depicting baby tiger character from the series. Shown with figure in our photo is back panel of box that illustrates other vinyl figures in the set. Box front has clear cellophane display window. **$125.**

FLIPPER

NBC: September 19, 1964 – September 1, 1968

Aquatic adventure series starring a dolphin and his human keepers at Coral Key Park in Florida. The series was created by Ivan Tors Productions and will normally have this copyright.

FLP-1   FLP-2

FLP-1. "FLIPPER FLIPS" BOXED BOARD GAME by Mattel © 1965. **$25.**

FLP-2. "FLIPPER" MUSIC BOX by Mattel © 1966. Box is 5.25x5.25x5.5" lithographed metal and winds by a crank which produces a tune before vinyl/fabric figure of Flipper pops out. **$50.**

FLP-3   FLP-4

FLP-3. "FLIPPER/DEEP-SEA PHOTOGRAPHER" Whitman Big Little Book #2032 © 1969 in 4x5" size with 248-page illustrated story. **$8.**

FLP-4. "FLIPPER" PLUSH TOY by Knickerbocker © 1976. Figure is 13" long, mostly of gray plush with pink mouth plus plastic jiggley-eye disks. The outfit is a fabric sailor's vest and naval cap. **$15.**

THE FLYING NUN

ABC: September 7, 1967 – September 18, 1970

Situation comedy starring Sally Field as Elsie Ethrington who joins a convent where she becomes Sister Bertrille and discovers she can fly. Items will normally have copyright of Screen Gems Inc.

FYN-1   FYN-2

FYN-1. "THE FLYING NUN GAME" by Milton Bradley ©1968 in 9.5x19" box. **$30.**

FYN-2. "THE FLYING NUN BUBBLE GUM" 5x6" waxed paper wrapper from 1967 © gum card series issued by Donruss. **$12.**

FYN-3   FYN-4

FYN-3. "THE FLYING NUN" PAPER DOLL KIT © 1969 by Saalfield in 11x14.25" box. Kit includes punch-out doll figures of Sister Bertrille, Sister Jacqueline (Marge Redmond), Sister Sixto (Shelly Morrison), Mother Superior (Madeline Sherwood), Carlos Ramiriz (Alejandro Rey), plus four youngsters. There are no clothing pieces for the nun figures, as intended, and four sheets of clothing for the other figures. **$30.**

FYN-4. "THE FLYING NUN PAPER DOLLS" punch-out doll book by Artcraft © 1969. **$30.**

FOODINI THE GREAT

ABC: August 25, 1951 – December 29, 1951

A spinoff filmed puppet show from earlier show, "Lucky Pup," both created by Hope and Morey Bunin. The star puppets were an inept magician, Foodini, and his equally inept assistant Pinhead. Items are normally copyrighted R.P.Cox.

FDI-1   FDI-2   FDI-3

FDI-1. "TELEVISION GUIDE" New York City issue for week of April 16, 1949 with black/white cover photo of Foodini pulling an Easter Bunny from top hat as Pinhead looks on. Inside has short article about the show under its original "Lucky Pup" title which did not change until 1951. **$40.**

FDI-2. "FOODINI'S TRIP TO THE MOON" RECORD on Caravan label ©1949. Record is single 45-rpm in 7x7" paper album cover. **$25.**

FDI-3. PINHEAD HAND PUPPET with fabric body and large rubber head. Puppet is in 1.5x3x3" carton marked "Television's Original Living Puppets" circa late 1940s – early 1950s. Front of carton in our photo also has a character name "Hot Shot" although puppet is actually Pinhead. **$75.**

FDI-4

FDI-4. "FOODINI" CHARACTER HAND GAMES. Each is a 3.5x5" red tin frame with clear cover over full color lithographed picture of either Foodini, Pinhead or clown Jolo. Each has tiny balls to be rolled into recesses on the playing surface. Each has © of R.C. Cox. **EACH $20.**

FDI-5

FDI-5. "THE GREAT FOODINI MAGIC SET" by Pressman Toys ©1951 in 10.5x18" box. Set comes with "Magic Set Secrets" instruction booklet for 10 tricks plus materials for performing each illusion. **$50.**

FURY

NBC: October 15, 1955 – September 3, 1966

Saturday live action show, syndicated in 1960 under new title of "Brave Stallion," also aired on NBC. Starred in addition to the Black Stallion were Bobby Diamond as Joey Newton, an orphan, and Peter Graves as Jim Newton, the policeman who adopted Joey. Items are normally copyrighted Vision Productions Inc. or Television Programs of America Inc., or Independent Television Corp.

FRY-1   FRY-2   FRY-3

FRY-1. FIRST ISSUE "FURY" COMIC BOOK, issue #1 from November, 1962 by Gold Key comic. **$5.**

FRY-2. "FURY TAKES THE JUMP" 1958 Little Golden Book. **$8.**

FRY-3. "FURY COLORING BOOK" 8.5x11" Whitman #1199 © 1958. **$15.**

GABBY HAYES SHOW

NBC: December 11, 1950 – January 1, 1954

Series featuring George "Gabby " Hayes, usually with clips from his many early western movie films. Under NBC, the show was 15 minutes in length and was aired immediately before the Howdy Doody show. The show became 30 minutes in length under ABC which ran it on Saturday mornings from May 12 – July 14, 1956. Item licensor was NBC Merchandising Inc.

GBH-1   GBH-2

GBH-1. "GABBY HAYES TALL TALES FOR LITTLE FOLKS" 6.25x8" stiff cardboard book with riveted die-cut cardboard pieces on inside front cover which open to produce a 17" tall figure of him. The pages are designed so that when each is turned, he appears in a different outfit from tip of his beard to top of his knees. Book's text is his tales and he has six different outfit changes including one spaceman suit and one Santa Claus costume. Book is ©1954 by Samuel Lowe Co. from its "Bonnie Jack-In-The-Box" series. **$30.**

GBH-2. "GABBY HAYES CHAMPION SHOOTING TARGET" SET by Haecker Industries © 1950. Set consists of 18x18" stiff cardboard target, a 6.5" plastic dart pistol designed like .45 caliber automatic, and two rubber cup plastic darts. Set is in 18x18" box which has lengthy inscription on lid in typical Gabby Hayes dialect. **$100.**

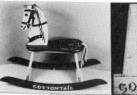

GBH-3

GBH-3. GABBY HAYES "COTTONTAIL" ROCKING HORSE. Child's wooden horse based on Gabby's horse, "Cottontail," circa early 1950s. The rockers have 30.5" length with 10.5" width between them. Height is 22.5" from floor level to top of head. The design is painted mostly in tan/red/black/white. The tail is braided white cord. The seat has a bandanna-like painted design, and front panel has Cottontail name decal plus 4x6" decal portrait of Gabby. **$125.**

GBH-4

GBH-4. GABBY HAYES "WESTERN GUN COLLECTION" early 1950s premium from Quaker Puffed Wheat and Puffed Rice consisting of 6.5x12" cardboard display board plus six miniature replica metal guns, each finished in bright gold color. Display board has small die-cut tabs for holding replicas plus text about them. Replicas are Winchester 1873 rifle, Harper's Ferry Flintlock, Wells Fargo Colt, Colt Peacemaker, Remington Breech-Loader Pistol, Sharp's Creedmore Buffalo Gun. Display board folds to 6x6.5" size. **$75.**

GBH-5

GBH-5. "GABBY HAYES CARRY ALL FISHING OUTFIT" circa early 1950s in 3" diameter by 23.5" lithographed tin carrying case. Kit contains child's actual rod and reel plus fishing cord, bobber, lead weights and hooks. The carrying case has vivid full color depiction of Gabby and a hooked fish plus inscription in typical Gabby Hayes dialect. Case comes with a carrying cord mounted at each end. **$75.**

| GBH-6 | GBH-7 | GBH-8 |

GBH-6. GABBY HAYES 10.25x14.5" frame tray inlay jigsaw puzzle with Kagran © circa early 1950s. Puzzle scene is full color illustration of him with gun threatening a cartoon-like rabbit who has invaded "Gabby's Carrot Farm/No Rabbits Allowed!" Puzzle maker is Milton Bradley. **$20.**

GBH-7. "GABBY HAYES" 11x13" coloring book by Abbott Publishing ©1954. Book has 14 coloring pages and Gabby is shown on each in cartoon-like illustrations, mostly in non-western activities. **$25.**

GBH-8. "GABBY HAYES TALL TALES/MAGIC DIAL FUNNY COLORING BOOK" 8x10.5" undated circa early 1950s book by Samuel Lowe Co. Book has stiff paper cover with die-cut opening in shape of television screen. A disk wheel is turned to produce black/white cartoon pictures of Gabby in various activities although rest of cover is bright full color. Coloring pages each depict Gabby in cartoon form as part of a "Tall Tales" adventure. **$25.**

GAME SHOW GAMES

High ratings and low budgets made game shows a popular network staple from the 1950s on. Game shows had various formats and were hosted by a popular master of ceremonies who generally became synonymous with the show. Numerous shows produced a boxed game but few other collectibles. Our selection shows twelve of the most popular shows and games based on them.

GSG-1   GSG-2

GSG-1. "ART LINKLETTER'S HOUSE PARTY GAME" by Whitman ©1968 based on long-running daytime variety show which began in 1952 and continued until 1969. Game parts include a playing board, small plastic 3-D house, die-cut character plastic playing pieces, game cards, spinner board, play money. Box is 3x13.5x18.5". **$25.**

GSG-2. "BREAK THE BANK" GAME by Bettye-B ©1955 based on one of earliest and longest-running game shows which appeared at various times on all three major networks and was still extended into syndication in 1976. The first version of the show started late in 1948 and the NBC version in the mid-1950s was retitled "Break The $250,000 Bank." Bert Parks hosted the ABC and NBC versions and is pictured on box lid of this game version. Bud Collyer hosted the CBS version. Box is 1.5x12.5x18". **$25.**

GSG-3   GSG-4

GSG-3. "DOLLAR A SECOND" GAME by Lowell Toys, undated but circa mid-1950s based on game show which first appeared on Dumont Network for the fall season of 1953 and later was aired on either NBC or ABC with final telecast September 28, 1957. Host of the show was Jan Murray who is pictured on box lid. Game parts include cards, envelopes, paper cups, face masks, whistle, plastic measuring tube, all designed for required stunts for incorrect answer. Box is 2x14x17". **$25.**

GSG-4. "EYE GUESS" THIRD EDITION of Milton Bradley game © 1966 based on daytime game show hosted by Bill Cullen which tested contestants' abilities to memorize. Game features a plastic gameboard with windows which expose correct answers to eight upcoming questions before being covered to begin play. The series aired on NBC January 3, 1966 – September 26, 1969. Box is 1.5x9.5x19". **$15.**

GSG-5   GSG-6

GSG-5. "JAN MURRAY'S TREASURE HUNT" GAME by Gardner Games circa late 1950s based on September 7, 1956 – May 24, 1957 (ABC) and August 12, 1957 – December 4, 1959 (NBC) game show hosted by Murray who is pictured on box lid. In 1974 the show was placed into syndication under another host. Game parts include ten question folders, treasure chest cards, a category spinner, a game timer and play money. Box is 1.5x13x20". **$40.**

GSG-6. "JAN MURRAY'S CHARGE ACCOUNT TV WORD GAME" by Lowell Toys © 1961 based on the September 5, 1960 – September 28, 1962 NBC game show hosted by Murray. Game is played by forming words from a group of 16 letters. Game parts include two large full-dimensioned plastic charge account recorders plus alphabet letter cards, and a cardboard cylinder which is cranked manually to shuffle the letters. Box is 3.5x13.25x18". **$25.**

GSG-7   GSG-8

GSG-7. "MASQUERADE PARTY" GAME by Bettye-B © 1955 based on game show aired at different times by all three major networks beginning July 14, 1952 through syndication in 1974. The game was issued during the 1954-1956 ABC years. The game parts feature 16 cardboard folders that have an inside photo of celebrity, with the outside showing the costume they wore on the actual Masquerade Party show. The pictured celebrities are all real-life individuals mostly from the entertainment field. Box is 1.5x13.5x22". **$25.**

GSG-8. "NAME THAT TUNE" SECOND EDITION GAME by Milton Bradley © 1959 based on music identification show which first appeared July 6, 1953 on NBC. The show had several different formats and hosts during its initial run through October 19, 1959 on CBS. Host George DeWitt is pictured on box lid. The show returned in syndication in 1970 and continued for almost another decade. Game parts include a single 33 1/3-rpm record, a spinner board and tokens. Box is 1.5x10.25x16.5". **$30.**

GSG-9. "THE PRICE IS RIGHT" GAME by Milton Bradley © 1964 based on November 26, 1956 – September 3, 1965 show which aired first on NBC and then ABC before reappearing in syndication in 1972. The entire nine-year original run was hosted solely by Bill Cullen. Game is a card version based on actual game format of winning merchandise by guessing nearest estimated cost. Box is 1.5x6x10". **$15.**

GSG-10. "$64,000 QUESTION" GAME by Lowell Toys © 1955 based on the June 7, 1955 – November 9, 1958 CBS quiz show sponsored by Revlon and hosted by Hal March. The show was one of those which ceased due to the quiz show scandals of 1958. Game parts include six large question cards containing 660 questions plus a roulette wheel to select questions. Box is 1.5x13x18.5". **$40.**

GSG-11   GSG-12

GSG-11. "2 FOR THE MONEY" GAME by Hasbro © 1955 based on the September 30, 1952 – September 7, 1957 series aired first on NBC and later on CBS. The show was a general knowledge type and started with Fred Allen as host although Herb Shriner served as host for most of the series. Game parts include a "Tick-Timer" and a "Money Calculator" plus question books and play money. Box is 3x13.5x18". **$20.**

GSG-12. "WHAT'S MY LINE?" GAME by Lowell Toys © 1956 based on February 2, 1950 – September 3, 1967 CBS evening game show which featured a panel of four celebrities trying to guess the occupations of guest contestants. The show then entered syndication between 1968-1975. The show was hosted throughout by John Charles Daly and the usual panelists were Dorothy Kilgallen, Arlene Francis, Bennett Cerf and a weekly guest celebrity. Game parts include a simulated TV screen equipped with a drop slot for contestant picture cards, paper masks to be worn by the players and a flip board which keeps track of number of questions asked. Box is 2x10x21". **$40.**

GARRISON'S GORILLAS

ABC: September 5, 1967 – September 17, 1968

World War II drama about four convicts recruited to be commandos under the leadership of Lt. Greg Garrison played by Ron Harper. Items are normally copyrighted Selmur Productions Inc.

GRG-1   GRG-2

GSG-9   GSG-10

GRG-1. "GARRISON'S GORILLAS COLORING BOOK" 8x10.5" Whitman book #1149 ©1968. **$10.**

GRG-2. "GARRISON'S GORILLAS BUBBLE GUM" 5x6" waxed paper wrapper from gum card set issued by Lead ©1967 by Selmur Productions. **$12.**

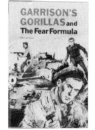

GRG-3   GRG-4

GRG-3. "GARRISON'S GORILLAS GAME" by Ideal Toys © 1967 in 9x17.5" box. Game parts include playing board, card deck, small figures of enemy generals, riflemen, machine gunners, plus a spinner. **$25.**

GRG-4. "GARRISON'S GORILLAS AND THE FEAR FORMULA" 5.25x8" Whitman hardcover book ©1964 with 210-page story. **$10.**

THE GENE AUTRY SHOW

CBS: July 23, 1950 – August 7, 1956

Series of 104 half-hour episodes featuring western film star Autry and produced by his own company, Flying A Productions. Autry played himself and Pat Buttram was a regular sidekick on the show. Also featured was Autry's horse, Champion, which led to another spinoff series, "The Adventures of Champion." The Autry series was syndicated after initial run. Most items usually have a "Gene Autry" copyright.

GNA-1   GNA-2   GNA-3

GNA-1. "TV GUIDE" issue for week of May 17, 1952 with black/white photo cover and single page article, "The Inside On Gene Autry," which is mostly a biography sketch plus photo of him with wife Ina Mae. **$35.**

GNA-2. "HORSESHOE NAIL RING" on 3.25x5.25" display card with facsimile signature plus symbol of Flying A Ranch. The ring is silvered metal and also repeats Autry name and symbol. Circa late 1940s – early 1950s. **$60.**

GNA-3. "GENE AUTRY & CHAMP" 1.75" celluloid button with fabric ribbons plus die-cut brass pendant of a bronc rider. Autry photo is black/white and color background comes in various shades. **$25.**

GNA-4   GNA-5

GNA-4. "GENE AUTRY" WALLET 4x4.5" zippered leather-like billfold with colorful printed scene on cover. Back cover has his name in script lettering. Wallet is zippered on three sides. **$30.**

GNA-5. "GENE AUTRY/MELODY RANCH" 8.25" lithographed steel thermos by Universal circa 1954-1955. Portrait illustration of Autry and Champion with a lithographed depiction of cowhide around the sides. Thermos came originally with lunch box **GNA-6. $50.**

GNA-6   GNA-7   GNA-8

GNA-6. GENE AUTRY "MELODY RANCH" STEEL LUNCH BOX by Universal circa 1954-1955. Full color lid art and other surfaces have lithographed design of cowhide. Box came originally with thermos **GNA-5. $100.**

GNA-7. "GENE AUTRY" ANIMATED WRIST WATCH with full color dial portrait of Autry. At bottom of dial is a small die-cut hand which holds a six-shooter. As time is kept, the hand bobs up and down. Inscribed on back of silvered metal case is "Always Your Pal/Gene Autry." By New Haven circa 1951 with original tan leather straps. **$150.**

GNA-8. "GENE AUTRY" WRIST WATCH with similar portrait on dial as **GNA-7** although this is version by Wilane circa 1948 without the animated hand. Both dial and back of case are inscribed "Always Your Pal/Gene Autry." **$125.**

GNA-9   GNA-10

GNA-9. "GENE AUTRY/44" CAP PISTOL by Leslie-Henry circa early 1950s. Gun is 11" silver-finished metal with ivory colored plastic grips, each with his name and "44" designation. The pistol uses roll caps and the left side opens to load. **$75.**

GNA-10. "GENE AUTRY" CAP PISTOL by Leslie-Henry circa early 1950s. Pistol is 9.5" of silvered white metal with ivory colored plastic grips. The Autry name is on both sides of gun with depiction of a rearing horse. Each grip has a raised illustration of a horse's head. The gun uses roll caps. **$60.**

GNA-11

GNA-11. "GENE AUTRY OFFICIAL COWBOY SPURS" circa late 1940s – early 1950s in 2x4x6.5" box. Spurs are white metal with leather straps and a metal link chain for fastening under boot sole. Box design is yellow/brown. **$60.**

GNA-12   GNA-13

GNA-12. "GENE AUTRY'S CHAMPION SLATE" 8x12.5" cardboard panel holding a gray film erasable slate sheet plus wood stylus. By Lowe Co. circa early 1950s. **$30.**

GNA-13. "GENE AUTRY PISTOL HORN" with box circa late 1940s – early 1950s. Horn is gray metal with red rubber squeeze bulb plus attachment clamp for a bicycle handlebar. "Official Gene Autry Pistol Horn" is on the metal part and the rubber bulb has a likeness of Gene and Champion plus their names. Set is in 2x2x7.5" box. **$50.**

GET SMART

NBC: September 18, 1965 – September 13, 1969
CBS: September 26, 1969 – September 11, 1970

Secret agent spoof spy show starring Don Adams as Maxwell Smart (Agent 86) and Barbara Feldon as his assistant, Susan Hilton, better known as Agent 99. Both worked for CONTROL, an intelligence agency that perpetually fought the evil KAOS organization. Items are normally copyrighted Talent Associates – Paramount Ltd.

GTS-1   GTS-2

GTS-1. "GET SMART! (MAXWELL SMART, THAT IS)" 8x11" Saalfield coloring book #4519 ©1965. **$60.**

GTS-2. "GET SMART" ELECTRONIC QUIZ GAME by Lisbeth Whiting Co. circa late 1960s featuring a battery-operated electrode format to determine correct answers to quiz questions. A correct answer flashes a red light. Game has set of six cardboard playing sheets designed for the electrode system. Box is 2x9x14". **$60.**

GTS-3   GTS-4

GTS-3. "GET SMART/SECRET AGENT 86/PEN-RADIO" by Multiple Toy Makers ©1966 in 6.5x7.5" box. Set is a fountain pen plus an earpiece and small clip. Pen is designed to be an actual working radio to receive AM stations. **$35.**

GTS-4. "GET SMART" PLASTIC CAR MODEL KIT by AMT © 1967 in 4x5x9" box. Assembled car is 1/25 scale replica of car used in the series. **$60.**

GTS-5

GTS-5. "GET SMART" STEEL LUNCH BOX with 6.5" metal thermos by King-Seeley Thermos ©1966. **LUNCH BOX $50. THERMOS $25.**

GILLIGAN'S ISLAND

CBS: September 26, 1964 – September 4, 1967

Comedy series about seven people stranded on a small island in the Pacific following the grounding of their boat, The Minnow, by first mate Gilligan (Bob Denver) and Skipper Jonas Grumby (Alan Hale). Other cast members: Thurston Howell III (Jim Backus), Mrs. Howell (Natalie Schafer), Ginger Grant (Tina Louise). Mary Ann Summers (Dawn Wells), Professor Roy Hinkley (Russell Johnson). A spinoff cartoon version by Filmation, "The New Adventures Of Gilligan" aired on CBS September 7, 1974 – September 4, 1976. Items are normally copyrighted United Artists TV.

GIL-1   GIL-2   GIL-3

GIL-1. "GILLIGAN'S ISLAND" unopened 2.5x3.5" bubble gum package containing cards from set of 55 issued by Topps gum ©1965. **$60.**

GIL-2. "ALAN HALE – BOB DENVER" 8x10" school tablet with full color cover photo circa 1965. **$20.**

GIL-3. "TV GUIDE" weekly issue for May 8, 1965 with cover color photo of Bob Denver and Tina Louise. Article is about five pages long and is part one of a two-part review of the show. **$10.**

GIL-4   GIL-5

GIL-4. "GILLIGAN'S ISLAND GAME" by Milton Bradley ©1965 in 9.5x18.5" box. **$90.**

GIL-5. GILLIGAN CHARACTER FIGURES. Three hollow soft vinyl plastic figures depicting Gilligan, Skipper and Mary Ann Summers from 1977 © set. Each is nicely colored and Skipper is the slightly tallest figure at 4". **LOT $25.**

GIL-6

GIL-6. "THE NEW ADVENTURES OF GILLIGAN" GAME by Milton Bradley ©1974 in 8x15.5" box. Game is based on mid-1970s animated cartoon version and features a box insert which serves as platform for the slotted stand-up die-cut background pieces of tropical scenery and a small primitive hut. Other game parts are deck of cards, pawns, single die. **$45.**

THE GIRL FROM U.N.C.L.E.

NBC: September 13, 1966 – August 29, 1967

Spinoff secret agent adventure series from the popular "The Man From U.N.C.L.E." series starring Stefanie Powers as agent April Dancer of the title role. Also featured was Noel Harrison as agent Mark Slate. Items will usually have copyright of Metro-Goldwyn-Mayer.

GFU-1   GFU-2

GFU-1. "THE GIRL FROM U.N.C.L.E. ANNUAL" English-published 8x10.5" hardcover book by World Distributors with 96 pages of text stories, comic-style stories, puzzles, fashion stories, ©1969. **$20.**

GFU-2. "THE GIRL FROM U.N.C.L.E. GARTER HOLSTER" SET on a 7x8" retail card. English made set is by Lone Star ©1966 and consists of a black stretch garter with small black/white checkered vinyl holster that holds a 3" metal cap gun. Also attached on card is a smaller checkered holster that holds caps plus instruction sheet. **$100.**

GOMER PYLE, U.S.M.C.

CBS: September 25, 1964 – September 9, 1970

Marine Corps comedy series about Pvt. Gomer Pyle (Jim Nabors) and his platoon leader Sgt. Vince Carter (Frank Sutton). Items will normally have copyright of Ashland Productions Inc.

GMP-1

GMP-2

GMP-1. "GOMER PYLE GAME" by Transogram © 1965 in 9x17.5" box. **$40.**

GMP-2. "GOMER PYLE USMC" unopened 2.5x3.5" bubble gum pack from set issued by Fleer Gum ©1965 with 66 cards in complete set. **$40.**

GMP-3   GMP-4

GMP-3. "GOMER PYLE USMC" GUM CARD SET of 66 cards issued by Fleer Gum ©1965. Each is 2.5x3.5" with black/white scene from TV series. **SET $30.**

GMP-4. "GOMER PYLE USMC" EMBOSSED STEEL LUNCH BOX by Aladdin Industries ©1966. **$60.**

THE GRAY GHOST

Syndicated 1957 (39 Episodes)

Civil War drama series distributed by CBS Film Sales starring Tod Andrews as Major John Mosby, a Confederate officer of the First Virginia Cavalry. Items are normally copyrighted CBS Television Film Sales.

GRY-1

GRY-2

GRY-1. "THE GRAY GHOST" GAME by Transogram ©1958 in 9x17.5" box. Game parts include a deck of "Secret Mission" cards, other small cards or disks representing Confederate flags and caps, small "Raid" or "Ambush" paper pieces, spinner board and four small plastic figures depicting Cavalrymen, plus colorful playing board designed like map of Civil War territory. **$45.**

GRY-2. "THE GRAY GHOST" 64-PAGE BLACK/WHITE COMIC BOOK © 1958 by C.B.I. Television Film Sales for distribution in Australia. **$35.**

GRY-3

GRY-3. "THE GRAY GHOST GUN AND HOLSTER SET" by Carnell Roundup circa 1957 in 2x10x12" box. Holster and belt are thin leather finished in solid gray with Confederate flag design on holster cover. Belt has covered bullet clip and three plastic bullets plus silvered metal buckle inscribed "CSA" (Confederate States Of America). Cap gun, by Hubley, is 10" long of silvered white metal with grained dark amber plastic grips. **$300.**

GREEN ACRES

CBS: September 15, 1965 – September 7, 1971

Comedy series about a wealthy married couple who left city life to live in the very rural small community of Hooterville. Stars were Eddie Albert as Oliver Douglas, a New York attorney turned farmer, and his high society wife Lisa, played by Eva Gabor. Items will normally have copyright of Filmways TV Productions Inc.

GRA-1   GRA-2   GRA-3

GRA-1. "GREEN ACRES" 10x13" paper doll cardboard album by Whitman ©1967. Album includes 10.5" stand-up cardboard doll figures of Lisa and Oliver plus six pages of uncut clothing. **$35.**

GRA-2. "EDDIE ALBERT – EVA GABOR" 8x10" school tablet with full color cover photo circa 1966. **$10.**

GRA-3. "GREEN ACRES" 8x11" coloring book by Whitman © 1967. **$25.**

THE GREEN HORNET

ABC: September 9, 1966 – July 14, 1967

Television series based on popular masked crime fighter of radio and movie serials of the 1930s - 1940s. The series starred Van Williams as Britt Reid and The Green Hornet, plus Bruce Lee as his aide Kato. Items will normally have copyright of Greenway Productions Inc.

GNH-1   GNH-2   GNH-3

GNH-1. "THE GREEN HORNET" SET OF 44 BUBBLE GUM CARDS issued by Donruss ©1966. Each card is 2.5x3.5" with color photo scene on front. Backs are printed with puzzle piece to form complete poster when set is assembled. **$150.**

GNH-2. "THE GREEN HORNET ANNUAL" 8x10.5" English-published hardcover by World Distributors Ltd. ©1967. Book has 64 pages with 13 text stories and one comic book-style story. **$45.**

GNH-3. "TV GUIDE" WEEKLY ISSUE for October 29, 1966 with color cover photo and three-page article, "Banker With A Sting" about Van Williams as The Green Hornet. **$20.**

GNH-4   GNH-5

GNH-9

GNH-4. "GREEN HORNET WRIST RADIOS" SET by Remco © 1966 in 2x6.5x10" box. Each radio is green hard plastic about 4" long, designed for use with battery. Set comes with a roll of insulated connecting wire. **$150.**

GNH-5. "THE GREEN HORNET" PLASTIC FILM VIEWER with boxed films on 5.5x7" retail blister pack card. Set is by Chemtoy ©1966. **$40.**

GNH-9. "THE GREEN HORNET QUICK SWITCH GAME" © 1966 by Milton Bradley. Box is 9.5x19" and holds 4 markers, 1 die, cardboard disks and a playing board with 4 mounted "Hornet" cardboard disk wheels. **$75.**

GNH-6

GNH-10   GNH-11

GNH-6. "THE GREEN HORNET" STEEL LUNCH BOX ©1967 by King-Seeley Thermos. **$200.**

GNH-10. "THE GREEN HORNET'S BLACK BEAUTY" REPLICA CAR by Corgi Toys © 1966. 2.25x2.25x6" long box holds detailed metal car with hornet decal on the roof, swiveling figure of The Green Hornet in the back seat and figure of Kato driving. Toy comes with 4 missles and 4 flying radar scanners which are launched from the front grille and trunk areas. **$250.**

GNH-11. "THE GREEN HORNET" MUG 3" tall of white milk glass with green and black illustrations of The Green Hornet, Kato and Black Beauty ©1966. **$25.**

GNH-7

GRIZZLY ADAMS

See The Life And Times Of Grizzly Adams

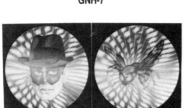

GNH-8

GNH-7. "THE GREEN HORNET" STEEL THERMOS 6.5" tall that came with lunch box **GNH-6. $75.**

GNH-8. GREEN HORNET FLASHER DISK 7.5" diameter © 1967 GPI. Colorful disk shows large illustration of The Green Hornet's head and when disk is tilted a large green hornet insect appears. **$35.**

GROUCHO MARX

See You Bet Your Life

THE GUMBY SHOW

NBC: March 16, 1957 – November 16, 1957

A spinoff from Howdy Doody, Gumby and his horse Pokey were animated clay figures. Bobby Nicholson, a former portrayer of Clarabell, was the first host, a role assumed later by Pinky Lee.

GUM-1   GUM-2

GUM-1. "GUMBY" 9" hand puppet with vinyl head and cloth handcover with original tag by Lakeside Toys © 1965. **$20.**

GUM-2. "THE ADVENTURES OF GUMBY ELECTRIC DRAWING SET" © 1966 by Lakeside Toys in 4x10x15" box. Contents include a plastic drawing stand lighted from small bulb underneath, 12 black/white illustrated drawing sheets picturing Gumby and Pokey, an eraser in the shape of Gumby, plus pencils and pencil sharpener. **$30.**

GUNSMOKE

CBS: September 10, 1955 – September 1, 1975

The longest-running television western, also credited as the longest-running prime time series with continuing characters. The original major cast members were James Arness as Marshal Matt Dillon, Amanda Blake as (Miss) Kitty Russell, Milburn Stone as Dr. Galen (Doc) Adams, and Dennis Weaver as Chester Goode. In 1964, Weaver left the show and was replaced by Ken Curtis as Festus Haggen. Items normally are copyrighted CBS Television Enterprises or Columbia Broadcasting System.

GNS-1   GNS-2   GNS-3

GNS-1. "MATT DILLON/GUNSMOKE" 3.5" celluloid button in unopened 4x6" "Top Western TV Stars" retail display bag © 1959. Button has black/white photo on yellow background. **$35.**

GNS-2. "L&M" 21x21" full color cardboard advertising sign with photo portraits and cigarette endorsements by Arness and Blake. Undated but circa 1960s prior to the 1971 banning of cigarette advertising on television. **$40.**

GNS-3. "GUNSMOKE" 6.5x8" hardcover Little Golden Book © 1958 with full color cover illustration and 24-page story with color art. **$8.**

GNS-4   GNS-5

GNS-4. "GUNSMOKE" BOXED BOARD GAME by Lowell Toy, undated circa late 1950s - early 1960s in 10x20" box. Playing board has design of Dodge City at one corner and Fort Riley at the opposite corner with Indian territory between. Game parts also include ten miniature plastic cowboys, twelve miniature Indians, four full-dimensioned cardboard and plastic stand-up stockade buildings. **$75.**

GNS-5. "GUNSMOKE" TOY STEEL HANDCUFFS on 5.25x8.75" black/white/red retail display card with photo of Arness as Dillon. By John-Henry Products circa late 1950s or early 1960s. **$25.**

GNS-6   GNS-7

GNS-6. "GUNSMOKE JIGSAW PUZZLE" by Whitman circa 1960s in 8x11" box. Assembled puzzle is 14x18" with scene of Dillon holding off a lynch mob at a prisoner's jail cell. **$15.**

GNS-7. "GUNSMOKE" STEEL LUNCH BOX © 1959 by Aladdin Industries. **$100.**

GNS-8   GNS-9

GNS-8. "GUNSMOKE" EMBOSSED STEEL LUNCH BOX AND PLASTIC THERMOS by Aladdin Industries © 1972. **LUNCH BOX $50. THERMOS $25.**

GNS-9. "GUNSMOKE TARGET GAME" by Park Plastic Co. © 1958 in 16x22" display box. Game parts consist of a dimensional diecut heavy cardboard back-drop piece, two 9" heavy cardboard diecut villain targets, two 10" plastic dart pistols, and six rubber-cupped darts. **$75.**

GNS-10   GNS-11

GNS-10. MATT DILLON REPLICA FIGURE from full-sized series by Hartland Plastics circa early 1960s. The figure is depicted in painted yellow shirt, brown vest, tan trousers and comes with white hat. The horse is beige with black markings plus saddle. **$75.**

GNS-11. "MATT DILLON OF GUNSMOKE" REPLICA FIGURE by Hartland Plastics © 1960 on unopened 7x11.5" retail card. The figure is from the smaller-sized series by Hartland and is depicted in orange outfit with black vest and white hat. The horse is gray with black marking. **$75.**

HAPPY DAYS

ABC: January 15, 1974 – August 1980

Late 1970s nostalgic comedy series based on teenage and high school life of the mid-1950s. The show featured a large cast which grew more in the later years, although central characters were Richie Cunningham (Ron Howard), and Arthur "Fonz" Fonzarelli (Henry Winkler). Howard left the show before start of 1980 season although new episodes were produced after that in addition to daytime re-runs on ABC. A spinoff Saturday morning animated cartoon version titled "Fonz And The Happy Days Gang" also originated in 1980. Items will normally have copyright of Paramount Pictures Corporation.

HPD-1   HPD-2

HPD-1. FONZ BUTTON 3.5" full color photo button of Winkler as Fonzarelli with inscription of one of his popular sayings. © 1976. **$8.**

HPD-2. "HAPPY DAYS" BOXED BOARD GAME by Parker Brothers © 1976. **$15.**

HPD-3   HPD-4

HPD-3. "HAPPY DAYS PICTURE CARDS BUBBLE GUM" BOX by Topps Gum Co. © 1976 which originally held packs containing set of 44 cards and 11 picture stickers. **BOX ONLY $15.**

HPD-4. "THE FONZ" STEEL LUNCH BOX AND "HAPPY DAYS" PLASTIC THERMOS issued as set by King-Seeley Thermos © 1976. **LUNCH BOX $25. THERMOS $10.**

HPD-5   HPD-6

HPD-5. FONZ 1.5x5x9" hard plastic battery-operated radio with full color paper sticker label picturing him at a jukebox with one of his phrases, "A-A-A-Y-Y-Y." Radio comes with original packaging. **$15.**

HPD-6. HAPPY DAYS DOLLS from 1976 series © by Mego with 8" height, soft vinyl molded head and hard plastic body plus original clothing. **EACH $20.**

THE HARDY BOYS MYSTERIES

ABC: January 30, 1977 – August 26, 1979

Youthful adventure series which originally premiered on television as two separate series with "The Nancy Drew Mysteries" which alternated biweekly in the same time slot. At the start of the 1978 season, The Hardy Boys Mysteries continued alone. The series was based on the popular fictional characters created in the 1920s. The principal characters in the TV series were Frank Hardy (Parker Stevenson) and Joe Hardy (Shaun Cassidy). The live action version was preceded by a Saturday morning September 6, 1969 – September 4, 1971 animated cartoon series titled "The Hardy Boys." Items will normally have copyright of Universal City Studios Inc.

HBM-1   HBM-2

HBM-1. "HARDY BOYS MYSTERIES" STEEL LUNCH BOX AND PLASTIC THERMOS issued as a set by King-Seeley Thermos © 1977. **LUNCH BOX $25. THERMOS $10.**

HBM-2. "THE HARDY BOYS MYSTERY GAME / THE SECRET OF THUNDER MOUNTAIN" by Parker Brothers © 1978 in 9.5x18" box. Game parts include playing board, cardboard stand-up figures and playing cards. **$10.**

HBM-3

HBM-4

HBM-3. "HARDY BOYS' VAN" PLASTIC ASSEMBLY KIT by Revell Plastics in 3.5x7.5x10" box circa 1977-1978. **$20.**

HBM-4. "HARDY BOYS/CORGI TOYS" REPLICA SET of vehicle and five miniature figures in 2x3x8.5" display box ©1969 although set is circa late 1970s. The replica vehicle is a 1912 Rolls Royce Silver Ghost touring car with diecast metal and plastic construction. The miniature figures are plastic and represent the Hardy Boys and others in their rock group, Chubby Morton, Pete Jones and Rhonda Kay. Set is #805 in the Corgi Toy series. **$90.**

HAVE GUN, WILL TRAVEL

CBS: September 14, 1957 – September 21, 1963

Adventure series starring Richard Boone as Paladin, a professional soldier of fortune who based his operation from the Hotel Carlton in San Francisco. His services were offered on a business card depicting a chess knight with inscription "Have Gun, Will Travel. Wire Paladin, San Francisco." Items will normally have copyright of either CBS Television Enterprises or CBS Inc.

HAV-1   HAV-2

HAV-1. "TV GUIDE" issue for week of May 10, 1958 with color cover photo of Boone as Paladin plus four-page article including biography and comments about his transition to the show from his previous "Medic" medical series. **$20.**

HAV-2. "HAVE GUN, WILL TRAVEL" STEEL LUNCH BOX WITH METAL THERMOS issued as 1960 © set by Aladdin Industries. **LUNCH BOX $125. THERMOS $40.**

HAV-3

HAV-3. "HAVE GUN, WILL TRAVEL" BOXED GUN AND HOLSTER SET © 1958 by Halco Industries. Holsters are thin leather with a glossy black finish and a die-cut metal depiction of a chess knight symbol on each holster cover. The belt is also black leather with a white plastic bullet clip on the reverse containing 18 toy plastic bullets. Each gun is silvered white metal with white plastic grips, each inset with a four-leaf clover symbol. Each gun has "Paladin" name on both sides. Box is 2x12x14". **$350.**

HAV-4

HAV-5

HAV-4. "PALADIN" SINGLE GUN AND LEATHER HOLSTER SET circa late 1950s. Holster and belt are dark leather with a white metal chess knight symbol on holster cover. The cap gun is silvered white metal with white and black plastic grips. Belt reverse has bullet clip. **$100.**

HAV-5. "HAVE GUN, WILL TRAVEL" BOXED BOARD GAME ©1959 by Parker Brothers. Game parts include playing board, spinner, bullet and horsemen playing pieces, and cards. Box is 10x19". **$50.**

HAV-6   HAV-7

HAV-6. "HAVE GUN, WILL TRAVEL" BLACK FELT HAT modeled after the one worn by Boone as Paladin. Front of crown has a black/silver fabric label with chess knight design and inscription "Wire Paladin/San Francisco." Hat has black cord drawstring and attached to this paper packet containing four "Paladin" calling cards. Also included is a peel-off Paladin mustache. Hat has original stitched label on brim by maker, Arlington Hat Co., New York, circa late 1950s. Hat dimensions are about 13x13x3.5" tall at the crown. **$75.**

HAV-7. PALADIN AND HORSE REPLICA PLASTIC FIGURE from series of television western hero figures by Hartland Plastics circa late 1950s – early 1960s. Paladin figure has painted depiction of dark blue outfit with matching hat. The horse is white with black markings. Figure set is from the full-sized series by Hartland and is complete with miniature pistol. **$125.**

HAV-8   HAV-9

HAV-8. "PALADIN/HAVE GUN, WILL TRAVEL" SMALL SIZED REPLICA FIGURE AND HORSE on unopened 6.5x11" retail card © 1960 by Hartland Plastics. Figure is depicted in dark blue outfit with black hat, and horse is white with black markings and saddle. **$100.**

HAV-9. "HAVE TUMS ... WILL TRAVEL!" METAL CASE issued by makers of antacid tablets circa late 1950s – early 1960s. Case is .75x1.75x3.5" with gold-colored finish plus a silver-colored metal depiction of chess knight symbol on lid. Inside of pill case is lined with black felt. **$20.**

HAWAII FIVE-O

CBS: September 26, 1968 – April 26, 1980

Long-running crime show with episodes actually filmed in Hawaii, often with adventures featuring exotic oriental villains. Featured characters were Jack Lord as Detective Steve McGarrett and James MacArthur as his assistant, Detective Dannie Williams. Items are normally copyrighted Columbia Broadcasting System Inc.

HWF-1

HWF-2

HWF-1. "HAWAII FIVE-O GAME" by Remco Industries © 1968 in 10x19.5" box. Game parts are a playing board designed with various Hawaiian sights plus depiction of Hawaii Five-O headquarters building, plus small figural character figures, playing cards and single die. **$40.**

HWF-2. "HAWAII FIVE-O/THE OCTOPUS CAPER" hardcover © 1971 Whitman book #1553 in 5.25x7.75" format with 212-page story. **$12.**

HAWAIIAN EYE

ABC: October 7, 1959 – September 10, 1963

Detective series by Warner Bros. with episodes based in Honolulu. Series was very similar in nature to Warner Bros.' earlier series "77 Sunset Strip" except for tropical setting. Featured original characters were freelance detectives Tom Lopaka (Robert Conrad) and Tracy Steele (Anthony Eisley). Supporting characters were Cricket Blake (Connie Stevens) plus Troy Donahue who joined the cast in 1962, the year Eisley left the series. Items generally will have copyright of Warner Bros. Pictures Inc.

HWY-1   HWY-2

HWY-1. "HAWAIIAN EYE" BOARD GAME by Lowell Toy © 1963 in original box. Game parts include playing board, separate decks of large and smaller cards, small wooden playing pieces. **$40.**

HWY-2. "HAWAIIAN EYE" MUSIC SOUND TRACK RECORD issued by Warner Bros. with 1960 © in 12.25x12.25" cardboard album. Record is 33 1/3-rpm with a total of 13 selections from original music of the show. **$12.**

HWY-3

HWY-3. "HAWAIIAN EYE STARRING TROY DONAHUE" 2.5" black/white flasher button which changes image when tilted from a depiction of palm tree and island design to portrait photo of him. Circa 1962-1963. **$10.**

THE HECKLE AND JECKLE SHOW

Syndicated 1955, CBS, NBC

Animated cartoon series based on the pair of conniving magpies originated in earlier Terrytoons movie cartoons before syndication for television. The series started October 14, 1956 on CBS and also spent two later years on NBC before ending September 12, 1982 back on CBS under title "New Adventures Of Mighty Mouse And Heckle And Jeckle." Other segments during the series featured Dinky Duck and Little Roquefort and others. Items will normally have copyright of Terrytoons or CBS, or both.

HJS-1   HJS-2

HJS-1. "HECKLE AND JECKLE" children's 6.5x8.25" Wonder Book ©1957 with 20-page story that has full color story art on each page. **$12.**

HJS-2. HECKLE AND JECKLE SOFT FOAM FIGURE PAIR each 7" tall and mounted on internal wire for rigidity. Each is a light yellow foam color with black accent on chest, tip of head and toes, fists and tail. **PAIR $30.**

HJS-3   HJS-4

HJS-3. "TERRYTOONS HIDE 'N SEEK GAME" by Transogram © 1960 in 9x17.5" box. Depicted on box lid or playing board are characters Heckle and Jeckle, Dinky Duck, Mighty Mouse, Deputy Dawg, Tom Terrific, Little Roquefort. **$25.**

HJS-4. "LITTLE ROQUEFORT" WOOD FIGURE of mouse character ©1959 with head mounted on a heavy wire spring. Figure is 2.5" diameter by 8.5" tall with movable arms plus a slot in the back to serve as a bank although no trap is in the base. **$30.**

THE HECTOR HEATHCOTE SHOW

NBC: October 5, 1963 – September 25, 1965

Saturday morning cartoon series featuring Heathcote, a scientist with a time machine used to re-write history. His assistants were Hashimoto, a mouse trained in the martial arts and an elephant named Sydney. Items will normally have copyright of Terrytoons division of CBS Films.

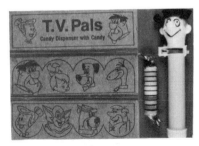

HHS-1

HHS-1. "T.V. PALS CANDY DISPENSER WITH CANDY" 1.5x1.5x4.5" illustrated box holding a 4" figural plastic candy dispenser depicting Hector Heathcote. Dispenser comes with original unused candy pack. Maker is Lions Novelty, Brooklyn, New York. Circa 1963-1965. **$50.**

HHS-2

HHS-2. "HECTOR HEATHCOTE" STEEL LUNCH BOX ©1964 by Aladdin Industries. **$60.**

HIGHWAY PATROL

Syndicated 1955 – 1959 (156 Episodes)

Popular syndicated crime-detection show with realistic adventures based on the activities of state police officer Chief Dan Matthews (Broderick Crawford). Items will normally have copyright of Ziv-TV.

HWP-1   HWP-2

HWP-1. "HIGHWAY PATROL" 3.5x5.5" fan post card with colorful design and full color photo of Broderick Crawford in his role from the show. The card back has a form message urging viewership of the show and this has a facsimile Crawford signature. **$25.**

HWP-2. "HIGHWAY PATROL" 8" lithographed tin friction car that produces a siren sound when pushed. Car has lithographed image of Broderick Crawford in the passenger seat with a policeman as driver. Each of these figures has a die-cut tin arm holding a gun, and these arms move up and down as the car moves. Car is in original box marked only "SM-Made In Japan." **$125.**

HWP-3   HWP-4

HWP-3. "HIGHWAY PATROL/OFFICIAL DAN MATTHEWS HOLSTER/REVOLVER & BADGE SET" produced in England and packaged in colorful 8x9" box. Contents are a plastic cap pistol with shoulder strap and a holster with silver Highway Patrol insignia. Completing the set is a 2" lithographed tin button inscribed "Highway Patrol Chief." **$100.**

HWP-4. "HIGHWAY PATROL SIREN" lithographed tin and plastic noise maker toy with a rear plunger which activates the "siren" mechanism in a 2.75" metal canister mounted on the top. Canister picture is in several colors with actual photo of Broderick Crawford. © 1957. **$35.**

HOGAN'S HEROES

CBS: September 17, 1965 – July 4, 1971

Comedy series set during World War II with premise of captured Americans running a prisoner of war camp without the knowledge of their inept German captors. Main characters: Col. Robert Hogan (Bob Crane), Col. Wilhelm Klink (Werner Klemperer), Sgt. Hans Schultz (John Banner), Cpl. Louis LeBeau (Robert Clary), Cpl. Peter Newkirk (Richard Dawson), Cpl. James Kinchloe (Ivan Dickson/Kenneth Washington), Sgt. Andrew Carter (Larry Hovis). Items will normally have copyright of Bing Crosby Productions Inc.

HGN-1   HGN-2   HGN-3

HGN-1. "TV GUIDE" issue for week of November 19, 1966 with color cover photo of Bob Crane and Robert Clary plus 3.5-page article, mostly about Clary who was an actual concentration camp prisoner as a youth. **$10.**

HGN-2. "JOHN BANNER" 8x10" school tablet with cover photo of him in his role as Sgt. Schultz. Circa 1966. **$20.**

HGN-3. "HOGAN'S HEROES SING THE BEST OF WORLD WAR II" 33 1/3-rpm record in 12.25x12.25" cardboard album. Songs are by Robert Clary, Richard Dawson, Ivan Dickson and Larry Hovis of the show cast and selections include "Hogan's Heroes March." Record is on Sunset label from Liberty Records. **$25.**

HGN-4   HGN-5

HGN-4. "HOGAN'S HEROES/BLUFF OUT GAME" by Transogram ©1966 in 9x17.5" box. The playing board has black/white inset photos of Hogan, Klink and Schultz which are repeated in illustration form on box lid. **$50.**

HGN-5. "HOGAN'S HEROES' WORLD WAR II JEEP" plastic model assembly kit by MPC Models ©1968 in 3.5x6.5x9" original box. **$50.**

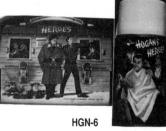

HGN-6

HGN-6. "HOGAN'S HEROES" DOMED STEEL LUNCH BOX WITH METAL THERMOS issued as set by Aladdin Industries ©1966. **LUNCH BOX $100. THERMOS $50.**

HOKEY WOLF

See The Huckleberry Hound Show

HONEY WEST

ABC: September 17, 1965 – September 2, 1966

Crime show starring Anne Francis in the title role of a female private detective who took over her father's detective agency after his death. Episodes featured a number of amazing or exotic weapons devices used by her. Items will normally have copyright of Four Star Television.

HWT-1

HWT-1. "HONEY WEST" BOARD GAME by Ideal Toys ©1965 in 10x18.5" box. Game parts include playing board, spinner board, plastic game pieces, and a total of 62 small playing cards. **$30.**

HWT-2   HWT-3   HWT-4

HWT-2. HONEY WEST 11.5" hard plastic doll with soft vinyl head and rooted life-like blonde hair plus black fabric stretch suit. Unmarked but by Gilbert Toys circa 1965-1966. **$75.**

HWT-3. "HONEY WEST" ACCESSORIES in original 9.25x12.25" retail box ©1965 by A.C. Gilbert Toys. Accessories are designed for use with action figure doll **HWT-2** and include a miniature cap-firing pistol, trick compact, telescope lens necklace, model's bag, comb and brush set with mirror and high-heeled pumps. Items are under original clear cellophane seal. **$50.**

HWT-4. "HONEY WEST" ACCESSORIES on 6.5x8.5" retail display card ©1965 by A.C. Gilbert Toys. Unopened accessories for use with action figure doll **HWT-2** are a miniature secret lipstick whistle, telescope lens necklace, handcuff bracelet, and telephone purse. **$25.**

HOPALONG CASSIDY

NBC: June 24, 1949 – December 23, 1951

One of earliest television western series featuring early William Boyd/Hopalong Cassidy movie films edited to time segments to fit television scheduling by Boyd himself, who purchased television rights to his earlier films. Another 52 new episodes were filmed for syndication by Boyd in 1951-1952. The series generally ran on NBC's 6:00-7:00 Sunday evening time slot and was immensely popular, producing a wealth of licensed products. Items are normally copyrighted Wm. (or) William Boyd 1950.

HPA-1   **HPA-2**

HPA-1. "HOPALONG CASSIDY AND LUCKY AT COPPER GULCH" 8x11" stiff cardboard "Television Book" by Doubleday ©1950 and published by Garden City. Front cover has die-cut square opening around a cardboard wheel which produces changing "flasher" western images when turned. Book also has 24-page story with large story art in color. **$35.**

HPA-2. HOPALONG CASSIDY FIGURE SET with box by Ideal Toys circa early 1950s. Set consists of 4" plastic figure of Hopalong and a 5" tall plastic figure of his horse Topper. Hopalong figure is depicted in black outfit and has removable hat plus jointed right arm. The box is 2.25x5x5" with colorful designs on all surfaces except bottom. **$75.**

HPA-3

HPA-3. "HOPALONG CASSIDY ROLLER SKATES" WITH BOX from Rollfast. Skates are steel with ball bearing wheels and mechanism for adjusting size. Each skate has cowhide straps and removable metal spurs. Straps each have "Hopalong Cassidy" name plus three cut glass jewels. The Cassidy name is engraved on the toe of each skate. Each spur has a turning rowel although spur attachments are not marked with his name. Set comes with skate key and instruction card in 3.5x6x10" illustrated box. **$300.**

HPA-4   **HPA-5**

HPA-4. "HOPALONG CASSIDY" CHILD'S TV ROCKER CHAIR by Comfort Lines, Inc. circa 1949-1950. Chair is 14.5" wide by 23" deep and has a 21" height to the top of the back rest. The back rest and seat are padded vinyl with the seat in a solid red color. The back rest is an ivory white with Hoppy portrait and facsimile signature in rope script plus various cowboy and western symbols, all on a large decal with black and white coloring. The chair support pieces are aluminum tubing and the rockers are steel. Stapled on the bottom of the seat is the maker's tag which shows an actual delivery date for the item to the store. **$150.**

HPA-5. "HOPALONG CASSIDY" DESK RADIO by Arvin circa 1950. Radio is 4x5.5x8.25" with black (or red) metal case and an embossed silver/black foil front die-cut in design of Hopalong on Topper. This die-cut area is over a background of red fabric which covers the internal speaker mechanism. The front panel also has embossed depictions of covered wagons, a longhorn steer and cactus. Radio is for electrical use rather than batteries. **$200.**

HPA-6   **HPA-7**

HPA-6. "HOPALONG CASSIDY GAME" by Milton Bradley © 1950 in 9.5x19" box. Game parts include playing board, miniature metal cowboy playing pieces, cardboard "outlaw" disks, and $90,000 in play money. **$60.**

HPA-7. "HOPALONG CASSIDY" PAIR OF CHILD'S RUBBER RAIN BOOTS mostly in black with tan toe, heel and rear spur design. On outer side of each boot is a printed colorful Hopalong portrait. **PAIR $60.**

HPA-8   **HPA-9**

HPA-8. "HOPALONG CASSIDY" CHILD'S WESTERN JACKET of black cotton twill with white stitching and silvered metal "Hopalong Cassidy" snaps on the front, both patch pockets and wrists. Also on each patch pocket is a stitched outline of a steer head. Made by "Blue Bell" circa 1950s and original maker label, also shown in our photo example, is stitched to inside collar. **$75.**

HPA-9. "HOPALONG CASSIDY" 3.5" steel pocketknife with black plastic insert panels on each side. One panel has black/white photo image of Hopalong holding pistol in upraised hand while seated on Topper. Knife has two steel blades and single utility blade plus a metal loop is attached at one end. The knife is by "Hammer Brand" of U.S.A. $40.

HPA-10

HPA-10. "HOPALONG CASSIDY AUTOMATIC PICTURE GUN AND THEATER" SET in 1.5x8.5x12.5" in original box. Set consists of a 6" gray metal picture gun with colorful Hopalong decals on each side of the barrel, plus two illustrated boxes containing a total of six black/white films. Also included is a cardboard fold-out screen. The box is designed to serve as a theater setting. The picture gun is operated by battery. $100.

HPA-11   HPA-12

HPA-11. "HOPALONG" 9" silvered metal cap pistol with ivory colored plastic grips. Gun is by Wyandotte Toys circa early 1950s and has "Hopalong" in raised letters on both sides. Each grip has an etched black illustration of Hoppy and his name. The gun is the same type which came with holster set HPA-12. $75.

HPA-12. "HOPALONG CASSIDY" BLACK LEATHER HOLSTER SET designed to fit pair of 9" cap guns. Holster belt is also black leather, and both holsters and belt have many silvered brass rivet accents. Each holster cover has a silvered metal design piece that has raised depiction of Hopalong. The back of the belt has his name imprinted in ink. $100.

HPA-13

HPA-13. "HOPALONG CASSIDY" WRIST WATCH with "saddle stand" display box, issued as set by U.S. Time in 1950. The watch is in a silvered metal case inscribed on the back "Good Luck From Hoppy." The dial face design is black/white/red with portrait of Hopalong below. The box is 3x4x4.25" and contains an insert cardboard display saddle for the watch. $200.

HPA-14   HPA-15   HPA-16

HPA-14. "HOPALONG CASSIDY" ALARM CLOCK by U.S. Time circa 1950. Clock is 5" in diameter by 5.5" tall with 2" depth and enameled black metal case holding key-wind clock. Clock crystal is glass with the dial face depiction of Hopalong on Topper in black/white. Background is gray with red numerals and clock hands. $250.

HPA-15. "HOPALONG CASSIDY" HOLSTER NIGHT LIGHT by Aladdin Lamps circa early 1950s. The light is molded heavy glass formed in image of a holstered gun. The light is about 4x9.5" with a depth of 3". A small electric bulb inserted in the back causes the light to glow when turned on. The coloring is a creamy white and tan with full color decal picture of Hopalong at center. $150.

HPA-16. "HOPALONG CASSIDY" NIGHT LIGHT designed as 7.5" tall, white glass cylinder with a full color picture decal on front side. The bulb holder in the hollow cylinder is attached to electric cord that has original maker's tag from Aladdin Lamps. Early 1950s. $200.

HPA-17   HPA-18

HPA-17. "HOPALONG CASSIDY" STEEL LUNCH BOX WITH METAL THERMOS issued as set by Aladdin Industries in 1950-1953. The box comes either in a red or blue enameled version with full color decal picture on the lid. The decal came either in a scalloped border design, as shown in our example, or in a square design. The thermos has full color lithographed picture on yellow background. LUNCH BOX $75. THERMOS $35.

HPA-18. "HOPALONG CASSIDY" STEEL LUNCH BOX by Aladdin Industries ©1954. Lid has a full color lithographed picture in border design to simulate a television screen. $125.

HPA-19   HPA-20

HPA-19. "HOPALONG CASSIDY" 3" white china cup with colorful illustration of Hopalong on one side. Bottom has a maker's signature, "Hopalong Cassidy By W.S. George" with depiction of a cowboy boot. Early 1950s. **$40.**

HPA-20. HOPALONG CASSIDY WHITE CHINA BOWL marked on bottom with same signature of maker as **HPA-19.** Bowl is 5.25" diameter by 2.25" tall with colorful illustration of Hopalong on Topper. **$35.**

HPA-21

HPA-22

HPA-21. "HOPALONG CASSIDY" COMPLETE SET OF FOUR MILK-GLASS MUGS each with different illustration in different single color of blue, green, black or red. Early 1950s. **EACH $20.**

HPA-22. "HOPALONG CASSIDY" COMPLETE SET OF THREE DIFFERENT MILK GLASSES circa 1952. Each is 5" tall with white background and different illustration in black on one side. Reverse of each has designation of either "Breakfast Milk," "Lunch Milk," or "Dinner Milk." **EACH $25.**

HOW THE WEST WAS WON

ABC: February 12, 1978 – April 23, 1979

Epic western series about a family's journey to the Northwest Territory in the 1860s. Starred was James Arness (formerly Matt Dillon of the Gunsmoke series) as Zeb Macahan, the leader of the arduous trek. The series was based on the 1963 motion picture of the same title. Items will normally have a 1978 copyright by Metro-Goldwyn-Mayer.

HWW-1

HWW-1. "HOW THE WEST WAS WON" STEEL LUNCH BOX by King-Seeley Thermos ©1976. The box came originally as a set with thermos **HWW-2. $20.**

HWW-2   HWW-3   HWW-4

HWW-2. "HOW THE WEST WAS WON" PLASTIC THERMOS by King-Seeley ©1976 and issued originally with lunch box **HWW-1.** **$10.**

HWW-3. "HOW THE WEST WAS WON" BOXED PLAYSET by Timpo ©1977 in original 3.5x11x18" box with colorful lid design. Plastic playset consists of 10 standing figures, 4 mounted figures, 2 mustang ponies, 2 sitting Indians and a single campfire, wigwam, vehicle, building and canoe. **$25.**

HWW-4. "HOW THE WEST WAS WON" BOXED JIGSAW PUZZLE by HG Toys ©1978. Box is 1.5x8x10" and contains 150-piece full color photo puzzle with assembled size of 10x14". Puzzle scene is the same as depicted on the box lid. **$10.**

HOWDY DOODY

NBC: December 27, 1947 – September 30, 1960
NBC 1976

Television's most famous children's show created by "Buffalo" Bob Smith. The show ran for 2,343 performances featuring the puppet characters of Howdy Doody and his friends Mr. Bluster, Flub-A-Dub, Dilly-Dally, Princess Summerfall-Winterspring, and others. The first Clarabell portrayer was Bob Keeshan, later to become Captain Kangaroo. An enormous variety of character merchandise was licensed. From 1948 to 1951, items are normally marked "Bob Smith" plus a copyright symbol. Beginning 1951 and continuing throughout the 1950s, merchandise was copyrighted with the name "Kagran Corp." Beginning in 1960, items were marked "N.B.C. Copyright."

HDY-1   HDY-2   HDY-3

HDY-1. "TV DIGEST" issue for week of December 27, 1952 with cover photo of Howdy and Bob Smith in black/white/red. Cover article contains more black/white photos of Howdy and friends including one with Gabby Hayes. **$35.**

HDY-2. "TV GUIDE" for week of June 25, 1954 with full color photo of Howdy and Bob Smith plus two-page article including another color portrait of Howdy. Article is about the show's continued popularity after nearly seven years. **$30.**

HDY-3. HOWDY DOODY CHINA FIGURAL BUST BANK with head and shoulders in a glossy off-white color accented by reddish-brown hair, reddish-pink soft accents on nose and cheeks, dark pink lips, and brown eyes and scattered freckles. The neckerchief is depicted in blue with the stripes on his shirt in a matching blue plus a reddish-pink matching the lips. The coin slot is in top of the head, and bottom of base has a rectangular trap. Overall size is about 4x7x8" tall. Unmarked but early 1950s. **$350.**

| HDY-4 | HDY-5 | HDY-6 |

HDY-4. HOWDY DOODY CHINA COOKIE JAR WITH LID and total size of about 8x8x8". The face and ears are an off-white accented by blue eyes, brown eyelashes, eyebrows, freckles plus pink-tinted cheeks, tip of nose and lips. The hair is a dark soft red approaching rust color. Unmarked but early 1950s. **$175.**

HDY-5. HOWDY DOODY CHINA PIGGY BANK about 3x4.5x7.5" tall, finished in soft tones of reddish-pink, light blue and tan on white. The red accents are on the face, cowboy hat and boots. Light blue is on the neckerchief and trousers, and the gloves are tan. The coin slot is in Howdy's back. Bob Smith ©circa 1950. **$175.**

HDY-6. "HOWDY DOODY" 5x7.5x11.5" stuffed plush replica doll of his dog "Windy." The doll is formed in a permanent seated position, and stitched on top of the head is a boating cap of white drill fabric which has Howdy name and picture printed in black around the brim. The head has glossy black plastic eyes plus a stitched soft rubber muzzle in tan. The nose is black and a bright red tongue is molded to perpetually hang out. By Rushton Co., Atlanta, circa early 1950s. **$200.**

| HDY-7 | HDY-8 |

HDY-7. "HOWDY DOODY MARIONETTE" by Peter Puppet Playthings Inc. circa early 1950s in original 4x5.5x15.5" box. The marionette is 15" tall and formed from wood with composition head and colorful cloth outfit. The head has a movable mouth. **BOXED $200. UNBOXED $100.**

HDY-8. "PRINCESS SUMMERFALL-WINTERSPRING" COMPOSITION AND WOOD MARIONETTE by Peter Puppet Playthings circa early 1950s in original box. Marionette is 12" tall with movable mouth, tufted yarn hair, colorful cloth outfit, and brass link necklace with plastic disks bearing symbols of the seasons. **BOXED $200. UNBOXED $100.**

| HDY-9 | HDY-10 |

HDY-9. GIRL'S "HOWDY DOODY" WRISTWATCH in 1" silvered metal case with leather straps covered in red vinyl. The dial face has Howdy portrait in fleshtone with red hair, lips, freckles and neckerchief. The portrait face has tiny die-cut holes around the eyes which slowly change position as time passes. The dial face numerals from 1 through 5 and 7 through 11, each have the added design of a letter of his name in gold color. Bob Smith ©circa 1950. **$100.**

HDY-10. CLARABELL MARIONETTE by Peter Puppet Playthings circa early 1950s in original 3.5x5.5x14" box. The marionette is 13" tall and formed from composition and wood with fabric outfit and movable mouth. **BOXED $250. UNBOXED $150.**

| HDY-11 | HDY-12 |

HDY-11. BOY'S "HOWDY DOODY" WRISTWATCH, similar to **HDY-9** except for slightly larger 1.25" silvered metal case plus leather straps are covered by green vinyl. The dial face appearance and operation are identical to **HDY-9** except for slightly larger size. Bob Smith ©circa 1950. **$150.**

HDY-12. DILLY-DALLY MARIONETTE by Peter Puppet Playthings circa early 1950s in original 3.5x5.5x14" box. Marionette is 13" tall of composition and wood with movable mouth and fabric clothing. **BOXED $300. UNBOXED $200.**

| HDY-13 |

HDY-13. MR. BLUSTER MARIONETTE by Peter Puppet Playthings circa early 1950s in original 3.5x5.5x14" box. The marionette is 13" tall of composition and wood with movable mouth and fabric clothing. **BOXED $350. UNBOXED $250.**

HDY-14

HDY-14. FLUB-A-DUB MARIONETTE by Peter Puppet Playthings circa early 1950s in original 4x6x14" box. The marionette has a 6.5" body length from rear to neck and when the head is upright, the height is about 9". The figure is wood with a movable lower jaw and tongue. The head has inset eyes that open and close with small artificial eyelashes. Attached to the body is a fabric name blanket, die-cut felt feet and ears, and a flannel neck. Kagran ©circa 1951. **BOXED $350. UNBOXED $250.**

HDY-15   **HDY-16**   **HDY-17**   **HDY-18**

HDY-15. HOWDY DOODY 8.5" hand puppet with soft vinyl head and red/white checkered hand cover. Bob Smith ©circa 1950. **$25.**

HDY-16. MR. BLUSTER 8.5" hand puppet with vinyl head plus fabric hand cover. Bob Smith ©circa 1950. **$25.**

HDY-17. HOWDY DOODY 13" stiff paper marionette multi-jointed by small metal grommets at neck, shoulders, legs and knees. A thread is attached at top and figure can be made to dance by dangling it to a flat surface. Nicely colored and ©Kagran. **$40.**

HDY-18. PRINCESS SUMMERFALL-WINTERSPRING 13" stiff paper die-cut marionette multi-jointed by small grommets at neck, shoulders, legs and knees. A thread is attached at top so figure can be made to dance by dangling it to a flat surface. Nicely colored and © Kagran. **$40.**

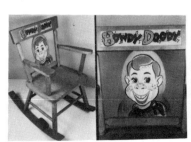

HDY-19   **HDY-20**

HDY-19. "HOWDY DOODY" CHILD'S MUSICAL ROCKING CHAIR with a music box-like unit on one of the rockers which produces the Howdy Doody theme music when chair is rocked. The chair is mostly a varnished light oak color with colored portrait and name decals on front side of the backrest. The overall size is 15" wide by 21.5" rocker length by 23" tall. Bob Smith ©circa 1950. **$150.**

HDY-20. HOWDY DOODY ELECTRICAL NIGHT LIGHT consisting of full-dimensioned 5.25" tall (from seated position to top of head) hard hollow plastic figure on 5.25" diameter wood base. The figure is nicely colored and the simulated neckerchief has his name printed on it. The head is socketed to enable movement of the face to any direction. The figure lifts from the base for installation of a small low-watt bulb which causes the figure to glow softly when turned on. Early 1950s. **$100.**

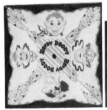

HDY-21   **HDY-22**

HDY-21. "HOWDY DOODY" 11x11" frosted glass lightbulb cover for ceiling fixture. The shade has a 2" concave depth of inner surface, and the edges are formed in a wavy beveled fashion. The graphic design is of colorful curtains and character portraits of Howdy, Clarabell, Flub-A-Dub and Mr. Bluster. The center of the shade is holed as made for the hanging bolt of a ceiling electrical fixture. Kagran © circa 1952. **$150.**

HDY-22. "HOWDY DOODY" 8x9" molded thin rubber mask depicting him in fleshtones with dark red hair, freckles and mouthline. Attached to the mask is a small original tag picturing Howdy and Clarabell with Bob Smith © notice. Both mask and tag are shown. **$60.**

HDY-23   **HDY-24**

HDY-23. "SEASON'S GREETINGS FROM HOWDY DOODY AND HIS FRIENDS." 5x20" red flannel stocking with full color softly-flocked design including Howdy and Clarabell around a decorated Christmas tree. Kagran ©circa 1952. **$150.**

HDY-24. "HOWDY DOODY CAMPAIGN CAP" cut and assembled from paper sheet issued as premium by Poll-Parrot Shoes circa early 1950s. Hat is mostly a dark red color trimmed in white and yellow plus a full color depiction of Poll-Parrot trademark. Maker is Ken Giles Tuk-A-Tab Toys. **$25.**

HDY-25

HDY-26

HDY-31

HDY-25. HOWDY DOODY CHARACTER FIGURES comprising a set of five issued originally in box designed to serve as small theater stage. Each figure is hollow hard plastic and about 4" tall with a movable mouth operated by a small lever in back of the head. Each is pink color accented by reds and blues. Figures normally have a "Tee-Vee" © and may have additional © of Bob Smith or Kagran. **EACH $15.**

HDY-26. "FLUB-A-DUB" PACKAGED "FLIP-A-RING" TOY in 6x12.5" original packaging. Toy is 9.5" long of thick die-cut cardboard. Attached at the chin is a length of string which holds a 2.5" diameter wood ring at the other end. Object of toy is to toss the tethered ring and catch it on the figure's beak. Kagran ©circa 1955. **$25.**

HDY-31. HOWDY DOODY 3.75" mug with full color depiction around side of six different characters. Mug has 1971 © National Broadcasting Co. **$15.**

THE HUCKLEBERRY HOUND SHOW
Syndicated 1958 – 1962

One of the first television cartoon series by William Hanna and Joseph Barbera, founders of Hanna-Barbera Productions, and items will normally have this copyright. Huckleberry Hound, a noble blood-hound with a southern accent, led to many other Hanna-Barbera characters. Cartoon segments also featured Pixie and Dixie, Hokey Wolf, plus Yogi Bear which went on to become a series on its own (see Yogi Bear). In 1960, Huckleberry Hound became the first television cartoon series to win an Emmy award.

HDY-27   HDY-28   HDY-29

HDY-27. "HOWDY DOODY SAVINGS BANK" circa 1960s with © National Broadcasting Co. Figure is 7" tall and covered entirely with flocked colors of pink, red and light blue plus flocked brown boots. The figure stands on a 1.5x2.5x4" black vinyl base which has coin slot at rear edge. **$25.**

HDY-28. "CLARABELL SAVINGS BANK" from same series as **HDY-27** with similar 7.5" flocked pink/red/blue figure on black vinyl base. **$25.**

HDY-29. "PHINEAS T. BLUSTER SAVINGS BANK" from same series as **HDY-27** with similar 7" flocked figure in pink/red/blue with flocked brown jacket and derby. Figure is on black vinyl base. **$25.**

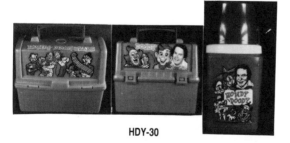

HDY-30

HDY-30. "HOWDY DOODY & PALS" PLASTIC LUNCH BOX AND THERMOS circa 1970s © National Broadcasting Co. Box and thermos are both red with full color character pictures. **LUNCH BOX $40. THERMOS $20.**

HUK-1   HUK-2   HUK-3

HUK-1. "HUCKLEBERRY HOUND" 18" stuffed plush doll with vinyl hands and face. The doll is by Knickerbocker Toy Co. ©1959 and features a red body with white chest area. Accents are a stitched felt hat, bow tie and chest buttons, all in aqua blue. Doll comes with maker's tag attached. **$60.**

HUK-2. HUCKLEBERRY HOUND 10" hard plastic figural bank with paint finish mostly in solid red accented by black and tan. The top hat has coin slot and head is removable. By Knickerbocker Toys circa 1960. **$20.**

HUK-3. HUCKLEBERRY HOUND'S HUCKLE-CHUCK" BOXED TARGET GAME © 1961 by Transogram in original 3x15.5x32" illus-trated box. Target is 15x31" formed from thick die-cut masonite which has bright lithographed paper target images. Game is played by either tossing plastic rings over the ears, beanbags into the mouth, or by throwing rubber-tipped darts at the chest target. Each of the accessory pieces comes in a set of four. The target is held upright by a pair of wood base supports which are also included. **$60.**

HUK-4   **HUK-5**   **HUK-6**

HUK-11   **HUK-12**   **HUK-13**

HUK-4. HUCKLEBERRY HOUND 6" glazed china figure mostly in glossy light blue coloring with accent colors of red and black. Bottom of base has sticker label from Ideas, Inc. Circa early 1960s. **$35.**

HUK-5. HUCKLEBERRY HOUND WIND-UP LITHOGRAPHED TIN TOY by Line Mar copyright 1962. Toy is 2x3x4" and winding causes it to hop up and down while moving in a circular fashion. **$175.**

HUK-6. HUCKLEBERRY HOUND LITHOGRAPH TIN FRICTION TOY depicting him on a go-cart. The toy is 4x4x6.5" and the figure has a vinyl head. By Line Mar Toys circa early 1960s. **$225.**

HUK-11. "HUCKLEBERRY HOUND PRESENTS TV SCENES" BOXED MINIATURE FIGURE SET by Marx Toys © 1961. Box is 1x3x3.25" and miniature figure of Hokey Wolf is held against a colorful background panel picturing a teepee and rail fence. **$35.**

HUK-12. "HOKEY WOLF" TV-TINYKIN FIGURE by Marx Toys ©1961 in original 1x1.5x2" display box. **$20.**

HUK-13. "DING-A-LING" TV TINYKIN by Marx Toys ©1961 in original 1x1.5x2.25" display box. Figure is 1.5" tall and hand painted. **$20.**

HUK-7   **HUK-8**

HUK-14   **HUK-15**

HUK-7. "HUCKLEBERRY HOUND AND HIS FRIENDS" STEEL LUNCH BOX AND THERMOS. Issued as set © 1961 by Aladdin Industries. **LUNCH BOX $60. THERMOS $30.**

HUK-8. "HUCKLEBERRY HOUND WESTERN GAME" by Milton Bradley ©1959 in original 8.5x16.5" box. **$50.**

HUK-16

HUK-9   **HUK-10**

HUK-9. "HUCKLEBERRY HOUND TV-TINYKINS BY MARX TOYS" on unopened 3.5x5.5" background card ©1961. Tinykin figure is Huckleberry with an underwater treasure chest background scene. **$35.**

HUK-10. "HUCKLEBERRY HOUND TV PLAYSET" by Marx Toys © 1961 in original 3.5x6.5" display carton. Boxed are miniature hand-painted plastic figures of him, Hokey Wolf, Ding-A-Ling, Mr. Jinks, Pixie and Dixie. **$100.**

HUK-14. "MR. JINKS/PIXIE AND DIXIE" 10" hard plastic bubble soap container bottle by Purex circa early 1960s. The figure is mostly orange with white and black markings plus the depicted figures of the mice are in gray. **$15.**

HUK-15. PIXIE AND DIXIE ORIGINAL "CEL" inked and painted art from a Mr. Jinks cartoon series by Hanna-Barbera circa 1960s. Total art size is 4x6" on 10.5x12.5" clear acetate sheet. The figures are each in two shades of gray plus black. **$75.**

HUK-16. MR. JINKS 13" stuffed plush figure toy by Knickerbocker Toys ©1959. Figure is formed in permanent seated position and has soft vinyl face. Body is black plush accented by white stomach and pink felt buttons and bow tie. Doll comes with attached tag for maker. **$60.**

I DREAM OF JEANNIE

NBC: September 18, 1965 – September, 1970

Situation comedy about a beautiful genie whose bottle was found by a crashed astronaut. Jeannie attempts to reward him by using magic, but most of her ideas backfire. Principal characters were Barbara Eden as Jeannie and Larry Hagman as Capt. Tony Nelson. A Saturday morning animated version followed on CBS from September 8, 1973 – August 30, 1975 under the title "Jeannie" which was based loosely on the original series but tailored to teenage interests. Items from the live action series will normally have copyright of Screen Gems Inc. or Sydney Sheldon Productions Inc. or both. Items from the animated version will normally have copyright of Columbia Pictures Industries Inc.

IDJ-1   IDJ-2   IDJ-3

IDJ-1. "I DREAM OF JEANNIE" 3.5x5.5" full color photo fan card picturing stars Eden and Hagman. Reverse has facsimile signatures of both. Circa 1965-1966. **$25.**

IDJ-2. JEANNIE 19" hard plastic doll with soft vinyl head. Doll is ©1966 by maker Libby and has life-like blonde rooted hair and sleep eyes. Doll was issued with various but similar outfits and our example shows it in a see-through pink fabric dress and top with thin veil over the face. **$150.**

IDJ-3. "JEANNIE JADE JEWELRY" on 6x9.5" store card ©1975. Jewelry is green plastic necklace and three charms, based on the animated cartoon version rather than real life version of the series. **$25.**

IDJ-4   IDJ-5

IDJ-4. "I DREAM OF JEANNIE" 6.5" poseable doll in original retail box. Doll is soft vinyl and hard plastic with movable arms and legs. Accessories are a fabric outfit, plastic pocketbook and shoes. By Remco Toys ©1977. **$75.**

IDJ-5. "I DREAM OF JEANNIE" BOARD GAME by Milton Bradley ©1965 in 9.5x19" box. **$35.**

I LOVE LUCY

CBS: October 15, 1951 – September 24, 1961

Probably the most consistently popular situation comedy in television history starring Lucille Ball as Lucy, a wacky, slapstick housewife. The early years of the series also starred her real-life husband Desi Arnaz, as her television husband Ricky Ricardo. In 1962 she returned to television, without ex-husband Arnaz and starred in "The Lucy Show" from October 1 of that year through September 16, 1968. For many years, the show also featured the neighbor couple of Fred and Ethel Mertz (William Frawley and Vivian Vance). One of the highlights of the series occurred January 19, 1953 when Lucy Ricardo gave birth to Little Ricky in the television series, the same night that Lucille Ball gave actual birth to her second child, Desi Arnaz IV. The Little Ricky television character was added to the cast in 1956-1957. The show had several other title and format changes during the years. Popularity with viewers remains high to the present day due to syndicated reruns. Items normally will have either copyright of "Lucille Ball and Desi Arnaz" or "Desilu."

ILY-1   ILY-2   ILY-3

ILY-1. "LUCY'S NOTEBOOK!" 6x9" softcover 44-page book of menus, recipes and entertaining tips by Lucy Ricardo. The recipes include comic text about Lucy and Ricky. Circa 1957-1960. **$25.**

ILY-2. "NEWSWEEK" issue for January 19, 1953 with color cover photo and four-page article about the "I Love Lucy" show. **$20.**

ILY-3. LUCY 27" stuffed cloth doll with molded plastic face and red/white fabric outfit. The head is accented by yellow yarn hair, and the apron has heart-shaped pockets. Inscription on the apron is "I Love Lucy-Desi." 1950s. **$150.**

ILY-4   ILY-5

ILY-4. "DESI'S CONGA DRUM" of heavy cardboard with vinyl strap. The drum is 19" tall with the larger end 11" in diameter which tapers to 6.5" diameter at the smaller end. The drum head is taut thin paper held in place by a metal ring. Graphics around the side are red/black/white. Drum comes with original four-page leaflet that includes photo of Desi Arnaz using the drum, and this picture is included in our photo example. **$175.**

ILY-5. "TV DIGEST AND GUIDE" issue for week of March 20, 1953, the last issue to be published under this title before changing to shorter "TV Guide" in April of that year. The front cover has tinted photo of "Lucy's Neighbors," the Mertzes, and related article has more small scenes from the I Love Lucy Show. **$100.**

ILY-12

| ILY-6 | ILY-7 | ILY-8 |

ILY-12. "I LOVE LUCY" PICTURE BOOK by 3 Dimension Publications ©1953. Book is 8x10" and inside front cover has small tip-in envelope holding set of cardboard 3-D glasses. Included are four pages of photos printed in 3-D process to be viewed through the glasses plus more than 20 pages featuring large black/white scenes from the TV series. The back cover has photo of Ricky, Jr. Our photo example shows both covers plus a typical page scene. **$75.**

ILY-6. "TV GUIDE" first issue under that title published for week of April 3, 1953 with color cover photo of Lucy and Desi's new son, Desiderio Alberto Arnaz IV. Cover article is titled "Lucy's $50,000,000 Baby" with color portrait photo of the parents plus black/white scenes from the I Love Lucy Show. **$250.**

ILY-7. "TV GUIDE" for week of December 10, 1955 with color cover photo and three-page article about the continued popularity of the I Love Lucy Show. Article includes both color and black/white photos. **$25.**

ILY-8. "LIFE" weekly magazine for April 6, 1953 with black/white cover photo plus five-page photo article about Lucy and her television and real life families. **$15.**

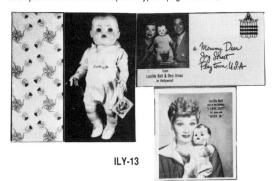

ILY-13

ILY-13. "RICKY JR." 20" doll by American Character Doll circa 1953-1954 in original box. Doll is lifelike vinyl and drinks, wets, blows bubbles and has moving eyes. The doll comes with clothing outfit plus instruction folder. Our photo example shows doll plus box lid, cover of the instruction leaflet, and a side panel from the box. **$300.**

I SPY

NBC: September 15, 1965 – September 2, 1968

Espionage adventure series starring Robert Culp and Bill Cosby as Kelly Robinson and Alexander Scott, a team of American agents. Cosby's role in the series is believed to be the first starring role for a black performer in a regular dramatic series on American television. Items will normally have copyright of Triple F Productions.

| ILY-9 | ILY-10 | ILY-11 |

ILY-9. "RICKY-JR." 8" finger puppet doll with soft vinyl head, hands and feet sewn into flannel pajamas which in turn are sewn into a 10x13" flannel wrapping blanket. Underside has opening in blanket and pajamas for placement of fingers in the doll's neck and arms. Blanket has "I Am Ricky, Jr." tag ©Lucille Ball and Desi Arnaz. By Zany Toys from 1953. **$50.**

ILY-10. "LUCILLE BALL/DESI ARNAZ/LITTLE RICKY" COL-ORING BOOK by Dell Publications ©1955. Front cover has reference to "I Love Lucy" show and book has 80 pages. **$30.**

ILY-11. "LUCY AND THE MADCAP MYSTERY" 1963 Whitman TV book #1505 with colorful cover art plus 212-page story based on the television series. **$15.**

ISY-1 ISY-2

ISY-1. "I SPY/MESSAGE FROM MOSCOW" hardcover Whitman TV book ©1966 with 210-page story. **$8.**

ISY-2. "TV GUIDE" for week of March 25, 1967 with color cover photo plus article about the real-life adventures of the co-stars while filming episodes in different countries. **$10.**

ISY-3   ISY-4

ISY-3. "I SPY" BOARD GAME ©1965 by Ideal in original 10x19" box. Game pieces include playing board, small plastic character figures, cardboard die-cut agent figures. **$20.**

ISY-4. "I SPY" BOXED CARD GAME by Ideal Toy ©1966 in original 1.5x6.5x10.5" box which is partially a styrofoam tray holding the card deck and mini-board stiff paper playing surface. Game is played with 4 small marker pegs. **$25.**

INH-3   INH-4

INH-3. "THE INCREDIBLE HULK" 6x7x15" large molded green plastic bank with black accent markings. Each side of bank has a picture sticker which is included in our photo example. Bank is by AJ Renz Corp. ©1978. **$25.**

INH-4. "THE INCREDIBLE HULK" 8" action figure on unopened original store card. Figure is green plastic with vinyl head plus purple fabric shorts. By Mego Corp. ©1979. **$30.**

J. FRED MUGGS

See Today

THE INCREDIBLE HULK

CBS: March 10, 1978 – May 19, 1982

Adventure drama series adapted from the Marvel Comic character of same name. The television version was based on the recurring transformation of research scientist David Banner into a huge green-colored monster man, when unduly angered. The part of Banner was played by Bill Bixby and his alter-ego, The Incredible Hulk by Lou Ferrigno. The character appeared in an earlier 1966 cartoon version under the title "Marvel Superheroes" and also in a later animated cartoon version beginning in 1982 "The Incredible Hulk And The Amazing Spider-Man." Items will normally have copyright of Marvel Comics Group.

THE JACKIE GLEASON SHOW

CBS: September 20, 1952 – September 12, 1970

Gleason's long television career included shows of various titles, always on CBS. The Honeymooners series, with Art Carney, Audrey Meadows and Joyce Randolph, is the most remembered series of his career. Items normally will have copyright or license agreement name of VIP Corp.

JGS-1   JGS-2   JGS-3

JGS-1. "TV DIGEST" issue for week of January 3, 1953 with cover photo and two-page photo article about the various characters portrayed by Gleason. **$20.**

JGS-2. "JACKIE GLEASON – THE PICTORIAL STORY OF TV'S GREATEST STAR" 8.5x11" special issue magazine published in 1955 with color cover design and many black/white page photos. **$20.**

JGS-3. "JACKIE GLEASON HONEYMOONERS COCKTAIL NAPKINS" in 2x5.5x5.5" box containing 50 napkins with cartoon scenes based on the Honeymooners, ©1955. **$40.**

INH-1   INH-2

INH-1. "THE INCREDIBLE HULK" MODEL ASSEMBLY KIT by Aurora Plastics ©1966 in original sealed 2x5x13" box. **$250.**

INH-2. "THE INCREDIBLE HULK" BOARD GAME by Milton Bradley ©1983 in original 9.5x16" box. **$7.**

JGS-4   JGS-5   JGS-6

JGS-9

JGS-4. "JACKIE GLEASON AW-A-A-AY WE GO CLIMBING TOY" on 6x8.5" store card. Toy is a plastic figure depicting "The Poor Soul" character of Gleason which can be made to climb by manipulating the attached strings. Mid-1950s. **$100.**

JGS-5. "JACKIE GLEASON AW-A-A-AY WE GO" from the same series as **JGS-4** on 6x8.5" store card. Toy figure depicts "The Loud Mouth" character of Gleason. **$100.**

JGS-6. "JACKIE GLEASON AW-A-A-AY WE GO CLIMBING TOY" from same series as **JGS-4** on 6x8.5" store card. Depicted toy figure is "Reggie Van Gleason III." **$100.**

JGS-9. "JACKIE GLEASON'S BUS DRIVER'S OUTFIT"by Empire Plastic Corp. circa mid-1950s in original 3x10x15" box. Costume set includes thin plastic gray hat with small simulated "Jackie Gleason Bus Lines" badge, plus plastic money changer, 15 plastic coins, a small booklet of bus transfer sheets and a ticket punch. **$400.**

JGS-7

JGS-10

JGS-7. "JACKIE GLEASON'S AWA-A-A-A-Y WE GO" BOXED BOARD GAME by Transogram ©1956 in original 10x19.5" box. Our photo example shows box lid and playing board. **$125.**

JGS-11   JGS-12

JGS-8

JGS-8. "JACKIE GLEASON BUS" by Wolverine Toys ©1955. Bus is 4.5x4.5x14" pressed steel with wood wheels plus metal drive mechanism on rear axle. When the rear roof is pressed down and released, the bus travels independently in a straight line for about 12 feet on a smooth surface. The design in red/white/blue with fleshtone faces of Honeymooner characters depicted at windows. Our photo example shows front, back, example side and roof. **$400.**

JGS-10. JACKIE GLEASON COLORING BOOK ORIGINAL ART black ink drawing on 8x11" stiff white paper circa mid-1950s. Art depicts Gleason as Ralph Kramden speeding his bus on Madison Avenue with caption "Ralph Kramden Has A Whole Bus To Himself." **$50.**

JGS-11. "JACKIE GLEASON AND HIS TV TROUPE STORY STAGE" by Utopia Enterprises Inc. ©1955 in colorful 2x12.5x18.5" box designed to serve as a stage setting for the contents. Contents include punch-out figures of Gleason as a Honeymooner, the Poor Soul and Reggie in addition to other figures for the major cast characters. Other parts are a pair of stage sets, a stage curtain of cardboard, paper costume changes, player scripts and studio tickets. **$100.**

JGS-12. "SONGS I SING ON THE JACKIE GLEASON SHOW" RECORD ALBUM by Frank Fontaine who regularly portrayed the "Crazy Guggenheim" character on the show. He is pictured on front of 12.25x12.25" album which holds single 33 1/3-rpm record. On each side of the record are six selections by him. Mid-1950s. **$25.**

THE JETSONS

ABC: September 23, 1962 – September 8, 1963

Prime time animated cartoon series by Hanna-Barbera Productions, and items will normally have this copyright. The series was about the 21st century adventures of the space age Jetson family consisting of parents George and Jane, children Judy and Elroy, their dog Astro, and Rosey the Robot, the family maid. The show went into reruns on ABC beginning September 21, 1963 with reruns on other networks as well continuing into the 1980s.

| JET-1 | JET-2 | JET-3 |

JET-1. "THE JETSONS" 10x13.5" Big Golden Book by Golden Press © 1963 with 24-page illustrated story. **$40.**

JET-2. "THE JETSONS/BIRTHDAY SURPRISE" 1963 © Whitman hardcover book. **$20.**

JET-3. "THE JETSONS" STEEL THERMOS by Aladdin Industries © 1963. Thermos was issued originally with lunch box **JET-4.** **$125.**

JET-4

JET-4. "THE JETSONS" DOMED STEEL LUNCH BOX by Aladdin Industries © 1963. Lunch box came originally with thermos **JET-3.** **$800.**

 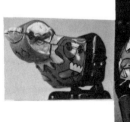 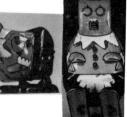

| JET-5 | JET-6 |

JET-5. JETSONS 1.5x2.5x3.25" plastic ramp walker toy by Marx Toys circa 1962. Depicted are Rosey the Robot and Astro. **$60.**

JET-6. JETSON "ROSEY THE ROBOT" 2x2x4" lithographed tin wind-up toy by Marx © 1963. Toy is formed in permanent stooped position and, when wound, the body rocks up and down. **$400.**

| JET-7 | JET-8 |

JET-7. "JETSON EXPRESS" LITHOGRAPHED TIN TOY TRAIN WIND-UP by Marx Toys circa 1962-1963. Total size is 1.5x2.5x12.5" length. Both engine and cars depict cast members. **$250.**

JET-8. "THE JETSONS" JIGSAW PUZZLE by Whitman © 1962 in 1.5X8.5X11" box. Puzzle has 70 pieces and assembled size of 14X18" with scene of George Jetson in bubble spaceship being chased by a policeman on a magnetized space motorcycle. **$30.**

| JET-9 | JET-10 |

JET-9. "THE JETSONS (OUT OF THIS WORLD) GAME" by Transogram © 1962 in 10x19.5" box. Game parts include playing board, die-cut cardboard stand-up figures of George, Astro, Jane, Judy, Elroy, Rosey the Robot, plus four miniature plastic space cars and two plastic comets. A cardboard spinner disk represents the Jetsons' revolving house. **$75.**

JET-10. "THE JETSONS ROSEY THE ROBOT GAME WITH ASTRO THE SPACE DOG" by Transogram © 1962 in 9x17" box. Game parts include playing board, four cardboard character figures, 16 cardboard playing pieces, spinner board, and small plastic playing pieces. **$75.**

JET-11

JET-11. "THE JETSONS FUN PAD GAME" by Milton Bradley © 1963 in 11x14" box. Game parts feature a space dome which is balanced on center of a central shaft so the dome tilts easily. The outer edge of the dome has three circular plastic pads for placement of small space car playing pieces. Game parts also include 18 miniature space cards and a spinner board. **$75.**

JET-12

JET-12. "THE JETSONS" COLORFORMS KIT ©1963 in 8x12.5" box. Set consists of die-cut thin vinyl stick-on character pieces plus jet-age cartoon airport background scene for placement of characters which then can be removed and re-positioned. **$75.**

JIM BOWIE
See The Adventures of Jim Bowie

JULIA
NBC: September 17, 1968 – May 25, 1971

Comedy/drama series starring Diahann Carroll as Julia Baker, a widowed nurse with a young son Corey (Marc Copage). Her role is generally considered the first for a black female on televieion as a serious character as opposed to a domestic or supporting role. Her son's perpetual friend was Earl J. Waggedorn (Michael Link). Items will normally have a 20th Century-Fox Film Productions Inc. copyright.

JUL-1   JUL-2   JUL-3

JUL-1. "DIAHANN CARROLL AS JULIA PAPER DOLLS" 11x14" boxed set by Saalfield ©1970. Doll figures are of Julia, Corey, Marie and Earl J. Waggedorn. **$15.**

JUL-2. "DIAHANN CARROLL AS JULIA" 8.5x11" coloring book #9523 by Saalfield ©1968 with cover photo repeated on front and back. **$15.**

JUL-3. "DIAHANN CARROLL AS JULIA" 8.5x11" Saalfield coloring book #4522 ©1969 with same front cover design as **JUL-2** but with back cover changed to show Corey and Earl J. Waggedorn. Book has some, but not all, pages repeated from **JUL-2. $15.**

JUL-4   JUL-5

JUL-4. "JULIA" VIEW-MASTER SET of three stereo photo reels plus 16-page story booklet in 4.5x4.5" envelope packet ©1969. **$15.**

JUL-5. "JULIA" STEEL LUNCH BOX AND THERMOS by King-Seeley Thermos ©1969. **LUNCH BOX $50. THERMOS $25.**

KIT CARSON
See The Adventures of Kit Carson

KOJAK
CBS: October 24, 1973 – April 15, 1978

Police detective series starring Telly Savalas as Lt. Theo Kojak, a street-smart chief of detectives for the 13th Precinct in Manhattan South district of the New York Police Department. Items will normally have copyright of Universal Studios Inc.

KOJ-1   KOJ-2

KOJ-1. "KOJAK/THE STAKE OUT DETECTIVE GAME" by Milton Bradley ©1975 in 19.5x24" box. Game parts include cardboard platform playing board and full-dimension cardboard buildings to be placed on the board which has full color photo design of actual buildings in a large city. **$15.**

KOJ-2. "KOJAK CARD GUM" DISPLAY BOX filled with Kojak bubble gum packs, each containing eight cards. Display box is 3x4.5x9.75". No maker or date indicated but circa mid-1970s. **$25.**

KOJ-3   KOJ-4

KOJ-3. "KOJAK BUICK" REPLICA CAR IN BOX by Corgi Toys ©1976. Retail display box holds 1.5x2.5x5.5" detailed die-cast metal car featuring doors that open, a figure with gun in rear seat which swings about, and a gunshot sound produced by small ratchet wheel at rear bumper. **$75.**

KOJ-4. "KOJAK" 8" fully-jointed action figure on original 7.5x9" retail card by Excel Toy Corp. ©1976. Action figure is hard plastic and comes with clothing outfit, miniature glasses, lollipops, cigar, and holster with police revolver. **$30.**

KUKLA, FRAN AND OLLIE

NBC: November 29, 1948 – June 13, 1954

Very popular and long-running children's puppet show which was still aired after initial run on NBC by ABC, NBC, PBS (Public Broadcasting System). The show was last syndicated in 1976. The show, originally known as "Junior Jamboree" actually began locally in Chicago on October 13, 1947 and then to the rest of the Midwest in 1948, east coast in 1949, and west coast in 1951. The puppets were the creation of Burr Tillstrom and the featured puppets were Kukla, a somber bulb-nosed worrier, and Oliver J. (Ollie) Dragon, a carefree one-toothed dragon. The show was always done live with actress-singer Fran Allison serving as hostess. Items will normally have the name or copyright of Burr Tillstrom.

| KFO-1 | KFO-2 |

KFO-1. "KUKLA, FRAN AND OLLIE SING THE MUSICAL ALPHABET" pair of 3.5x5.25" premium post cards by sponsor Curtiss Candy Co. circa 1957. Each card has color photo and is designed as a small 78-rpm record with song titles "Sleep Baby Sleep" and "The Musical Alphabet." Back of each has illustrated candy bar ad. **EACH $30.**

KFO-2. KUKLA, FRAN AND OLLIE TRU-VUE CARD with full color stereo viewer photos of a Wild West Show adventure that also includes Burr Tillstrom. Card is in 3.5x5.5" envelope ©1953. **$20.**

| KFO-3 | KFO-4 | KFO-5 |

KFO-3. "BURR TILLSTROM'S KUKLA, FRAN AND OLLIE" SET of two 45-rpm records in 7.25x7.25" paper album folder. Records are on RCA Victor "Little Nipper" label circa early 1950s. **$40.**

KFO-4. "KUKLAPOLITAN COURIER" 6.25x9.5" black/white eight-page fan club newsletter published in October 1949 for second anniversary celebration of the series. Issue is Volume 2, Number 1 and includes 8 photos plus center spread with 12 more. **$25.**

KFO-5. "OLLIE" PUPPETEER LACING DOLL KIT in 2x9x13" box. Kit includes pre-cut cloth hand puppet doll to be finished with enclosed yarn. Circa 1950s. **$50.**

KFO-6

KFO-6. "BURR TILLSTROM'S KUKLA AND OLLIE" STAGE SET by Parker Brothers ©1962 in 14.5x18.5" box. Set consists of six character punch-out figures on stiff cardboard plus a TV stage, cue cards and props. **$60.**

KUNG FU

ABC: October 14, 1972 – June 28, 1975

A rather esoteric western series starring David Carradine as Kwai Chang Caine, a fugitive Buddhist monk roaming the western United States and correcting injustices along the way. The "Kung Fu" title is derived from the Chinese term for martial arts which were used by Kwai Chang when unduly angered. Items will normally have copyright of Warner Bros. Inc.

KFU-1

KFU-1. "KUNG FU" GUM CARD SET of 60 cards issued by Topps Gum ©1973. Each is 2.5x3.5" with color photo scene and red border. Cards 1-44 have poster pieces on back and cards 45-60 have a martial arts scene. **SET $60.**

KFU-2

KFU-2. "KUNG FU" STEEL LUNCH BOX AND PLASTIC THERMOS issued as set by King-Seeley Thermos ©1974. **LUNCH BOX $35. THERMOS $15.**

DOLLS *(left to right, top to bottom)*

"I Love Lucy," 26", fabric with molded vinyl face, circa early 1950s; **$150.**   Batman, 26", felt with molded vinyl face, circa 1966, **$100.**   Hopalong Cassidy, 26", taffeta outfit with composition head and hands, circa 1950; **$250.**   Jeannie, 19", hard plastic, by Libby, 1966; **$150.**   Popeye, 20", fabric with vinyl head and arms, by Gund, 1958; **$100.**   Fred Flintstone, 17", fabric with vinyl head, 1961; **$75.**   "Ricky Jr.," 14", rubber with body formed in a seated position, by American Character Doll, circa 1953; **$150.** Underdog, 16", fabric by J. Swedlin, 1970; **$35.**   "Howdy Doody," 20", fabric with movable eyes and mouth, plastic head, by Ideal Doll, circa early 1950s; **$350.**

LUNCH BOXES *(left to right, top to bottom)*

"Yogi Bear And Friends" by Aladdin, 1963; **$75.** "The Rifleman" by Aladdin, 1960; **$200.** "Get Smart" by King-Seeley, 1966; **$50.** Satellite bottle by American Thermos, 1958; **$30.** "Lost In Space" by American Thermos, 1967. **$300.** "Emergency!" (dome variety) by Aladdin, 1977; **$60.** Cartoon Zoo bottle by Universal, 1962; **$40.** "Cartoon Zoo Lunch Chest" by Universal, 1962; **$200.** "The Brady Bunch" by King-Seeley, 1970; **$50.** "Mike Mercury's Supercar Orbital Food Container" by Universal, 1962; **$200.**

FIGURES *(left to right, top to bottom)*

"Ringo Starr/Colgate's New Personality Bath" plastic bottle with box, 1965; **$100.**   "Maynard" Krebs bobbing head figure, Japanese, circa 1960; **$100.**   "Zorro" 9″ porcelain figure with metal sword by Enesco, circa late 1950s; **$125.**   Underdog 7″ vinyl bank by Play Pal Plastics, circa 1970; **$25.**   Superman 15″ painted plaster statue, circa 1950; **$150.**   Dick Tracy 13″ composition figure with movable head and mouth, circa late 1930s; **$300.**   "Hopalong Cassidy" 15″ composition store display for Timex watches, circa 1950; **$500.**   Foodini The Great 10″ hand puppet, circa 1951; **$35.**   Charlie Brown 7″ glazed ceramic bank, "Hand Painted In Italy," 1968; **$75.**   Shari Lewis' Charlie Horse 13.5″ rubber squeak toy, 1962; **$35.**   Mr. Peabody 8.5″ rubber squeak toy, 1960; **$50.** Yogi Bear bubblebath/bank container by Purex, 1967; **$35.**

MODEL KITS *(left to right, top to bottom)*

"The Rat Patrol" by Aurora, 1967; **$100.**   "My Mother the Car" by AMT, 1965; **$35.**   "Monkeemobile" by MPC, 1967; **$90.**
"TV'S Rawhide Western Cowpuncher" by PYRO, circa 1960; **$35.**   "Six Million Dollar Man" by MPC, 1975; **$20.**   "Flash Gordon
And The Martian" by Revell, 1965; **$125.**   "The Man From U.N.C.L.E." (Napoleon Solo) by Aurora, 1966. **$150.**

LAND OF THE GIANTS

ABC: September 22, 1968 – September 6, 1970

Science-fiction fantasy series about a seven-member space crew from Earth whose spaceship "Spindrift" crashes in another world where inhabitants and creatures are Earth-like except a dozen times larger. The Earth crew was continually menaced or hunted by giant people, pets, insects, etc. Items will normally have copyright of 20th Century-Fox Television Inc., 20th Century-Fox Film Corp., Kent Productions Inc., or a combination of these. The series was later syndicated for reruns.

| LND-1 | LND-2 | LND-3 |

LND-1. "LAND OF THE GIANTS" 5.25x8" © 1969 Whitman hardcover book #1516 from "Authorized TV Adventure" series with 212-page story titled "Flight Of Fear." **$10.**

LND-2. "LAND OF THE GIANTS" 8x10" Whitman coloring book #1138 © 1969. **$25.**

LND-3. "LAND OF THE GIANTS" PLASTIC MODEL ASSEMBLY KIT by Aurora Products © 1968 in sealed 2x7x13" box. **$400.**

| LND-4 | LND-5 |

LND-4. "LAND OF THE GIANTS GAME" by Ideal Toys © 1968 in 10x19.5" box. **$50.**

LND-5. "LAND OF THE GIANTS SPACESHIP SPINDRIFT" TOOTHPICK CRAFT KIT by Remco Industries © 1968 in 2x10x10" box. Kit consists of toothpicks and four full color die-cut cardboard sheets to be assembled into a replica model of the spaceship. **$100.**

LND-6

LND-6. "LAND OF THE GIANTS SHOOT 'N STICK TARGET RIFLE" SET by Remco Industries © 1969 in 4x12x32" box. Set includes a 28" plastic mechanical rifle, six firing missles, and a 9x9" target board. **$200.**

| LND-7 | LND-8 | LND-9 |

LND-7. "LAND OF THE GIANTS CARTOON KIT" by Colorforms © 1968 in 8x12" box. Contents are thin die-cut vinyl character parts and accessories to be applied on a scene board featuring a huge cat. **$50.**

LND-8. "LAND OF THE GIANTS" HAND MOVIE VIEWER with two boxes of films on 5.5x7.5" retail card © 1969. **$35.**

LND-9. "LAND OF THE GIANTS" VIEW-MASTER SET of three stereo photo reels plus 16-page story booklet © 1968 in original 4.5x4.5" cover envelope. **$25.**

LND-10

LND-10. "LAND OF THE GIANTS" EMBOSSED STEEL LUNCH BOX AND PLASTIC THERMOS issued as set © 1968 by Aladdin Industries. **LUNCH BOX $75. THERMOS $40.**

LARAMIE

NBC: September 15, 1959 – September 17, 1963

Western series set in the 1870s Wyoming Territory about a younger and older brother attempting to run a ranch, assisted only by a friend of their late father plus a drifter who settled in. Original cast members included John Smith as Slim Sherman, the older brother; Bobby Crawford Jr. as Andy Sherman, the younger brother; Hoagy Carmichael as Jonesy, the long-time friend; and Robert Fuller as Jess Harper, the drifter. Items will normally have copyright of Revue Productions Inc.

| LAR-1 | LAR-2 |

LAR-1. "TV GUIDE" for week of April 23, 1960 with color cover photo and three-page article about the series. **$10.**

LAR-2. "LARAMIE" 8.5x11" hardcover 1964 © book with 96 pages including black/white comic strips and illustrated stories. Publisher is Dean & Son Ltd., London. **$20.**

LAR-3   LAR-4

·**LAR-3. "LARAMIE GAME"** by Lowell Toy ©1960 in 9x17.5" box. Game parts include playing board, die-cut cardboard playing pieces, cards, spinner board and small plastic cowboy figures. **$50.**

LAR-4. "LARAMIE" 10" lithographed tin gun for firing a cork attached on a string. Lithographed design is black/white/gold. Circa mid-1960s and unlicensed. **$35.**

LASSIE

CBS: September 12, 1954 – September 12, 1971

Long-running series in changing format, featuring resourceful and intelligent collie owned and trained by Rudd Weatherwax. The concept of Lassie existed from earlier film and radio versions and the original television version was based on a boy, his widowed mother and grandfather living in a rural community. The featured child stars in the early years were Tommy Rettig as Jeff Miller (1954-1957) and Jon Provost as Timmy Martin (1957-1964). In later years, the show's title was changed at least three times to reflect the changing story situation. The show was also syndicated for reruns in the 1970s plus a CBS animated Saturday morning series titled "Lassie's Rescue Rangers" ran from September 1973 – August 1975. Items will normally have copyright of Wrather Corp. or licensed copyright of Rankin and Bass Productions or Jack Wrather Productions.

LAS-1   LAS-2

LAS-1. LASSIE PHOTO CARD issued as 1960s premium by Recipe Brand Dinners with full color Lassie photo. Back has printed Lassie paw print autograph plus facsimile autograph of trainer Rudd Weatherwax. **$20.**

LAS-2. "TV GUIDE" for week of July 4, 1959 with color cover photo of Lassie and Jon Provost plus three-page article about the changes in cast since the series began. **$12.**

LAS-3

LAS-3. "LASSIE THE ORIGINAL" DETAILED HARD PLASTIC REPLICA FIGURE in 2x6.5x9.5" box. Figure has original cardboard tag inscribed "Lassie – Wonder Dog Of TV." 1955. **$50.**

LAS-4

LAS-4. "LASSIE THE WONDER DOG OF TELEVISION AND MOVIES" 3x8x12" soft rubber squeaker figure in original 4x9x13" box © 1955 by Rempel Industries. Figure is realistically colored and detailed and box is designed to serve as a display stand. **$75.**

LAS-5

LAS-5. "THE MAGIC OF LASSIE" FLAT STEEL LUNCH BOX ©1978 by King-Seeley Thermos and Lassie Productions. **$35.**

LAS-6   LAS-7

LAS-6. "LASSIE COLORING BOOK" by Whitman ©1958. **$20.**
LAS-7. "LASSIE GAME" ©1968 in 9.5x18" box. **$20.**

LAS-8

LAS-8. "LASSIE & TIMMY ERASABLE-PIX" COLORING KIT © circa 1957-1958 by Standard Toykraft in 15x18" box. Kit includes four 6x7.5" black/white pictures plus a crayon slate, all with glossy slick surface to be colored and then wiped clean. Kit includes five crayon markers. **$25.**

LAS-9

LAS-9. "ADVENTURES OF LASSIE" GAME by Lisbeth Whiting ©1955 in 13.5x16.25" box. Game parts include playing board, spinner board, four die-cut cardboard character stand-up figures of Lassie, and four rubber squeakers designed to make a barking sound. Our photo example shows lid, playing board, and example stand-up figure. **$40.**

LAUGH-IN

NBC: January 22, 1968 – May 14, 1973

Classic comedy variety show with official title "Rowan and Martin's Laugh-In" with fast-moving format of short skits, sight gags, satire sketches, blackouts, etc. The show was co-hosted by Dan Rowan and Dick Martin with a cast listing that eventually reached over 40 members plus frequent cameo guest stars. Among the regular original cast members were comedians and comediennes Gary Owens, Ruth Buzzi, Judy Carne, Eileen Brennan, Goldie Hawn, Arte Johnson, Henry Gibson. Items will normally have copyright of George Schlatter-Ed Friendly Productions and Romart Inc.

LIN-1   LIN-2

LIN-1. "LAUGH-IN" 8.25x11.5" Saalfield paper doll book #1325 ©1969. Front cover has punchout dolls of Rowan, Martin, Worley and back cover has similar dolls of Carne, Johnson, Hawn. Pages include costumes for the characters plus many printed slogans popularized by the show. **$20.**

LIN-2. "LAUGH-IN" MAGAZINE Volume 1, Number 2 second issue from November 1968 of fan magazine devoted to the show with 68 pages of features, art and photos. **$15.**

LIN-3   LIN-4

LIN-3. "LAUGH-IN" EMBOSSED STEEL LUNCH BOX ©1970 by Aladdin Industries. **$35.**

LIN-4. LAUGH-IN "SQUEEZE YOUR BIPPY" GAME by Hasbro ©1968 in 12x18" box. Game parts include playing board, card deck, a ping-pong ball and circular tray for it, dice, and four miniature plastic bottles. **$35.**

LIN-5   LIN-6

LIN-5. "LAUGH-IN" STEEL WASTE CAN ©1968 with colorful lithograph design including photos, illustrations, and popular phrases from the show. Can is 13" tall. **$25.**

LIN-6. "LAUGH-IN KNOCK-KNOCK JOKES" GAME by Romart ©1969 in 11x14.5" box. The game features a "window" cardboard folder for insertion of knock-knock joke cards. Each card also depicts one of the main characters. The windows are opened to reveal the joke answer and another character. **$25.**

LAUREL AND HARDY

Syndicated 1966 (156 Episodes)

Animated cartoon version featuring the rotund Oliver Hardy and the thin Stan Laurel team, based on actual comedian team of 1930s-1940s. Segments were produced in five-minute cartoon episodes by Hanna-Barbera Productions and co-produced by Larry Harmon Pictures. Items will normally have one or both of these copyrights plus copyright of Wolper Productions Inc.

LHY-1   LHY-2

LHY-1. "LAUREL AND HARDY GAME OF MONKEY BUSINESS" by Transogram © 1962 in 9x17.5" box. Contents include a playing board, card deck and four wooden tokens. **$20.**

LHY-2. "LAUREL & HARDY" COMPLETE SET OF 50 ENGLISH CANDY INSERT CARDS issued by Primrose Confectionery, Great Britain, based on Larry Harmon animated cartoon series. Each card is printed on thin 1.5x2.5" paper with full color cartoon scene. Back of each has brief joke related to the scene. **SET. $35.**

LHY-3   LHY-4

LHY-3. "LAUREL & HARDY '25 T ROADSTER" PLASTIC MODEL ASSEMBLY KIT by AMT circa 1970s in sealed 4x6x9" box. **$30.**

LHY-4. STAN LAUREL FULL-DIMENSIONED VINYL FIGURAL BANK 14" tall on 5" diameter base © 1972. **$25.**

LHY-5   LHY-6

LHY-5. "LARRY HARMON'S LAUREL AND HARDY" 78-RPM THEME SONG Little Golden Record © 1963 in original 6.5x8" cover envelope. The record features voices of Harmon as Laurel and Henry Calvin as Hardy. **$10.**

LHY-6. "LARRY HARMON'S LAUREL AND HARDY FEELABLE AND MOVABLES" unopened kit containing materials for assembly of flocked velour die-cut puppets. Circa 1970s in 8.5x11" box. **$15.**

THE LAWMAN

ABC: October 5, 1958 – October 2, 1962

Western series starring John Russell as the stern Marshal Dan Troop of Laramie, Wyoming. The series was one of several western shows produced by Warner Bros. and items will normally have this copyright.

LAW-1   LAW-2

LAW-1. THE LAWMAN 8" plastic figure depicting John Russell as Dan Troop from the series. Figure is by Hartland Plastics circa early 1960s and has movable arms plus accessories of hat and gun. **$125.**

LAW-2. "TV GUIDE" for week of July 25, 1959 with color cover photo and three-page article about John Russell and his starring role in the series. Back cover of issue has cigarette ad featuring Steve McQueen in his "Wanted Dead or Alive" television role. **$12.**

LAW-3

LAW-4

LAW-3. "LAWMAN COW PUNCHER BOOTS" in original 3x8x8" retail box that has paper label on side picturing co-stars Russell and Peter Brown with title of series and © Warner Bros. Boots are leather and sized for a young child with generic western design in colors including red, white, orange and black. **$75.**

LAW-4. "LAWMAN" 24" length western chaps of cloth and leather accented by tin die-cut symbols with glass jewels. On each leg is a large illustration of "The Lawman" along with the logo of the show. Attached at the waist are two brown leather holsters. Circa early 1960s. **$25.**

THE LAWRENCE WELK SHOW

ABC: July 2, 1955 – September 4, 1971

Long-running musical variety show still being aired in new programs through syndication formed by Welk himself. The show features "Champagne Music" of basic unadorned style with dozens of regular cast entertainers during the regular network years. Among the most popular show members from the early years were "Champagne Lady" Alice Lon, accordion player Myron Floren, and the Lennon Sisters (Diane, Peggy, Kathy, Janet). Items are normally copyrighted Bob Plunkett or MRW Associates.

LWK-1   LWK-2

LWK-1. "LAWRENCE WELK ALBUM" 8.5x11" 52-page magazine © 1956 devoted exclusively to photos and features about Welk, cast members Alice Lon as Champagne Lady, each member of the orchestra, members of the Welk family, etc. Magazine is published by Skyline Features but probably sponsored by Dodge Motor Corp. which has back cover ad. **$20.**

LWK-2. "LAWRENCE WELK" 3x4x6" light green ceramic planter designed as an accordian with the Welk name in raised letters above the simulated keyboard. The back side has raised depictions of a champagne glass and bubbles plus musical notes. Circa late 1950s. **$10.**

LWK-3   **LWK-4**

LWK-3. LAWRENCE WELK/LENNON SISTERS 9x13.5" lithographed tin television tray with full color photos and glossy black/yellow border design of musical notes and champagne bubbles. Undated, circa 1957. **$20.**

LWK-4. "THE LENNON SISTERS COLORING BOOK" by Whitman ©1959 in 8.5x11" size. **$20.**

LEAVE IT TO BEAVER

CBS: October 4, 1957 – September 17, 1958
ABC: October 2, 1958 – September 12, 1963

Family comedy series based on the middle-class adventures and misadventures of Theodore (Beaver) Cleaver, youngest son of the Cleaver family of suburban community "Mayfield" with his older brother Wally (Tony Dow). Featured as their parents were Barbara Billingsley as mother June and Hugh Beaumont as father Ward Cleaver. Items will normally have copyright of Comalco Productions Inc.

LTB-1   **LTB-2**

LTB-1. LEAVE IT TO BEAVER "ROCKET TO THE MOON SPACE GAME" by Hasbro ©1959 is 8.5x16.5" box. Game features a colorful space travel playing board plus insert board which serves as a launching station. **$35.**

LTB-2. LEAVE IT TO BEAVER "AMBUSH GAME" by Hasbro © 1959 in 8.5x16.5" box. Jerry Mathers as Beaver is pictured on box lid but contents are actually a western adventure game which does not mention or picture him further. Game parts include a playing board, spinner board, 7 molded plastic rock formations and small marker pieces for five players. **$35.**

LTB-3

LTB-3. LEAVE IT TO BEAVER "MONEY MAKER" GAME by Hasbro ©1959 in 8.5x16.5" box. The game features a colorful playing board depicting various money-raising schemes plus backfire situations for losing money as it is earned. This is the scarcest version of the three games issued by Hasbro in 1959. **$70.**

LTB-4   **LTB-5**

LTB-4. "LEAVE IT TO BEAVER" 4x6.5" Berkley Medallion 1960 © book with 160-page illustrated story. Our photo example shows cover and example story art. **$25.**

LTB-5. "LEAVE IT TO BEAVER" HARDCOVER WHITMAN TV ADVENTURE BOOK with 212-page story. Circa 1958. **$20.**

LTB-6   **LTB-7**   **LTB-8**

LTB-6. "LEAVE IT TO BEAVER" 8x11" coloring book by Whitman ©1958. **$50.**

LTB-7. "LEAVE IT TO BEAVER" 8.5x11" Saalfield coloring book ©1963 with 24 pages. **$50.**

LTB-8. "LEAVE IT TO BEAVER" 8x11" Saalfield coloring book ©1963 with about 192 pages. **$75.**

THE LIBERACE SHOW

NBC/Syndicated/ABC/CBS:
July 1, 1952 – September 16, 1969

Musical variety series starring flamboyant pianist who distinguished himself by his showy playing style, glittery sequined wardrobe, and the candelabra positioned on his piano. The show ran in its original format through the 1955 season and in revised fashion with more guest performers through the late 1950s and 1960s.

LIB-1   **LIB-2**

LIB-1. "LIBERACE" 2.25x3.75" plastic pocket card calendar issued with name of Pittsburgh television station with ad line for Pittsburgh bank. Front is blue/white photo and reverse is calendar. **$10.**

LIB-2. "LIBERACE" AUTOGRAPH. Our example is a Western Union telegram announcing to the recipient that she has won tickets to a Liberace concert in Philadelphia. The telegarm invites the winner to a TV Guide tea with Liberace at a Philadelphia television station. The telegram has Liberace signature and his quick sketch of a grand piano in black ink. **$20.**

LIB-3   LIB-4

LIB-3. "LIBERACE" 11x14" souvenir program for live stage performance circa 1970s. Program is die-cut in shape of a grand piano cover, and contents include many photos of his home life, past concerts, show business friends, his wardrobe and jewelry collection, etc. **$15.**

LIB-4. "LIBERACE" 4.5x6x7" realistically-detailed plastic jewelry box formed in image of a grand piano with hinged lid that raises similar to an actual lid. Coloring is mostly an off-white with his facsimile signature above keyboard in gold. Circa mid-1950s. **$30.**

THE LIFE AND LEGEND OF WYATT EARP

ABC: September 6, 1955 – September 26, 1961

Western adventure series based on the real life 19th century lawman, starring Hugh O'Brian as Earp, the Marshal of Dodge City, Kansas (same locale as concurrent series "Gunsmoke" but different network.) In 1959, the Earp locale shifted to Tombstone, Arizona where Earp was again Marshal but with a different supporting cast. Items will normally have copyright of Wyatt Earp Ent. Inc.

LWE-1   LWE-2   LWE-3

LWE-1. "WYATT EARP COLORING BOOK" © by Whitman 1958 in 8.5x11" size with unusual thickness of about 1". **$15.**

LWE-2. WYATT EARP LARGE-SIZED REPLICA FIGURE by Hartland Plastics circa 1960-1961. Figure is from a Hartland series based on popular television western stars. The painted clothing is in olive green/dark green/ivory/black and the figure comes with hat and two guns. The horse is brown accented with black and white. **$75.**

LWE-3. "WYATT EARP" REPLICA FIGURE from Hartland Plastics series on original 7x11.5" retail card circa 1960-1961. Figure is from the smaller sized series by Hartland and Earp's painted outfit is white shirt, dark green trousers, black boots, gun belt and hat. The horse is brown. **$50.**

LWE-4   LWE-5

LWE-4. "MARSHAL WYATT EARP" WHITE METAL BADGE on original 3x4" card which has illustration of O'Brian as Earp. Circa late 1950s-early 1960s. **$15.**

LWE-5. "JUNIOR WYATT EARP" GUN AND HOLSTER SET on original 9x10" yellow/black/white store display card. The set consists of a cowhide leather holster and belt set, matched pair of silvered metal pistols and a red/silver plastic "Marshal" star badge. The display card refers to the television series and O'Brian is pictured twice. **$100.**

LWE-6   LWE-7

LWE-6. "WYATT EARP U.S. MARSHAL" PLASTIC MODEL ASSEMBLY KIT for 10" replica figure. Kit is by Pyro Plastics circa 1958 in 2x4.25x12" box. Our photo example shows both front and back of box. **$75.**

LWE-7. "WYATT EARP" CHEERIOS BOX cut and flattened with an ad on front for Wyatt Earp "Peacemaker" pistol and target game which is printed on back panel in full color. Each panel is 7.5x10". Circa late 1950s. **$100.**

LWE-8   LWE-9

LWE-8. "HUGH O'BRIAN/WYATT EARP/DODGE CITY WESTERN TOWN" Marx playset circa late 1950s in 3x10x35" illustrated carton. Contents include miniature figure of O'Brian as Earp plus western town buildings, cowboys and Indians, buckboard, horses, fence and accessories. **$600.**

LWE-9. "MARSHAL WYATT EARP/HUGH O'BRIAN" 3x4" vinyl wallet with cover design in blue/black/white/fleshtone. ©1957. **$20.**

THE LIFE AND TIMES OF GRIZZLY ADAMS

NBC: February 9, 1977 – July 26, 1978

Hour-long prime time adventure series set in the late 1800s about an unjustly-accused criminal James "Grizzly" Adams (Dan Haggerty) who then seeks refuge in the northwest wilderness. His associates there are a big grizzly bear called Ben plus occasional human acquaintances of Mad Jack (Denver Pyle) and Indian blood brother Nakuma (Don Shanks). The television series was based on an earlier film of same title, also starring Haggerty. Items will normally have copyright of Schick Sunn Productions Inc.

LGA-1

LGA-2

LGA-1. "GRIZZLY ADAMS" GAME by House of Games, Canada, ©1978. **$15.**

LGA-2. "THE LIFE AND TIMES OF GRIZZLY ADAMS" DOMED STEEL LUNCH BOX AND PLASTIC THERMOS issued as set © 1977 by Aladdin Industries. **LUNCH BOX $30. THERMOS $15.**

LIPPY THE LION

Syndicated 1962

Animated cartoon series by Hanna-Barbera Productions featuring the jungle adventures of the braggart Lippy and his hyena buddy, Hardy Har Har. Items willl normally have copyright by Hanna-Barbera.

LIP-1

LIP-2

LIP-1. "LIPPY THE LION" 11.5" hard plastic soap container figure from the "Bubble Club" series by Purex Corp. in 1960s. Figure is mostly in tan color with brown and ivory face markings plus lavender vest. **$25.**

LIP-2. "LIPPY THE LION" GAME by Transogram ©1962. Both lid and playing board picture Lippy and Hardy Har Har. **$35.**

LITTLE HOUSE ON THE PRAIRIE

NBC: September 11, 1974 – September 20, 1982

Rural family drama series set in the 1870s which continued on NBC September 27, 1982 – September 5, 1983 under title change to "Little House: A New Beginning." Episodes featured the adventures of the Ingalls family of Walnut Grove, Minnesota, headed by the farmer father Charles Ingalls, played by Michael Landon who was also the show's executive producer, director and frequent writer. Other original cast members: wife Caroline Ingalls (Karen Grassle), daughters Laura (Melissa Gilbert), Mary (Melissa Sue Anderson), and Carrie (twins Lindsay Greenbush/Sidney Greenbush, alternating). Items will normally have copyright of Ed Friendly Productions Inc. or licensing name JLM Licensing Associates, or both.

LHP-1　　　　　　　　LHP-2

LHP-1. "LITTLE HOUSE ON THE PRAIRIE" 12" "Laura" doll in original box that includes photo of the show's cast members. Doll has vinyl head and stuffed cloth body plus fabric clothing. From a 1978 © series of dolls based on the television series. **$25.**

LHP-2. "LITTLE HOUSE ON THE PRAIRIE" 12" "Carrie" doll in original box, from same series as **LHP-1. $25.**

LHP-3

LHP-3. "LITTLE HOUSE ON THE PRAIRIE" STEEL LUNCH BOX by King-Seeley Thermos ©1976. **$35.**

LITTLE ROQUEFORT

See The Heckle and Jeckle Show

THE LONE RANGER

ABC: September 15, 1949 – September 12, 1957

Western adventure series based on the highly popular masked man hero of 1930s-1940s radio and film versions. The television version starred long-time portrayer Clayton Moore as the Lone Ranger from 1949-1957 with the exception of 1952-1954 years when veteran actor John Hart stepped in. The character of Tonto was played throughout the series by Jay Silverheels. An animated version by Filmation was aired on CBS between September 10, 1966 and September 6, 1969 under the same title, "The Lone Ranger." He reappeared briefly during 1980 in a new cartoon series "Tarzan/Lone Ranger Adventure Hour." Items will normally have copyright of Lone Ranger Inc., Lone Ranger Television Inc., or Wrather Corp.

| LRG-1 | LRG-2 | LRG-3 |

LRG-1. "TV DIGEST" for week of October 29, 1949 with black/white cover illustration plus one-page article about the premiere of The Lone Ranger series on television. Issue is for the Philadelphia area and also includes television schedule listings for Philadelphia stations. **$40.**

LRG-2. LONE RANGER AND SILVER REPLICA FIGURE by Hartland Plastics with a 1954 Lone Ranger © stamped on the leg of the Lone Ranger. The figure is from the large-size series by Hartland and this is the earliest version of two large Lone Ranger figures. He is depicted in a light blue outfit with black mask. Figure comes with a white hat and two guns. **$150.**

LRG-3. TONTO AND SCOUT REPLICA FIGURE by Hartland Plastics with 1954 Lone Ranger © on Tonto's seat. Figure is from the large-sized series of Hartlands and this is the earliest of two versions from the series. Tonto is depicted in orange buckskin outfit trimmed in burnt orange. Figure comes with headband feather, knife, and single gun. **$150.**

LRG-4. LONE RANGER AND SILVER REPLICA FIGURE by Hartland Plastics circa late 1950s-early 1960s. Figure is large-sized second version with outfit depicted in light blue with red neckerchief and white hat. Figure comes with two guns. **$75.**

LRG-5. LONE RANGER AND SILVER REPLICA FIGURES © 1960 by Hartland Plastics on 7x11.5" retail card. Figures are from the smaller sized series by Hartland and Lone Ranger is depicted in light blue outfit with black mask and white hat. **$100.**

LRG-6. "LONE RANGER 6-SHOOTER RING" FULL COLOR POSTER sponsored by Kix cereal which offered the premium ring in 1948. Poster is 17x22" on stiff paper. **$75.**

| LRG-7 | LRG-8 |

LRG-7. "THE LONE RANGER" 21.5x22.5" linen-like bandanna offered as premium by Cheerios cereal circa 1949-1950. Background color is bright red with illustrations and inscriptions accented in white and blue. Our example shows corner detail and entire design includes depictions of crossed guns, horseshoe, bullets. **$40.**

LRG-8. LONE RANGER/TONTO 8x10" full color photo with facsimile signatures of each. Clayton Moore is pictured as the Lone Ranger and Jay Silverheels as Tonto. 1950s. **$20.**

| LRG-9 | LRG-10 |

LRG-9. "THE LONE RANGER/THE PEACE PATROL" 11x14" poster sheet issued as promotion circa 1956 for U.S. Savings Stamps program in schools and post offices. Poster background color is red with accent colors in white and black. **$150.**

LRG-10. LONE RANGER "U.S. SAVINGS BOND PEACE PATROL" 2.5x4" membership card from circa 1956 promotion by the Treasury Department to encourage bond sales. Card is printed in black/white with the Peace Patrol member's creed and pledge on the reverse. **$20.**

| LRG-4 | LRG-5 | LRG-6 |

LRG-11

LRG-11. LONE RANGER JUNIOR DEPUTY KIT offered as premium circa 1949-1950 by Wheaties, Cheerios, Kix, Sugar Jets or Trix. Kit consists of black linen half-mask, copper colored tin Junior Deputy badge, silver bullet with secret compartment, membership card which serves as I.D. card on reverse plus a single Invisible Writing Clues slip with original 1x4x7" mailing box from General Mills. **$150.**

LRG-12   LRG-13

LRG-15

LRG-15. 1950 "RODEO AND RANCH EXPOSITION" 8.5x11" 36-page souvenir program from show held in International Ampitheater, Chicago. Front cover has pink/green/black/white illustration, and inside pages include Lone Ranger photos for featured Event 5 of the show, the Lone Ranger and Silver. Our photo example shows a detail photo from that page plus detail from another full page ad for Lone Ranger boots. **$50.**

LRG-12. "LONE RANGER HIKE-O-METER" Wheaties box circa 1951-1956 with colorful front illustration on front and back panels plus order coupon on a side panel. Box is 2.5x7.5x10" tall. **$100.**

LRG-13. "LONE RANGER ROUND-UP" 3" diameter clear glass snow dome containing miniature figures of the Lone Ranger with rope in hand, a small calf, and clear fluid with tiny loose flakes. When shaken, the flakes swirl and appear to be a snowstorm. The dome is on a plastic base which has colorful decal. Total height is 4". Circa 1950s. **$60.**

LRG-16   LRG-17

LRG-16. "LONE RANGER BOOTS" in original 4x10x11" box by Endicott-Johnson ©1948. Boots are a conventional western leather design in brown/red/white although "Official Lone Ranger Cowboy Boots" is printed on each pull strap at the top. **$100.**

LRG-17. "THE ADVENTURES OF THE LONE RANGER" 45-RPM RECORD ©1951 by Decca Records in original 10x10" paper cover. This is record No. 1 from a series of 4, titled "He Becomes The Lone Ranger." **$20.**

LRG-14

LRG-18   LRG-19   LRG-20

LRG-14. LONE RANGER AND TONTO LIFE-SIZED POSTERS offered as Wheaties premium circa 1957. Each poster is 25x75" on stiff paper and each character depiction is about 6' tall. The Lone Ranger is pictured in a light blue outfit with red neckerchief. Tonto is pictured in a yellowish-tan buckskin outfit. **PAIR $250.**

LRG-18. "THE ADVENTURES OF THE LONE RANGER" 45-RPM RECORD from same series as **LRG-17** but this is No. 2 titled "He Finds Silver" **$20.**

LRG-19. "THE ADVENTURES OF THE LONE RANGER" 45-RPM RECORD from same series as **LRG-17** but this is No. 3 titled "He Finds Dan Reid." **$20.**

LRG-20. "THE ADVENTURES OF THE LONE RANGER" 45-RPM RECORD from same series as **LRG-17** but this is No. 4 titled "He Helps The Colonel's Son." **$20.**

LRG-21

LRG-22

LRG-25   LRG-26   LRG-27

LRG-25. LONE RANGER/TONTO 11.25x15" frame tray inlay jigsaw puzzle by Whitman © 1954. Puzzle picture is in full color. **$25.**

LRG-26. LONE RANGER/SILVER 11.25x14.5" frame tray inlay jigsaw puzzle by Whitman © 1955. Puzzle picture is full color. **$25.**

LRG-27. "I'M LONE RANGER PUSH-BUTTON PUPPET" PLASTIC TOY © 1968. Toy has a 2" diameter base with large foil sticker, and actual figure is 3" tall. The figure moves when the plunger in bottom of base is pushed. **$25.**

LRG-21. "THE LONE RANGER" RECORD PLAYER in all-wood, hinged cabinet with turntable to play 78, 45, 33 1/3-rpm records. Both sides of lid have a burned wood illustration, as pictured in our photo example. A burned wood name "The Lone Ranger" is in rope script on each side. The record player is by Decca circa late 1940s. Closed size is 12.5" wide by 10" deep by 6" tall. **$150.**

LRG-22. "THE LONE RANGER BINOCULARS" complete with black plastic neck strap. Binoculars are 5x5.5" black plastic with colorful decals on each hand grip. Circa late 1940s-1950s. **$50.**

LRG-23

LRG-23. "THE LONE RANGER" FLAT STEEL LUNCH BOX by ADCO Liberty circa 1954-1955. **$100.**

LRG-28   LRG-29   LRG-30

LRG-28. "THE LONE RANGER AND HIS GREAT HORSE SILVER" PLASTIC MODEL ASSEMBLY KIT by Aurora Plastics © 1967 in 2x7x13" box. **$150.**

LRG-29. "TONTO" PLASTIC MODEL ASSEMBLY KIT by Aurora Plastics © 1967 in 2.25x7x13" box. **$150.**

LRG-30. "TONTO" 11.5" hand puppet © 1966 with soft vinyl head plus plastic hand cover which depicts his outfit in tan with black and yellow accent colors on green background. **$25.**

LRG-24

LRG-24. "LONE RANGER GUN AND HOLSTER SET" in "Official Outfit" 2x7.5x11" box by Esquire Novelty Co. © 1947. Holsters and belt are a braided-texture black leather with smooth black leather holster covers, each trimmed in white with silvered tin decorative disks centered by small red glass cut stones. Matching cap pistols are each 7.5" long of silvered white metal with ivory plastic grips that have raised depiction of a reindeer head on each side. Both guns are by Kilgore and fire single caps. **$150.**

LRG-31   LRG-32

LRG-31. "THE LONE RANGER" BLACK FELT HAT with 12" oval brim and 3" crown height. The brim is edged in stitched red vinyl with matching chin cord. On the front of the crown is a black/white/red fabric label with 1956 © and name of maker, Arlington Hats. **$35.**

LRG-32. "THE LEGEND OF THE LONE RANGER" EMBOSSED STEEL LUNCH BOX by Aladdin Industries © 1980. **$25.**

LOST IN SPACE

CBS: September 15, 1965 – September 11, 1968

Science-fiction adventure series about the Space Family Robinson, a stowaway espionage agent, a spaceship pilot and a robot, all marooned in uncharted but inhabited space. Main characters: Professor John Robinson (Guy Williams), wife Maureen Robinson (June Lockhart), children Judy and Will Robinson (Marta Kristen and Billy Mumy), Penny Robinson (Angela Cartwright), pilot Don West (Mark Goddard), stowaway Dr. Zachary Smith (Jonathan Harris), the robot (voice of Bob May). Items will normally have copyright of either Space Productions or 20th Century Fox Film Corp.

LIS-6. "LOST IN SPACE ROBOT" by Remco Industries circa 1965 in 8x10x14" original box. Robot is 12" tall and battery operated. The body is combination of red and black plastic with a clear plastic dome on the head. Each side of the base has a sticker. The toy moves forward and has a blinking light. The arms can be opened and closed by levers on the back and the top part can be swiveled. **$400.**

LIS-7. LOST IN SPACE ASSEMBLED ROBOT REPLICA FROM KIT ©1968 by Aurora Plastics. The base is 5x7" and actual robot figure is 2.5x2.5x7" tall. The figure and base in our example are in unpainted original solid silvery gray color with clear plastic parts at the neck and head. **$200.**

LIS-1   LIS-2   LIS-3

LIS-8

LIS-9

LIS-1. "LOST IN SPACE" October 1967 first printing edition of paperback by Pyramid Books with 160-page story. **$20.**

LIS-2. "LOST IN SPACE" 3.5x5.5" fan post card showing the cast in full color. Mailing side has facsimile autograph of each. Circa 1966. **$25.**

LIS-3. "LOST IN SPACE" 8x10" autographed full color photo of entire cast with signatures of cast members Lockhart, Harris, Mumy, Cartwright, Kristen. This example is not signed by Williams or Goddard. Circa 1965-1967. **$80.**

LIS-4   LIS-5

LIS-4. "LOST IN SPACE" GAME by Milton Bradley © 1965 in 8.5x16.5" box. Game parts include playing board, insert board with dial spinner and small plastic playing pieces. **$65.**

LIS-5. "LOST IN SPACE" 10.25x14.25" inlay jigsaw puzzle by Milton Bradley ©1965 with full color puzzle scene. **$85.**

LIS-8. LOST IN SPACE LOT OF 8 HARD PLASTIC FIGURES from the Mattel Switch And Go set ©1966. Included are the seven human cast members plus the robot. The set also came originally with figure of Bloop the monkey. Each human figure is about 2" tall in solid metallic silver. The robot figure is 3" tall in silver with clear plastic dome. **LOT $200.**

LIS-9. "LOST IN SPACE" SET OF 3 VIEW-MASTER REELS plus 16-page story booklet in unopened 4.5x4.5" packet envelope. Title of adventure is "The Condemned Of Space" and set is ©1967. **$50.**

LIS-6   LIS-7

LIS-10

LIS-10. "LOST IN SPACE 3D ACTION FUN GAME" by Remco Industries ©1966. The game features colorful thick die-cut cardboard parts to be assembled by tabs and slots to form a 3-level planetary scene. Game parts also include four 2" spaceman figures. **$250.**

LIS-11   LIS-12

MSH-2

LIS-11. "LOST IN SPACE WALKIE TALKIE PLAY SET on original 6.5x10" display card, © 1977. Set consists of pair of plastic walkie talkies plus vinyl "Talk -Through Wire." **$40.**

LIS-12. "LOST IN SPACE ROBOT" by Azrak-Hamway International (AHI) ©1977 in original 4.5x5x11" box. Robot is 10" tall in black and silver with clear green dome at the top. Toy is battery operated for stop-and -go action with blinking lights and a clicking sound. **$150.**

MSH-2. M*A*S*H GREETING CARD LOT OF 16 each 5x7" with full color photo front ©1981. Inside of each card has message greeting corresponding to the front picture. **EACH $1.**

MSH-3   MSH-4

MSH-3. M*A*S*H SET OF THREE VIEW-MASTER REELS plus story booklet in 4.5x4.5" cover envelope ©1978. **$15.**

MSH-4. M*A*S*H COSTUME by Ben Cooper ©1981 in original 2.5x8.5x11" box. Costume consists of thin face mask representing Cpl. Klinger plus vinyl one-piece outfit with "M*A*S*H 4077th" chest inscription. **$30.**

M*A*S*H

CBS: September 17, 1972 – March 2, 1983

Long-running and very popular comedy/drama series with title derived from the 4077th Mobile Army Surgical Hospital unit based behind the lines in the early 1950s years of the Korean War. The final episode on March 2, 1983 was watched by more viewers – other than possibly sports events – than any other single program to that time, according to pollsters. Major characters among a lengthy list of characters over the years included Capt. Benjamin Franklin "Hawkeye" Pierce (Alan Alda), Capt. John "Trapper John" McIntyre (Wayne Rogers), Maj. Margaret "Hot Lips" Houlihan (Loretta Swit), Maj. Frank Burns (Larry Linville), Cpl. Walter "Radar" O'Reilly (Gary Burghoff), Lt. Col. Henry Blake (McLean Stevenson), Father John Mulcahy (William Christopher), Cpl. Maxwell Klinger (Jamie Farr), Col. Sherman Potter (Henry Morgan), Capt. B. J. Hunnicutt (Mike Farrell), Maj. Charles Emerson Winchester (David Ogden Stiers). Items will normally have copyright of 20th Century Fox Film Corp.

MSH-5   MSH-6

MSH-1

MSH-1. "M*A*S*H GAME" by Transogram © 1975 in original box. Game parts include playing board, card deck of assorted medical problems, die-cut stand-up cardboard figures of Trapper, Hawkeye, Radar and Hot Lips plus full-dimensioned toy helicopter, jeep and tent. **$25.**

MSH-5. M*A*S*H autographed 8x10" glossy black/white photo of seven cast members. Photo is autographed circa 1977 or later with signatures of Alda, Stiers, Morgan, Swit, Farrell, Christopher, Farr. **$75.**

MSH-6. "TV GUIDE" for week of February 12, 1983 dedicated to the final episode of M*A*S*H with several articles including a "favorite episodes" story by Alda. Issue has a fold-out cover that opens to 9" with color photos of cast members. **$15.**

THE MAGILLA GORILLA SHOW

Syndicated 1964 – 1965
ABC: January 1, 1966 – September 2, 1967

Animated cartoon about an enormous, mischievous gorilla who lives in a pet shop owned by Mr. Peebles who continually attempts to evict him. Additional cartoon segments included those for characters Punkin' Puss and Mushmouse, Droop-A-Long Coyote, Ricochet Rabbit. Series was by Hanna-Barbera Productions and will normally have this copyright.

| MAG-1 | MAG-2 | MAG-3 |

MAG-1. MAGILLA GORILLA 18.5" stuffed plush figure toy with entire head of realistically molded and colored soft vinyl. Body color is tan plush with color accents in brown and yellow felt. By Ideal Toys with company name and © on back of neck. Circa 1966-1967. **$40.**

MAG-2. "MAGILLA GORILLA" 9.5x13" hardcover Big Golden Book by Golden Press ©1964 with 28-page story with full-color story art on each page. **$15.**

MAG-3. "MAGILLA GORILLA" 8x11" Whitman coloring book © 1964 with 128 pages. **$25.**

MAG-4

MAG-5

MAG-4. "MAGILLA GORILLA CANNON" by Ideal Toy ©1964 in 6.5x11x12" retail box. Toy is a red plastic wheeled cannon with Magilla in the driver's seat. The cannon is loaded by pushing a cannonball into the barrel until a spring release is caught. The cannonball is fired when the toy is pushed. **$35.**

MAG-5. MAGILLA GORILLA 8" diameter white Melmac dinnerware plate with full color illustration of Magilla, Ricochet Rabbit, Droop-A-Long, Mush Mouse, circa 1964-1965. **$15.**

MAG-6

| MAG-7 | MAG-8 |

MAG-6. "MUSHMOUSE AND PUNKIN' PUSS GAME" by Ideal Toy ©1964 in original 10x19" box. Game parts include playing board, box insert with spinner board and playing cards depicting bullets. **$40.**

MAG-7. "PUNKIN' PUSS" 11.5" hard plastic soap container by Purex Corp. circa mid-1960s. Body of figure is orange and the head has orange face accented by tan. From the makers of the "Bubble Club" series. **$35.**

MAG-8. "DROOP-A-LONG COYOTE" 12" hard plastic soap container by Purex Corp. circa mid-1960s from the "Bubble Club" series. Body is pink with blue and orange accent colors. The head is white with painted green hat. **$15.**

| MAG-9 | MAG-10 | MAG-11 |

MAG-9. "RICOCHET RABBIT" 10.5" hard plastic soap container by Purex Corp. circa mid-1960s from the "Bubble Club" series. Paint colors are green, lavender, pink and tan on white. **$40.**

MAG-10. "RICOCHET RABBIT" 10.5" hard plastic soap container very similar fo **MAG-9** except this version has a movable arm which holds a six-shooter. Paint colors are the same as **MAG-9** although applied in a different variation. Circa mid-1960s. **$60.**

MAG-11. "RICOCHET RABBIT" 11" hand puppet with soft vinyl head and fabric body. Printed design on hand cover is mostly in green/red/brown. By Ideal Toy circa mid-1960s. **$75.**

THE MAN FROM U.N.C.L.E.

NBC: September 22, 1964 – January 15, 1968

Spy and secret agent adventure and spoof series centered around an international crime-fighting organization of U.N.C.L.E. (United Network Command for Law and Enforcement). Starred were Robert Vaughn as Napoleon Solo and David McCallum as his partner, Illya Kuryakin. The third major cast member was Leo G. Carroll as Alexander Waverly, the head of U.N.C.L.E. The series featured several exotic weapon gimmicks used in the eternal fight against the international crime syndicate THRUSH. Items will normally have copyright of Metro-Goldwyn-Mayer Inc.

MAN-5

MAN-5. "THE MAN FROM U.N.C.L.E." FLAT STEEL LUNCH BOX by King-Seeley Thermos © 1966. Box came originally with thermos **MAN-6. $100.**

MAN-1   **MAN-2**

MAN-6   **MAN-7**

MAN-1. "THE MAN FROM U.N.C.L.E." 12" plastic action figure by A.C. Gilbert Co. ©1965 in original 2.5x4.25x12.5" box. Figure has movable vinyl head plus hard plastic arms including right arm which raises and shoots small cap pistol. Figure is designed in image of Napoleon Solo and comes with fabric outfit, identity card, metal gun clip, and a triangular pocket insignia to be worn by the user. **$150.**

MAN-2. "THE MAN FROM U.N.C.L.E." 12.5" plastic action figure by A.C. Gilbert Co. © 1965 in 2.5x4.25x12.5" original box. Figure is designed in image of Illya Kuryakin with same mechanical feature as **MAN-1** plus fabric outfit and similar accessories. **$150.**

MAN-6. "THE MAN FROM U.N.C.L.E." STEEL THERMOS by King-Seeley Thermos ©1966. Thermos came originally with lunch box **MAN-5. $35.**

MAN-7. "THE MAN FROM U.N.C.L.E." SET OF 50 CARDS published in England ©1966. Each is 1.25x2.5" with full color photo on front plus text on the back. **SET $30.**

MAN-8

MAN-8. U.N.C.L.E. "GUN FIRING THRUSH-BUSTER" REPLICA TOY by Corgi ©1966 in original 2x2x6" retail box. Car is diecast metal finely detailed replica of the Oldsmobile Super 88 vehicle of the U.N.C.L.E. team. Miniature figures of Napoleon and Illya are in the front seat and these figures dart in and out of opened windows as a lever on the roof is pressed. The car comes with a silvered plastic finger ring that has flasher portrait image that changes from Napoleon to Illya when tilted. **$100.**

MAN-3   **MAN-4**

MAN-3. "U.N.C.L.E." FIGURE SET by Marx ©1966. Each figure is about 6" tall in solid gray color with very realistic facial and body likeness of Napoleon Solo and Illya Kuryakin. Base of each has U.N.C.L.E. insignia plus name of the particular character and ©1966. **EACH $20.**

MAN-4. "THE MAN FROM U.N.C.L.E." ACCESSORY PACK by A.C. Gilbert Co. ©1965 on original 6x8.5" display card. Accessories are designed for use with Gilbert 12" action figures and this set contains a cap-firing tommy gun with scope and a belt with four grenades. **$30.**

MAN-9

MAN-9. U.N.C.L.E. "SECRET CODE WHEEL PIN BALL GAME" by Marx Toys ©1966. Game is a large 10x11x22" pinball-style bagatelle device with a code wheel in the center that is turned by a large knob. The game object is to place marbles properly to enable the winning of charm pieces determined by the proper "code key" combination. The game comes with original illustrated box shown in our photo example with detail from the playing board. **$150.**

MAN-14   **MAN-15**

MAN-14. U.N.C.L.E. "ILLYA KURYAKIN CARD GAME" by Milton Bradley ©1966 in original 1.5x6x10" box . Game parts are two different sets of cards plus plastic playing chips. **$25.**

MAN-15. "THE MAN FROM U.N.C.L.E." PLASTIC MODEL ASSEMBLY KIT by AMT © 1967. Kit comes with assembly parts and decals for construction of vehicle like that used in the television series. **$125.**

MAN-10   **MAN-11**

MAN-16

MAN-16. U.N.C.L.E. "FOTO FANTASTIKS" PHOTO COLORING SET by Eberhard Faber © 1965 in original 9.5x16.5" box. Set consists of six photo sheets plus six colored pencils and a small art brush for coloring the sheets. Photo sheets are designed to be colored with the special water soluble pencils and then brushed with clear water to transform them into lifelike color. Our photo example shows box lid, opened contents with a single photo sheet and the other five sheets, all 8x10". **$60.**

MAN-10. "THE MAN FROM U.N.C.L.E." CIGARETTE LIGHTER GUN in 3x4" black hard plastic case with silver lighter unit plus red decal. When the top of the lighter is pushed down, a small gun barrel pops out. The case opens to expose a row of plastic cigarettes which are a cover for a secret simulated radio. By Ideal Toys ©1966. **$40.**

MAN-11. "THE MAN FROM U.N.C.L.E. PISTOL CANE" on 6x27" retail display card. Cane is 25" long with aluminum shaft and plastic handle plus a metal bullet cartridge and 8 plastic bullets to be loaded into the top of the cane. The bullets are fired from the barrel of the cane by a trigger mechanism in the handle which simultaneously fires a cap. By Marx Toys ©1966. **$100.**

THE MANY LOVES OF DOBIE GILLIS

CBS: September 29, 1959 – September 18, 1963

Comedy series about a pair of teenage buddies, Dobie Gillis (Dwayne Hickman) and his "beatnik" sidekick Maynard G. Krebs (Bob Denver) with occasional appearance of Hickman's brother, Darryl Hickman as the older brother Davey Gillis. The show title was derived from Dobie's unsuccessful attempts to woo high school girlfriends. Items are normally copyrighted 20th Century-Fox TV.

MAN-12   **MAN-13**

MAN-12. "THE MAN FROM U.N.C.L.E. GAME" by Ideal Toy © 1965 in 10x19.5" original box. Game parts are a playing board, assignment cards, THRUSH chief cards and four small figural plastic playing pieces. **$30.**

MAN-13. "THE MAN FROM U.N.C.L.E." CARD GAME by Milton Bradley ©1965 in original 1.5x6x10" box. Game consists of deck of 48 cards, blue plastic playing chips, and a card tray. **$25.**

MDG-1

MDG-1. "DOBIE GILLIS JEWELRY BAR" 4x21" wood sign with jagged cut ends as made. Illustrations of Gillis and Krebs are in black/white/yellow. Sign reverse has sticker for Patachou Jewelry Co. Inc. circa early 1960s. Holed as made at top and bottom for hanging. Our photo example shows sign with closeup detail of each portrait. **$50.**

MDG-2   MDG-3

MDG-2. "DOBIE" 7" composition bobbing head figure circa early 1960s. **$100.**

MDG-3. DARRYL HICKMAN AUTOGRAPH on 3.5x5" black/white photo. He is pictured in his series role as Davey Gillis. **$20.**

MAVERICK

ABC: September 22, 1957 – July 8, 1962

Western series starring James Garner as Bret Maverick, a rather dapper poker player who could be quite casual about other western traditions. He was joined early in the series by Jack Kelly as brother Bart Maverick who was a bit more straight-laced. The series was one of several westerns produced at the time by Warner Bros. and items will normally have copyright of Warner Bros. Pictures Inc.

MAV-1   MAV-2   MAV-3

MAV-1. "BRET AND BART MAVERICK" PAIR OF STRING NECKTIES, each on 7" tall die-cut black/white/red photo display card. The plastic clip on each string tie is an image of a small stagecoach or covered wagon. **PAIR $30.**

MAV-2. "MAVERICK TV ERAS-O-PICTURE BOOK" ©1958 in 9x11" spiral-bound format with stiff cardboard pages that can be colored and then erased. Book comes with crayons and erasing cloth. **$30.**

MAV-3. BRET MAVERICK REPLICA PLASTIC FIGURE from full sized series issued circa early 1960s by Hartland Plastics. Figure is depicted in painted black coat with ruffled white shirt and light blue trousers and comes with white hat and gun. The horse is tan with black saddle. **$200.**

MAV-4   MAV-5

MAV-6

MAV-4. BRET MAVERICK REPLICA PLASTIC FIGURE from smaller sized series issued by Hartland Plastics circa early 1960s. The figure is depicted in painted black jacket with white shirt and blue trousers plus white hat. The horse is gray with black markings. **$40.**

MAV-5. BRET MAVERICK 7.5" replica plastic figure from "Gunfighters" series featuring individual TV western stars by Hartland Plastics circa early 1960s. The figure has movable arms and is depicted in painted black jacket with frilled white shirt, khaki vest and gray trousers plus white hat. Figure also comes with miniature gun. **$125.**

MAV-6. "MAVERICK PRIVATE SCORE AND KEY CASE" brown vinyl 2x3.5" holder containing small note pad with black/white photo cover. Circa late 1950s - early 1960s. **$15.**

MAV-7   MAV-8   MAV-9

MAV-7. "MAVERICK" 11.5x14.5 frame tray inlay jigsaw puzzle © 1960. **$15.**

MAV-8. "MAVERICK" TOY WRIST PISTOL on 6x9.5" retail card with black/white photo of Garner. Toy consists of a 4.5" white metal single shot cap pistol in red/black vinyl wrist holster. Circa early 1960s. **$50.**

MAV-9. "MAVERICK HIDE-A-WAY DERRINGER" on 3x5" black/white/red retail card. Miniature replica gun is 3.25" long of white metal with red plastic grips. The gun fires single caps and was issued by Leslie-Henry Co. circa late 1950s-early 1960s. **$35.**

THE MICKEY MOUSE CLUB

ABC: October 3, 1955 – September 25, 1959

Daily late afternoon series from Walt Disney Studios featuring the live action Mouseketeers, Mouseketeer host Jimmie Dodd, and "The Big Mouseketeer" Roy Williams. Among the most popular Mouseketeers by first name were Sharon, Bobby, Lonnie, Tommy, Dennis, Annette, Darlene, Cubby, Karen, Doreen. The show featured cartoons and other short features plus live action serial episodes produced especially for the series. Among the most popular of the latter was "The Adventures Of Spin And Marty." Reruns were syndicated in 1962, again in 1975, and again in 1976 with new format, cast and title "The New Mickey Mouse Club." Items will normally have copyright of Walt Disney Productions.

MMC-6

MMC-6. "MOUSEKETEER FAN CLUB TYPEWRITER" in 5x7.5x11" black/white/red original box. Typewriter is colorful lithograph tin and performs actual typing function by means of typewriter keys and lettered pointer dial. Inscriptions include "Write To Your Favorite Mouseketeer." Circa late 1950s. **$50.**

MMC-1   MMC-2   MMC-3

MMC-7   MMC-8   MMC-9

MMC-1. MICKEY MOUSE 3x4.5x7.5" hard plastic figure bank by Knickerbocker Toys circa 1960. The sticker on the hat reads "This Is A Bank" and both coin slot and trap are on back of the figure. **$40.**

MMC-2. MICKEY MOUSE 2" colorful china figure by Hagen-Renaker positioned on original card inscribed "Mickey Mouse – The World's Best Loved Mouse/Grand Impresario Of The Mickey Mouse Club" circa late 1950s. **$150.**

MMC-3. "MOUSECLUBHOUSE" 5x7x8" colorful lithograph tin and plastic bank by Mattel Toys © 1957. **$65.**

MMC-7. "WALT DISNEY'S JIMMIE DODD COLORING BOOK" by Whitman © 1956 in 11x14" size with a cut-out pattern on back cover to make a Mouseketeer hat. **$20.**

MMC-8. "WALT DISNEY'S MOUSEKETEER CUT-OUTS" 10x12" cardboard folder by Whitman © 1957 featuring punch-out cardboard figures of Cubby and Karen plus clothing sheets for them. **$30.**

MMC-9. "WALT DISNEY'S MICKEY MOUSE CLUB MAGAZINE" Volume 1, Number 1 first issue from winter 1956 although possibly published late in 1955. **$50.**

MMC-4   MMC-5

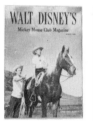

MMC-10   MMC-11   MMC-12

MMC-4. "MICKEY MOUSE CLUB" 7x8" full color die-cut cardboard sign issued by television sponsor "P-F Canvas Shoes/B.F. Goodrich" circa late 1950s. Sign has cardboard easel back with front inscription designed for filling in local television channel number. **$50.**

MMC-5. "MICKEY MOUSE CLUB GAME IN DISNEYLAND" by Whitman © 1955 in 2x12x17" box. Game parts include a playing board with Disneyland design centered by a Mickey Mouse Clubhouse plus four wood playing pieces die-cut in images of Minnie Mouse, Donald Duck, Practical Pig and Little Bad Wolf. **$45.**

MMC-10. "WALT DISNEY'S MICKEY MOUSE CLUB MAGAZINE" Volume 1, Number 2 for spring 1956. **$30.**

MMC-11. "WALT DISNEY'S MICKEY MOUSE CLUB MAGAZINE" Volume 1, Number 3 for summer 1956. **$20.**

MMC-12. "WALT DISNEY'S MICKEY MOUSE CLUB MAGAZINE" Volume 1, Number 4 for fall 1956. **$20.**

THE MIGHTY MOUSE PLAYHOUSE

CBS: December 10, 1955 – September 2, 1967

Saturday morning animated cartoon series starring Mighty Mouse, probably the most popular of the Terrytoons characters, and several of his sidekicks. The series was syndicated in 1967 following original run. Items will normally have copyright of either Terrytoons Inc., CBS Inc., or CBS Television Sales Inc.

MMP-1

MMP-2

MMP-1. "MIGHTY MOUSE" 9.5" hollow soft rubber squeaker figure with fleshtone face that blends into brown ears and head. Uniform is depicted in yellow with red tights and boots. 1950s. **$25.**

MMP-2. "MIGHTY MOUSE" 14" stuffed cloth doll by Ideal Toys circa mid-1950s with original tag stitched under one arm. Doll has realistic molded and colored soft vinyl face plus black plush head and outer ears. The inner ears and hands are pink corduroy. The uniform is a bright yellow slick synthetic fabric with red shorts and feet of same material. The cape is also a slick red fabric with his name in yellow gold. **$100.**

MMP-3

MMP-4

MMP-3. "MIGHTY MOUSE MAKE A FACE" 10x12.5" cardboard sheet with yellow/red/white/blue design plus four wood turning dials mounted around a central die-cut area that resembles a television screen. Dials are for changing the eyes, nose, mouth, and facial features which are printed on a series of four cardboard disk wheels mounted on the reverse. "Over 64,000 Faces" may be produced. Toy is by Towne Premiums ©1958. **$30.**

MMP-4. "MIGHTY MOUSE AND HIS TV PALS" TILE PUZZLE on 5x6" yellow/black/white/red display card circa 1950s. Actual puzzle is 2.5" square with black/white movable tiles to form different body images for Mighty Mouse, Sourpuss, Gandy and Sylvester. **$15.**

MMP-5   MMP-6

MMP-5. "TERRYTOONS" 28x28" silk-like bandanna scarf with brightly colored printed depictions of Mighty Mouse, Heckle & Jeckle, Dinky Duck and others. Circa mid-1950s. **$35.**

MMP-6. "MIGHTY MOUSE" HARD AND SOFT VINYL FIGURE with movable body parts in original 6x10.5" plastic display bag by R. Dakin & Co. ©1977. Figure is depicted in painted yellow costume with orange trunks and red boots plus a red fabric cape. **$30.**

THE MILTON BERLE SHOW

NBC: September 21, 1948 – June 9, 1953

Berle's first series, "The Texaco Star Theater," was immensely popular. He was dubbed "Mr. Television" and was credited with prompting more people to buy television sets than even the set manufacturers' advertising campaigns. Vaudevillian pitchman Sid Stone delivered the sponsor's commercials. He was later replaced by ventriloquist Jimmy Nelson and his dummy Danny O'Day. Nelson and his puppet character, "Farfel" the dog, are best known for ten years of Nestlé commercials. The Berle show underwent several title changes and continued in differing formats through the 1950s and on into the 1960s.

MBS-1   MBS-2

MBS-1. "TV GUIDE" Volume 5, Number 21 for week of May 23-29, 1952 with cover photo of Berle and related article "Berle Talks Back To His Critics!" **$25.**

MBS-2. "THE TEXACO STAR THEATER PRESENTS THE MILTON BERLE SHOW" 13x19.5" cardboard ad sign from 1948. Berle is pictured in black/white photo and rest of sign design is red with green stars on a white background that also has black and red lettering. **$75.**

MBS-3

MBS-3. "THE MILTON BERLE CAR" by Marx Toys circa early 1950s in original attractively designed and colored box. Toy is a lithographed tin wind-up 5.5" long by 6.5" tall. **$300.**

MBS-4

MBS-5

MBS-4. "THE SID STONE PITCHMAN KIT" 1950s MAGIC SET in original 3.5x11x17" illustrated box. The kit "Makes Any Kid A Star Pitchman And Amateur Magician" with set consisting of "Collapsible Wooden Stand, Ten Fascinating And Valuable Gadgets And Magic Tricks, Ten Scripts For Preparing Sales Talks, Genuine Imitation Gold Horseshoe Stickpin, Real Sid Stone Derby Hat." **$35.**

MBS-5. "FARFEL" 3.5" white china mug with full color portrait of him on one side. Smaller inscription is "Especially For You – Jimmy Nelson." **$40.**

MBS-6

MBS-6. "JIMMY NELSON'S TV FARFEL" 17" hand puppet in 3.5x8.5x8.5" corrugated cardboard illustrated box by Juro Celebrity Dolls circa mid-1950s. The puppet has a soft vinyl head with movable mouth plus flannel ears. A cloth bow is around the neck and the hand cover is also fabric. **$75.**

MISSION: IMPOSSIBLE

CBS: September 17, 1966 – September 8, 1973

Series featuring a team of specialized government agents which resolved international assignments by devious and exotic gadgetry and intrigue. Main cast members: James Phelps (Peter Graves), Rollin Hand (Martin Landau), Cinnamon Carter (Barbara Bain), Willie Armitage (Peter Lupus), Barney Collier (Greg Morris). Items will normally have copyright of Paramount Pictures Corp.

MIS-1   MIS-2   MIS-3

MIS-1. "MISSION: IMPOSSIBLE" 3.5x5.5" fan photo card with full color photo of the co-stars. Back of card has facsimile signature of each. Circa late 1960s. **$15.**

MIS-2. "MISSION: IMPOSSIBLE" 5.25x7.75" hardcover Whitman novel ©1969 with 212-page story "The Priceless Particle." **$8.**

MIS-3. "MISSION: IMPOSSIBLE" VIEW-MASTER SET of three stereo photo reels plus 16-page story booklet in original 4.5x4.5" cover envelope ©1968. **$12.**

MR. ED

CBS: October 1, 1961 – September 8, 1965

Comedy series about a talking horse discovered in the barn of architect Wilbur Post (Alan Young), the only human that Mr. Ed would confide in. The television voice of Mr. Ed was provided by former western cowboy star Allan "Rocky" Lane. Items will normally have copyright of Mr. Ed Company.

MRE-1   MRE-2   MRE-3

MRE-1. "MISTER ED/THE TALKING HORSE" 8x11" Whitman coloring book ©1963. **$35.**

MRE-2. "MISTER ED" 10" hand puppet with soft vinyl head and cloth hand cover body by Knickerbocker Toys ©1962. The head is light tan with black/white eyes. The hand cover is striped in red and blue and has original maker's tag attached. **$75.**

MRE-3. "MISTER ED" 11.5" talking hand puppet by Mattel Toys with original maker's tag © 1962. Head is a soft vinyl mostly in tan accented by painted white forehead stripe, brown halter, plus white yarn mane. Inside of hand cover has voice box activated by a pullstring loop from outside. Phrases include "Isn't That Silly, Talking To A Horse?", "Oh, Horsefeathers!", "The Phone Is Ringing, Shall I Answer?", and others. **WORKING $85. NOT WORKING $40.**

| MRE-4 | MRE-5 | MRE-6 |

MRE-4. "TV GUIDE" issue for week of March 31, 1962 with full color cover photo plus three-page article "Mister Ed Gets The Last Laugh" about continued success of the series. **$15.**

MRE-5. "MISTER ED/THE TALKING HORSE" 5x7.25" full color 16-page premium comic book #260 from a series of similar books titled "Boys' and Girls' March Of Comics" © 1964. Comic story is a single adventure "Stop, Book And Listen." **$18.**

MRE-6. "MISTER ED/THE TALKING HORSE" 6.5x8" first edition Little Golden Book published by Golden Press © 1962 with 24-page story that has large full color story art on each page. **$18.**

MRE-7

MRE-7. "MISTER ED/THE TALKING HORSE" GAME by Parker Brothers © 1962 in 9x17" box. Parts include colorful playing board, a deck of Mister Ed cards, plus "TV Show" cards. Our photo example shows box lid and detail from the playing board. **$40.**

MR. MAGOO

See The Famous Adventures Of Mr. Magoo

MR. PEABODY

See The Bullwinkle Show

MR. PEEPERS

NBC: July 3, 1952 – June 12, 1955

Live situation comedy starring Wally Cox as Robinson J. Peepers, the shy and unassuming science teacher at Jefferson High. A highlight of the series was the television marriage May 23, 1954 between him and Nancy Remington, the school nurse (Patricia Benoit). Items will normally have copyright of National Broadcasting Corp.

MRP-1

| MRP-2 | MRP-3 |

MRP-1. "TV PROGRAM WEEK" issue for week of February 26, 1955 with cover photo plus 7-page article about Cox as Mr. Peepers including four more color photos. **$10.**

MRP-2. "MR. PEEPERS" 5x8" soft cover 248-page book by Simon & Schuster © 1955 by Peepers Co. The subtitle is "A Sort Of Novel" by Cox. **$20.**

MRP-3. "TV GUIDE" issue for week of May 21, 1954 with full color front cover wedding photo of Cox and Benoit plus 3-page feature on their television wedding. **$15.**

MRP-4

MRP-4. "MR. PEEPERS SCHOOL BAG AND GAME KIT" by Pressman Toys © 1955 in 2.5x10.5x13.5" box. Kit consists of a 9x13" vinyl school bag and a framed crayon/chalk slate, report cards, attendance sheets, cut-out stencils, chalk, pencil and eraser, paint stands with brush, plus materials for a lotto game, arithmetic bingo game, and a word card game. **$40.**

THE MOD SQUAD

ABC: September 24, 1968 – August 23, 1973

Police drama featuring a trio of "hippie" cops, each a former offender of the law and all a "drop-out" from conventional society. Main characters: Pete Cochran (Michael Cole), Link Hayes (Clarence Williams III), Julie Barnes (Peggy Lipton), Capt. Adam Greer (Tige Andrews). Items will normally have copyright of Thomas Spelling Productions.

 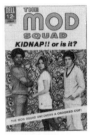

MOD-1   MOD-2

MOD-3

MOD-1. "THE MOD SQUAD" 5.25x7.75" hardcover © 1969 Whitman book #1538 with 212-page story "Assignment: The Arranger." **$12.**

MOD-2. "THE MOD SQUAD" Dell issue #2 of comic book for July 1969. **$8.**

MOD-3. "THE MOD SQUAD" JIGSAW PUZZLE by Milton Bradley ©1969 in 1.5x9.5x14.5" box. Completed puzzle is 14x20" with full color photo portrait of the co-stars. **$15.**

MOD-4   MOD-5

MOD-4. "THE MOD SQUAD" VIEW-MASTER SET of three reels and story booklet © 1968 in 4.5x4.5" cover envelope. Reels have stereo photo scenes for story "Bad Man On Campus." **$15.**

MOD-5. "MOD SQUAD STATION WAGON" PLASTIC MODEL ASSEMBLY KIT by Aurora Plastics ©1969 in original 3.5x10x10" box. Kit is for replica model of the late 1940s-early 1950s Mercury wood panel station wagon used by the Mod Squad. Model accessories include scaled dimensional figures of the three main characters plus three surfboards for the roof rack of the vehicle. **$75.**

THE MONKEES

NBC: September 12, 1966 – August 19, 1968

Teenage-oriented series, basically comedy but with assorted techniques like fast and slow motion or distorted focus featuring a rock music group formed hopefully as the U.S. answer to the English Beatles. The Monkees used their actual first names in the series and quartet members were Davy Jones (guitar), Peter Tork (guitar), Mike Nesmith (guitar) and Micky Dolenz (drums). Dolenz had previously appeared in the television starring role of "Circus Boy" under the name of Mickey Braddock. The series was rerun on Saturday morning by ABC September 9, 1972 – September 1, 1973. Items will normally have copyright of Raybert Productions Inc. or Screen Gems Inc.

MKE-1   MKE-2   MKE-3

MKE-1. "TV GUIDE" for week of January 28, 1967 with full color cover photo plus four-page article "Those Rambunctious Monkees" that includes another color photo of them. **$20.**

MKE-2. "MONKEES" 10" talking hand puppet featuring a molded vinyl head of each Monkee designed on inside for fitting over fingers of the user. The hand cover is fabric with yellow/red/black design. Under the cover is a voice box to be activated by a looped pullstring from the outside. Several phrases are said when the voice mechanism is working. Puppet is with original Mattel Toys tag ©1966. **WORKING $100. NOT WORKING $50.**

MKE-3. "MONKEES" 20" tall, hard plastic guitar by Mattel Toys © 1966. Guitar face has full color die-cut lithographed paper label depicting each Monkee on a background including musical notes. The guitar neck is black and entire underside is red. **$75.**

MKE-4

MKE-4. "MONKEE-MOBILE" ENAMELED METAL BATTERY-OPERATED MUSICAL FRICTION CAR © 1967. The car is 3.5x4.5 x12" in bright red with colorful plastic half-figures of each Monkee mounted in the seats. The battery operates the music feature only and friction car is pushed manually if desired. The car is a replica "GTO" Pontiac convertible. The battery compartment has an adjustment to slow or speed the music which is a song about 30 seconds long including the phrases "We Are The Monkees" and "The Monkees Are The Greatest." The car is made in Japan but is an authorized version with official Monkee symbol plus trademark. The box is 6x4.5x13.5" with full color design. **$600.**

MKE-5

MKE-6

THE MUNSTERS

CBS: September 24, 1964 – September 1, 1966

Macabre comedy about the ghoulish Munster family in their cobwebbed mansion at 1313 Mockingbird Lane. All family members had a monster-like appearance except Marilyn who was considered odd by the rest of the family because of her normal human appearance. Cast members: Herman Munster (Fred Gwynne), Lily Munster (Yvonne DeCarlo), Grandpa Munster (Al Lewis), Eddie Munster (Butch Patrick), Marilyn Munster (Beverly Owen, 1964; Pat Priest, 1964-1966). Items will normally have copyright of Kayro-Vue Productions.

MKE-5. "THE MONKEES MONKEEMOBILE" REPLICA VE-HICLE by Corgi Toys © 1967 in original 2x3x6.25" retail display box. Replica is a beautifully detailed and colored diecast vehicle mostly in dark red with white top. The engine, trim, and wheels are a simulated silver and the tires are black rubber. **$300.**

MKE-6. "MONKEES" VINYL LUNCH BOX WITH STEEL THER-MOS by King-Seeley Thermos © 1967. **LUNCH BOX $150. THER-MOS $30.**

MORK & MINDY

ABC: September 14, 1978 – August 12, 1982

Comedy series about a misfit alien from the planet of Ork who was equally as misfit on Earth, although supported here by an earthling girlfriend. Stars were Robin Williams as Mork and Pam Dawber as Mindy McConnell. A spinoff Saturday morning cartoon series, "The Mork & Mindy/Laverne & Shirley/Fonz Hour" followed on ABC, September 25, 1982 – September 3, 1983. Items will normally have copyright of Miller-Milkis Productions, Henderson Production Co. or Paramount Television.

MRK-1

MRK-1. "MORK AND MINDY GAME" by Parker Brothers © 1979 in 9x17" box. Game pieces include Grebbles (coins from the planet Ork) and game object is a test of "Splink" (bluffing your friends to get what you want). **$15.**

MRK-2

MRK-2. "MORK & MINDY" STEEL LUNCH BOX AND PLASTIC THERMOS by King-Seeley Thermos © 1979. Box has full color scenes on all surfaces including one large scene picturing Robby the Robot from Forbidden Planet. **$30.**

MTS-1   MTS-2   MTS-3

MTS-1. "THE MUNSTERS" WAXED PAPER WRAPPER FROM GUM CARD SERIES issued by Leaf © 1966. Wrapper design is green/black/red with folded size of 2.5x3.5". Opened size is 6x6". **$10.**

MTS-2. "THE MUNSTERS JIGSAW PUZZLE" by Whitman © 1965 in 1.5x9x11" full color box. Assembled puzzle is 14x18" with scene which is repeated on box lid. **$30.**

MTS-3. "THE MUNSTERS AND THE GREAT CAMERA CA-PER" 5.5x7.5" hardcover book published by Western Printing © 1965 with 212-page story. **$10.**

MTS-4   MTS-5

MTS-4. "THE MUNSTERS PAPERDOLLS" 9x12" cardboard folder containing paperdoll figures of Herman, Lily, Grandpa, Eddie and Marilyn plus six sheets of costumes. Set is by Whitman © 1966. **$60.**

MTS-5. "THE MUNSTERS STICKER FUN" 8.5x12" Whitman book © 1965 with pages of cut-out stickers to be applied over pre-printed picture pages. The book also features several coloring pages. Our photo example shows front and back cover. **$35.**

MTS-6   MTS-7   MTS-8

MTS-12   MTS-13   MTS-14

MTS-6. "LILY MUNSTER" 10.5" hand puppet © 1964 with realistic soft vinyl head plus fabric hand cover body. The hand cover has printed design of her bat-like dress in purple against light blue background. **$100.**

MTS-7. "GRANDPA" MUNSTER 10.5" hand puppet © 1966 with realistic soft vinyl plastic head plus fabric hand cover printed with design of his coat-and-tails outfit in purple/black on pink background. **$100.**

MTS-8. GRANDPA MUNSTER 5" figure with hard plastic body and soft vinyl plastic head that has rooted lifelike artificial hair. The face is a vivid chartreuse green with markings in black plus red mouth line. The body is depicted mostly in a painted black/white combination and a small red pendant medal is depicted on the chest. From a Munsters figure set © 1964 by Remco. **$75.**

MTS-12. YOUTHFUL LILY 8.5" vinyl doll with movable body parts by Ideal Toys © 1965, from same "Mini-Monster" series as **MTS-11.** The fabric outfit consists of pink undershorts plus pink dress that has a die-cut felt design of a bat in maroon/black applied to the front. **$60.**

MTS-13. YOUTHFUL EDDIE 8.5" vinyl doll with movable body parts by Ideal Toys © 1965, from same "Mini-Monster" series as **MTS-11.** Fabric outfit is a black jacket trimmed in white plus short black trousers. **$60.**

MTS-14. YOUTHFUL VAMPIRE BOY 8.5" vinyl doll with movable body parts by Ideal Toys © 1965, from same "Mini-Monster" series as **MTS-11.** Doll comes with fabric outfit. **$60.**

MTS-15   MTS-16

MTS-15. "THE MUNSTERS" FLAT STEEL LUNCH BOX by King-Seeley Thermos © 1965. **$100.**

MTS-16. "THE MUNSTERS" STEEL THERMOS by King-Seeley Thermos © 1965. Pictured around the side are Lily, Herman, Eddie, Grandpa, Marilyn. Thermos came with **MTS-15. $35.**

MTS-9   MTS-10   MTS-11

MTS-9. "HERMAN MUNSTER" 12" talking hand puppet by Mattel Toys © 1964. Puppet has soft vinyl head and hands with cloth body that has original maker's tag. The vinyl parts are green and face is accented by black hair and yellow eyes. The talking mechanism produces several phrases. **WORKING $150. NOT WORKING $75.**

MTS-10. "HERMAN MUNSTER" 20" talking stuffed cloth doll by Mattel Toys © 1964. The head and hands are an olive green vinyl with black accent markings on the head and face. The cloth body is a blue upper torso with black arms and legs. When working, the doll says several phrases by pulling a voice cord. Original maker's tag is attached. **WORKING $175. NOT WORKING $100.**

MTS-11. YOUTHFUL HERMAN 8.5" vinyl doll with movable body parts from a "Mini-Monster" series by Ideal Toys © 1965. The outfit is a fabric white jacket with blue collar plus blue shorts. Youthful image but strong resemblance of Herman Munster. **$60.**

MTS-17

MTS-17. "THE MUNSTERS CARTOON KIT" by Colorforms © 1965 in 12.5x16" box. Set consists of die-cut vinyl character figures and accessories plus a background scene board of the Munsters' living room. Our photo example shows box lid and example character pieces of Eddie and his Wolfman doll. **$150.**

MTS-18

MTS-21

MTS-18. "THE MUNSTERS CARD GAME" by Milton Bradley © 1964 in 1.5x6x10" colorful box. Game parts include deck of 42 cards, a stiff paper playing board and plastic markers. **$25.**

MTS-21. "THE MUNSTERS MASQUERADE PARTY" GAME © 1964 by Hasbro in 9.5x19" box. Game features a full color and vividly-designed playing board. Other game parts are a deck of cards plus die-cut stand-up character figures of Edward, Lily, Herman and Grandpa with a slotted base for each character. **$125.**

MTS-19

MTS-22

MTS-23

MTS-19. "THE MUNSTERS PICNIC" GAME by Hasbro ©1965 in 9.5x19" box. The game features a playing board with large full color, vivid illustration of the family enjoying their picnic in a graveyard. Other game parts include an insert spinner board, die-cut character playing pieces of Herman, Eddie, Lily, Grandpa, plus a set of 20 playing cards, each with a character picture. **$125.**

MTS-22. MUNSTERS "DRAG-U-LA" PLASTIC MODEL AS-SEMBLY KIT by AMT ©1964 in 2.5x5x9" box. Assembly parts are for a racing rod which would measure about 2x3x6" when assembled. **$175.**

MTS-23. "MUNSTER KOACH" PLASTIC MODEL ASSEMBLY KIT by AMT © 1964 in 2.5x5x9" box, from same series as **MTS-22.** Plastic assembly parts are for a sporty hearse vehicle that would be about 2.5x3x7" when assembled. **$125.**

MTS-20

MTS-24

MTS-20. "THE MUNSTERS DRAG RACE GAME" by Hasbro © 1965 in 9.5x19" box. The game features a full color vivid playing board depicting drag race scene. Other game parts are an insert spinner board, 20 playing cards and 4 die-cut cardboard figures plus small slotted wood base for each. **$125.**

MTS-24. "MUNSTER KOACH TOY" finely-detailed plastic replica pre-assembled by AMT ©1964 in 5.5x6x14.5" display box. The car features a rear mechanism which simulates motor noise. Coloring is a black exterior, red interior, and several chrome-colored body parts and features. **$200.**

MY FAVORITE MARTIAN

CBS: September 29, 1963 – September 4, 1966

Comedy series about a young newspaper reporter who takes in a Martian whose spaceship crashed on Earth. The Martian, Uncle Martin (Ray Walston), revealed his true identity only to his rescuer, Tim O'Hara (Bill Bixby) and appeared to be a human being to everyone else. Uncle Martin was capable of many Martian tricks, including immediate sprouting and retracting of antennae on each side of his head. Items will normally have copyright of Jack Chertok Television Inc. A Filmation cartoon series adapted loosely from the original live series, "My Favorite Martians" followed on CBS September 8, 1973 – August 30, 1975.

MFM-1

MFM-1. "MY FAVORITE MARTIAN GAME" by Transogram © 1963 in 9x17" box. Game parts consist of a playing board and 4 Martian figures. Our photo example shows box lid and detail from the board. **$40.**

MFM-4

MFM-2   MFM-3

MFM-2. "UNCLE MARTIN THE MARTIAN" 8.5x11" cut-out coloring book by Golden Press ©1964. Our photo example shows front cover and two example pages. **$35.**

MFM-3. "MY FAVORITE MARTIAN" MOLDED RED FELT SKULLCAP ©1963 with a metal wire spring attached on each side. Each spring is tipped by a small silvered metal bell. Attached on front is a fabric patch picturing Walston. **$50.**

MFM-4. "MY FAVORITE MARTIAN" 8x11" coloring book by Whitman ©1964. **$25.**

MFM-5

MFM-5. "MARTIAN MAGIC-TRICKS" KIT circa 1963-1964 in 2x14x20.5" box. Contents are trick and illusion materials plus instructions for 16 tricks, each with a Martian or space-related title. Typical trick titles are Penetrating Meteorite, Moon Maid Mystery, Disappearing Martian, Galaxial Guillotine. **$75**

THE OUTER LIMITS

ABC: September 16, 1963 – January 16, 1965

Hour-long science fiction anthology filmed in 49 episodes without a regular cast. Each episode opened with a blurred image and the assurance "There is nothing wrong with your TV set" with explanation that the television picture was controlled from "The Outer Limits." Episode content was about various extraterrestrial beings. Items will normally have copyright of Daystar-Villa Di Stefano-United Artists Television.

OTL-1   OTL-2

OTL-1. "THE OUTER LIMITS ANNUAL" 7.5x10.5" hardcover 96-page English-published annual with seven full color comic strip stories. **$50.**

OTL-2. "THE OUTER LIMITS" COMIC BOOKS published by Dell. Our photo example shows issues #2,3,4, all from 1964. **EACH $10.**

OTL-3

OTL-3. "THE OUTER LIMITS" GAME by Milton Bradley ©1964 in 9.5x19" box. Game parts include playing board illustrated by a laboratory, operating room, rocketship control room, rocket televiewer screen. Game is also played with cards, most to be matched with others in the deck to form a complete picture of a creature. **$90.**

OZZIE AND HARRIET

See The Adventures Of Ozzie And Harriet

PALADIN

See Have Gun, Will Travel

THE PARTRIDGE FAMILY

ABC: September 25, 1970 – August 31, 1974

Musical situation comedy about a mother and her family of six who become a professional rock group touring the country in a vividly-colored family bus. Featured were Shirley Jones as Shirley Partridge, David Cassidy as Keith, Susan Dey as Laurie, Danny Bonaduce as Danny, Jeremy Gelbwaks and Brian Forster as Chris, Suzanne Crough as Tracy. Items will normally have copyright of Screen Gems Productions. An animated version based on the original series, but set in the future, titled "The Partridge Family 2200 A.D." followed on CBS from September 7, 1974 to March 1, 1975.

PAR-1

PAR-2

PAR-1. "THE PARTRIDGE FAMILY ANNUAL 1975" 8x11" hardcover English-published 80-page book by World Distributors Ltd. containing full color comic stories, color photos, other illustrated text stories, short features. **$15.**

PAR-2. "THE PARTRIDGE FAMILY" FLAT STEEL LUNCH BOX AND STEEL THERMOS by King-Seeley Thermos © 1971. **LUNCH BOX $25. THERMOS $15.**

PAR-3   PAR-4

PAR-3. "SUSAN DEY (LAURIE) PAPERDOLLS" Saalfield kit © 1972 in 11x14.5" box. The set is based on her role in the television series and includes two 8.5" stand-up dolls plus cardboard accessories and paper clothing sheets designed in the fashion of Kate Greenaway costumes. **$20.**

PAR-4. "THE PARTRIDGE FAMILY PICTORIAL ACTIVITY AL-BUM" 10x12.5" activity book ©1973 by Columbia Pictures Industries with pages to color, puzzles, facts on cast members, full color stand-ups of the family members. **$20.**

THE PATTY DUKE SHOW

ABC: September 18, 1963 – August 31, 1966

Family comedy show starring Patty Duke in the dual role of identical teenage cousins Patty Lane, an American, and Cathy Lane, from Scotland. Items will normally have copyright of Chrislaw and United Artists TV.

PDK-1   PDK-2

PDK-1. "PATTY DUKE AND THE MYSTERY MANSION" hardcover 1964 Whitman book #1514 with 212-page story. **$15.**

PDK-2. "PATTY DUKE AND THE ADVENTURE OF THE CHI-NESE JUNK" hardcover 1966 Whitman book #2334 with 192-page story. **$20.**

PDK-3   PDK-4

PDK-3. "PATTY DUKE JR. JIGSAW PUZZLE" by Whitman © 1963 in 1.5x8.5x11" box. Puzzle consists of 100 pieces for assembly of 14x18" puzzle scene which is pictured on box lid. **$15.**

PDK-4. "PATTY DUKE" GAME by Milton Bradley © 1963 in 9.5x19" box. Game parts include playing board and miniature plastic figure pieces. **$15.**

PETER GUNN

NBC: September 22, 1958 – September 26, 1960
ABC: October 3, 1960 – September 25, 1961

Private eye series starring Craig Stevens in the title role as a suave detective. Also featured were Herschel Bernardi as Lt. Jacoby and Lola Albright as Edie Hart, a nightspot singer and Gunn's romantic interest. The show was also noted for its outstanding jazz themes by Henry Mancini. Items will normally have copyright of Spartan Productions.

PERRY MASON

CBS: September 21, 1957 – January 27, 1974

Television's longest-running lawyer series starring Raymond Burr as the trial lawyer who seemingly never lost a case. Also featured in the original cast were Barbara Hale as his assistant Della Street, William Hopper as his special investigator and William Tallman as Hamilton Burger, the district attorney and Mason's weekly opponent in the courtroom who seemingly never won a case. Items will normally have copyright of Paisano Productions or CBS Films Inc.

PTG-1

PTG-1. "PETER GUNN DETECTIVE GAME" by Lowell Toys © 1960 is 9x17.5" box. Game parts include playing board, deck of assignment cards, die-cut criminal and weapon figures. **$60.**

PER-1   PER-2

PER-1. "PERRY MASON CASE OF THE MISSING SUSPECT GAME" by Transogram © 1959 in 10x19.5" box. **$35.**

PER-2. "TV GUIDE" for week of March 4, 1961 with color cover photo of Burr and 4-page photo feature article about him and his Perry Mason role. **$10.**

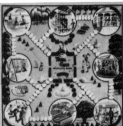

PTG-2

PER-3   PER-4

PER-3. "PERRY MASON" Dell comic book #2 for October-December 1964. **$8.**

PER-4. "TIME" weekly magazine issue for October 26, 1959 with composite illustration on front cover of television detectives Mason, Peter Gunn, Philip Marlowe, Richard Diamond, Stu Bailey. The cover article is five pages long about the popularity of the various detective series with scenes from several shows. **$8.**

PTG-2

PTG-3

PTG-2. CRAIG STEVENS AUTOGRAPH on 4x5" glossy black/white photo circa 1958-1960. **$10.**

PTG-3. "GUNN" 27x41" one-sheet movie poster for 1967 Paramount Pictures film based on televsion's Peter Gunn series. The film version also starred Stevens as Gunn and other film cast members are Laura Devon, Ed Asner, Sherry Jackson. **$20.**

THE PETER POTAMUS SHOW

Syndicated 1964 – 1965
ABC: January 2, 1966 – January 24, 1967

Animated cartoon series featuring a purple hippopotamus and his humorous adventures with his trusted monkey assistant, So So. Other cartoon segments featured a bear, Breezly, and a seal, Sneezly plus a trio of dogs, Yippee, Yappee and Yahooey. Items will normally have copyright of Hanna-Barbera Productions.

PPS-1   PPS-2

PPS-1. "PETER POTAMUS" 10.5" hard plastic soap container unmarked except for character name on base and "Mexico" on bottom although probably a Purex issue. Figure has a lavender body with tan muzzle and black eyes. The jacket is depicted in yellow. Circa mid-1960s. **$25.**

PPS-2. "BREEZLY" 9" hard plastic soap bottle with paper advertising holder by Purex Corp., circa 1967. The figure is of polar bear character in white with painted pink hat and neck scarf. This version has a plastic trap in the bottom rather than removable head. The paper display ring offers other illustrated "Bubble Club Liquid" and "Powder Fun Bath" characters from the Hanna-Barbera series. **$75.**

PETTICOAT JUNCTION

CBS: September 24, 1963 – September 12, 1970

Rural comedy about the widowed owner of the Shady Rest Hotel in Hooterville, along the railroad line carrying the Cannonball engine, and her three attractive young daughters. Starred were Bea Benaderet as Kate Bradley, the mother, and Linda Kaye, Pat Woodell, and Lori Saunders as her daughters Betty Jo, Bobbie Jo, and Billie Jo. Items will normally have copyright of CBS Enterprises.

PTJ-1   PTJ-2

PTJ-1. "PETTICOAT JUNCTION" 9.5x12" Whitman paperdoll album #1954 ©1964 including 9.5" stiff paper stand-up doll for Kate Bradley and her three daughters plus paper clothing sheets for each doll. **$50.**

PTJ-2. "THE PETTICOAT JUNCTION GAME" by Standard Toykraft in 9.5x18.5" box. Featured is a playing board with cartoon-like graphics picturing the hotel surrounded by incoming railroad tracks. Other game parts include cardboard disks, plastic pieces and a single die. **$25.**

THE PINK PANTHER SHOW

NBC: September 6, 1969 – September 2, 1978
ABC: September 9, 1978 – September 1, 1979

Long-running animated cartoon show which changed titles four times during its original duration. Featured was a suave panther, plus a jazz theme by Henry Mancini. Items will normally have copyright of DePatie-Freleng Production or United Artists.

PKP-1   PKP-2

PKP-1. "THE PINK PANTHER" VINYL LUNCH BOX AND PLASTIC THERMOS by Aladdin Industries ©1980 by United Artists. **$40.**

PKP-2. "PINK PANTHER AND SONS" FLAT STEEL LUNCH BOX by King-Seeley Thermos ©1984 picturing characters from spinoff animated series. **$30.**

PKP-3

PKP-4

PKP-3. PINK PANTHER 3.5" celluloid advertising button ©1984 with picture in pink/black/white on yellow background with black lettering. **$5.**

PKP-4. PINK PANTHER "ONE MAN BAND" BATTERY TOY by Illco Toys ©1980 in original 5.5x7.5x10.5" colorful box. Toy figure is 10" tall with pink plush body plus head of pink soft vinyl. When activated by batteries, the toy plays three drums and two cymbals while moving its body to the rhythm. **$60.**

THE PINKY LEE SHOW

**NBC: April 19, 1950 – November 9, 1950
January 4, 1954 – May 11, 1956**

Daily children's show starring Lee. His costume was a baggy black and white checkered suit with matching pants, coat and hat. The show was later syndicated for reruns. Items will normally be copyrighted National Brodacasting Co. Inc.

PLE-1   PLE-2   PLE-3

PLE-1. "PINKY LEE" 10.5x14.5" full color lithographed tin serving tray circa 1954. **$20.**

PLE-2. "PINKY LEE'S HEALTH AND SAFETY CUT-OUT COLORING BOOK" published by Pocket Books © 1955 in 8.5x11" format. **$15.**

PLE-3. "PINKY LEE" 2.75" tall, hard white plastic detailed miniature figure by Marx Toys although unmarked except for NBC © plus his name on front of base. 1950s. **$45.**

PLE-4   PLE-5

PLE-4. "PINKY LEE" large 24" animated doll from "Juro Celebrity Doll" series circa early 1950s in original 4.5x9x26" illustrated cardboard box designed to also serve as a carrying case. The doll has very realistic soft vinyl head with molded cap plus stuffed cloth body outfitted in black/white checkered fabric suit plus large red cloth bow tie. The chest of his jacket has a stitched "Pinky Lee NBC-TV" cloth label. In the doll's back are strings to be pulled for waving its arms and kicking its legs. Doll comes with original picture folder from Juro Novelty Co. that includes the words for Pinky's song, "Yoo-Hoo, It's Me," plus pictures of other dolls offered in the animated series. **$175.**

PLE-5. "PINKY LEE GAME TIME" early 1950s game by Pressman Toys in 13x18" box. Game parts include a large paper poster picturing Pinky plus masks, straws, ping-pong balls, balloons, bowling pins, a timer, and game book. **$30.**

PIXIE AND DIXIE

See The Huckleberry Hound Show

THE PLANET OF THE APES

CBS: September 13, 1974 – December 27, 1974

Science-fiction series based on popular movie of same title although the television version was short-lived. Featured in the television cast were Ron Harper and James Naughton as astronauts Alan Virdon and Pete Burke, Roddy McDowall as Galen, an ape who befriended the astronauts; and Booth Colman as Zaius, leader of the apes. Items are normally copyrighted 20th Century-Fox TV. The live action series was followed by a Saturday animated version, "Return To The Planet Of The Apes" on NBC from September 6, 1975 – September 4, 1976.

PLT-1   PLT-2   PLT-3

PLT-1. "PLANET OF THE APES" 2.5x3.5" folded waxed gum wrapper from gum card series by Topps Gum © 1967. Wrapper design is yellow/red/black/tan/fleshtone. **$8.**

PLT-2. "DR. ZAIUS/PLANET OF THE APES" PLASTIC SNAP-TOGETHER MODEL ASSEMBLY KIT by Addar © 1973 in 4x5x9" sealed box. **$20.**

PLT-3. "PLANET OF THE APES" EMBOSSED STEEL LUNCH BOX by Aladdin Industries © 1974. **$40.**

PLT-4   PLT-5

PLT-4. "PLANET OF THE APES VILLAGE" 1967 BOXED PLAYSET by Mego Corp. with parts for erecting the "Headquarters For All Planet Of The Apes 8" Action Figures" which were sold separately. The set includes a laboratory table, weapons bench, capture net and carry pole, detention pen, three control sticks, three rifles, plus illustrated catalogue for action figures. **$90.**

PLT-5. "PLANET OF THE APES MINI-PLAYSET" by Multiple Toymakers © 1967 by APJAC Productions in 1.5x7x10.5" box. Contents include small hand-painted hard plastic figures of Dr. Zaius, Zira, Cornelius, two ape warriors and two horses. The background panels behind the figures depict full color Planet Of The Apes village. **$35.**

POPEYE

Syndicated 1958 – 1963
CBS: September 9, 1978 – September 10, 1983

Animated cartoon version based on the durable, popular comic strip star of the 1920s on. The show had various title changes and was known as "The All-New Popeye Hour" in the series beginning in 1978. Featured were the traditional Popeye characters of Olive Oyl, Swee'Pea, Wimpy and others plus a perpetual villain named either Bluto or Brutus. Items are normally copyrighted King Features Syndicate with many types of collectibles issued both during the television and pre-television eras.

POP-5   POP-6

POP-5. "OLIVE OYL WITH A VOICE" HAND PUPPET by Gund Toys from same series as **POP-4** in original 4x5x6" display box. Puppet has soft vinyl squeaker head with fabric hand cover. **$25.**

POP-6. "POPEYE DAILY QUARTER BANK" by Kalon Co. circa 1950s. Bank is 3x4x4.5" of lithographed metal construction. Our photo example shows front and back side. **$125.**

POP-1   POP-2

POP-7   POP-8   POP-9

POP-1. "POPEYE PIPE / IT LITES / IT TOOTS" on 5.5x8.5" colorful retail display card ©1958. The pipe has a 5" wood stem and a 2" bowl with a "Popeye Pipe" decal on one side. A push button is on the bottom of the bowl, and in the top is a red plastic replica insert formed to resemble glowing coals. The pipe comes equipped with a small battery that causes the coals to glow when the push button is pressed. **$35.**

POP-2. "POPEYE LANTERN" by Line Mar Toys circa 1960s in original and very colorful 2.5x3.5x7.5" box. The lantern is formed in figural image of Popeye with metal parts except for the clear glass bulb shade in the center and a black rubber pipe inserted in the mouth. The arms are axled at the shoulders and may be raised to serve as a carrying bail. The lantern glows by a small bulb when activated by a battery. **$200.**

POP-7. "POPEYE COLOR AND RE-COLOR BOOK" by Jack Built Toys ©1957 in 9x10.5" spiral-bound format printed entirely with stiff cardboard covers plus 8 stiff pages, each with a black/white illustration on each side to be colored by crayons and then erased to be colored again. A box of washable crayons is included. All illustrations are attributed to Tom Sims and Bill Zaboly. **$25.**

POP-8. POPEYE 10" hard plastic painted soap container from the "Soaky" series circa 1960s. The figure has a fleshtone face with white cap plus a white body accented in blue on the collar and anchor. **$20.**

POP-9. BRUTUS 10" painted hard plastic soap container from "Soaky" series circa 1960s. Figure has a fleshtone face accented by black beard and hair plus a bright red/white painted outfit. **$20.**

POP-3   POP-4

POP-3. "POPEYE AND WIMPY" WALKER TOY by Marx Toys © 1964 in full color 2x4.5x5" box. Toy is a one-piece brightly colored plastic pull toy with weighted and jointed feet for each character which causes them to walk when pulled or placed on an inclined surface. Each figure has a spring-mounted head which bobs as the toy moves. **$25.**

POP-4. "WIMPY WITH A VOICE" HAND PUPPET by Gund Toys in original 4x5x6" display box. Puppet has a soft vinyl squeaker head plus fabric hand cover. Circa 1950s. **$25.**

POP-10

POP-10. "POPEYE" FLAT STEEL LUNCH BOX AND STEEL THERMOS by King-Seeley Thermos © 1964. **LUNCH BOX $75. THERMOS $35.**

POP-11   POP-12

POP-14. "THE POPEYE GETAR" by Mattel circa mid-1950s in 2x6x14" box illustrated in black/white/red. The guitar is 13.5" tall of black plastic with a full color lithographed paper die-cut picture of Popeye on the guitar front. On the right side is a manual crank which plays "Popeye The Sailor Man." The other side holds a yellow plastic pipe which may be removed to serve as a guitar pick. **$35.**

POP-15. POPEYE GUMBALL DISPENSER TOY by Hasbro © 1968. Toy is 5.5x5.5x9" formed in image of his head on a base. The head removes for insertion of gumballs which are then dispensed at the front by a lever on the base. A yellow plastic simulated corncob pipe extends from the mouth. **$25.**

POP-16. POPEYE SNOW DOME 4x4.5x5" hard plastic figure of Popeye in seated position holding a 2.5" diameter clear plastic sphere. Inside the sphere is a miniature replica scene of Olive Oyl, Swee' Pea and Wimpy around a small boat. The sphere has tiny white crystals in fluid which give snow effect when shaken. Popeye is depicted in painted outfit of white cap, black shirt with red collar, blue trousers and brown shoes. **$50.**

POP-11. "POPEYE SPINACH" POP-UP TOY by Mattel ©1957. Toy is formed like a 4.5" can of spinach with full color lithographed steel design. The can holds a hard plastic Popeye head to be depressed and then held in place inside the can by a small catch on the lid cover. When the catch is released, Popeye's head rises slowly from the can with an airy sound. The lithographed design around the can also pictures Olive Oyl and Wimpy plus Popeye again. **$75.**

POP-12. "POPEYE THE WEATHERMAN" COLORFORMS KIT ©1959 in 8.5x13" box. Box holds an insert board picturing Popeye with a small youngster who stands in front of a window with nature scene outside. Also included are press-down vinyl pieces to form a hot weather or cold weather scene through the window plus appropriate clothing pieces for the youngster. **$35.**

THE PRISONER
See Secret Agent

PUNKIN' PUSS AND MUSH MOUSE
See Magilla Gorilla

POP-13

POP-13. "POPEYE IN THE MUSIC BOX" MUSICAL TOY by Mattel ©1957 in original 5.5x5.5x6.5" illustrated carton. The box is a full color lithographed metal crank-wound music box which produces the tune "Popeye The Sailor Man" before a simulated spinach can pops up from under the lid. On top of the can is a plastic Popeye head with pipe. **$100.**

QUICK DRAW McGRAW
Syndicated 1959 – 1962

Animated cartoon series starring a slow-witted horse, based on Red Skelton's Clem Kaddiddlehopper, and his Mexican burro pal Babba Looey. Stories focus on their adventures tracking down villains. Other segments featured detectives Snooper and Blabber along with son and father Augie Doggie and Doggie Daddy (who spoke like Jimmy Durante). The show was run as a regular Saturday morning feature by CBS from 1963-1966. Items are normally copyrighted Hanna-Barbera Productions.

POP-14   POP-15   POP-16   QDM-1   QDM-2   QDM-3

QDM-1. "QUICK DRAW McGRAW" 16" stuffed plush figure toy with soft vinyl face. Doll has attached tag for Knickerbocker Toys with the Quick Draw name plus ©1959. The body is mostly light blue plush with white paws and feet. The figure has a removable red felt cowboy hat plus colorful polka dot neckerchief. At the waist is a thin plastic gun belt depicting cartridges and a gun holster which pictures him in profile. **$100.**

QDM-2. QUICK DRAW McGRAW 9.5" hard plastic figural bank with coin slot in top of hat which twists off for coin removal. Body is solid orange with accent markings in white and blue. 1960 Hanna-Barbera ©but maker is not identified. **$30.**

QDM-3. "QUICK DRAW McGRAW PRIVATE EYE GAME" by Milton Bradley © 1960 in 9.5x19" box. Game parts include playing board, small die-cut stand-up character figures, sets of cards. **$40.**

| QDM-4 | QDM-5 |

QDM-4. "QUICK DRAW McGRAW PLAYBOOK" by Whitman © 1960 with six beautifully colored punch-out sheets of character figures and accessories. **$35.**

QDM-5. "TV-TINYKINS QUICK DRAW McGRAW" MINIATURE HAND-PAINTED PLASTIC FIGURE SET by Marx © 1961 on very colorful 3.5x5.5" background card with unopened plastic blister. **$35.**

| QDM-6 | QDM-7 | QDM-8 |

QDM-6. BABBA LOOEY 20" stuffed plush doll with soft vinyl face with original Knickerbocker Toys tag ©1959. The face is molded into a pair of vinyl donkey ears which add another 4" of height. The body is green plush with orange feet. An orange felt sombrero is placed over the ears. **$40.**

QDM-7. BABBA LOOEY 9" soft vinyl figure bank with hard plastic removable head for coin removal. Bank is from a series by Knickerbocker Toys circa 1960s. The figure has orange body with brown sombrero. **$30.**

QDM-8. AUGIE DOGGIE 10" stuffed plush doll with soft vinyl face and floppy black felt ears plus a small black topknot of looped cord. Doll has original Knickerbocker Toys tag © 1959 and is designed in permanent seated position. The body is orange plush with a white tummy and the face is mostly orange with tan nose and blue eyes. **$30.**

| QDM-9 | QDM-10 |

QDM-9. "AUGIE DOGGIE" 10" hard plastic soap container with original cardboard tag around the base which offers "Bubble Club" records featuring Hanna-Barbera characters. Container originally held bubble bath soap issued by Purex Corp. circa mid-1960s. The container is orange with accent markings in green, tan and black. **$40.**

QDM-10. SNOOPER 20" stuffed plush doll with vinyl face and felt clothing pieces by Knickerbocker Toys with original 1959 ©tag. Body is yellow gold plush with black paws and feet. The felt pieces are an aqua blue detective cap and small necktie with white collar plus black felt vest cape. **$60.**

| QDM-11 | QDM-12 |

QDM-11. BLABBER 15" stuffed plush doll with soft vinyl face plus felt cap and bow tie. Doll has original Knickerbocker Toys tag ©1959. The body is purple plush with white tummy and cap plus a green bow tie. **$60.**

QDM-12. "BLABBER BUBBLE CLUB" 10.5" hard plastic soap container by Purex Corp. circa mid-1960s. Figure has a white body plus gray head accented by yellow and black plus a purple hat. **$15.**

RAMAR OF THE JUNGLE

Syndicated 1952 – 1954 (52 Episodes)

Very popular and widely syndicated children's adventure series starring Jon Hall in the title role as Dr. Tom Reynolds, a doctor and scientist in the wilds of Kenya. Items are normally copyrighted Arrow Productions and TPA.

| RAM-1 | RAM-2 | RAM-3 |

RAM-1. "RAMAR OF THE JUNGLE" FRAME TRAY JIGSAW PUZZLE SET of four in original 8.5x12" box that has large colorful lid portrait of him. **SET $35.**

RAM-2. RAMAR 4x5" glossy black/white advertising photo with margin inscription text for a television sponsor, Good & Plenty Candy. The photo is of him feeding candy to a monkey. **$20.**

RAM-3. "RAMAR OF THE JUNGLE" set of four different 9.5x12" full color jigsaw puzzles in same-sized box by Gabriel Toys © 1955. Puzzle scenes are action shots from the series. **SET $25.**

RAM-4

RAM-5

RAM-4. "RAMAR OF THE JUNGLE COLORING BOOK" by Saalfield © 1955 in 11x14" size with 16 coloring pages. **$20.**

RAM-5. "RAMAR OF THE JUNGLE SPECIAL MODEL GENUINE LEATHER DAISY HOLSTER SET" by Daisy Manufacturing Co. circa 1953 in the original 10x12.5" colorful box. Contents are a gold plastic canteen plus a leather belt and holster with simulated leopard skin. The canteen has carrying straps and the belt has bullet loops with toy bullets. **$75.**

RAM-6   RAM-7

RAM-6. "RAMAR OF THE JUNGLE" BOXED GAME including playing board, "Safari Scout" membership card, cardboard spinner, six wooden game pieces. Game is by Dexter Wayne Co. circa 1952-1954. **$35.**

RAM-7. "RAMAR OF THE JUNGLE" 19x34.5" beautifully colored stiff cardboard target from a blow gun game based on the television series. The target is scored to fold into a 15x19" easel with four die-cut holes in the center. Mounted in each hole by elastic string is a die-cut head of a scowling jungle beast. These are the targets for the blow gun which comes with four rubber pellets as ammunition. Game is by Gabriel Toys © 1955. **$50.**

THE RANGE RIDER

Syndicated 1951 – 1952 (78 Episodes)

Children's western adventure series featuring cowboy star Jock Mahoney in the title role with Dick Jones as his youthful sidekick Dick West. Items are normally copyrighted Gene Autry Flying A Productions. Reruns of the show were aired Sunday afternoons by ABC during the last four months of 1965.

RGR-1

RGR-2

RGR-1. THE RANGE RIDER 8x10" black/white premium photo of co-stars Mahoney and Jones with facsimile signature of each. Reverse side has ad for sponsor Langendorf Bread. Circa early 1950s. **$20.**

RGR-2. "THE FLYING A'S RANGE RIDER" English-published 7.25x10" hardcover book with 124 pages of black/white comic strips or illustrated stories. Cover text includes title of BBC Television (Great Britain). Circa 1960. **$18.**

RGR-3   RGR-4

RGR-3. "RANGE RIDER" 100-PIECE JIGSAW PUZZLE by Gabriel Toys © 1955 in 1.5x6.5x9.5" box with full color lid picture that repeats the puzzle scene. Assembled puzzle is 10x12". **$30.**

RGR-4. "RANGE RIDER AND DICK WEST" 5.5x8.5" colorful folder that opens to 11x17" for mounting 16 bread wrapper labels issued as set by ButterKrust Bread circa mid-1950s. The completed 16 labels comprise "Adventure Story No. 2" titled "Mystery Of The Dead Bandit." **$25.**

RAT PATROL

ABC: September 12, 1966 – September 16, 1968

War fiction adventure series set in the North African desert during World War II featuring four young commandos known as the Long Range Desert Group. Starred were Christopher George as Sgt. Sam Troy, Gary Raymond as Sgt. Jack Moffitt, Lawrence Casey as Pvt. Mark Hitchcock, Justin Tarr as Pvt. Tully Pettigrew, and Hans Judegast as Cpt. Hans Dietrick of the German Afrika Korps. Items are normally copyrighted Mirisch-Rich TV Productions.

RAT-1	RAT-2

RAT-1. "TV GUIDE" issue for week of December 3, 1966 with color cover photo of cast members plus five-page article titled "The War In The Desert" about the series. **$25.**

RAT-2. "RAT PATROL" SET OF 66 GUM CARDS issued by Topps Gum ©1966. Each card is 2.5x3.5" with color scene from the series. Back of each has brief description of pictured scene plus a picture piece to form a large poster by using the complete set. **SET $60.**

RAT-3	RAT-4

RAT-3. "THE RAT PATROL DESERT COMBAT GAME" by Transogram ©1966 in original box. Game parts include playing board with vivid desert battle scenes, plus small die-cut stand-up jeep and German tank figures. $50.

RAT-4. "THE RAT PATROL" PLASTIC MODEL ASSEMBLY KIT by Aurora Plastics ©1967 in original 2.5x10x15" box. Assembly parts are for two jeeps and accessories, two tanks, four palm trees, a sand dune with sand bags, plus 15 soldier figures. **$100.**

RAT-5

RAT-5. "THE RAT PATROL MIDGET MOTORS JEEP" by Remco Industries ©1966 in original box. Jeep is a 3x4x6" motorized hard plastic vehicle with rubber wheels. A machine gun is on a swivel base and a "Rat Patrol" sticker is on the left side of the vehicle. The jeep makes an engine noise while climbing steep grades. Jeep color is mostly tan with black markings. **$75.**

RAT-6

RAT-6. "THE RAT PATROL" EMBOSSED STEEL LUNCH BOX AND STEEL THERMOS by Aladdin Industries ©1967. **LUNCH BOX $50. THERMOS $25.**

RAT-7

RAT-7. "RAT PATROL" JEEP AND SOLDIERS SET by Marx Toys ©1967 in original box. Jeep is 7x8x14" hard plastic with a swivel machine gun that spring-fires bullets. Included are two 7.5" scaled hard plastic fully jointed figures, each with accessories including rifles, scabbards, canteen, pistol, cartridge belt and holster, walkie-talkie, binoculars plus military clothing. **$250.**

RAWHIDE

CBS: January 9, 1959 – January 4, 1966

Western adventure series about a traveling cattle drive team starring Clint Eastwood as Rowdy Yates and Eric Fleming as trail boss Gil Favor. The show also featured a popular theme song sung by Frankie Laine. Items are normally copyrighted CBS Films Inc.

RAW-1	RAW-2	RAW-3

RAW-1. "RAWHIDE" BROWN PLASTIC TOY CANTEEN attached to 3.5x6" retail display header tag picturing Eric Fleming as Gil Favor. Canteen has a 6" diameter by 1.5" thickness. By Carnell Mfg. Co. ©1959. **$35.**

RAW-2. GIL FAVOR PLASTIC REPLICA FIGURE from full-sized series circa early 1960s by Hartland Plastics. The figure has painted outfit of yellow vest, blue shirt, brown chaps plus a white hat. The horse figure is tan. Accessories include saddle and miniature six-shooter. **$250.**

RAW-3. "RAWHIDE" OUTFIT of chaps and vest circa early 1960s. The chaps have a 29" length and are formed from plastic and leather in two shades of tan. The vest is red/gray plastic with leather cut-outs representing pockets. The outfit is accented by several silvered tin decorative medallions with red glass cut stones. Our photo example shows the vest laid on the chaps. **$25.**

RAW-4   RAW-5

RAW-4. "RAWHIDE" GAME by Lowell Toys ©1960 in original box. Box lid has full color portrait of Eric Fleming as Gil Favor but there is no further picture reference on the playing board. **$35.**

RAW-5. "RAWHIDE" COWPUNCHER PLASTIC MODEL ASSEMBLY KIT by Pyro Plastics ©1958 in original 2x4.5x11.5" box. Assembly parts are for a 10" tall replica figure of Gil Favor. Our photo example shows box lid plus opened box with instruction sheet. **$65.**

THE REAL McCOYS

ABC: October 3, 1957 – September 20, 1962
CBS: September 30, 1962 – September 22, 1963

Television's first successful rural comedy about a mountain family relocated from the east to a ranch in California. Starred were Walter Brennan as Grandpa Amos McCoy, Richard Crenna as grandson Luke McCoy, Kathy Nolan as Luke's wife Kate, Lydia Reed as Aunt Hassie, and Michael Winkleman as Little Luke. Items are normally copyrighted Brennan-Westgate Productions or V T & L Productions. In its last year, reruns were shown on weekday mornings under the shortened title, "The McCoys" concurrent with the regular evening version.

RMC-1   RMC-2

RMC-1. "THE REAL McCOYS AND DANGER AT THE RANCH" 6x8" hardcover 1961 Whitman book #1577 with 212-page story. **$8.**

RMC-2. "THE REAL McCOYS" FABRIC IRON-ON PATCHES KIT ©1961 on 4x4.5" header card. The card holds a plastic bag of 50 soft knit patches with a darning tool. **$20.**

THE REBEL

ABC: October 4, 1959 – September 12, 1962

Western series starring Nick Adams as Johnny Yuma, an ex-Confederate soldier who roamed the West after the Civil War. The show also featured a popular theme song sung by Johnny Cash. NBC aired reruns from June to September 1962. Items are normally copyrighted Goodson-Todman Productions, Celestial Productions, or Fen-Ker-Ada Productions.

REB-1   REB-2   REB-3

REB-1. "JOHNNY YUMA'S JOURNAL/THE REBEL" DELL COMIC BOOK #1138 for October-December 1960 with color cover photo of Adams as Yuma. **$10.**

REB-2. "THE REBEL" 6x8" hardcover 1961 Whitman book with 212-page story. **$12.**

REB-3. NICK ADAMS "THE REBEL" 45-RPM RECORD on RCA Victor label circa early 1960s. Side 1 is song "Tired And Lonely Rebel" sung by Adams and Side 2 is song "It Could Have Been Different," also sung by him. Record is in 7x7" paper sleeve. **$25.**

REB-4   REB-5

REB-4. THE REBEL PLASTIC REPLICA FIGURE from the small-sized series circa early 1960s by Hartland Plastics. The Johnny Yuma figure has painted turquoise shirt with brown trousers and brown Rebel cap. **$75.**

REB-5. "THE REBEL" GAME by Ideal Toys ©1961 in original 10x20" box. Game parts include playing board plus small plastic figures of a cowboy and three Indians. Box lid design is black/white/pink/blue with photo of Adams as Johnny Yuma. **$45.**

THE RESTLESS GUN

NBC: September 23, 1957 – September 14, 1959

Western adventure series about a quiet loner cowboy, Vint Bonner (John Payne) who roamed the Southwest after the Civil War. Bonner was frequently called on to settle disputes, against his will, by his proficient gunfighting ability. Items are normally copyrighted MCA Corp. ABC later aired reruns of the original series.

RST-1　　　　　　　RST-2

RST-1. "THE RESTLESS GUN" 45-RPM RECORD in 7x7" dust sleeve that has full color photo of John Payne as Vint Bonner. Both sides are sung by The Sons Of The Pioneers, and Side 2 title is "Bunkhouse Bugle Boy." Record is on RCA Victor label circa late 1950s. **$10.**

RST-2. "THE RESTLESS GUN" GAME by Milton Bradley ©1959 in original box. Game parts include a playing board with a trail of die-cut holes for insertion of marbles which are provided with the game, plus a spinner board and play money. **$30.**

RST-3　　　　　　　RST-4

RST-3. "VINT BONNER" PLASTIC REPLICA FIGURE from the "Gunfighter" series by Hartland Plastics circa late 1950s in original 2x3x9.5" retail box. Figure has jointed arms and comes with miniature six-shooter. The painted outfit is brown vest, white shirt, blue trousers and black hat. **COMPLETE UNBOXED $150. BOXED $250.**

RST-4. "TV'S RESTLESS GUN" PLASTIC FIGURE ASSEMBLY KIT by Pyro Plastics circa 1958 in original 2x4.5x11.5" box. Assembly parts are for a 10" figure. Our photo example shows box lid with opened box and instruction sheet. **$65.**

RST-5

RST-5. "JOHN PAYNE/RESTLESS GUN" PACKAGED GUN AND HOLSTER SET by Esquire Novelty Corp. © 1958 in original 12x15" carton. The basic gun is a 9" metal standard western cap pistol which can be converted by a 12" brown plastic stock into a pistol rifle. The holster and belt are black/white/gold leather with the name of the show across the holster. The set comes with 12 toy bullets. **$150.**

RST-6　　　　　　　RST-7

RST-6. "JOHN PAYNE/RESTLESS GUN" 3.5" celluloid button in unopened 4x6" "Top Western TV Stars" retail package ©1959. Payne is pictured in black/white photo on light green background. **$35.**

RST-7. "THE RESTLESS GUN" 6x8" hardcover Whitman book ©1959. **$10.**

RICOCHET RABBIT

See Magilla Gorilla

THE RIFLEMAN

ABC: September 30, 1958 – July 1, 1963

Western adventure series starring Chuck Connors in the title role as Lucas McCain, a rancher raising his son Mark (Johnny Crawford) near the trouble-filled town of North Fork, New Mexico. McCain was called upon weekly to settle the town's problems with the help of his .44 Winchester rifle modified with a large cocking ring for extremely quick firing. Items are normally copyrighted Four Star-Sussex Productions.

RFL-1　　　　　　　RFL-2

RFL-1. "TV GUIDE" issue for week of October 23, 1965 with color cover photo plus 3-page article about Connors' television career to date. **$10.**

RFL-2. "TV GUIDE" issue for week of February 7, 1959 with color photo cover plus 3-page article about Connors' transition from professional baseball to movie and television roles. **$15.**

RFL-3   RFL-4

RFL-3. RIFLEMAN REPLICA PLASTIC FIGURE from full-sized series by Hartland Plastics circa early 1960s. Figure depicts Connors as Lucas McCain with painted outfit of light blue shirt, mustard yellow trousers, plus white hat and rifle. **$100.**

RFL-4. RIFLEMAN PLASTIC REPLICA FIGURE from small-sized series by Hartland Plastics circa early 1960s. Figure is of Connors as Lucas McCain with painted outfit of dark blue vest and trousers with white shirt and hat. **$50.**

RFL-5   RFL-6

RFL-5. "THE RIFLEMAN GAME" by Milton Bradley © 1959 in 10x19" box. Connors as Lucas McCain is pictured on box lid and playing board. **$40.**

RFL-6. "THE RIFLEMAN" 32" brown plastic and metal cap-firing rifle by Hubley circa late 1950s. **$150.**

RFL-7   RFL-8

RFL-7. "THE RIFLEMAN RANCH" PLAYSET by Marx Toys in original 4x13x22" illustrated carton. A very extensive plastic playset including figures of Lucas and Mark McCain, eight other cowhand figures, a lithographed tin ranch house with porch and chimney, a lithographed tin log cabin, 11 sections of fencing, ranch gate with swinging gates, hitching post, grinding wheel, water pump with bucket, forge, anvil, axe on stump, steers, turkey, chickens, 9 horses and a covered wagon drawn by two horses, a buckboard with driver, and many other smaller accessory parts. **$700.**

RFL-8. "THE RIFLEMAN" STARCHED RED FELT HAT formed to resemble the one worn by Connors as Lucas McCain. Front of crown has a fabric picture label in silver/yellow/red. The hat is about 11x13" with a 3" crown, and comes with original label stitched to brim by maker Tex-Felt © 1958. Our photo example shows entire hat and label detail. **$75.**

RIN TIN TIN
See The Adventures Of Rin Tin Tin

THE ROAD RUNNER SHOW
CBS: September 10, 1966 – September 7, 1968
ABC: September 11, 1971 – February 9, 1972

Animated cartoon series featuring the Road Runner's perpetual outwitting of his inept nemesis Wile E. Coyote. The show was aired on Saturday mornings under its own title but also was paired with Bugs Bunny in "The Bugs Bunny/Road Runner Hour." Items are normally copyrighted Warner Bros. Productions.

RRS-1

RRS-1. "THE ROAD RUNNER GAME" by Whitman © 1969 in 2x11.5x14" box. The game features eight large cardboard figures of Wile E. Coyote and Road Runner plus a deck of cards and small picture disks of the two characters. **$20.**

RRS-2   RRS-3

RRS-2. ROAD RUNNER AND COYOTE HAND PUPPETS each 10" tall with soft vinyl head plus thin plastic hand cover. Road Runner is depicted mostly in purple with markings in yellow and black. The Coyote is mostly in tan and brown with accent markings of yellow. Each has Warner Bros. © and are made in Japan circa 1970s. **EACH $5.**

RRS-3. "THE ROAD RUNNER" STEEL LUNCH BOX by King-Seeley Thermos circa 1970-1973. Different chase scenes are on all exterior surfaces. **$50.**

RRS-4

RRS-4. ROAD RUNNER/COYOTE LAMP WITH SHADE © 1977. The lamp is 12.5" tall including a 2" base and 3" bulb socket. Mounted on the plastic base are full color vinyl figures plus a green vinyl cactus plant. Behind the cactus is a small bulb for night light and a conventional bulb goes into the upper socket. The lamp shade is stiff paper with full color action scene. The bottom diameter of the shade is 11" and its height is 8". **$50.**

ROBIN HOOD

See The Adventures Of Robin Hood

ROCKY AND HIS FRIENDS

See The Bullwinkle Show

ROCKY JONES, SPACE RANGER

Syndicated 1953
NBC: February 27 – April 17, 1954

Short-lived children's space show set in the 21st century starring Richard Carne in the title role as Captain of the Space Rangers. Items are normally copyrighted Space Ranger Enterprises.

RJS-1   RJS-2

RJS-1. "ROCKY JONES, SPACE RANGER COLORING BOOK" by Whitman © 1951 in large 11x15" size with 32 pages. **$25.**

RJS-2. "ROCKY JONES/SPACE RANGER/COLORING BOOK" by Whitman © 1953 in 11x15" size with 32 pages. **$40.**

ROOTIE KAZOOTIE

NBC: December 9, 1950 – November 1, 1952
ABC: December 22, 1952 – May 7, 1954

Children's puppet show hosted by Todd Russell featuring puppet characters of Rootie, Polka Dottie, Gala Poochie, El Squeako (mouse) and Poison Zoomack. Items are normally copyrighted Rootie Kazootie Inc.

RKZ-1   RKZ-2   RKZ-3

RKZ-1. "TV JR" Volume 1, Number 1, April 25, 1953 first issue of child's magazine with browntone cover photo of Rootie. Magazine has 48 pages of monthly suggestions for children's parties and there is no further inside reference to Rootie Kazootie or the show. 6x9". **$12.**

RKZ-2. "ROOTIE KAZOOTIE" 1953 Dell first issue of 3-D comic series with 32 pages of specially printed pictures to be viewed through set of 3-D enclosed glasses. **$15.**

RKZ-3. "ROOTIE KAZOOTIE" HAND PUPPET 11" tall with vinyl head and cloth body that has printed design of him in a baseball uniform. Circa 1953. **$25.**

RKZ-4   RKZ-5   RKZ-6

RKZ-4. "POLKA DOTTIE" HAND PUPPET 10" tall in original plastic retail display canister by National Mask & Puppet Corp. circa early 1950s. Puppet has vinyl head and lavender fabric hand cover. **$35.**

RKZ-5. "GALA POOCHIE PUP" 8.5x9" colorful fabric handkerchief picturing the pup in a doghouse inscribed "Rootie Kazootie Club" on the edge of the roof. Early 1950s. **$15.**

RKZ-6. "ROOTIE KAZOOTIE WORD GAME" consisting of 36-card playing deck in 2.5x3.5" box. Game is by Ed-U-Cards © 1953. Each card has full color character illustration and game is designed to aid spelling and word recognition. **$10.**

ROUTE 66

CBS: October 7, 1960 – September 18, 1964

Adventure series about a pair of young men who traveled about the country in their 1960 Corvette. Original stars were Martin Milner as Tod Stiles and George Maharis as Buzz Murdock. In the spring of 1963, Glenn Corbett succeeded Maharis as the new partner, Lincoln Case. The show also featured a very popular theme song by Nelson Riddle. Items are normally copyrighted Screen Gems Productions.

RTE-1   RTE-2

RTE-1. "ROUTE 66 TRAVEL GAME" by Transogram ©1962 in 9x17.5" box with colorful box lid including photos of the co-stars. Game consists of a playing board, a box insert that has road map instructions and spinner, four miniature plastic cars, and two small plastic cones. Game is also ©by Lancer Productions Inc. **$60.**

RTE-2. "TV GUIDE" issue for week of July 6, 1963 with color cover photo of co-stars Milner and Corbett plus 4-page article about Corbett's move to the show replacing George Maharis. **$15.**

ROWAN AND MARTIN'S LAUGH-IN
See Laugh-In

THE ROY ROGERS SHOW
NBC: December 30, 1951 – June 23, 1957

Western variety show starring durable 1930s-1940s cowboy star Rogers and wife Dale Evans. The show was reintroduced briefly in 1962 under the title "Roy Rogers & Dale Evans Show." Also featured regularly were sidekick Pat Brady, western singing group Sons of the Pioneers, Roy and Dale's horses Trigger and Buttermilk, and their German shepherd, Bullet. The Roy-Dale series predated the "adult" western era and produced a very extensive line of licensed merchandise, usually copyrighted Roy Rogers Enterprises.

| ROY-1 | ROY-2 | ROY-3 |

ROY-1. "ROY ROGERS" 6.5" composition bobbing head figure with spring-mounted head. Figure is on a square green base and the painted outfit is mostly in aqua/dark red/white. The face is very realistically colored and detailed. The front of the base has a facsimile signature decal. Circa 1960s. **$75.**

ROY-2. "ROY ROGERS" 4.5" plastic premium mug offered by Quaker Cereals circa 1950. Mug has a bright full color likeness of Roy and on his hat band is small inscription "Roy Rogers/The King Of The Cowboys." **$20.**

ROY-3. "DALE EVANS/QUEEN OF THE WEST" 7x8" white terrycloth washing mitt with design in brown, red, green, blue and fleshtone. Mid-1950s. **$25.**

| ROY-4 | ROY-5 | ROY-6 |

ROY-4. ROY ROGERS AND TRIGGER REPLICA PLASTIC FIGURE from the full sized series by Hartland Plastics circa late 1950s-early 1960s. Roy is depicted in painted outfit of light blue and dark red plus white hat and comes with two guns. **$125.**

ROY-5. DALE EVANS AND BUTTERMILK PLASTIC REPLICA FIGURE from the full sized series by Hartland Plastics circa late 1950s-early 1960s. The figure is depicted in painted olive green outfit with white hat and one gun. **$100.**

ROY-6. ROY ROGERS AND TRIGGER PLASTIC REPLICA FIGURE from the small sized series by Hartland Plastics circa late 1950s - early 1960s. Figure of Roy is depicted in painted outfit of white trimmed in red plus white hat. The figure of Trigger is a palomino gold. **$100.**

| ROY-7 | ROY-8 |

ROY-7. BULLET, REPLICA PLASTIC FIGURE OF ROY AND DALE'S DOG, by Hartland Plastics circa late 1950s - early 1960s and scaled to the full sized other Hartland figures. Coloring is a mellow white with black markings. **$25.**

ROY-8. "ROY ROGERS" 8.5" tall lithographed metal ranch lantern with clear plastic center chimney. Lithographed design is mostly in bright red/blue/yellow with Roy portrait illustrations and other Roy-related symbols. The lamp is operated by a battery. Mid-1950s. **$60.**

ROY-9

ROY-9. "ROY ROGERS FIX-IT CHUCK WAGON AND JEEP" PLASTIC SET by Ideal Toys circa mid-1950s in original 4.5x7.5x24" illustrated cardboard carton. Major parts are 3" seated character figures of Roy, Dale and Pat Brady plus a scaled horse-drawn chuckwagon with accessories and replica of the Nellybelle jeep. Accessory pieces include a figure of Bullet plus various items of cooking equipment, bucket, storage chest and team of horses for the wagon. The wagon and jeep consist of over 60 different parts to be assembled and disassembled at will. **$150.**

ROY-10

**ROY-10. "ROY ROGERS FIX-IT STAGECOACH" PLASTIC
SET** by Ideal Toy ©1955 in original 5.5x6.5x15" illustrated carton. "Fix-
It" features are horses to be hitched or unhitched, changable wheels,
doors that open and close and complete assembled size is about
5x6.5x15". A seated Roy figure is included for the stagecoach seat, and
other accessories include a tool box, money chest, rifle, wrench, and
other small tools. **$200.**

ROY-11

**ROY-11. "ROY ROGERS STAGECOACH WAGON TRAIN"
WIND-UP TOY** by Marx circa mid-1950s in original 2.5x3x14.5"
brightly illustrated carton. Toy consists of a single unit plastic stagecoach and horse team plus three trailing lithographed metal wagons,
each in very bright full color design. The wagons are joined to each
other so the entire unit moves in a circular motion when wound. The
total unit size is 2.5x2.5x14" long. **$100.**

ROY-12

ROY-12. "NELLYBELLE JEEP WITH FIGURES" TOY by Marx
circa mid-1950s in original 5x6.5x13.5" illustrated carton. Jeep is gray
pressed steel with yellow "Nellybelle" name decal on each side. The
jeep is about 5x5x11" and features a hood which raises to expose
detailed plastic engine. Other features are a windshield which raises
and lowers, removable side panels and wire roll bar. The jeep is with
three hard plastic scaled figures of Dale, Pat Brady and Bullet. **$250.**

ROY-13

**ROY-13. "ROY ROGERS HAULER AND VAN TRAILER"
BATTERY TOY** by Line Mar circa 1957 in original 4x6.5x11" colorfully
illustrated carton. The toy consists of lithographed metal trailer van and
metal cab hauler which has cord to a remote control unit with forward
and reverse button. Total length of the joined cab and trailer is about
13". Very colorful lithography design is on the van trailer which also has
side and rear doors that open and close. **$500.**

ROY-14

ROY-14. "ROY ROGERS RODEO RANCH" PLAYSET by Marx
circa early 1950s in original 4x9x22" colorfully illustrated carton. Set
features a full color lithograph tin ranch house to be assembled plus
white plastic rail fence sections for the ranch and rodeo chute plus a
matching gateway inscribed "Roy Rogers/Double R Bar Ranch." The
figure of Roy and 9 other cowboys are each about 2.5" tall in a single
color of plastic. Other figures include those of various livestock,
saddles and bridles, tree and cactus, wishing well, wood pile, chopping
block, grill, anvil, whetstone, barrel, and other similar items. Our photo
example shows box lid and the figure of Roy. **$300.**

ROY-15

ROY-15. ROY ROGERS "BIG GAME RIFLE" by Marx Toys circa
mid-1950s in original 2x5x35" illustrated carton. Rifle is a 34" nicely
detailed cap-firing replica of a .348 caliber game rifle with metal or
simulated metal parts in black plus a stock of simulated dark red wood.
"Roy Rogers" is in gold script on one side of the stock. The rifle has a
webbed strap and uses roll caps. A panel of the box has the Roy Rogers
Pledge To Parents. **$150.**

ROY-16   ROY-17   ROY-18

ROY-16. "ROY ROGERS & TRIGGER" POCKET WATCH by Bradley Time circa 1959. Watch has a silvered metal case with clear crystal over dial face which has portrait illustration of Roy in a yellow hat with black shirt and red neckerchief plus fleshtone face. The portrait is against a background full color scene of him on Trigger at the ranch fence. The watch has mechanism for regular timekeeping plus stopwatch use. **$350.**

ROY-17. "ROY ROGERS & TRIGGER" WRIST WATCH by Ingraham circa 1951. Watch has silvered metal case and clear crystal over colorful dial face portrait illustration of Roy and Trigger surrounded by green border with black numerals. **$75.**

ROY-18. "DALE EVANS" WRIST WATCH by Ingraham circa 1951. Watch has silvered metal case and clear crystal over colorful dial face illustration of Dale and Buttermilk within a horseshoe design surrounded by orange border with black numerals. **$75.**

ROY-19   ROY-20

ROY-19. "ROY ROGERS AND TRIGGER" ANIMATED WIND-UP CLOCK by Ingraham Co. circa 1951. Clock is 1.5x4x4.5" in enameled ivory metal case with bright brass frame around clear crystal over dial face. Dial face has full color illustration of a western desert scene with rising sun rays. Mounted on the scene is a small die-cut figure of Roy on Trigger which rocks back and forth as time passes. A small inscription "Roy Rogers And Trigger" is near the center of the scene. This inscription may not appear on all versions, and some versions may come in a different colored metal case. **$150.**

ROY-20. "ROY ROGERS HOLSTER SET" by Classy Products Corp. © 1956 in original 2x13x13" box with full color lid illustration. Set consists of leather belt and holsters with pair of 10.5" silvered metal cap pistols with white painted metal grips. The pistols use roll caps. Both sides of each pistol have a "RR" symbol and "Roy Rogers" name in script. The holsters and belt have many silvered brass decorative rivets, each with the "RR" symbol. The belt is 4" wide at the front and tapers smaller at the rear where the two belt pieces are joined by a rawhide cord. **$250.**

ROY-21   ROY-22

ROY-21. "ROY ROGERS HOLSTER SET" by Classy Products Corp. © 1955 in original 13x13" box with full color lid illustration. The belt and holsters are brown leather with a holster cover design of silver foil stamped with Roy's initials, horseshoe and name which are then outlined in red cut glass stones. The guns are silvered metal with various Roy brand symbols on the barrel. The pistol grips are gray plastic with a horse head design. Each grip has Roy's initials and his name is on one side of each gun. **$300.**

ROY-22. "TRIGGER" FLAT STEEL LUNCH BOX by American Thermos circa 1956. **$100.**

ROY-23

ROY-23. "ROY ROGERS AND DALE EVANS DOUBLE R BAR RANCH" STEEL LUNCH BOX AND STEEL THERMOS by King-Seeley Thermos circa 1955-1956. **LUNCH BOX $80. THERMOS $40.**

ROY-24   ROY-25

ROY-24. "ROY ROGERS AND DALE EVANS DOUBLE R BAR RANCH" FLAT STEEL LUNCH BOX AND STEEL THERMOS by American Thermos circa 1953-1954. **LUNCH BOX $80. THERMOS $40.**

ROY-25. "ROY ROGERS SADDLEBAG" TAN VINYL LUNCH BOX by King-Seeley Thermos © 1960. **$150.**

ROY-26   ROY-27   ROY-28

ROY-26. "TV GUIDE" issue for week of November 7, 1952 with black/white cover photo of Roy plus two-page article "TV Cowboy At Home" including three family photos. **$60.**

ROY-27. ROY/TRIGGER "WORLD CHAMPIONSHIP RODEO" 8x11" soft cover 36-page souvenir program for the October 19-30, 1955 appearance in Boston Garden during the 25th year of the rodeo. Roy and Trigger were featured in the rodeo and are on the program cover. There is also an illustrated two-page article, "King Of The Cowboys," plus photo stories about Pat Brady, Sons Of The Pioneers, and a center ad picturing Roy, Trigger, and Dale for Post's Sugar Crisps. **$50.**

ROY-28. "ROY ROGERS AND DALE EVANS COLORING BOOK" by Whitman © 1951 in 8.5x11" size. **$35.**

ROY-29   ROY-30

ROY-29. "ROY ROGERS AND DALE EVANS" 10x15" punch-out book by Whitman ©1952 with both covers and inside six pages of heavy cardboard. Roy and Dale are the punch-outs on the front cover while Trigger and Buttermilk are punch-outs on the back cover. The inside pages have very colorful punch figures of ponies, Indian, tents and Indians, cactus and ranch scenes, cook wagon with horses, burros and steers, gold miner and more. **$100.**

ROY-30. "ROY ROGERS AND DALE EVANS CUT-OUT DOLLS" 10.5x12" cardboard folder with inside pockets holding stiff cardboard stand-up dolls of Roy and Dale with paper sheets of clothing for each. Beautifully designed and colored folder by Whitman ©1954. **$60.**

ROY-31

ROY-31. "ROY ROGERS' COOKIES" 8" stiff paper premium pop gun with colorful illustrations printed on each side. Circa mid-1950s. **$25.**

RUFF AND REDDY

NBC: December 14, 1957 – September 26, 1964

The first TV animated cartoon series by Hanna-Barbera Studios, featuring a dog and cat team which battled evil forces. The show continued in syndicated reruns following the original version.

RUF-1   RUF-2

RUF-1. "RUFF AND REDDY GO TO A PARTY" 5.5x6.5" Whitman ©1958 Tell-A-Tale hardcover children's book. **$15.**

RUF-2. "RUFF AND REDDY AND THEIR FRIENDS" 45-RPM LITTLE GOLDEN RECORD ©1959 in 7x8" cardboard dust jacket. Song titles are Ruff and Reddy, Professor Gizmo, Ubble and Ubble, Killer and Diller, Captain Greedy & Salt-Water Daffy, Hairy Safari. **$20.**

RUF-3

RUF-3. "RUFF AND REDDY TV FAVORITE SPELLING GAME" by Exclusive Playing Card Co. ©1958 in 1x4x7.5" box. Our photo example shows box lid and sealed contents. **$20.**

SECRET AGENT

CBS: April 3, 1965 – September 10, 1966

Espionage drama series produced in Great Britain starring Patrick McGoohan as John Drake. The show was an outgrowth of the earlier "Danger Man" series also starring McGoohan. He later created and produced a series, "The Prisoner," considered to be a sequel to "Secret Agent." Items are normally copyrighted ATV Productions or Television Products, Ltd.

SEC-1   SEC-2

SEC-1. FIRST ISSUES "SECRET AGENT" COMIC BOOK by Gold Key Comics, each with front cover color photo. Each back cover has tinted scene from the series and black/white scenes are on inside covers. Issues are Number 1, 1966 and Number 2, 1967. The two issues are the entire series published by Gold Key. **EACH $15.**

SEC-2. "SECRET AGENT" PAPERBACK NOVEL authored by Howard Baker and published by Macfadden Publications ©1966 with 128-page adventure story "Departure Deferred." **$15.**

SEC-3

SEC-3. "SECRET AGENT GOLDEN SNIPER" GUN TOY made in England by Crescent Toy Co. circa mid-1960s in original 1x8x11" illustrated box. Gun is 6" diecast metal formed like a Luger pistol finished in bright gold with brown plastic grips. Accessory parts for the gun are a plastic silencer, telescope sight, metal/plastic shoulder butt. **$50.**

SEC-4

SEC-5

SEC-4. "JOHN DRAKE/SECRET AGENT GAME" by Milton Bradley © 1966 in 9.5x19" box. The playing board has action scenes at each corner plus a small picture of Drake at bottom edge. The game is also © Independent Television Corp. **$35.**

SEC-5. "JOHN DRAKE/DANGER MAN" CARDS from set of 72 printed in Denmark circa early 1960s under © of Television Products Ltd. London. Each is 2.25x3" with black/white scene from the series which became "Secret Agent" for U.S. viewing. Back of each card has synopsis of depicted scene and entire set constitutes a single continuous adventure. Our photo example shows front and back of a single card. **EACH $3.**

SEC-6   SEC-7

SEC-6. "DANGER MAN ANNUAL" hardcover 7.5x10.5" adventure book © 1965 by Television Products Ltd. and published by World Distributors Ltd., England. Contents are nine text stories with full color illustrations. **$20.**

SEC-7. "THE PRISONER" PAPERBACK NOVEL published by Ace Books © 1969 with 160-page story based on the spinoff television series from "Secret Agent." The story is #2 of a series published by Ace. **$15.**

SECRET SQUIRREL

See Atom Ant

SERGEANT BILKO

See You'll Never Get Rich

SERGEANT PRESTON
OF THE YUKON

CBS: September 29, 1955 – September 25, 1958

Adventure series starring Richard Simmons as Sergeant Frank Preston of the Royal Canadian Mounted Police, a character which originated on radio in the 1940s. The series also featured his faithful dog, King, and horse Rex. The show was filmed originally in monochrome and 22 new shows were filmed in color beginning late in 1958 for syndication. The television series was sponsored by Quaker cereals which issued numerous premium collectibles. Items are normally copyrighted Wrather Corp.

SGT-1   SGT-2   SGT-3

SGT-1. SERGEANT PRESTON LARGE PORTRAIT PRIZE POSTER sent to winners in a 1950 Sergeant Preston contest sponsored by Quaker. Portrait illustration is superb full color and 16x22" with additional white margin. **$200.**

SGT-2. "SERGEANT PRESTON COLORING BOOK" by Whitman © 1953 with 8.5x11" size. **$20.**

SGT-3. "SERGEANT PRESTON OF THE YUKON" 8.25x11" coloring book by Treasure Books © 1957 with 52 pages. **$15.**

SGT-4   SGT-5

SGT-4. "SERGEANT PRESTON" 100-PIECE JIGSAW PUZZLE by Milton Bradley circa mid-1950s in 1x7x10" box. Assembled puzzle is 10x18" with choice color scenes of him on Rex crossing a lake with King in the water alongside the horse. A detail of the puzzle scene is on the box lid. **$25.**

SGT-5. "SGT. PRESTON'S YUKON TRAIL" Quaker Puffed Wheat box with complete uncut back, front and side panels. This example is Package 7 from set of eight packages to complete a miniature Yukon community. This package included Trading Post, Trading Post Interior, Wells Fargo Office, Hotel and Interior, Dog Sled, Dog Team, Husky. One of the earliest Sergeant Preston premiums from 1949. Flattened size of box is 9x9". **SET OF 8, EACH $50.**

SGT-6   SGT-7

SGT-6. SERGEANT PRESTON "KLONDIKE BIG INCH LAND CO., INC." 5.5x8" paper Deed Of Land certificate citing legal terms and authorizing the bearer to a single square inch of territory in the Yukon. The deed is printed on both sides and was a 1955 Quaker cereal premium. Our example has not been inked or penciled with the owner's name. **$20.**

SGT-7. "SGT. PRESTON PEDOMETER" with instruction paper and original mailing box from Quaker cereals circa 1952-1954. The pedometer is 2.5" aluminum with black/white/red dial. **$65.**

77 SUNSET STRIP

ABC: October 10, 1958 – September 9, 1964

Private eye adventure series starring detective pair of Efrem Zimbalist, Jr., as Stu Bailey and Roger Smith as Jeff Spencer. The pair operated their agency from the street address of 77 Sunset Strip although adventures took them around the world. Also featured was Edd Byrnes as Gerald Lloyd (Kookie) Kookson III, a parking lot attendant whose hair-brushing routine prompted a very popular novelty song "Kookie, Kookie, Lend Me Your Comb." Byrnes was replaced temporarily during the series by Troy Donahue. Items are normally copyrighted Warner Bros. Pictures Inc.

SSS-1   SSS-2

SSS-1. "77 SUNSET STRIP" GAME by Lowell Toys © 1960 in 10x20" box. Game parts include a playing board with design of motel rooms exposed openly from above, miniature figure pieces plus die-cut clue figures, pencils and a notepad. **$35.**

SSS-2. "TV GUIDE" issue for week of August 27, 1960 with color cover photo of original stars plus a newly-added partner, Richard Long. Cover article has brief summary about the series but is mostly a biography sketch of Edd Byrnes. **$10.**

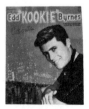

SSS-3   SSS-4

SSS-3. "KOOKIE YEARBOOK" 8.5x11" 1959 fan magazine with 52 pages devoted exclusively to Edd "Kookie" Byrnes with many large photos, dozens of smaller photos, plus articles and facts about him. This is first issue, Volume 1, Number 1 of the publication. **$20.**

SSS-4. "EDD 'KOOKIE' BYRNES" 9.5x12.5" doll cut-out book by Whitman © 1959. **$50.**

THE SHARI LEWIS SHOW

NBC: October 1, 1960 – September 28, 1963

Saturday morning children's puppet show hosted by ventriloquist Lewis and her hand puppets Lamb Chop, Hush Puppy, Charlie Horse, Wing Ding. Items normally are copyrighted Tarcher Productions.

SRL-1   SRL-2   SRL-3

SRL-1. "SHARI LEWIS & HER FRIENDS PRINTER SET" by Colorforms © 1962 in 1x8.5x13" box. The set includes six wooden-handled plastic character stamps, each 1x1.25" and depicted characters are Shari, Lamb Chop, Charlie Horse, Hush Puppy, Wing Ding, Little Boy. The set also includes a small pad of blank stamp sheets plus a stamp pad. **$20.**

SRL-2. LAMB CHOP STUFFED PLUSH WHITE DOLL with realistic vinyl plastic head. Doll has original tag by Ideal Toys circa early 1960s and is formed in a permanent seated position with height of 8.5" and leg length of about 7". The face is a rosy flesh-tone with black eyebrow and nose marks plus simulated white wool hair. The body has three pink fabric simulated buttons on the chest, and the hands are each a die-cut pink felt. **$50.**

SRL-3. CHARLIE HORSE STUFFED CLOTH DOLL with realistic soft vinyl head and original tag from Ideal Toys circa early 1960s. Doll is designed in permanent seated position with a seated height of 7" to the tip of the ears. The fabric outfit is an orange/white polka dot bandanna neckerchief, yellow shirt, blue jeans with red suspenders, and a red felt hanky stitched to a back pocket. **$35.**

SRL-4   SRL-5   SRL-6

SRL-4. LAMB CHOP 9" hand puppet with realistic soft vinyl head with mouth which may be opened and closed by fingers of the user underneath a fabric neck piece. The head is fleshtone with simulated white wooly short hair and the hand cover is red fabric with blue trim. The neck has ©1960 Tarcher Productions and puppet is believed to be by Ideal Toys, although not marked, probably from a set of four consisting of this item through **SRL-7. $20.**

SRL-5. CHARLIE HORSE 9" hand puppet from same series as **SRL-4.** The head is a rosy fleshtone with a simulated bright yellow straw hat. The hand cover is red with blue trim. **$20.**

SRL-6. HUSH PUPPY 9" hand puppet from same series as **SRL-4.** The head is light blue with a red tongue and bow tie. The hand cover is blue with red trim. **$20.**

SRL-7   SRL-8

SRL-7. WING DING 9" hand puppet from same series as **SRL-4.** The head is black with jutting white eyeballs under a blue hat. The beak is yellow and may be opened and closed by fingers of the user under the hand cover that is blue with red trim. **$20.**

SRL-8. "SHARI LEWIS PARTY GAMES" by Lowell Toys ©1962 in 2x13x18" box. Set is a child's party kit including a single record by her and her puppet friends, plus materials, instructions and props for ten games. **$25.**

THE SHERIFF OF COCHISE

Syndicated 1956 – 1960 (156 Episodes)

Contemporary western adventure series starring John Bromfield as Sheriff/Marshal Frank Morgan who headed a team of three deputies in Cochise County, Arizona. The show was syndicated under titles The Sheriff Cochise, Man From Cochise, or U.S. Marshal.

SOC-1

SOC-1. "THE SHERIFF OF COCHISE" FULL COLOR 16-PAGE PREMIUM COMIC BOOK issued by Mobil Oil ©1957. Front cover has full color artwork and inside front cover has black/white photo of Bromfield. **$20.**

SOC-2   SOC-3

SOC-2. JOHN BROMFIELD 8x10" black/white premium photo with his facsimile signature, issued circa late 1950s or 1960s by Budweiser Beer. **$8.**

SOC-3. JOHN BROMFIELD AUTOGRAPH on 8x10" black/white fan photo of him with his sheriff's station wagon. In addition to the autograph is printed script "Thanks For Watching Our Show/Best Wishes Always/John Bromfield." **$25.**

THE SIX MILLION DOLLAR MAN

ABC: January 18, 1974 – March 6, 1978

Science-fiction action adventure series starring Lee Majors as Colonel Steve Austin, a former astronaut rebuilt from an injury with a $6 million futuristic, cybernetic body to perform government assignments for the Office of Strategic Information (O.S.I.), headed by Oscar Goldman, played by Richard Anderson. Items are normally copyrighted Universal City Studios Inc. and some collectibles may also be copyrighted General Mills Fun Group Inc.

SMD-1   SMD-2

SMD-1. "THE SIX MILLION DOLLAR MAN" GAME by Parker Brothers ©1975 in 9x18" box. **$15.**

SMD-2. "THE SIX MILLION DOLLAR MAN" EMBOSSED STEEL LUNCH BOX AND PLASTIC THERMOS by Aladdin Industries © 1974. **LUNCH BOX $30. THERMOS $10.**

SMD-3

SMD-3. "THE SIX MILLION DOLLAR MAN" SLIDE PROJECTOR SET by Chad Bally ©1976 in original 2x11x14" colorful box. Set consists of a 9" plastic slide projector and 16 full color filmstrips. **$20.**

SMD-4   SMD-5   SMD-6

SMD-4. "THE SIX MILLION DOLLAR MAN BANK BY ANIMALS PLUS" circa late 1970s. Bank is a full-dimensioned 10" vinyl figural image depicting him bursting through a wall of bricks. Figure is nicely colored including a painted bright orange uniform, red bricks and gray base. The coin slot is in back and the bottom has a plastic trap. **$15.**

SMD-5. "THE SIX MILLION DOLLAR MAN" 13" action figure in original colorful display box by Kenner Toys © 1977. Figure is fully posable with special features of snap-off arms and legs, rolled skin with hidden bionic module arms, bionic eye, bionic grip, plus a button in the back to raise the right arm. The figure comes in a red/white jumpsuit with matching sneakers. **$60.**

SMD-6. "OSCAR GOLDMAN" 12" action figure in original colorful display box by Kenner Toys ©1973. Figure is fully posable with added features of a plastic briefcase with detailed interior and capacity to explode into several pieces by pressing detonator. The fabric clothing is plaid jacket, green turtleneck sweater and tan trousers. **$50.**

SKY KING

NBC: September 16, 1951 – October 26, 1952

Contemporary western adventure series starring Kirby Grant as Sky King, owner of the Flying Crown Ranch and pilot of his plane, The Songbird, used weekly to patrol the ranch, usually to rescue or capture individuals. Co-starred was Gloria Winters as his niece Penny. The series was based on a radio series of the late 1940s and the television version was rerun later on both ABC and CBS into the mid-1950s. Items normally are copyrighted Jack Chertok Productions and several premium collectibles were issued by television sponsors Nabisco and Peter Pan Peanut Butter.

SKY-1   SKY-2   SKY-3

SKY-1. SKY KING/PENNY 8x10" black/white matte photo with facsimile signature in white "To All Of Our Friends Of The Zembo Shrine Circus/Happy Landing/Sky King And Me Too! Penny." Late 1940s or early 1950s. **$50.**

SKY-2. "SKY KING AND PENNY IN PERSON" 14x22" brown/white thin cardboard poster for their appearance as part of the Zembo Temple Shrine Circus performance in Harrisburg, Pa, circa late 1940s-early 1950s. **$60.**

SKY-3. "SKY KING DETECTO-MICROSCOPE" early 1950s premium of small but actual microscope with specimens for viewing plus original mailing box. The microscope is with a cardboard stand and the specimens are mesquite wood, painted desert sand, gold ore, and horsehair. Set is with an instruction sheet. **$200.**

SKY-4   SKY-5

SKY-4. SKY KING 3.5x5.5" unused post card with full color photo of him and his aircraft "Songbird III." Back has Nabisco logo and brief text about the show. Circa early 1950s. **$30.**

SKY-5. "SKY KING AZTEC EMERALD CALENDAR RING" 3.75x5.25" instruction sheet including large illustration of the premium ring circa 1952. Sheet is white with brown inking. **$60**

SMILIN' ED McCONNELL AND HIS BUSTER BROWN GANG

NBC: August 26, 1950 – May 19, 1951

Children's show based on similar radio show of 1940s, also hosted by McConnell. Both radio and television versions were sponsored by Buster Brown Shoes. The television version featured a variety format including regular appearance of puppets Froggy the Gremlin, Midnight the Cat, Squeekie the Mouse, Old Grandie the Talking Piano, plus Uncle Fishface, a teller of tall tales. Items are normally copyrighted J. Ed. McConnell. The television version appeared after its initial run on both CBS and ABC into the mid-1950s. On McConnell's death in 1955, Andy Devine replaced him as host with the show re-titled "Andy's Gang."

SEM-1   SEM-2

SEM-1. "FROGGY THE GREMLIN" 8.25x10.25" die-cut stiff paper mask printed in realistic full colors, mostly shades of green, with depiction of a black bow tie. Front mask has his printed name plus 1946 McConnell © and printed inscription "The Buster Brown Gang Is On The Air Every Saturday On NBC." **$40.**

SEM-2. "BUSTER BROWN T.V. THEATRE" 2x2.75" cardboard designed like a woodgrain/yellow/brown/gold television set. Inserted in the screen is a black/white flasher image of Froggy which jumps, down and a bit sideways as the card is tilted. On the back is "Hi, Kids! Be Sure To See Me, Buster And Tige, Andy Devine And The Rest Of The Gang On Televison Every Week." Undated but probably 1955. **$30.**

SEM-3   SEM-4

SEM-3. FROGGY THE GREMLIN 5" soft rubber squeaker toy figure with 1948 McConnell © and name of maker, Rempel Mfg. Inc. Figure is nicely colored with most of the body in shades of green with a flexible mouth that holds a small red flexible tongue. The jacket is depicted in red over a white dress shirt with simulated black buttons. The oversized shoes are depicted in black. This is the smallest size of at least one other known version. **$100.**

SEM-4. FROGGY 5x10" die-cut thick cardboard paddle board © 1946 McConnell with string and rubber ball attached on reverse. Depiction of Froggy is green/red/white and a Buster Brown/Tige at bottom of handle is red/white. **$60.**

THE SMOKEY BEAR SHOW
ABC: September 6, 1969 – September 12, 1971

Animated ecology cartoon series featuring the spokesbear of the National Forest Fires Commission and related groups. The series was by Rankin-Bass Productions. Items frequently will have Smokey's motto, "Only You Can Prevent Forest Fires," or a variation of the motto. Domestic-made items are normally licensed by a national or state government agency.

SBS-1   SBS-2   SBS-3

SBS-1. "SMOKEY" 9" hard plastic soap container figure from the "Soaky" series circa mid-1960s. The removable cap is formed like a forest ranger's yellow hat. The body front is light brown with tan muzzle and eyes. The trouser fronts and shovel are in light blue. The back side is entirely solid brown. **$10.**

SBS-2. "SMOKEY" 6.25" composition bobbing head figure with head mounted on a spring in the neck. The figure is on a round white base with very brightly colored body including tan and dark orange simulated fur, blue overalls and a yellow hat. Bottom of base has "Hand Made In Japan" sticker circa mid to late 1960s. **$35.**

SBS-3. "SMOKEY" 2.5x3x6" china figure bank with sticker on bottom for "Norcrest-Crafted In Japan." The body is a rich glazed brown with light yellow muzzle and darker yellow ranger hat plus light blue trousers. The bottom has a rubber disk trap. **$30.**

SBS-4   SBS-5

SBS-4. "SMOKEY" CHINA SET OF SALT & PEPPER SHAKERS each 3.5" tall with depiction of Smokey in glossy brown body with yellow hat and blue trousers. One shaker is depicted holding a white bucket and the other holds a shovel. Circa late 1960s. **SET $20.**

SBS-5. "SMOKEY BEAR WRIST WATCH" in original display box by Hawthorne Watch Co. circa late 1960s. Watch is in 1.25" silvered metal case with clear crystal over dial face with portrait of a standing Smokey. He is depicted wearing yellow ranger hat with brown upper body and dark blue trousers. The watch hands are formed like tiny shovels. Dial face inscription includes his name and "Prevent Forest Fires." The watch is in 1.5x2.5x9" colorful display box with clear plastic cover sleeve. **$75.**

SNAGGLEPUSS
See Yogi Bear

SNOOPER AND BLABBER
See Quick Draw McGraw

THE SOUPY SALES SHOW
ABC: July 4, 1955 – April 13, 1962

Children's show later syndicated in 1965 and again in 1979 featuring a variety format of story telling, jokes, songs, film segments and puppets. A frequent occurrence of the series was a pie thrown in the face of Sales. Items normally are copyrighted Soupy Sales – W.M.C. (Weston Merchandising Corp.)

SPS-1   SPS-2

SPS-1. "SINCERELY SOUPY SALES" AUTOGRAPH on a 3.5x5.5" black and white glossy photo post card. **$20.**

SPS-2. "SOUPY SALES MINI BOARD CARD GAME" ©1965 by Ideal in 1.5x6.5x10.5" box. A colorful lid covers a styrofoam base holding a deck of cards, 4 plastic pegs and a small cardboard playing board made up of whipped cream pie designs. **$25.**

SPS-3   SPS-4

SPS-3. "SOUPY SALES SEZ GO-GO-GO!" MILTON BRADLEY BOARD GAME circa 1960 in 1.5x9.5x19" box. Game includes punchout markers designed like cars and the object is to win a car race across mountainous terrain. **$30.**

SPS-4. SOUPY SALES PENCIL CASE. Light blue vinyl zippered pencil case 3.75x8" with black illustration of Soupy and the inscription "Soupy Sez Let's Do The 'Mouse'." Circa 1960. **$15.**

SPS-5   SPS-6

SPS-5. "CHARTER MEMBER SOUPY SALES SOCIETY" 3.5" black, white and red pinback button circa 1960. **$12.**

SPS-6. "SOUPY SALES" FIRST EDITION FAN MAGAZINE. Volume 1, Number 1 issue from Fall, 1965 with 68 pages. 8.5x11" with full color close-up photos on the covers and many black and white photos inside. **$30.**

SPACE: 1999

Syndicated 1974 – 1976 (48 Episodes)

English-produced science-fiction series about the dwellers in a lunar space colony known as Moonbase Alpha, who are thrown into outer space as the result of a nuclear explosion on the moon. The cast starred the real-life husband and wife team of Martin Landau as Commander John Koenig and Barbara Bain as Dr. Helena Russell. Items normally are copyrighted ATV Corp.

SPA-1

SPA-1. "SPACE: 1999" FLAT STEEL LUNCH BOX by King-Seeley Thermos ©1976. **$25.**

SPA-2

SPA-2. "SPACE: 1999" COLORFORMS SET © 1976 in a 8x12x1" box with a color glossy insert depicting the interior of the Eagle I Spaceship. **$15.**

SPA-3   SPA-4

SPA-3. "SPACE: 1999 MOON CAR" ON CARD. 6.5x7.5" retail card holds 3x5x4" tall plastic moon vehicle made of yellow plastic with 3 black tires on each side accented by silver wheel covers. Two astronauts in orange outfits are positioned in the seat and each side of the vehicle has a small "Space: 1999" paper sticker. Issued by Ahi with © 1976. **$60.**

SPA-4. "SPACE:1999 MOON BASE ALPHA" BOXED PLAY-SET ©1976 by ATV Licensing Ltd. and Mattel. Set includes a large vinyl play area which opens to 18x30x11" tall forming a control room and launch monitor center. Set includes white hard plastic furniture pieces for the control room and a sheet of decals. Set comes in a 12.5x13.5x4" box. **$35.**

SPA-5   SPA-6

SPA-5. "SPACE: 1999" COLORING BOOK 8.5x11" © by Saalfield and designated #C1881. **$10.**

SPA-6. "SPACE:1999 EAGLE I" 1975 MODEL KIT by Fun Dimension in 7.5x10x4" box which features several color photos from the TV show on the sides. **$25.**

SPACE MOUSE

See The Woody Woodpecker Show

SPACE PATROL

ABC: September 11, 1950 – February 26, 1955

Futuristic science-fiction adventure series set in the 30th century starring Ed Kemmer as Commander Buzz Corry, Lyn Osborn as Cadet Happy, Ken Mayer as Major Robbie Robertson. They and other crew members were based on Earth and traveled through space to defend the United Planets Organization by means of their spaceship Terra. The series was aired on both an early evening and daily/Saturday schedule. Items normally are copyrighted Mike Moser Enterprises. Ralston cereals was the program's sponsor and issued numerous premium collectibles.

SPT-1   SPT-2

SPT-1. "OFFICIAL SPACE PATROL ROCKET LITE" issued circa early 1950s by the Ray-O-Vac Co. The 5x5x13" box pictures Commander Corry on one side with illustrations of his rocket ship on other sides of the box. The 12" long silvered metal flashlight is designed to resemble the Space Patrol rocket ship with a clear plastic nosecone that illuminates. This piece is finished off with a thin red rubber nose while at the opposite end are tailfins and rockets of blue plastic. Each fin has an "Official Space Patrol Rocket Lite" decal on one side. **$200.**

SPT-2. "SPACE PATROL COSMIC SMOKE GUN" premium from Ralston circa early 1950s. 5" long metallic green gun that will shoot puffs of powder when the trigger is pulled provided the inside rubber bladder which holds the powder has not hardened with age. **$150.**

SPT-3   SPT-4

SPT-3. "SPACE PATROL MICROSCOPE" Ralston premium circa 1950-53. 4" tall green and black plastic microscope that came with small plastic slides including one described as showing "Atomic Particles." Complete premium includes a 4x8" instruction sheet and a 1.25x3x4" mailing carton. **$250.**

SPT-4. "NEPTUNE" RALSTON PREMIUM TRADING CARD from a set of 40 issued circa early 1950s by Ralston Wheat Chex and Rice Chex. Cards are 2.25x3.5" with color pictures on the front and text on the reverse. **EACH CARD $15.**

SPT-5   SPT-6

SPT-5. "SPACE PATROL MAGIC SPACE PICTURE" CARD from a set of 24 issued by Ralston cereals circa early 1950s. Each 3x4.5" black and white paper card features an optical illusion image. **EACH CARD $25.**

SPT-6. "SPACE PATROL COSMIC RAYN (sic) PROTECTOR." Clear plastic bag holds a mostly red and yellow 5.5x6.5" paper label along with a silvered gray and red hood-like plastic rain hat with "Space Patrol Commander" inscription on the forehead section above a 3x5" clear plastic viewing window. The item was licensed by Space Patrol Enterprises and made by Marketon Co., Los Angeles. Early 1950s. **$150.**

SPT-7

SPT-7. "SPACE PATROL WALKIE-TALKIE SPACE-A-PHONES" from 1952 in a box with a return address of "Space Patrol Toys." The sides and back of the 4x7.5x1" box depict an interplanetary space travel scene. Each 4.5" tall red and white plastic phone unit has a small plastic antenna and the set includes a long red string wrapped around a small board. **$150.**

SPT-8

SPT-8. "SPACE PATROL COMMANDER" HELMET. Early 1950s 21" diameter by 11" tall clear hard plastic helmet with a blue plastic inflatable piece that fits over the neck, shoulders and back. There is a 5x6.5" window cut out from the front and back of the helmet and on the forehead there is a colorful decal with illustrations of planets and spaceships. **$400.**

SPIDER-MAN

ABC: September 9, 1967 – September 6, 1970

Animated series based on character that first appeared in Marvel Comics in 1962. A similar version with a succession of titles was introduced by NBC in the early 1980s. Items from either version normally are copyrighted Marvel Comics.

| SPD-1 | SPD-2 | SPD-3 |

SPD-1. SPIDER-MAN 8" JOINTED HARD PLASTIC FIGURE with soft vinyl head. The figure has traditional red and blue costume and is marked on the reverse Mego Corp. 1974. **$30.**

SPD-2. "THE AMAZING SPIDER-MAN" 1966 Aurora model kit in 5x13x2" colorful box. **$150.**

SPD-3. "THE AMAZING SPIDER-MAN" HARD PLASTIC FIGURAL BANK 11" tall by Renzi with © 1979 Marvel Comics Group. Spider-Man is done in traditional colors while the background is in green designed like a spider web. **$25.**

SPD-4

SPD-4. "THE AMAZING SPIDER-MAN SUPER-HERO WATCH" by Dabs ©1977 Marvel Comic Group. The 1.25" diameter watch has a gold metal case with full color Spider-Man picture on the dial against a bright yellow background. Watch comes with a warranty leaflet in a 1x2.25x6.25" red plastic display case held in a colorful cardboard sleeve. **$125.**

| SPD-5 | SPD-6 |

SPD-5. "THE AMAZING SPIDER-MAN GAME WITH THE FANTASTIC FOUR!" 1977 Milton Bradley game in a 9.5x16x1.5" box that includes a playing board, travel cards and villain cards. **$12.**

SPD-6. "THE AMAZING SPIDER-MAN ADVENTURE SET" © 1974 by Colorforms with an 8x12x1" box containing a cardboard back drop of a city with die-cut vinyl pieces to form figures of Spider-Man and his enemy, the Vulture. **$12.**

STAR TREK

NBC: September 8, 1966 – September 2, 1969

Science-fiction series with great popularity during original run as well as later syndication in the 1970s. An animated cartoon version, also titled Star Trek, featuring the voices of the original cast, was aired by NBC from September 8, 1973 – August 30, 1975. Starred in the original cast were William Shatner as Captain James Kirk, Leonard Nimoy as Officer Spock, DeForest Kelley as Dr. Leonard "Bones" McCoy, James Doohan as Chief Engineer Montgomery (Scotty) Scott, Nichelle Nichols as Lt. Uhura, George Takei as Mr. Sulu, Walter Koenig as Ensign Chekov, plus other crew members. All traveled from one space adventure to another in the 22nd century starship U.S.S. Enterprise. Items normally are copyrighted Paramount Pictures Corp.

| STR-1 | STR-2 |

STR-1. "STAR TREK GAME" 1977 boxed board game by Ideal Toys. Box is 10x19.5x2" and contains a playing board, plastic markers, single die, deck of 40 fuel cards and 4 mission cards. **$75.**

STR-2. "STAR TREK" 6.5" tall litho metal thermos © 1968 by Aladdin. Thermos came with the following lunch box **STR-3.** **$75.**

STR-3

STR-3. "STAR TREK" DOME STEEL LUNCH BOX © 1968 by Paramount Pictures and produced by Aladdin. Item **STR-2** came with this box. **$350.**

STR-4   **STR-5**

STR-9   STR-10   STR-11

STR-4. "STAR TREK NUMBERED PENCIL AND PAINT SET" ©
1967 by Hasbro. Colorful 11x15x1" box contains eight colored pencils,
eight water color paint tablets and twelve pre-sketch pictures to color
and paint. **$75.**

STR-5. "STAR TREK" VIEW-MASTER REELS ©1968 depicting
the adventure "Omega Glory." Set of 3 reels plus 16-page story booklet all in 4.5" square package. **$15.**

STR-6

STR-7

STR-9. "STAR TREK ALIENS" ACTION FIGURE © 1975 by
Mego Corp. with an 8" jointed plastic action figure under a clear plastic
blister on a full color 8.5x9" retail dislay card. This item is a figure of "The
Keeper" who has a light blue body clothed in a white fabric gown
trimmed in orange. **$150.**

STR-10. "NEPTUNIAN" STAR TREK ALIEN FIGURE from
same series as **STR-9.** This figure is in green with yellow accents on
the head. The clothing is designed to depict black skin scales and figure
wears a red vest. **$150.**

STR-11. "CHERON" STAR TREK ALIEN FIGURE from the
same series as **STR-9.** One-half of the body is designed in black while
the other half is in white and the figure wears a matching outfit. **$150.**

STR-12   STR-13   STR-14

STR-6. "STAR TREK TRACER GUN" 8x11" retail blister pack
containing 6.5" long green hard plastic gun with brown handle and
small red plastic jet disks. By Grand Toys ©1966. **$30.**

STR-7. "STAR TREK PHASER GUN" 8x11x2.5" colorful box that
holds an 8" long black plastic gun with silver Star Trek logo on the side.
The gun comes with three beam disks and makes a battery operated
phaser sound. Top of the gun has a secret compartment. By Remco ©
1975. **$40.**

STR-12. "ANDORIAN: STAR TREK ALIEN FIGURE from same
series as **STR-9.** The head is light blue with white hair and horns plus
tiny red eyes. Outfit is silver stretch fabric with tan buckskin vinyl jacket,
gloves and boots. **$150.**

STR-13. "THE GORN" STAR TREK ALIEN FIGURE from same
series as **STR-9.** Figure has beast-like head in brown plus brown
hands. Outfit is brown fabric with black knee boots and a maroon vest.
Figure wears a gun belt with small red space gun. **$150.**

STR-14. "TALOS" STAR TREK ALIEN FIGURE from same
series as **STR-9.** Figure has fleshtone body parts with an enlarged
head. Outfit is yellow fabric trimmed with a black belt and collar plus red
boots. **$150.**

STR-8

STR-8. "STAR TREK U.S.S. ENTERPRISE" MEGO PLAY SET
©1975. Cardboard carrying case with a handle on the top and clear
plastic film covering used with the 8" Mego Star Trek Action Figures.
When closed, the case is 10x16x10" tall and it opens to 32" wide by 10"
tall depicting a replica of the U.S.S. Enterprise control room.The play
set features a spin-action transporter for moving the figures back and
forth into space and the set came with loose items which include the
captain's chair, navigation console, two crew seats and three cardboard telescreen cards. **$50.**

STR-15   STR-16

STR-15. "STAR TREK SOFT POSABLE FIGURE" by Knickerbocker ©1979. Display box holds 12" tall cloth doll with nicely-molded and colored vinyl head depicting Captain Kirk. The uniform is in blue and white with gold trim and a Star Trek symbol on the chest. The figure has 'mitt' hands with small velcro spots on the palms to hold the arms in different posable positions. **$25.**

STR-16. "STAR TREK SOFT POSABLE FIGURE" same as item **STR-15** but this is Mr. Spock. **$25.**

| STR-17 | STR-18 |

STR-17. "DINKY/U.S.S. ENTERPRISE" 4.5x9x3" tall die cast metal and plastic replica ©1976. Bottom of the ship has two hatch doors which open and a small plastic spaceship can be removed. The set includes five plastic disks which are placed in the top of the ship and then a metal crank can be turned to fire the disks. **$75.**

STR-18. "STAR TREK THE MOTION PICTURE" FLAT STEEL LUNCH BOX WITH PLASTIC THERMOS by King-Seeley Thermos © 1979. **LUNCH BOX $20. THERMOS $10.**

STARSKY & HUTCH

ABC: September 3, 1975 – August 21, 1979

Police action series featuring a pair of undercover officers, Detective Dave Starsky (Paul Michael Glaser) and Detective Ken "Hutch" Hutchinson (David Soul). Supporting cast members were Bernie Hamilton as Capt. Harold Dobey and Antonio Fargas as Huggy Bear, a street informant. Items normally are copyrighted Spelling-Goldberg Productions.

| STH-1 | STH-2 | STH-3 |

STH-1. "STARSKY & HUTCH" 7.25x10.25" soft cover 36-page adventure book ©1977 with the imprint "Golden All-Star Book." **$8.**

STH-2. "STARSKY & HUTCH .357 MAGNUM" WATER PISTOL ©1976 by Fleetwood Toys. The 6.5" long black plastic water pistol has no inscriptions but the header card on the clear plastic bag has a color photo of the co-stars. **$15.**

STH-3. "STARSKY & HUTCH 9MM AUTOMATIC" WATER PISTOL. From same series as item **STH-2. $15.**

| STH-4 | STH-5 |

STH-4. "STARSKY & HUTCH/DOBEY" FIGURE 8x9" display card holding 8" tall plastic posable figure with soft vinyl head ©1976 by Mego. Figure is in a blue suit with brown shoes. **$15.**

STH-5. "STARSKY & HUTCH/HUGGY BEAR" FIGURE. From same series as **STH-4.** Figure is dressed in a blue jean jacket with blue pants, red and white scarf and black shoes. **$15.**

STEVE CANYON

NBC: September 13, 1958 – September 8, 1959

Air Force adventure series based on character created by cartoonist Milton Caniff in 1948, starring Dean Fredericks as Lt. Col. Canyon, a command pilot and trouble shooter based at Big Thunder Air Force Base. The series was aired in summer reruns, also by NBC, in 1960. Items are copyrighted Field Enterprises Inc.

| STV-1 | STV-2 | STV-3 |

STV-1. "MEET STEVE CANYON – NBC-TV" full color photographic 21x22" advertising poster for Chesterfield cigarettes. Close-up portrait of Canyon in his Air Force helmet with a pack of Chesterfields in his hand as four jets streak through the sky in the background. Circa 1950s. **$50.**

STV-2. "STEVE CANYON" LITTLE GOLDEN BOOK ©1959 by Golden Press. 6.5x8" with 24 pages. **$5.**

STV-3. "STEVE CANYON'S INTERCEPTOR STATION" PUNCH-OUT BOOK circa late 1950s by Golden Press. The book's four 7.5x13" thin cardboard pages have punch-out parts for assembling Air Force building, character pieces, large jet fighter, jeep, ground crew vehicles, headquarters shack, etc. **$50.**

STV-4   STV-5

STV-4. STEVE CANYON MASK AND COSTUME. Circa 1959 set by Halco in 9x11x3" box containing 8.5x9" thin molded plastic mask depicting Canyon along with a synthetic fabric costume designed like a jump suit with bright yellow/black depictions printed on the front of parachute gear. **$20.**

STV-5. "STEVE CANYON" 10x20" boxed board game ©1959 by Lowell Toys. Included are gameboard, instruction booklet, 4 cardboard instrument panels and 4 plastic jet plane playing pieces. **$35.**

STV-6

STV-6. "STEVE CANYON" FLAT STEEL LUNCH BOX ©1959 by Aladdin with matching 6.5" steel thermos. The inside box lid has black/white printed pictures of various jets with brief descriptions of each Air Force command group's duties. **LUNCH BOX $150. THERMOS $50.**

STINGRAY

Syndicated 1965

English-produced puppet adventure show utilizing the Super Marionation process developed by Gerry and Sylvia Anderson. The series featured a futuristic submarine, Stingray, and its commander puppet Troy Tempest plus various villain puppets. Items normally are copyrighted A.P. Films Ltd. and ITC Ltd.

STG-1   STG-2

STG-1. "STINGRAY GAME/THE UNDERWATER GAME" © 1966 by Transogram with 9x17" box containing colorful playing board along with a plastic maze overlay, four cardboard Stingrays, and a set of playing cards. **$150.**

STG-2. "STINGRAY FRAME TRAY PUZZLE" © 1965 by Whitman. Cardboard puzzle 11x14" featuring Troy Tempest in a flying space vehicle with the Stingray sub below him. **$30.**

STG-3   STG-4   STG-5

STG-3. "TROY TEMPEST" ©1966 Lakeside Toys 9" tall hand puppet with cloth body and soft vinyl head. Body is mostly gray with red lettering and red and yellow accents. Face is fleshtone with color details and the hat is gray and yellow. **$30.**

STG-4. "AQUAPHIBIAN" HAND PUPPET from the same series as **STG-3.** Cloth body is green and blue with blue lettering. The head is green with black eyes and mouth. **$30.**

STG-5. "X2-ZERO" HAND PUPPET from the same series as **STG-3.** Body is yellow, blue and green with green lettering. The face is blue with black hair and eyebrows and red lips. **$30.**

SUPER CIRCUS

ABC: January 16, 1949 – June 3, 1956

Children's circus variety show produced from ABC's Chicago station, WBKB (now WLS-TV). The show host was ringmaster Claude Kirchner assisted by baton leader and band mistress Mary Hartline plus clowns Scampy, Cliffy and Nicky. In 1955, the show moved to New York City with Jerry Colonna replacing as ringmaster and Sandy Wirth replacing as baton twirler.

SRC-1   SRC-2   SRC-3

SRC-1. "SUPER CIRCUS" Whitman 11.5x15" frame tray puzzle ©1954. Pictured are ringmaster Claude Kirchner, his assistant Mary Hartline and the clowns Cliffy, Scampy and Nicky. **$15.**

SRC-2. "WEATHER-BIRD SHOES" 7x8.5" premium photo circa 1950 picturing Claude Kirchner with a facsimile signature. The company emblem appears on the bottom corners of the photo. **$15.**

SRC-3. "MARY HARTLINE" 7.5" tall premium hand puppet from Three Musketeers candy. The fabric hand cover is in brown with a facsimile signature and the head is soft rubber. The puppet originally came with an instruction sheet in a mailing box, circa 1950. **$30.**

SRC-4   SRC-5

SRC-4. "SUPER CIRCUS" Volume 1, Number 1 Weather-Bird Shoes premium comic from January 1951. The book is 7.25x10.25" with 52 full color pages. **$15.**

SRC-5. SUPER CIRCUS IRON-ON TRANSFERS. Four different tissue premium transfer sheets, each with a 3.5x4" illustration of the characters, their names and the inscription "Weather-Bird Weatherized Shoes." Circa 1951. **$20.**

SUPERCAR

Syndicated 1961

English-produced marionette series developed by Gerry and Sylvia Anderson featuring character Mike Mercury and his multipurpose vehicle, Supercar. One of the earliest series developed by the Andersons who later refined the Super Marionation technique. Items normally are copyrighted A.P. Films Ltd.

SPC-1   SPC-2

SPC-1. "SUPERCAR TO THE RESCUE GAME" BOXED BOARD GAME © 1962 Milton Bradley with a 16x16" playing board featuring adventure scenes and several views of the Supercar in action. **$60.**

SPC-2. "SUPERCAR" 1962 Little Golden Book 6.5x8" with 24 pages. **$10.**

SPC-3

SPC-3. "MIKE MERCURY IN SUPERCAR" PRINTING KIT in 2.5x3.5" box © 1962 by Tillman Toy. Package contains materials for developing film negatives on magic paper either by sunlight or artificial light to produce a small "Sun-Eze"print. **$15.**

SUPERMAN
See The Adventures Of Superman

SYLVESTER AND TWEETY
CBS: September 11, 1976 – September 3, 1977

Animated cartoon series featuring adversary cat and canary which began their own series in the fall of 1976, although they made many earlier appearances on other cartoon series. Items normally are copyrighted Warner Bros. Productions.

SYL-1   SYL-2   SYL-3

SYL-1. "SYLVESTER THE CAT" 9x12" sheet music with black/white illustration of dark blue cover © 1955 M. Witmark & Sons, N.Y. **$15.**

SYL-2. SYLVESTER THE CAT CEL. 3x5" painted image on 10.5x12.5" animation cel circa 1963-65. **$100.**

SYL-3. TWEETY CEL. 2x5" image on 10.5x12.5" animation cel circa 1963-65. **$100.**

SYL-4   SYL-5   SYL-6

SYL-4. SYLVESTER AND TWEETY COMIC BOOK COVER ORIGINAL ART. 11x12" stiff white paper sheet with black ink art work that was used for the cover of Gold Key Comics issue No. 42 circa early 1970s. **$30.**

SYL-5. "I'M TWEETY PIE" 6" tall rubber squeeze toy by Oak circa 1950. The box is designed like a bird cage with an illustration of Sylvester on the reverse. **$25.**

SYL-6. TWEETY PLASTIC FIGURE designed to slip over the top of a plastic "Soaky" bubble bath container. The figure is in soft vinyl and depicts Tweety perched on a molded tree stump. The figure is 8.5" tall but when mounted on the bottle the height is 11.5" tall. Circa late 1960s-early 1970s. **$20.**

TALES OF THE TEXAS RANGERS

CBS: September 3, 1955 – May 25, 1957
ABC: December 22, 1958 – May 25, 1959

Western adventure series which was loosely an actual historical account of the Texas Rangers over the past century. The era of adventure varied from week to week from the mid-1850s to contemporary Texas, although the same co-stars of Willard Parker as Ranger Jace Pearson and Harry Lauter as Ranger Clay Morgan remained the same in each episode with crime-fighting techniques displayed from the particular time period. The series was aired Saturday morning by CBS and moved to prime time on ABC. Items normally are copyrighted Screen Gems Inc.

TTR-1   TTR-2

TTR-1. "TO MY DEPUTY PAL – JACE PEARSON" FACSIMILE INSCRIPTION at the top of a 5x7" semi-glossy black/white photo fan card circa mid-1950s. **$15.**

TTR-2. "TALES OF THE TEXAS RANGER/DEPUTY" 2.5x3.75" blue and white member's identity card with member's description on the front and the "Ranger Oath" on the reverse. Card has a facsimile Jace Pearson signature and comes with a 2.25" five-pointed silver finished tin star badge inscribed "Texas Ranger Deputy." Circa mid-1950s premium from unknown sponsor. **PAIR $30.**

TTR-3

TTR-3. "JACE PEARSON'S TALES OF THE TEXAS RANGERS" BOARD GAME in 8.5x16.5" box ©1956 by All-Fair. **$25.**

TALES OF WELLS FARGO

NBC: March 18, 1957 – September 8, 1962

Western adventure series starring Dale Robertson as Jim Hardie, an agent for the 19th century stage transport company of Wells Fargo. Items normally are copyrighted Overland Productions.

TWF-1   TWF-2   TWF-3

TWF-1. "TALES OF WELLS FARGO COMIC ALBUM" first issue of a 7x10" English published book printed circa 1955 with 96 black/white comic strip pages. **$15.**

TWF-2. "DALE ROBERTSON/TALES OF WELLS FARGO" 3.75x5" silver/red fabric patch with peel-off cardboard backing. Issued by the TV sponsor and dated "Buick '59." **$15.**

TWF-3. "TALES OF WELLS FARGO" 45-RPM GOLDEN RECORD in 7" square sleeve. Songs are by the Sandpipers with Mitch Miller & Orchestra. Circa 1957. **$10.**

TWF-4   TWF-5

TWF-4. "TALES OF WELLS FARGO PAINT BY NUMBER" 13x16.5" boxed water color set ©1959 by Transogram. Set came with about 10 picture sheets as well as water color paints. **$40.**

TWF-5. "WELLS FARGO GAME" ©1959 by Milton Bradley with 9.5x19" box containing gameboard plus die-cut miniature metal cowboy figures. **$35.**

TWF-6   TWF-7   TWF-8

TWF-6. JIM HARDIE AND HORSE HARTLAND FIGURE. Full size figure from the Hartland series depicting western TV show stars. The horse is in brown with white feet and Hardie is in a dark tan jacket with blue trousers. Accessories include saddle, hat and six-gun. **$100.**

TWF-7. "SPECIAL AGENT JIM HARDIE" SMALL SIZE HARTLAND FIGURE AND HORSE on original 7x11.5" retail card with plastic blister. Hardie's outfit is orange with a brown hat and the horse is solid brown. From 1960. **$100.**

TWF-8. JIM HARDIE 8" tall Hartland figure from the Gunfighter Series with a dark tan jacket and dark blue trousers. The figure has movable arms and comes with a gun and hat, although the hat should be black rather than white as shown in the illustration. **$100.**

TWF-9   TWF-10

TWF-9. "WELLS FARGO" ©1959 Whitman set of three boxed 9x12" jigsaw puzzles. Puzzle scenes depict a Wells Fargo robbery attempt. **$25.**

TWF-10. "TALES OF WELLS FARGO" circa 1950s gun and holster set by Esquire in 10x13x3" box. The two 10" long nickel-plated guns use roll caps and have plastic grips. The holsters are nicely embossed leather each with a "Wells Fargo" imprint and the cartridge belt contains 18 silver colored bullets. **$200.**

| TWF-11 | TWF-12 |

TWF-11. "TALES OF WELLS FARGO" DOUBLE BARREL SHOTGUN ©1959 by Marx Toys. The plastic and metal gun is 36" long with breakdown barrel action and a chamber to hold a roll of caps. The stock has a yellow/red/brown "Tales Of Wells Fargo" illustrated sticker and the front of the trigger housing has dog and bird hunting scenes. The original carton has black and red illustrations along with a black/white photo portrait of Dale Robertson. **$125.**

TWF-12. "WELLS FARGO" ENGLISH-ISSUED GUN AND HOLSTER SET on card with ©1960 Overland Productions imprint. 11.5x14.5" display card holds black leather holster with "Wells Fargo" imprint plus a cartridge belt. Belt has white plastic clip with four silver plastic bullets. The 9" silvered white metal cap gun uses roll caps. Each side of the gun is marked "Lone Star" and "Cisco Kid" appears on each side of the barrel although this is the original issue gun for the set. Gun grips are black plastic with raised depictions of a horse's head. **$125.**

TWF-13

TWF-14

TWF-13. "DALE ROBERTSON/TALES OF WELLS FARGO" 3.5" button in black/white with an orange background in an unopened 4x6" plastic bag with a header card marked "Top Western TV Stars" © 1959. **$35.**

TWF-14. "TALES OF WELLS FARGO/WELLS FARGO AGENT" 2" white metal badge in black and silver on 3.5x4" red,white and blue card. Circa 1958. **$20.**

TARZAN

NBC: September 8, 1966 – September 13, 1968

Jungle hero adventure series based on durable fiction character first created circa 1915 by Edgar Rice Burroughs. The original television version was live action starring Ron Ely in the title role. Other versions, all in animation, later appeared on CBS under various titles from 1976 through the early 1980s. Items normally are copyrighted Edgar Rice Burroughs Inc.

| TZN-1 | TZN-2 |

TZN-3

TZN-1. "TARZAN" ©1967 Aurora model kit in 5x13" box. **$175.**

TZN-2. "TARZAN COLORING BOOK" 8x11" by Whitman © 1966 with full color photo front and back covers. **$50.**

TZN-3. "TARZAN" FLAT STEEL LUNCH BOX by Aladdin © 1966 Banner Productions Inc. **$60.**

| TZN-4 | TZN-5 | TZN-6 |

TZN-4. "TARZAN CARTOON KIT" © 1966 Colorforms set in 8x12" box with cardboard insert featuring a jungle scene to be used with the small vinyl die-cut pieces to form various pictures. **$30.**

TZN-5. "TARZAN/KING OF THE JUNGLE" © 1967 figures by Aurora on 11x15.25" retail display card. The 9 figures under a clear blister are Tarzan, chimpanzee, serpent, gorilla, tiger, lion, ibex-like goat, zebra and crocodile. Figures are nicely detailed in a solid tan color with the figure of Tarzan 3" tall and the others to the proper scale. **$65.**

TZN-6. "TARZAN/LORD OF THE JUNGLE POSTER ART" KIT ©1977 by Avalon Industries. Retail 12x17" package contains six felt tip markers plus three black/white action scene poster sheets to be colored. Packaging includes three smaller copies of the posters in full color as examples. **$10.**

TZN-7   TZN-8

TZN-7. "TARZAN TO THE RESCUE" © 1977 Milton Bradley board game in 9.5x19" box with gameboard depicting a colorful jungle scene. $20.

TZN-8. "TARZAN PAINT 'N WEAR" KIT ©1976 by Avalon with 8x9" box that holds two reusable iron-on transfers. Each colorful transfer features Tarzan. $10.

TELEVISION COMMERCIAL CHARACTERS

A variety of character figures have been developed by television program sponsors to attract and maintain viewer identification with the advertised product. Several such characters represent collectible items.

TCC-1   TCC-2

TCC-1. "BUD MAN" 17" tall soft foam rubber figure with thin blue plastic cape. Figure is in traditional red/blue uniform colors with a Budweiser sticker on the bow tie plus sticker lettering on the chest. The cape also has a portrait sticker. Circa early 1970s. $40.

TCC-2. "BUD MAN/BUDWEISER" pair of two different 6.5" tall hard plastic mugs in red/blue on white circa 1970. EACH $10.

TCC-3. "CAMPBELL KIDS" SALT AND PEPPER SET. Brightly colored plastic figures each 4.5" tall issued circa 1950s and marked on the reverse "Permission Of Campbell's Soup Company." $20.

TCC-4. "CHARLIE THE TUNA" ELECTRIC LAMP © 1970 by Star-Kist. The 9" tall painted plaster figure is in shades of blue accented by an orange cap which has his name on the bill. The lampshade is textured white cardboard trimmed in light blue. $40.

TCC-5   TCC-6

TCC-5. CHARLIE THE TUNA 10" tall hard plastic film viewer © 1971 by Star-Kist. Viewer requires a battery for operation. $25.

TCC-6. CHARLIE THE TUNA 7" vinyl squeeze figure © 1973 Star-Kist. Figure was issued with either a removable or non-removable hat. $25.

TCC-7   TCC-8

TCC-7. "SORRY CHARLIE" ACTUAL BATHROOM WEIGHT SCALE ©1972 by Star-Kist Foods. Scales are a 13" oval by 1.5" deep with a colorful depiction of Charlie on the vinyl covering. $40.

TCC-8. "SORRY CHARLIE" WRIST WATCH WITH CASE. Colorful watch has gold colored case with dial showing Charlie in metallic blues on a silver background depicted next to a barbed fish hook. Watch is ©1971 by Star-Kist Foods and comes in a 1x2x5" pink plastic display case with gold lettering on the lid. $75.

TCC-3   TCC-4   TCC-9   TCC-10   TCC-11

TCC-9. "SORRY CHARLIE" ALARM CLOCK ©1969 made by the Lux Time Div. of Robertshaw Controls Co. Clock is 4" in diameter and 6" tall with a brass case and blue/orange/red image of Charlie. **$40.**

TCC-10. COL. SANDERS 7" tall painted composition bobbing head figure depicting the Colonel holding a bucket of chicken in one hand with his cane in the other. Circa 1960s with a tiny silver foil sticker under the base. **$75.**

TCC-11. COL. SANDERS BANK. Hollow hard plastic figural bank 12.5" tall inscribed on the front "Col. Harland Sanders/Kentucky Fried Chicken." Reverse has a coin slot but there is no coin trap as made. Circa 1960s. **$30.**

| TCC-12 | TCC-13 | TCC-14 |

TCC-12. HUMBLE TIGER BANK. 8.5" tall hard plastic bank in orange and tan depicting the character first introduced in 1962 by the Humble Oil & Refining Company. The tiger was revived about ten years later when the Exxon name was introduced. Coin slot is on the reverse and there is a plastic trap under the base. **$12.**

TCC-13. KRAFT TELEVISION CAMERAMAN. 4x4" black and yellow plastic premium toy that served to introduce the popular 1950s Kraft Television Theater. **$50.**

TCC-14. "MARKY MAYPO" 9.5" tall hollow soft vinyl squeaker figure depicting the trademark character of Maypo Cereal circa 1960s-1970s. Figure is in blue outfit and red hat with other color accents. **$40.**

| TCC-15 | TCC-16 |

TCC-15. "OSCAR MAYER-ALL MEAT WIENERS" colorful 3x10x3.5" tall plastic "Wienermobile" with a die-cut plastic figure of Little Oscar who pops up and down through a slot in the top as the toy is pushed along. A recent re-issue of this toy does not have the moving figure. **$100.**

TCC-16. PILLSBURY DOUGH BOY FIGURES. Set of white soft vinyl squeeze figures with light blue eye accents. Larger figure is 7.25" tall and the figures are ©1971-1972 on the reverse. **$25.**

| TCC-17 | TCC-18 |

TCC-17. QUAKER CEREALS PREMIUM MILK PITCHER. 3.5" tall colorful plastic pitcher in the shape of the Quaker man's head circa 1950s. **$20.**

TCC-18. RICE KRISPIES' FIGURE SET. Set of three soft vinyl squeaker figures circa 1960s representing the characters Snap!, Crackle! and Pop! Each figure is about 8" tall and finished in colorful outfit with the appropriate name on the cap. **SET $120.**

| TCC-19 | TCC-20 | TCC-21 |

TCC-19. "SPEEDY ALKA-SELTZER" 5.5" soft rubber figure from the 1960s designed as a coin bank with a slot in the top of the hat although there is no trap. **$100.**

TCC-20. SPROUT ADVERTISING FIGURE. 6" tall soft vinyl figure depicting the youthful counterpart of the jolly Green Giant circa 1970s. Figure is in two shades of green and has a movable head. **$12.**

TCC-21. "TEDDY SNOW CROP" 8" tall hand puppet with soft white plush fabric hand cover and molded rubber face. This trademark character represented a frozen foods line by Snow Crop circa 1950s. The chest has a fabric label with his name and a copyright "CF," probably Consolidated Foods. **$35.**

| TCC-22 | TCC-23 | TCC-24 |

TCC-22. "KELLOGG'S" LIGHTLY EMBOSSED STEEL LUNCH BOX by Aladdin ©1969. Cereals advertised include Sugar Frosted Flakes, Rice Krispies, Corn Flakes, Sugar Smacks, Puffa Puffa Rice, Froot Loops and Apple Jacks. **$75.**

TCC-23. "TRIX" CEREAL CHARACTER ALARM CLOCK circa 1970s. 4" diameter metal wind-up clock with bright brass bell ringers mounted on the top. Dial depicts the "Trix" rabbit who was constantly denied the cereal because "Trix Are For Kids." **$50.**

TCC-24. "TRIX" 9" tall soft vinyl squeaker figure with movable head depicting the General Mills advertising character circa 1970s. Figure is solid white with colorful facial accents. **$25.**

TELEVISION SET FIGURALS

The basic square or rectangular shape of a television set prompted novelty manufacturers, particularly in the 1950s, to create miniature TV replica pieces serving as banks, planters, salt & pepper sets, film viewers, etc.

| TSF-1 | TSF-2 | TSF-3 |

TSF-1. "TELEVISION BANK" circa 1950 litho tin bank 4x5.5x2" deep. Colorful design features a young girl in the screen area flanked by two soldiers. The bank is by Television Toys, Inc. **$50.**

TSF-2. "BEST WISHES – BETTY FURNESS" 3x3x5" tall plastic flower planter designed as a "Westinghouse" television. The planter is in black and gold with a black/white photo under plastic on the front of the screen with four movable metal legs below that can be swiveled. Circa 1950s. **$30.**

TSF-3. JACK BENNY SAVINGS BANK. 4x5x5" tall tan hard plastic bank shaped like a TV set but really designed as a combination safe. The center dial with a 1.25" paper color photo of Benny is attached to a long spindle core which fits into the face of the bank and the core has maze-like patterns which are part of the dialing combination. Circa 1950s. **$75.**

| TSF-4 | TSF-5 | TSF-6 |

TSF-4. TV ADVERTISING BANK. 2.5x2.5x2.75" deep ivory-colored plastic bank with bright full color paper picture of a bathing beauty on the screen. Below is the inscription "Your TV Bank" while the top surface has the imprint of a local TV dealer. Circa 1950s. **$25.**

TSF-5. "EMERSON ULTRA-WAVE TELEVISION" BANK WITH BOX. The 4x2.5x2.5" tall marbled mahogany colored plastic bank has a black/white insert photo of a clown on the screen. This original photo could be removed and replaced by a personal photo. Circa early 1950s. **$40.**

TSF-6. TV SET REPLICA TOY by Ideal Toys. 2x3.75x3.5" dark mahogany plastic replica of a floor model television set with small die-cut screen area. Below the screen is a knob to change the pictures and six different scenes may be viewed showing a cowboy, puppet show, boxing match, circus scene, ice skater and an island dancer. Circa early 1950s. **$75.**

| TSF-7 | TSF-8 |

TSF-7. "YOUTH ON THE MARCH" TV BANK. 2.25" diameter by 3" tall cylinder bank with a paper label around the side. The label advertises the "Youth On The March" religious Sunday evening TV show which ran from 1949-1952. The green and white label has browntone illustrations of two television sets, one picturing the Rev. Percy Crawford, although he is not identified as such. The other set pictures a lady who may be Mrs. Crawford. The label includes the cost of each week's TV and radio time and "Please Place Bank On Top Of Your Radio Or Television Set And Pass It Around While The Program Is In Progress." **$30.**

TSF-8. "BEST WISHES FROM ART LINKLETTER/ MINIATURE TV SALT & PEPPER SET" 1.5x3.5x3" tall in white plastic trimmed with gold. Front of the set has a small on/off knob which is turned to elevate the salt and pepper sections which are housed in the right side of the TV set. The photo of Linkletter is removable so a more personal photo can be inserted. Circa early 1950s. **$25.**

TSF-9

TSF-9. "EXCEL TOY TELEVISION" 11x11.5x9.75" tall bright red plastic 16mm film projector designed like a TV set. The unit has an 8" diagonal screen framed in white plastic with black plastic "picture" and "sound" knobs below the screen. Inside is a 16mm projector and the instruction sheet lists films including the Three Stooges, Krazy Kat, Our Gang, Buck Jones and others. **$75.**

TSF-10

TSF-10. "HOLLYWOOD TOY TELEVISION" 6x7x9.5" deep red plastic film viewer with a 5" diagonal screen. The set comes with eight filmstrips, including three in color, each with about 28 frames. The set is electrically powered and a viewing light is turned on with a knob on the front. Two of the color films feature Gene Autry and the third features Woody Woodpecker. The black/white films feature Gene Autry, Super-Duper Duck (2), Woody Woodpecker and Andy Panda. Circa 1950s. **$75.**

TEXACO STAR THEATER

See The Milton Berle Show

THUNDERBIRDS

Syndicated 1966

English-produced puppet adventure series about the Tracy family of a worldwide International Rescue organization. The series utilized the Super Marionation process developed by Gerry & Sylvia Anderson. Items normally are copyrighted A.P. Films Ltd.

| THN-1 | THN-2 |

THN-1. "THUNDERBIRDS JIGSAW PUZZLE" in 8.25x11" box © 1966 by Whitman Publishing Company with 100 pieces. **$20.**

THN-2. "THUNDERBIRDS" ©1967 Parker Brothers 9x18" boxed board game. Our illustration shows the box lid plus a photo detail from one corner of the 18x18" gameboard which is mostly designed as a global map surrounded by rocketship game route squares. Game parts include miniature metal Thunderbird planes plus character playing cards, small wood disks and dice. **$35.**

| THN-3 | THN-4 |

THN-3. "THUNDERBIRDS GAME" 8x15.5" boxed board game © 1965 A.P. Films Ltd. The board is a colorful map of the world and other parts include a direction finder, four Thunderbird spaceships, a figure of "the Hood," eight Hood cards, nine red alarm markers, and a die. **$35.**

THN-4. "THUNDERBIRDS" GUN © 1965 and made by the English Company "Lone Star." Retail card is 6x9" and the space pistol is 8.5" in red plastic with a small blue plastic front sight. The gun fires a spring-loaded dart. **$50.**

| THN-5 |

THN-5. "THUNDERBIRDS 2 & 4" BOXED DINKY TOYS ©1966. The replica of the Thunderbird 2 is 4x5.5x1.5" tall standing on four 1" plastic stilts. This ship is green with red plastic afterburner jets. At the center of the ship is a detachable metal hanger pod with a ramp door that opens. Inside is a tiny miniature yellow plastic replica of Thunderbird 4. **$65.**

| THN-6 |

THN-6. "LADY PENELOPE'S FAB 1" FRICTION CAR made in Hong Kong for J. Rosenthal Toys Ltd. circa 1960s. The car is 3.5x10.5x2.5" tall with the body in solid pink with silver plastic grille and trim. Lady Penelope figure sits in the seat behind chauffeur's seat which holds figure of Parker and both are under a clear plastic canopy. Two guns are ejected from the front of the car by pushing a button. Car has a friction mechanism and develops a nice whirring sound when pushed. **$150.**

| THN-7 |

THN-7. "LADY PENELOPE'S FAB 1" circa 1966 diecast metal car 2x6x1.5" tall by Dinky Toys, England. Car is finished in deep pink with silver grille and trim plus tiny diamond-like headlights. The radiator opens to fire a forward rocket and the rear of the car is designed to fire four harpoons. A clear plastic canopy opens and inside are figures of Lady Penelope and Parker, her chauffeur. **$75.**

THE TIME TUNNEL

ABC: September 9, 1966 – September 1, 1967

Science-fiction series about a pair of research scientists who find themselved trapped in their own time tunnel experiment, causing them to move forward and backward in history to participate in historic or futuristic events. Starred were James Darren as Dr. Tony Newman and Robert Colbert as Dr. Doug Phillips. Items normally are copyrighted Kent Productions Inc. and 20th Century-Fox TV Inc.

| TTT-1 | TTT-2 | TTT-3 |

TTT-1. "THE TIME TUNNEL" ©1966 Saalfield book designated #9561 measuring 8.25x11". **$25.**

TTT-2. "TIME TUNNEL ADVENTURE #2/TIMESLIP!" 1967 paperback book published by Pyramid Books with a story by Murray Leinster. Book is 4.25x7" with 144 pages. **$15.**

TTT-3. "THE TIME TUNNEL" VIEW-MASTER PACKAGE containing three reels and a 16-page story booklet. Circa 1967. **$40.**

TDY-3

TTT-4   TTT-5

TTT-4. "THE TIME TUNNEL" 1966 BOXED BOARD GAME by Ideal Toys. Playing board design depicts characters and events from the prehistoric era into the future. The box insert has a spinner board and other parts include playing cards, tokens and marker disks. **$40.**

TTT-5. "THE TIME TUNNEL SPIN-TO-WIN" 10x15.5" boxed board game by Pressman Toys from 1967. Game features a box insert playing board which has a target-like design representing different past years in history and plastic tops are spun on the playing board to determine "Time Travels." **$50.**

TDY-3. "J. FRED MUGGS" DOLL WITH BOX AND TAG. 14" tall stuffed cloth doll with molded rubber head and hands and artificial brown hair. He wears a brightly striped shirt plus bright yellow trousers. The doll is by Ideal Toys and the tag has his name on both sides plus "Famous Chimp Featured On NBC 'Today' Show." The doll comes in a 6x8x10" tall box which has a colorful chimp and bamboo cane design and the box is designed so that it can be cut and folded to form a chair for the doll. The tag is marked "Copyright 1955 J. Fred Muggs Enterprises." **$60.**

TODAY

NBC: January 14, 1952 – Present

Network television's first early morning program made famous originally by Dave Garroway. The chimpanzee, J. Fred Muggs, appeared for four years regularly on the show and became an immensely popular animal celebrity. Items normally are copyrighted National Broadcasting Co. Inc.

TDY-4

TDY-4. "DAVE GARROWAY'S GAME OF POSSESSION" 18.5x18.5" gameboard from the 1950s. Board was presumably boxed and with other playing accessories but this is the only part of the game we have come across. **$20.**

TOM AND JERRY

CBS: September 25, 1965 – September 17, 1972

Animated cartoon series based on cat and mouse characters created by William Hanna and Joseph Barbera in the 1940s for MGM Studios. The characters came to television in 1965 with several network and title changes following in later years. Items normally have either copyright of Hanna-Barbera Productions or MGM cartoons.

TDY-1   TDY-2

TDY-1. "TODAY WITH DAVE GARROWAY" 12.5x17.5" boxed game by the Athletic Products Co. of South Bend, Indiana. Game features a beautifully designed full colorTV studio layout with a 3-D backdrop that serves as the gameboard. The set comes with a control panel with a circuit indicator as well as time control tones, flip cards, and miniature metal TV cameras. There are at least two versions of the game and the earliest one has a battery operated control panel but on the later version this device must be operated manually. **$125.**

TDY-2. "J. FRED MUGGS" 9" tall hand puppet with a cloth body and soft rubber molded head. **$15.**

TAJ-1   TAJ-2

TAJ-1. "TOM AND JERRY GO KART WITH FRICTION DRIVE" 3.5x6x4" tall colorful plastic toy©1973 by Louis Marx. Toy depicts Tom in the driver's seat with Jerry seated behind him holding a pistol to the back of Tom's head. **$50.**

TAJ-2. "TOM AND JERRY SCOOTER WITH FRICTION DRIVE" 3x4.5x4" tall hard plastic friction toy © 1973 by Louis Marx. **$50.**

TAJ-3   TAJ-4

TAJ-3. TOM AND JERRY ENGLISH-MADE WHITE CHINA MUG 3.25" tall by Staffordshire Potteries with 1970 © and full color picture of Jerry swinging a mallet as Tom sets a mouse trap. Reverse has color picture of Tom's head. **$20.**

TAJ-4. "TOM AND JERRY" PORCELAIN CHINA FIGURES © 1973 by George Wade & Son Ltd., England. The figure of Tom is 3.75" tall and he is depicted leaning on a tree stump. The figure of Jerry is 2" tall and he stands on a light green colored base. Figures are in a 4.5x5x1.5" deep styrofoam holder with a colorful die-cut cardboard slip case. **$40.**

TOM CORBETT, SPACE CADET

CBS: October 2, 1950 – September 26, 1952

ABC: January 1, 1951 – September 26, 1952

NBC: July 7, 1951 – September 8, 1951 and December 11, 1954 – June 25, 1955

Dumont: August 29, 1953 – May 22, 1954

Early space adventure series, one of the few shows to appear on all four original commercial networks, and one of the few to appear on different networks simultaneously. The series was set during the 24th century at the Space Academy for Training of Solar Guards. Frankie Thomas starred in the title role. Fellow cadets were Jan Merlin as Roger Manning and Jack Grimes as T. J. Thistle. Other characters were Edward Bryce as Captain Strong and Al Markim as Astro, a crew member from Venus aboard the Academy's training ship, the Polaris. Items normally are copyrighted Rockhill Productions.

TCS-1   TCS-2   TCS-3

TCS-1. TOM CORBETT 1950s PREMIUM FAN CARD. 3.5x5.5" black/white glossy photo card with facsimile signature in white "Spaceman's Luck/Tom Corbett Space Cadet." From Kellogg's cereals with a blank reverse. **$20.**

TCS-2. "TOM CORBETT SPACE CADET SONG & MARCH" 78-rpm yellow plastic record in 7x7.5" colorful record sleeve with lyrics on the reverse to the Space Cadet theme song as well as four photos from the television show. From 1951. **$20.**

TCS-3. TOM CORBETT SPACE CADET GIRL'S COSTUME. Gray cloth top and skirt with a blue and yellow polka dot pattern around the neck and cuff areas. On a yellow felt section around the chest and back area is a red and blue Tom Corbett Space Cadet logo. The costume comes with a gray cloth hat trimmed in yellow. **$75.**

TCS-4

TCS-4. "OFFICIAL TOM CORBETT SPACE ACADEMY SET" by Louis Marx. Set is No. 7012 and includes many plastic and litho tin pieces in a 14x23x4.5" deep tan cardboard box with a blue illustration. **$400.**

TCS-5

TCS-6   TCS-7

TCS-5. "TOM CORBETT SPACE CADET BREAD AND LABEL ALBUM 1" 7.5x8" stiff paper folder ©1952 which opens to 8x22.5" with spaces for mounting a numbered set of 24 bread labels featuring Tom Corbett designs. This album has the imprint of "Koester's Bread" but most likely there were additional sponsors who marked the album with their imprints. **EACH LABEL $5. ALBUM ONLY $40.**

TCS-6. "TOM CORBETT SPACE CADET" FLAT STEEL LUNCH BOX in red (or blue) metal with full color picture on one side. By Aladdin © 1952. **$75.**

TCS-7. "TOM CORBETT SPACE CADET" 6.5" tall litho metal thermos by Aladdin that came with item **TCS-6. $40.**

TCS-8

TCS-8. "TOM CORBETT SPACE CADET" FLAT STEEL LUNCH BOX ©1954 by Aladdin. This box was issued with a thermos the same as **TCS-7**, although in the later issue the thermos has a yellow cup rather than a red cup. **LUNCH BOX $100. THERMOS $40.**

TCS-9

TCS-9. "TOM CORBETT SPACE CADET ATOMIC PISTOL FLASHLIGHT" by Louis Marx in 2.5x5.5x7.5" red, white, blue and yellow box. The red plastic flashlight gun is 8" long and comes with lenses to turn the light red or green. **$90.**

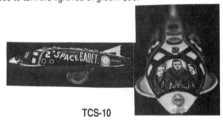

TCS-10

TCS-10. "TOM CORBETT SPACE CADET/POLARIS" 3.5x12.5x3.5" tall litho tin wind-up rocket ship by Louis Marx. Under the tail fin is a holder for a piece of flint that makes sparks as the toy moves. **$400.**

THE TONIGHT SHOW

NBC: September 27, 1954 – Present

Long-running talk and variety show that has undergone numerous transformations over the years. The most famous hosts include Steve Allen, Ernie Kovacs, Jack Paar and Johnny Carson. Items related to the show normally are copyrighted National Broadcasting Co. Inc.

TTS-1

TTS-2

TTS-1. "GOO-GOO STEVE ALLEN – STAR OF NBC-TV TO-NIGHT" 6.5" tall yellow balloon with inscription and sketch of Steve in blue. Circa mid-1950s. **$10.**

TTS-2. "BEECH-NUT GUM PRESENTS JACK PAAR" 5" tall stiff cardboard container used to give away samples of gum in grocery stores. Container has three black/white illustrations of Jack Paar and lettering is in red and yellow. 1950s. **$20.**

TTS-3

TTS-4

TTS-3. "CHARLEY WEAVER'S LETTERS FROM MAMA" 1959 book by Cliff Arquette with an introduction by Jack Paar. The book is 6x9" with 64 pages and black/white/red dust jacket. **$15.**

TTS-4. "JOHNNY CARSON" 8x10" pencil tablet circa 1960s with full color photo on a blue background decorated with silver stars. **$10.**

TOP CAT

ABC: September 27, 1961 – September 26, 1962

Animated cartoon show which originally appeared in prime time followed by Saturday morning airings on ABC from October 6, 1962 – March 30, 1963. The show also appeared in 1965-1966 on NBC and was then syndicated. The series featured a crafty street cat, with a Sgt. Bilko-type personality, and his gang which continually outwitted the local beat policeman, Officer Dribble. Items normally are copyrighted Hanna-Barbera Productions.

TOP-1

TOP-2

TOP-3

TOP-1. "TOP CAT" 10" tall vinyl container which held "Soaky" bubble bath by Colgate-Palmolive circa mid-1960s. Figure is mostly bright yellow with red and black accents. **$20.**

TOP-2. "TOP CAT TV-TINYKINS" ©1961 by Louis Marx. Small plastic figure is under a clear plastic bubble on a colorful 3.5x5.5" retail display card. **$35.**

TOP-3. "TOP CAT TV SCENES" ©1961 figure by Louis Marx in a 3x3.25x1" deep cardboard box designed like a TV set. Plastic pieces include a figure of Top Cat, a board fence and a "No Parking" sign. The background design is of a room with a lighted pool table. **$40.**

| TOP-4 | TOP-5 | TOP-6 |

TOP-4. "TOP CAT VIEWMARX MICRO-VIEWER" ©1963 small plastic house 2.5x3.25x1.5" deep by Louis Marx. House has a push button underneath and a viewing lens on the back so that eight different full color Top Cat cartoon scenes can be viewed. **$25.**

TOP-5. "TOP CAT" first issue Volume 1, Number 1 comic book from Charlton Comics November, 1970. **$20.**

TOP-6. "TOP CAT" ©1962 set of three View-Master reels with a story booklet. Reels are numbered B5131-5133 with titles "Medal For Meddling/Zoo Operation/No Cat Fishing." **$20.**

TOPO GIGIO

See The Ed Sullivan Show

THE TWILIGHT ZONE

CBS: October 2, 1959 – September 5, 1965

Science-fiction anthology series created, hosted and narrated by Rod Serling. Each episode was usually noted for its eerie or ironic twist of fate at the story's conclusion. Items are normally copyrighted CBS Television Inc.

| TWZ-1 | TWZ-2 |

TWZ-1. "ROD SERLING'S THE TWILIGHT ZONE" 7.5x10.25" hardcover Grossett & Dunlap book with 208 pages from 1963. The book has "13 New Stories From The Supernatural Especially Written For Young People." Our illustration shows the dust jacket plus the detail photo of Serling from the rear flap. **$20.**

TWZ-2. "ROD SERLING HOSTS 'TWILIGHT ZONE'". Cover photo on an issue of "TV Time" from June 6, 1965. Weekly magazine is 5.5x8.5" with 16 pages and this particular copy was a giveaway from a Madison, Wisconsin pharmacy. **$10.**

TWZ-3

TWZ-4

TWZ-3. "THE TWILIGHT ZONE" 10x19.5" boxed board game © 1964 by Ideal. Object of the game is to be the first player to move his marker "Along The Road To Reality Through The Twilight Zone" to his destination. **$75.**

TWZ-4. "THE TWILIGHT ZONE" 3.25x6.5" full color 16-page comic marked "No. 1" ©1977. **$15.**

UNDERDOG

NBC: October 3, 1964 – September 3, 1966

Weekend cartoon series which moved to CBS from September 10, 1966 – September 1, 1968 and then back to NBC for the years 1968-1973. Featured was a sometimes bumbling super hero canine who emerged from his disguise as a humble shoe shine boy to fight crime in Washington, D.C. or around the world or out in space as required. The voice of Underdog was by Wally Cox, the star of television's "Mr. Peepers" show. Items normally are copyrighted Leonardo Productions.

| UND-1 | UND-2 |

UND-1. "UNDERDOG GAME" © 1964 8.5x16.5" boxed board game by Milton Bradley with a playing board depicting characters Underdog, Shoe Shine, Simon Barsinister, Riff Raff, and Sweet Polly. Game also includes four playing pieces, 24 cards and a die. **$35.**

UND-2. "UNDERDOG" German-made 3x3" octagonal plastic wind-up alarm clock circa 1970s. **$60.**

UND-3   UND-4

UTH-3

UND-3. "UNDERDOG" 8.5x10.5" boxed 100-piece jigsaw puzzle ©1975 by Whitman. **$20.**

UND-4. "UNDERDOG DOT FUNNIES" KIT ©1974 by Whitman. Box is 9x11.5" containing 8 comic strip adventures with a total of 64 pictures to be finished by following the dots and then colored with the enclosed crayons. **$20.**

UTH-3. "ELIOT NESS AND THE UNTOUCHABLES" 10x19" boxed board game ©1961 by Transogram. Our illustration shows the box lid and a detail from the center of the 19x19" gameboard. Game also includes 120 playing tiles, 24 plastic gun markers and 24 gun cards. **$60.**

THE UNTOUCHABLES

ABC: October 15, 1959 – September 10, 1963

Crime drama show based on the actual deeds of 1930s Treasury agent Eliot Ness and his assistants, known as "The Untouchables." The show was set in the crime-ridden Chicago of the era and Ness was portrayed by Robert Stack. The series was narrated by long-time news personality Walter Winchell. Items normally are copyrighted Desilu or Langford Productions.

UTH-4   UTH-5

UTH-4. "THE UNTOUCHABLES PLAY SET" by Louis Marx © 1961. The 14x26x3" deep box is in shades of blue/white/orange. A complete set includes a large thin plastic layout sheet, two litho tin friction cars by Line Mar, two sections of tin buildings, marked character figures of Eliot Ness and Al Capone plus many additional accessories. **$1,500.**

UTH-5. "THE UNTOUCHABLES" 6x6.5" waxed paper wrapper from a gum package issued by Leaf Brands in 1962. Wrapper is in blue/white/pink/yellow colors with a premium offer on the margin for a personalized I.D. bracelet. **$35.**

UTH-1   UTH-2

UTH-6   UTH-7

UTH-1. ROBERT STACK FAN PHOTO. 5x7" glossy black and white photo of Stack portraying the character Eliot Ness. Circa early 1960s with facsimile signature in blue. **$10.**

UTH-2. "THE OFFICIAL UNTOUCHABLES MECHANICAL ARCADE" TARGET GAME by Louis Marx circa early 1960s. Target set consists of 13.5" long tapered clear hard plastic dome over a litho tin target area that features a wind-up rotating disk depicting a gangster car and gangster's head. In the opposite end of the toy is a 6" long black plastic pistol that fires small metal ball bearings at the target. The toy comes with a pair of thin wire supports. The box is 5x7.5x21" long with black/white/green/orange designs including a photo of Robert Stack. **$150.**

UTH-6. "THE OFFICIAL UNTOUCHABLES DETECTIVE SET" circa 1961 in an open 15.5x18.5x2" deep cardboard display frame. The set holds a 6" long snub nose cap revolver, vinyl holster, belt with 16 bullets and 1.75" badge on a 2x5" I.D. wallet. **$150.**

UTH-7. "ELIOT NESS AND THE UNTOUCHABLES SAWED OFF SHOTGUN" on 9x24" black/white/yellow cardboard picturing Robert Stack. The gun is sealed under plastic and the package contains two red plastic and two green plastic shotgun shells along with bullets. The gun is intended to shoot both bullets and water from both barrels. Undated but made by Transogram and ©by Desilu. **$200.**

THE VIRGINIAN

NBC: September 19, 1962 – September 8, 1971

Western adventure series, the first to be experimentally produced on a 90-minute episode basis, set on the Shiloh Ranch in Wyoming during the late 19th century. The series was continued on NBC during 1970-1971 under the title "The Men From Shiloh." Featured were James Drury in the title role, Doug McClure as Trampas and Lee J. Cobb as Judge Henry Garth. Items normally are copyrighted Universal Artists Inc. or MCA Enterprises.

VIR-1   VIR-2

VIR-1. "THE VIRGINIAN GAME" by Transogram © 1962 in 10x19.5" box. Game includes instructions, gameboard, reward money and cardboard stand-up figures as markers. **$50.**

VIR-2. "THE VIRGINIAN" MOVIE VIEWER on 5.5x7.5" retail card with plastic blister holding a hand viewer and two boxed films based on the TV series. Set is © 1966 by Chemtoy. **$25.**

VOYAGE TO THE BOTTOM OF THE SEA

ABC: September 14, 1964 – September 15, 1968

Science-fiction series about the underwater adventures aboard the Seaview, a research submarine under the command ot Admiral Harriman Nelson (Richard Basehart). The adventures included many with alien life forms or creatures in the depths of the oceans. Items normally are copyrighted Cambridge Productions Inc. or 20th Century-Fox Films.

VBS-1   VBS-2

VBS-1. "TV GUIDE" Voyage To The Bottom Of The Sea cover photo and article. Issue from June 19, 1965 with cover photo of star Richard Basehart with 4-page article about his transition from being a Shakespearean actor to starring in a TV role. **$8.**

VBS-2. "VOYAGE TO THE BOTTOM OF THE SEA SUBMARINE SCOUT SET" © 1965 by Remco Industries in 6x20.5x11" tall box. Set consists of 6.5" long hard plastic mini-sled and a 9.5" sea crawler. The sled is yellow with a clear plastic dome over a pair of small metallic blue plastic men. The sea crawler is yellow and metallic blue plastic holding two blue metallic men and a silver control panel. Each item has a "Mini-Sled" or "Sea Crawler" sticker on the side and the set includes a small metallic blue treasure chest. **$75.**

VBS-3   VBS-4

VBS-3. "VOYAGE TO THE BOTTOM OF THE SEA" 8.5x16.5" boxed board game © 1964 by Milton Bradley with a gameboard, spinner board, and cardboard disk playing pieces. **$25.**

VBS-4. VOYAGE TO THE BOTTOM OF THE SEA CAST PHOTO. 3.5x5.5" full color fan card featuring cast members with facsimile signatures on the reverse of Richard Basehart, David Hedison, Terry Becker, Allan Hunt and Bob Dowdell. **$10.**

WAGON TRAIN

NBC: September 18, 1957 – September 12, 1962
ABC: September 19, 1962 – September 5, 1965

Western series relating the adventures of a wagon caravan traveling from Missouri to California under the leadership of wagonmaster Major Seth Adams (Ward Bond) and his scout Flint McCullough (Robert Horton). Following Bond's death in 1960, his character was replaced by a new wagonmaster, Chris Hale (John McIntire). Items normally are copyrighted Revue Productions Inc.

WGT-1   WGT-2   WGT-3

WGT-1. "WAGON TRAIN COLORING BOOK" 8.5x11" by Whitman Publishing Co. © 1960. **$15.**

WGT-2. MAJOR SETH ADAMS OF WAGON TRAIN LARGE FIGURE by Hartland Plastics circa 1960s. Figure of the character portrayed by Ward Bond wears a dark red shirt, gray vest, tan trousers and black hat, gloves and boots. Other accessories include a saddle, gun and coiled rope. **$100.**

WGT-3. "WAGON TRAIN" 3.5" button with black/white photo of co-stars Robert Horton and Ward Bond on a light blue background. Button comes in clear plastic 4x6" bag with "Top Western TV Stars" cardboard label © 1959. **$35.**

WGT-4   WGT-5

WGT-4. "WAGON TRAIN" HEAVY GLAZED PORCELAIN ASH TRAY marked on the reverse "Wade Porcelain, Made In England, Copyright 1960 By Revue Studios." The heavy oval ashtray is 5" across with the coloring in various shades of brown. The rim is decorated with Indian designs and wagon trains appear at the center behind the portrait of "Seth Adams." **$25.**

WGT-5. "WAGON TRAIN GUN AND HOLSTER SET" © 1958 by Leslie-Henry Co. 9x14.5x2" deep black/white/ brown/yellow box pictures stars Robert Horton and Ward Bond. The silvered white metal guns are inscribed "Marshal" and have white plastic grips with black ovals at the center depicting raised four-leaf clovers. The guns have a small cover that swings back to reveal a cylinder that accepts six cap-firing metal bullets; however, no such bullets came with the set we've illustrated although there are six plastic bullets that fit into and look original to the holders on the back of the holster belt. The holsters have floral tooling in shades of brown on the high quality leather and each holster is inscribed "Wagon Train." **$200.**

WGT-6   WGT-7

WGT-6. "WAGON TRAIN COMPLETE WESTERN COWBOY OUTFIT"SET by Leslie-Henry in a 27" long box that is 8" on one side and 12" on the other. The box lid pictures Bond and Horton and the set contains a "Genuine Leather Gun And Holster Set And 50 Shot Repeater 'Flip' Rifle." The gun is in a brown and white leather holster with 3 wooden bullets and a belt. The rifle is made of brown and silver plastic and the set also contains a pair of metal spurs. **$200.**

WGT-7. "OFFICIAL WAGON TRAIN PLAY SET" in a 13x24 x4" deep beige box with brown and green illustrations by Marx Toys. The set is marked "No. 4788-Series 2000." The set includes character figures of Major Seth Adams and Flint McCullough along with bags of 54mm cavalry, frontiersmen and Indians along with many additional accessories. **$600.**

WGT-8   WGT-9

WGT-8. "WAGON TRAIN GAME" © 1960 Milton Bradley in 8.5x16.5" box. Game includes playing board and marker pieces. **$25.**

WGT-9. "WAGON TRAIN" FLAT STEEL LUNCH BOX ©1964 by King-Seeley Thermos. Box comes with a 7" tall litho metal thermos depicting a "Chuck Wagon." **LUNCH BOX $100. THERMOS $40.**

WALLY GATOR

Syndicated 1963

Animated cartoon series featuring a zoo alligator and his perpetual quest for freedom from his cage. Items normally are copyrighted Hanna-Barbera Productions.

WAL-1

WAL-2

WAL-1. "WALLY GATOR GAME" ©1962 by Transogram with 9x17.5" box containing gameboard, cardboard spinner, plus a large "Detecto-Fun" spinner wheel. **$30.**

WAL-2. "WALLY GATOR COLORING BOOK" 8x11" published by Whitman with © both 1959 and 1962. **$20.**

WAL-3   WAL-4

WAL-3. HANNA-BARBERA CHARACTER THERMOS. 8" tall litho steel thermos depicting Wally Gator, Touche Turtle and Lippy The Lion. Thermos is by Universal and came with its 1962 "Cartoon Zoo" lunch box. **$40.**

WAL-4. WALLY GATOR CEL ON BACKGROUND. 10.5x12.5" poster sheet with original painted sky background in light blue with gray stylized clouds. The overlay cel is the same size with the figure of Wally 3x3". Circa 1963. **$100.**

WALT DISNEY

See Disneyland, The Mickey Mouse Club, Walt Disney's Wonderful World Of Color, Zorro

WALT DISNEY'S WONDERFUL WORLD OF COLOR

NBC: September 24, 1961 – September 7, 1969

A switch from ABC to NBC allowed Disney to broadcast in color. The premiere show on NBC introduced Professor Ludwig von Drake. The show was re-titled three times and ended September 24, 1983. Items normally are copyrighted Walt Disney Productions.

WWW-1   WWW-2

WWW-1. "WALT DISNEY'S WONDERFUL WORLD OF COLOR" 12x17" litho tin tray © 1961 showing Disney characters watching Ludwig von Drake on a television set. **$35.**

WWW-2. LUDWIG VON DRAKE 8" rubber squeeze toy by Dell circa 1961. **$25.**

WWW-3   WWW-4

WWW-3. "WALT DISNEY'S PROFESSOR LUDWIG VON DRAKE" 3x6" boxed set by Marx Toys containing 2.5" tall plastic figure of Ludwig along with plastic animals, ivory tusks, several heads and a Buddha. The set is captioned "A Nearsighted Professor." **$75.**

WWW-4. "COURTESY OF YOUR RCA VICTOR DEALER" red and white cardboard container holding a pair of 3.5" tall white china mugs with raised color figures of Donald Duck and Ludwig von Drake. Set is circa 1961. **EACH MUG $15. PACKAGED SET $50.**

WWW-5   WWW-6

WWW-5. "WALT DISNEY'S WONDERFUL WORLD OF COLOR GAME" ©1961 by Whitman with a box lid depicting Ludwig von Drake coming through a television screen to make a move on the gameboard surrounded by other Disney characters. The game has a thin cardboard 15x22" gameboard and there are 4 die-cut frames designed like a front of a television set. There are also colorful stiff cardboard pieces picturing many different Disney characters and there is a large spinner. **$25.**

WWW-6. "PROFESSOR LUDWIG VON DRAKE PRESENTS WALT DISNEY'S WONDERFUL WORLD OF COLOR – A GAME BASED ON THE TV PROGRAM" ©1962 by Parker Brothers. 9x17" box holds a board, spinner, 28 cards, 4 small plastic ducks and a large die-cut figure of Ludwig. **$25.**

THE WALTONS

CBS: September 14, 1972 – August 20, 1981

Drama based on the Depression-era Walton family in the Blue Ridge Mountains of Virginia. The series had an extensive cast headed by Ralph Waite as John Walton, Michael Learned as his wife Olivia, Will Geer and Ellen Corby as Grandpa and Grandma Walton and Richard Thomas as John Boy Walton, to be replaced in 1979 by Robert Wightman. Items are normally copyrighted Lorimar Productions.

WLT-1   WLT-2

WLT-1. "THE WALTONS" diecast metal 1.5x3x2" tall replica of the family's vintage pickup truck on a 5x7" retail display card marked "road stars" © 1975. The truck is finished in dark green with black running boards and wheels plus a silver grille. **$20.**

WLT-2. "THE WALTONS PLAYSET" © 1974 by AMSCO of Milton Bradley. Box is 13.5x20x1.5" deep and set contains die-cut fiberboard pieces for assembly of the Walton home along with family members, truck, seesaw, porch swing and rocking chair. **$60.**

WLT-3   WLT-4

WLT-3. "THE WALTONS GAME" ©1974 by Milton Bradley with 9.5x19" box containing a gameboard and box insert, both with full color cast member illustrations. **$15.**

WLT-4. "THE WALTONS" EMBOSSED STEEL LUNCH BOX © 1973 by Aladdin. Box comes with a 6.5" tall plastic thermos. **LUNCH BOX $20. THERMOS $10.**

WANTED: DEAD OR ALIVE

CBS: September 6, 1958 – March 29, 1961

Western adventure series starring Steve McQueen as bounty hunter Josh Randall who chased down wanted individuals with his sawed-off carbine rifle referred to as his "Mare's Laig." Items are normally copyrighted Four-Star Malcolm Productions or CBS Films Inc.

WDA-1   WDA-2

WDA-1. "WANTED - DEAD OR ALIVE GAME" circa late 1950s by Lowell Toy with 9x17.5" box picturing star Steve McQueen. Game includes die-cut outlaw and Indian figures, plastic cowboys, a card deck and 17" square gameboard. McQueen is not pictured on the game pieces except for a drawing on a spinner board depicting a cowboy using a Mare's Laig gun. **$100.**

WDA-2. JOSH RANDALL FULL SIZE HARTLAND FIGURE from their circa 1960 series depicting western TV stars. The figure is depicted with an aqua shirt, gray trousers and black hat. The horse is mostly brown with a black saddle and the figure of Randall holds a Mare's Laig rifle. **$200.**

WDA-3

WDA-3. "OFFICIAL MARE'S LAIG TARGET GAME" ©1959 by Marx Toys with a 16x16" black/white/red/tan box that holds a double-barreled plastic dart rifle along with a 15x15" colorful litho tin target. Target features art work and an actual Steve McQueen photo on the far left side. **$200.**

WDA-4

WDA-5

WDA-4. "THE OFFICIAL MARE'S LAIG GUN AND HOLSTER SET" by Marx Toys in a 12x20" box that holds a 19" long plastic and metal rifle plus a plastic holster and a bag of metal and plastic bullets. There is also a plastic leg strap for the holster. **$150.**

WDA-5. "THE 'MARE'S LAIG' WESTERN RAPID FIRE RIFLE PISTOL" by Marx Toys with a 7x15" display card holding a 13.5" gun made of nicely detailed brown and black plastic with metal cocking lever. The gun fires roll caps. **$150.**

WDA-6

WDA-6. "THE 'MARE'S LAIG' WESTERN RAPID FIRE PISTOL" by Marx Toys and with a card identical to item **WDA-5** but the gun is 16" long and inscribed "Rayline 12" on one side without any Marx copyright. Also, this gun is all brown plastic with a silver plastic cocking lever and it does not fire caps. **$200.**

WDA-7

WDA-7. "THE 'MARE'S LAIG'/A MARX MINIATURE" 5.5" finely detailed metal and plastic gun on a 4x7.5" display card inscribed on the bottom edge "Collectors Series." The gun fires a single cap with shooting instructions printed on the card reverse. **$75.**

WDA-8

WDA-8. "THE PURSUER/WANTED A SHOOTING SAWED-OFF RIFLE" BOXED SET without copyright but obviously inspired by the "Wanted: Dead Or Alive" show. The brown plastic rifle is 16" long with a silver plastic cocking lever. The gun holds 6 plastic bullets and a package of 25 are included plus 18 on the holster belt. The gun features a clicker action and the cylinder moves as the trigger is pulled. The holster belt is black vinyl plastic and the holster is molded to hold the gun and allow it to be swiveled and fired without actually drawing the weapon. The display box is 8.5x17x3" deep with a clear cellophane covering. **$125.**

WELCOME BACK, KOTTER

ABC: September 9, 1975 – August 10, 1979

Realistic situation comedy about high school teacher Gabe Kotter (Gabriel Kaplan) who returns to his alma mater Buchanan High in Brooklyn to teach a tough remedial group of students known as the "Sweathogs" led by Vinnie Barbarino (John Travolta). Items normally are copyrighted Wolper Organization Inc. & Komack Co. Inc.

WEL-1   WEL-2

WEL-1. "KOTTER" STAND-UP FIGURE with clothing in 7.25x15.25" box ©1976 by Toy Factory. Box holds the figure plus two small stands to hold it upright along with five different sets of clothing and accesories which can be rubbed on and then peeled off. **$12.**

WEL-2. "WELCOME BACK KOTTER" ©1976 Colorforms set in 8x12.5" box with insert depicting school classroom scene to be used with the thin vinyl pieces to create various pictures. **$12.**

WEL-3

WEL-4

WEL-3. "WELCOME BACK, KOTTER" EMBOSSED STEEL LUNCH BOX AND PLASTIC THERMOS ©1977 by Aladdin Industries. **LUNCH BOX $20. THERMOS $10.**

WEL-4. "SWEATHOGS DREAM MACHINE" ©1976 model kit by "MPC" in 7.5x10x4" deep box. The kit is 1/25 scale and includes "Sweathogs Figures." **$25.**

WELLS FARGO

See Tales Of Wells Fargo

THE WILD, WILD WEST

CBS: September 17, 1965 – September 7, 1970

Western adventure series with a continuing fantasy twist involving a pair of undercover agents for the U.S. Government during the term of President Grant. Criminals were foiled or confused by an assortment of bizarre weapons, devices or ploys by agents James West (Robert Conrad) and Artemus Gordon (Ross Martin). Items normally are copyrighted Bruce Lansbury Productions or Columbia Broadcasting Systems Inc.

WIL-1   WIL-2   WIL-3

WIL-1. "THE WILD, WILD WEST" FIRST PRINTING PAPERBACK from January, 1966 by Signet Books. The book has 128 pages with a black/white cover photo of Robert Conrad as James West against a bright red background with yellow lettering. **$25.**

WIL-2. "TV GUIDE" issue for January 6, 1968 with cover photo of James Conrad with a 3-page article which is a tongue-in-cheek spoof of the levity of leading man Conrad as James West and the villains he faces. **$20.**

WIL-3. "TV TIMES" January 9, 1966 issue with black/white cover photo of stars Ross Martin and Robert Conrad. The magazine is 5.5x8.5" with 16 pages and these were used as giveaways by various businesses which imprinted their names on the lower portion of the front cover. **$20.**

WIL-4   WIL-5

WIL-4. "THE WILD, WILD WEST" GOLD KEY COMIC #5 from April, 1969. **$10.**

WIL-5. "THE WILD,WILD WEST" 7" tall black/white/red plastic thermos ©1969 by Aladdin. This item came with **WIL-6. $50.**

WIL-6

WIL-6. "THE WILD,WILD WEST" FLAT STEEL LUNCH BOX © 1969 by Aladdin Industries. This item came with **WIL-5. $150.**

WINKY DINK AND YOU

CBS: October 10, 1953 – April 27, 1957

Weekend children's show featuring format of cartoons and short skits, many involving the little boy character of Winky Dink. The show was hosted by Jack Barry and the televised adventures could be enhanced by viewers through use of a Winky Dink kit, available by mail, which was used to draw pictures on a plastic surface placed over the actual television screen. Items normally are copyrighted Marvel Screen Enterprises Inc. or CBS-TV.

WIN-1   WIN-2

WIN-1. "WINKY DINK AND YOU" 10x14" mailing envelope inscribed "Here It Is! Your Own Winky Dink Magic Television Kit." Set includes "Magic Window, Special Magic Crayons, Erasing Cloth." Circa mid-1950s. **$60.**

WIN-2. "WINKY DINK" LITTLE GOLDEN BOOK from 1956 with 24 pages. **$20.**

WIN-3   WIN-4

WIN-3. "WINKY DINK/WINKO MAGIC" 10x14.5x2" deep colorful boxed magic kit from the mid-1950s. The set includes an assortment of magic tricks plus a cardboard Winky Dink face mask and instruction book. **$40.**

WIN-4. "WINKY DINK AND YOU! SUPER MAGIC TV KIT" © 1968 by Standard Toy Craft in 10x15x1.5" box. Kit includes a boxed set of 8 magic crayons, plastic film cover for a TV screen and a wiping cloth. The kit also includes a large full color display board plus cards of thin plastic stick-on character pieces.**$25.**

WONDER WOMAN

ABC: December 18, 1976 – July 30, 1977
CBS: September 16, 1977 – September 11, 1979

Adventure series based on the comic book character created originally in the early 1940s. The television series starred Lynda Carter in the title role and that of her alter ego, Diana Prince. Items are normally copyrighted D.C. Comics Inc. or Warner Bros. TV.

WND-1

WND-2

WND-1. "WONDER WOMAN" BLUE VINYL LUNCH BOX with color illustration of Wonder Woman by Aladdin Industries ©1977 D.C. Comics. **$40.**

WND-2. "WONDER WOMAN" 1.5x7x2" tall blue and yellow hard plastic train car ©1977 by Tyco. Each side of car has colorful Wonder Woman illustration with the caption "Bullets vs. Bracelets" and a second caption reads "Another Car Load Of Wonder Woman D.C. Comics." **$15.**

WND-3

WND-3. "DABS SUPER HERO WATCH" with display box and cardboard sleeve. Watch is 1.25" diameter with a gold-colored metal case around a colorful dial depicting Wonder Woman on a light blue circular background. The dial numerals are in black and the watch hands are in yellow. Watch comes with a warranty leaflet in a 1x2.25x6.25" long solid blue plastic display box held in a same-size colorful cardboard sleeve. Watch is Swiss-made for "Super Time Inc." **$125.**

THE WOODY WOODPECKER SHOW

ABC: October 3, 1957 – September 25, 1958

NBC: September 12, 1970 – September 2, 1972 and September 11, 1976 – September 3, 1977

Animated cartoon show featuring brash woodpecker character created in the 1930s by Walter Lantz. Woody was featured as host and participant in the series with other segments featuring Andy Panda, Charley Bear, Gabby Gator, Space Mouse, Chilly Willy, Wally Walrus, Buzzy Buzzard, and several others. Items normally are copyrighted Walter Lantz Productions.

WDY-1   WDY-2

WDY-1. "WALTER LANTZ EASY WAY TO DRAW" © 1958 Whitman 8x11" hardcover book with 124 pages of black/white illustrated instructions for drawing various Lantz characters plus another section on action drawings and lettering. Instructions are given for drawing Woody Woodpecker, Andy Panda, Oswald The Rabbit, Wally Walrus and others. The last few pages of the book are blank for practicing and the back cover has an actual black/white photo of Lantz. **$20.**

WDY-2. "WOODY'S CAFE" ANIMATED ALARM CLOCK © 1959 by Columbia Time Products. 4.25" diameter metal case with a full color dial and animated figure of Woody depicted at the entrance to his cafe which is inside a hollow tree. Caution: In 1989 a reproduction of this clock was issued. Unfortunately, we don't have an example of the reproduction to provide a precise method of distinguishing it from the original but on the reproduction the colors on the dial are not as subtle and finely printed as on the original. **$150.**

WDY-3   WDY-4   WDY-5

WDY-3. WOODY WOODPECKER fully dimensioned 20" tall hollow plastic electrical lamp which glows softly from within when turned on. The figure is in vivid colors of red head, yellow beak and blue body with white front and neck. The eyes are white with green/black/white paper stickers representing eyeballs. The base is 6" in diameter and has a Walter Lantz ©1974. **$25.**

WDY-4. "TALKING WOODY WOODPECKER HAND PUPPET BY MATTEL" in 4.5x7x11.5" tall display carton. The puppet is ©1963 and done in white flannel with an aqua corduroy body plus a molded vinyl head. The puppet is designed so that fingers can move the beak from the inside as the voice activating string is pulled. **NOT WORKING $25. WORKING $75.**

WDY-5. "SPACE MOUSE COLORING BOOK" 8.25x10.5" book ©1962 by Saalfield. **$10.**

WDY-6

WDY-6. "SPACE MOUSE CARD GAME" by Fairchild ©1964 in 2.5x4" box with deck of 36 playing cards plus a title card and three other instruction cards for different game options. Most cards depict Space Mouse but one card in each suit pictures his girlfriend. **$20.**

WYATT EARP
See The Life And Legend Of Wyatt Earp

YAKKY DOODLE
See Yogi Bear

YOGI BEAR
Syndicated 1961 – 1963

Animated cartoon series featuring character which appeared first in 1959 on The Huckleberry Hound Show. Yogi's adventures are set in Jellystone National Park where he and his small sidekick companion Boo Boo devise ways to raid picnic baskets and create other havocs. Other segments of the series featured Snagglepuss and Yakky Doodle. Yogi and friends later appeared in a 1973-1975 ABC series titled "Yogi's Gang" and a 1978-1979 NBC spin-off series, "Yogi's Space Race." Items normally are copyrighted Hanna-Barbera Productions.

YGB-1   YGB-2   YGB-3

YGB-1. "YOGI BEAR" ©1961 "Big Golden Book" with 28 pages in a 8.5x11" hardcover. **$15.**

YGB-2. YOGI BEAR circa 1960s 9" tall figural bank by Knickerbocker with a soft vinyl body and hard plastic removable head with a coin slot on the top of the hat. The head twists off for coin removal. **$30.**

YGB-3. "YOGI BEAR" circa 1961 colorful 13.5" tall ceramic cookie jar depicting Yogi next to a sign reading "Better Than Average Cookies." The jar is mostly brown with a light yellow color on the face and Yogi wears a soft green necktie and hat. **$200.**

YGB-4   YGB-5

YGB-4. YOGI BEAR AND BOO BOO HOT WATER BOTTLE. 8x13" soft rubber hot water bottle mostly in tan with some color accents on the faces. A screw-in rubber stopper is in the top of Yogi's hat and the reverse of the bottle is marked ©1966. **$75.**

YGB-5. "YOGI BEAR" 5.5" tall painted hollow ceramic figure depicting Yogi next to a sign post that reads "Don't Feed The Bears." Unmarked but from the 1960s. **$35.**

YGB-6   YGB-7

YGB-6. "YOGI BEAR TV-TINYKINS" © 1961 by Marx Toys. Retail 3.5x5.5" card depicting Yogi's cave with an open front door that holds a small plastic figure of him under a clear plastic bubble. **$35.**

YGB-7. "YOGI BEAR TV SCENES" © 1961 by Marx Toys. 3x3.25x1" deep colorful display box holds a plastic figure of the ranger and an outdoor fireplace chimney. The background illustration depicts a forest "Camping Area." **$60.**

YGB-8   YGB-9   YGB-10

YGB-8. YOGI BEAR 19" TALL STUFFED PLUSH DOLL circa early 1960s by Knickerbocker. The body is brown plush with a gold colored felt tummy. The necktie and cap are both light blue felt and the face and hands are molded soft vinyl. **$50.**

YGB-9. CINDY BEAR © 1959 Knickerbocker stuffed plush doll 15" tall. In addition to the sewn-in fabric label there is a string-attached paper label showing a box of Kellogg's Corn Flakes with the inscription "TV" and "I Am Cindy Bear." The figure has a molded vinyl face and the plush body is brightly colored in blue, yellow and pink with a sewn ruffled and fringed net apron. **$75.**

YGB-10. BOO BOO 9.5" stuffed plush doll © 1959 by Knickerbocker. The plush is solid green with a pink felt bow tie at the neck. The face is molded vinyl and the figure has a sewn-in tag. **$35.**

YGB-11

YGB-11. "YOGI BEAR JELLYSTONE NATIONAL PARK" Marx Toys playset #4364 in a 14.5x22x4.5" deep white/ yellow/dark green box. The set includes the 8 character figures shown in our photo along with a ranger station, jeep, fence, gateway, trees, animals and many other accessories. **$400.**

YGB-12   YGB-13

YGB-12. "YOGI BEAR" unmarked circa 1960s pull toy with a 7.5" tall paper label on wood figure of Yogi positioned on a 5x8x2.5" tall wheeled frame. The front of the frame has a silvered brass bell chime and when the toy is pulled, Yogi uses wire spring drumsticks in each hand to beat on the chime. Base of the toy has color pictures of Yogi, Boo Boo, Pixie and Dixie. The wooden wheels have a bright red finish. **$400.**

YGB-13. "YOGI SCORE-A-MATIC BALL TOSS GAME WITH AUTOMATIC BALL RETURN" large boxed set © 1960 by Transogram with a 4x11x19.5" tall die-cut and formed thin hard plastic target in the image of Yogi's head. Game comes with plastic balls which are thrown into Yogi's open mouth. As the balls drop into the mouth, the score dial at the lower corner of his chest changes to indicate a new total. **$60.**

YGB-14

**YGB-14. "YOGI BEAR" FLAT STEEL LUNCH BOX AND PLAS-
TIC THERMOS** © 1974 by Aladdin Industries. **LUNCH BOX $30.
THERMOS $15.**

YGB-15   YGB-16

YGB-15. "YOGI BEAR" ©1963 wrist watch with light blue plastic
oval cylinder 2.25x3x6" long display case with a Yogi sticker label
inside the hinged lid. The 1.25" diameter silvered metal watch has a
Swiss movement and was offered by Bradley. Colorful dial depicts Yogi
walking with a hobo stick over one shoulder. **$90.**

YGB-16. YAKKY DOODLE 1.25" tall plastic figure by Marx Toys
from the early 1960s. **$10.**

  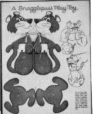

YGB-17   YGB-18

YGB-17. "SNAGGLEPUSS" circa 1960s 9" tall vinyl plastic
figural bottle from the bubble bath series by Purex Corp. Figure is
mostly pink with some facial accents in other colors and he holds a
green top hat in his hands. **$30.**

YGB-18. "SNAGGLEPUSS STICKER FUN" 10x12" Whitman
book ©1963. Book has sheets of stickers to cut out and apply to pre-
printed outlined pictures. **$25.**

YOU BET YOUR LIFE
NBC: October 5, 1950 – September 21, 1961

*Very popular game show hosted by Groucho Marx who inter-
spersed his humor throughout the quiz proceedings of each show. He
was ably assisted throughout the series by the show's regular
announcer, George Fenneman. The show was an outgrowth of a radio
program of the late 1940s and was re-introduced on a syndicated basis
by NBC in 1980 although the hosting of the new series was by Buddy
Hackett. Items normally are copyrighted National Broadcasting Co.
Inc.*

YBL-1   YBL-2

YBL-1. "TV GUIDE" issue for July 18, 1952 with cover photo of
Groucho and the article "The Truth About Groucho Marx's Ad-Libbing."
This book is Volume 5, Number 29 from the series published in the New
York City area. **$20.**

YBL-2. "TV DIGEST & GUIDE" issue for the Delaware area
March 7, 1953 with cover photo of Groucho Marx and George Fenneman with the article inside titled "Groucho's Fenneman Talks Back!"
$30.

YBL-3   YBL-4

YBL-3. "GROUCHO GOGGLES AND CIGAR" ©1955 retail card
holding a plastic cigar and a die-cut plastic face piece consisting of two
large eyeballs with black styrofoam balls that shake around inside. The
nose is flesh color and there is a hole in the black mustache to insert
the cigar. The piece is held in front of one's face by biting on a small
projection on the reverse covered with a rubber strip. Packaging
includes a tiny advertisement for the NBC show sponsored by DeSoto
Cars. **$40.**

YBL-4. "THAT'S ME – GROUCHO – 36 COCKTAIL NAPKINS"
in a 5" square black/white/orange box ©1954. Each napkin features a
Groucho cartoon in black/white with various background colors. **$30.**

YBL-5

YBL-5. "GROUCHO'S YOU BET YOUR LIFE" © 1955 Lowell
Toy Corp. game in a 12.25x18.25x1.5" deep box. Game contains cards
and playing tiles and features an insert board with a wind-up sixty-
second clock. The box lid pictures Groucho and includes the inscription
"DeSoto/Plymouth." **$100.**

YBL-6

YBL-6. "GROUCHO TV QUIZ" GAME by Pressman in a 13x18x1.5" deep box that contains a pair of Groucho spectacles, rubber cigar, mustache and eyebrows. The game has a 4" tall dimensional molded plastic figure of Groucho which rests in a center receptacle on one of the game dials, and this figure spins around to the correct answers for questions. Also included is a timer, magic word cards, and play money with Groucho's portrait. **$75.**

YOU'LL NEVER GET RICH

CBS: September 20, 1955 – September 11, 1959

Situation comedy starring Phil Silvers as a perpetual con-artist, Master Sergeant Ernie Bilko, on the military base at Fort Baxter, Kansas. Items normally are copyrighted CBS Television Enterprises.

YNG-1

YNG-2

YNG-1. "TV GUIDE" Volume 3, Number 44 from October 29, 1955 with cover photo of Phil Silvers plus a 4-page article on his new show "You'll Never Get Rich." **$10.**

YNG-2. "BILKO MARCHES" 33 1/3-RPM RECORD by Promenade from 1958 in a 12" square dust cover. Selections include "Bridge On The River Kwai, Semper Fidelis, Stars And Stripes Forever," and others. **$15.**

YNG-3

YNG-4

YNG-3. "PHIL SILVERS/SGT. BILKO...CBS TELEVISION'S YOU'LL NEVER GET RICH" circa 1955 game by Gardner Games in a 13x20x1.5" deep box. Game object is to establish a Bilko "Enterprise" and finish the game with the most money. **$50.**

YNG-4. "I'M A BILKO FAN" 1950s black/white/green stiff cardboard fan from "Amana – Sponsors Of The 'You'll Never Get Rich' Phil Silvers Show." The fan is 10x10.5" and the reverse has a picture of Bilko with the slogan "You'll Have To Wave This Fan 27,587 Times To Be As Cool As An Amana Air Conditioner Would Make You In 2 Seconds." **$20.**

ZORRO

ABC: October 10, 1957 – September 24, 1959

Popular Walt Disney series based on the fictional Spanish hero character created originally circa 1920. Guy Williams starred in the television title role. The series created a wide assortment of collectibles. Items are normally copyrighted Walt Disney Productions.

ZRR-1

ZRR-2

ZRR-3

ZRR-1. "TV JUNIOR – THE TV MAGAZINE FOR CHILDREN" September, 1958 issue (Volume 1, No. 7) with 64 pages in a 5x7.5" format. Magazine is for the Philadelphia area but may have had a wider distribution as well. Front cover features Zorro and the magazine includes an article on Cheyenne plus photos or information on many other personalities and characters such as Annette Funicello, Jack Webb, Superman, Leave It To Beaver, Lassie and others. **$35.**

ZRR-2. "ZORRO" 5x7" glossy black/white photo fan card from the Disney Studios with reverse designed as a post card. Front is inscribed "Guy Wlliams As Zorro And Don Diego In Walt Disney Studios Presentation The Sign Of Zorro." Reverse of the card has facsimile inscription "Thanks For Writing – Best Wishes Guy Williams" plus his "Z" signature. **$25.**

ZRR-3. "ZORRO" 2x3x7" tall painted china figurine with a gold foil tag, red and gold foil sticker and a 4" long metal sword. **$125.**

ZRR-4

ZRR-5

ZRR-4. "OFFICIAL WALT DISNEY'S ZORRO PLAY SET" #3758 by Marx Toys in a 15x23x5" deep white/blue/orange box. Set contains figure of Zorro, horses, litho tin building and many other accessories. **$800.**

ZRR-5. "WALT DISNEY'S ZORRO/A FUN GAME FOR ALL THE FAMILY" first issue of the game from 1958 in an 8x15.5x2" deep box. **$45.**

ZRR-6

ZRR-7

ZRR-6. "WALT DISNEY'S ZORRO GAME" © 1966 by Parker Brothers in a 9x17" box. **$30.**

ZRR-7. "ZORRO" VIEW-MASTER SET with three reels and a 12-page adventure story book. From 1958. **$35.**

ZRR-8   ZRR-9

ZRR-8. "ZORRO" FLAT STEEL LUNCH BOX by Aladdin © 1958 with a blue sky background on the box. The steel thermos has a black cup. **LUNCH BOX $80. THERMOS $35.**

ZRR-9. "ZORRO" EMBOSSED STEEL LUNCH BOX © 1966 by Aladdin with a red sky background. The steel thermos has a red cup. **LUNCH BOX $125. THERMOS $40.**

ZRR-10   ZRR-11   ZRR-12

ZRR-10. "WALT DISNEY'S ZORRO PUNCH-OUT FIGURES READY TO ASSEMBLE" 7x13" book with eight stiff cardboard sheets of punch-outs © 1958 by Pocket Books. **$50.**

ZRR-11. "WALT DISNEY'S ZORRO" LITTLE GOLDEN BOOK from 1958 with 24 pages. **$10.**

ZRR-12. "WALT DISNEY'S ZORRO AND THE SECRET PLAN" LITTLE GOLDEN BOOK from 1958. **$10.**

ZRR-13   ZRR-14   ZRR-15

ZRR-13. "WALT DISNEY'S ZORRO" 5.5x7.5" hardcover with 284 pages © 1958 by Whitman. **$12.**

ZRR-14. "WALT DISNEY'S ZORRO MAGIC SLATE - DRAWING, TRACING AND GAME." 8.5x13" black/white/pink/yellow die-cut stiff cardboard album that opens to reveal a spinner, game book and story, pencil and magic slate. Made by the Strathmore Company circa 1960. **$40.**

ZRR-15. "ZORRO" 9" tall hand puppet by Gund with a black fabric hand cloth and colorful molded rubber face. A blue plastic sword is held on one hand by small elastic straps and the figure comes with a black felt hat. **$40.**

ZRR-16   ZRR-17   ZRR-18

ZRR-16. "WALT DISNEY STUDIOS PRESENTS ZORRO OIL PAINTING BY NUMBERS" large 14x18x2" deep box with a beautiful color lid illustration by Hassenfeld Brothers circa 1960. Set contains four 10x14" black and white canvas pictures to paint. There is also a red and yellow die-cut card picturing Zorro that holds 24 small plastic paint capsules. **$50.**

ZRR-17. ZORRO PLASTIC WIND-UP made in Hong Kong © 1976. Toy is 4" long by 4" tall mostly in black plastic but with an orange saddle and some color detailing on Zorro's face, sword and cape. The horse moves along on its rather stubby legs. **$40.**

ZRR-18. "ZORRO" 3.5" black/white pinback button circa 1957. **$20.**

ZRR-19

ZRR-19. "ZORRO BEANBAG-DART GAME" 14.5x16.5x1.5" deep boxed target set circa 1960 by Gardner Toys. Set contains a pair of 14x16" targets featuring a Zorro picture design in gray/black/red on a yellow background. One target for beanbags has large die-cut circles while the second matching target to be used with rubber-tipped darts is a solid single picture. The set contains a pair of vinyl beanbags, each with a Zorro symbol printed on it, and there is a pair of plastic darts. Our example did not include a gun for shooting the darts but presumably a gun came with the set. **$90.**

ZRR-20

ZRR-20. "ZORRO ALL METAL TARGET BOARD WITH DART SHOOTING RIFLE" SET by T. Cohn, Brooklyn, circa 1960. Large 16x24x1.5" deep silver on black cardboard box holds a beautifully colored metal target showing Zorro fighting Mexicans. Set includes a 21" long black plastic rifle with a large black/white Zorro sticker on the stock. Rifle fires black plastic darts with rubber suction cups and two come with the set. Set stands up by means of a pair of cardboard easels. **$175.**

APPENDIX

TELEVISION HISTORY
A Chronology of Selected Events

1873   Discovery of selenium – a nonmetallic element first discovered in 1817 – changes electrical resistance due to intensity of light on it; several theories thus develop on sending pictures by electrical signals over a series of wires.

1875   Inventor G. R. Carey, using selenium cells, develops a single wire mechanical transmission concept. Refinements and improvements in optical and mechanical techniques are added by Shelford Bidwell and Maurice LeBlanc in the early 1880s.

1884   Paul Nipkow, a German, files a patent for the Nipkow Disk, a mechanical "scanning" device which continues to serve as the basic method of reproducing and sending pictures by wire into the next century.

1897   K. F. Braun creates a cathode ray tube as alternative to mechanical scanning.

1900   Two decades begin of intense research and development by U. S. and foreign scientists, engineers and inventors. Included are Bors Rosing, C. Francis Jenkins, John Logic Brand, Philo T. Farnsworth and Vladimer K. Zworykin – all to become credited in later years as an "inventor" of television.

1907   Word "television" appears in *Scientific American* magazine, one of earliest known appearances of the word.

1918   World War I interrupts research and development of television concepts until early 1920s revival.

1923   Iconoscope theory (first camera tube) invented by Zworkin with funding by Westinghouse, leading to the cathode ray picture tube and kinescope concepts, both patented by Zworkin in 1939.

1925   Scottish inventor Baird transmits recognizable human features by wireless television and forms his own company in 1929, later to become the British Broadcasting Company.

An early "radiovisor" developed by Jenkins sends a mechanical picture (without sound) of President Harding from Washington, D.C. to Philadelphia. Both events are perfections of the mechanical disk-scanning method.

Era wanes of disassociated inventors, as major radio companies begin television development. Public demonstrations of operating viewing systems are subsequently sponsored by AT&T (1927), General Electric (1928), RCA and Dumont (1930), Philco (1931).

1926   RCA forms National Broadcasting Company (NBC), the first major radio broadcasting network, by purchasing network facilities from AT&T. The NBC system is then divided into "Red" and "Blue" networks. The Blue Network begins January 1, 1927 and would become ABC in 1943.

1927   President Herbert Hoover and AT&T President Walter Gifford appear in first intercity telecast (both image and sound) by wire in a Washington, D.C. to New York City hookup which appeared on a 2.5" screen developed by Bell Telephone.

Columbia Broadcasting System (CBS) begins as United Independent Broadcasters merged with Columbia Phonograph and Records Co. Operations begin September 18 as the "Columbia Phonograph Broadcasting Systems," the second major network.

1928   WRNY, Coatsville, N.Y. is first station to regularly broadcast a television image.

General Electric begins first regularly scheduled programming over WGY, Schenectady, N.Y. September 11 is first TV drama, "The Queen's Messenger."

General Electric demonstrates what was probably the first home television set with a 3x4" screen.

Color motion pictures are exhibited by George Eastman, Rochester, N.Y.; RCA predicts application of color to television. RCA begins using popular cartoon comic strip character Felix the Cat statuette on a turntable for continuous experimental purposes.

1929   Bell Telephone Laboratories demonstrates color television transmission.

RCA, under David Sarnoff, begins work on all-electronic television systems.

1930   NBC projects a picture from W2XBS, its experimental television station in New York City, to a 6x8 foot downtown theater screen.

1931   NBC places a television transmitter antenna atop the tallest building in the world, New York City's Empire State Building.

1932   British Broadcasting Company (BBC), London, takes over English development of television from Baird company; BBC inaugurates television service in 1935.

1936   A coaxial transmission cable is constructed by Bell Telephone between New York City and Philadelphia.

1937   NBC introduces the first mobile television filming unit; a 1938 New York City fire is the first unscheduled news event filmed. About 20,000 television sets are in service in New York City; few elsewhere.

1938   Dumont places the first all-electronic home television set on the retail market.

1939   RCA demonstrates commercial television at New York World's Fair, announces plans to start regular network broadcasting and sale of home television sets. RCA President Sarnoff's dedication remarks at RCA Exhibit at New York World's Fair is the first scheduled news event covered by television.

President Franklin D. Roosevelt speaks from the New York World's Fair, the first head of state to appear on television.

NBC offers the first televised musical production, Gilbert & Sullivan's "Pirates Of Penzance."

Among the first televised sports events during the year are the boxing match between Max Baer and Lou Nova, a college football game between Fordham and Waynesburg State, a baseball game between Columbia and Princeton Universities, a professional baseball game between Brooklyn Dodgers and Cincinnati Reds.

1940   Color television is demonstrated by CBS in New York City.

First coverage by television of political conventions from Philadelphia (Republican) and Chicago (Democratic), first telecast of presidential election returns.

1941   On July 1, NBC begins commercial service in New York City area on WNBT (now WNBC-TV). The programs – on a spaced basis – are a Brooklyn Dodger-Philadelphia Phillie baseball game, Sunoco newscast by Lowell Thomas, a U.S.O. program, Uncle Jim's Question Bee, Fort Monmouth Signal Corps Show, Ralph Edwards' Truth or Consequences. First-day program sponsors were Bulova Watch, Lever Brothers, Proctor & Gamble (Ivory Soap). The program day began at 2:30 PM and lasted until 10:30 PM. In the following week, 19 hours of programming – 15 devoted to sports – were aired by WNBT.

Television growth is delayed for the next five years by World War II although Dumont continues commercial broadcasting. NBC also continues, but only about four hours a week, mostly for war-related home defense. At the time, 21 licensed television stations are in the United States.

Despite the War lull, more radio fan magazines begin adding the word "television" to the title.

1943   The Federal Communications Commission (FCC) orders divestiture of one of NBC's two-network "Red" and "Blue" Systems. The Blue Network is divested. It is purchased by Edward J. Noble, the maker of Life Savers Candy, resulting in the origin of the third major network, American Broadcasting Company (ABC).

1945   Federal Communications Commission allocates 13 channels as commercial television nears reality.

On V-E Day, May 8, WNBT, New York City (NBC), presents 15 hours of programming on the end of World War II in Europe.

1946   CBS sends color image from New York City to suburban Nyack.

The Milton Berle weekly series begins June 8 on NBC.

Gillette Razor Co. is first show sponsor on a network basis on telecast of Joe Louis vs. Billy Conn boxing match, June 19.

1947   An estimated 142,000 home sets are in use, quickly increasing to over one million sets the following year.

Howdy Doody show begins on NBC on December 27; other puppet shows and wrestling are also popular and common. Regular coverage of World Series begins. 1948 national election returns are first seen on mass television.

1948   Hopalong Cassidy movie films achieve great popularity on television, setting off the earliest mass retail merchandising program based on a personality, rather than a character such as Howdy Doody.

The dominant prime time shows are Milton Berle's Texaco Star Theater (NBC), Ed Sullivan's Toast of the Town, Arthur Godfrey's Talent Scouts (both CBS).

1949   First telecast of a presidential inauguration is for President Truman in January.

The first National Academy of Television Arts and Sciences award dinner is held with a single award for Best Film Made for Television, "The Necklace," on NBC's "Your Show Time." The "Emmy" award name is derived from "Immy," a nickname for the image orthicon tube.

New prime time shows include the Goldbergs, Captain Video, Life of Riley, and Kukla, Fran and Ollie. Friday and Saturday evenings are mostly boxing, wrestling, roller derby programs.

FCC begins hearings on color television standards.

1950   ABC, CBS, NBC begin Saturday morning children's market programs.

The January 27 Emmy Award winners announced for 1949, the first complete year of awards, are for the Ed Wynn Show (Best Live Show), Texaco Star Theater (Best Kinescope Show), Ed Wynn (Most Outstanding Live Personality), Milton Berle (Most Outstanding Kinescope Personality), The Life Of Riley (Best Film Made for and Viewed on Television). The awards banquet is not televised nationally, however, until 1955.

First market experiment of a pay television broadcasting system is tried in New York City.

All 156 episodes of "Cisco Kid" over the next five years are filmed in color by Ziv TV for eventual color syndication use, although stations are able to telecast them only in monochrome through the 1950s.

1951   CBS receives FCC authorization to begin color transmission, and first color broadcast is a four-hour program seen in New York City, Baltimore, Boston, Philadelphia and Washington, D.C., although few home sets are equipped to receive it. Early color television sets utilize an internal color wheel, and various devices of external nature are soon marketed with design intent of adding "color" to black-and-white sets.

President Harry Truman's address at the Japanese Peace Treaty Conference is the first coast-to-coast simultaneous black-and-white broadcast carried by 94 stations.

Groucho Marx receives "Most Outstanding Personality" Emmy Award for 1950 season.

ABC strengthens its assets and network through merger with United Paramount Theaters; the Dumont Network becomes a distant fourth in broadcasting capability.

CBS adopts its "eye" logo symbol.

1952   Presidential candidates Eisenhower and Stevenson are the first to significantly use television for campaigning.

FCC assigns 2,053 new stations across the country.

"I Love Lucy" receives "Best Situation Comedy" and "Best Comedienne" Emmy Awards for 1951 season. The first award is repeated in 1953. The show itself has the nation's top-rated viewership rating by Nielsen for the seasons of 1952-1955, 1957, with close second rating for 1956 season.

1953   Kukla, Fran & Ollie is NBC's first telecast in "Living Color" and receives "Best Children's Program" Emmy Award for 1952 season. "Dragnet" also is an Emmy awardee this year and next.

Chicago's *TV Forecast,* Philadelphia's *TV Digest,* and New York's *TV Guide* are purchased by Walter Annenberg to become the nationally distributed *TV Guide* with debut publication in April.

1954   Although Senator Kefauver Crime Hearings were telecast earlier, the Senate hearings on subversion and Communism led by Senator Joe McCarthy are the first public hearings of a prolonged nature.

1955   Dumont Network goes out of business.

President Eisenhower holds the first filmed presidential press conference January 19 in conjunction with inauguration ceremonies.

"The $64,000 Question" receives Emmy Award for "Best Audience Participation Series" and bumps "I Love Lucy" as top-viewed program for the 1955-56 season. The show is canceled in 1958 in a series of quiz show scandals.

1956   Era begins of taped, rather than live, programs.

1957   The first use of videotape on television is the west coast feed by CBS of "Douglas Edwards with the News."

"Gunsmoke" begins a four-year consecutive season run as the most-watched series according to Nielsen ratings.

1958   Contestant quiz programs "Dotto," "21," and "$64,000 Question" are canceled either in 1958 or the following year for contestant rigging.

NBC adopts its "peacock" symbol for color broadcasting.

1959   The fall season begins with about 27 westerns in prime time slots on the three networks.

1960   The Richard Nixon-John F. Kennedy presidential campaign debates are first to be televised nationally.

"The Huckleberry Hound Show" is the first TV cartoon series to win an Emmy Award.

Home television sets are now purchased nationally at a rate of 10,000 more units a day compared to 1950.

1961   Newton N. Minow, FCC Chairman, criticizes television programming as a "vast wasteland."

1962   "Wagon Train" and "Bonanza" move to first and second top-viewership ratings for 1961-1962 season by Nielsen. "Gunsmoke" drops to third.

1963   The assassination of President Kennedy is covered on all networks in an almost-continuous news coverage over four days.

"The Beverly Hillbillies" is the most-viewed 1962-63 series according to Nielsen ratings, and continues in top spot for 1963-64 season.

The 1963 season debut of "The Jetsons" is also the debut of color TV on ABC.

1964   Ed Sullivan introduces The Beatles on U.S. prime time television during his February 9 show. Nearly 44% of the nation's viewers watched.

New prime time programs include The Man from U.N.C.L.E., Bewitched, The Munsters, The Addams Family, Daniel Boone, Gomer Pyle U.S.M.C., Gilligan's Island, Flipper, The Famous Adventures of Mr. Magoo.

1965   "Bonanza" begins a consecutive three-year run as most-watched season series, according to Nielsen ratings.

"I Spy" premieres; co-star Bill Cosby is the first black in a regular drama series.

1966   By fall season, almost all network shows are broadcast in color; nearly half of all 11 million sets sold during the year are color models.

1967   The creation of the Corporation for Public Broadcasting, a non-profit public corporation to aid non-commercial television, is signed into law by President Johnson. PBS (Public Broadcasting System) results.

The first global television broadcast, "Our World," originates live from 19 countries on five continents, and is seen in 39 nations via satellite.

The first Super Bowl is telecast by both NBC and CBS; Green Bay Packers defeat Kansas City Chiefs, 35-10.

1968	"The Andy Griffith Show" is most-watched 1967-68 series according to Nielsen ratings; in the fall "Laugh-In" begins a consecutive two-year run as most-watched show for the 1968-69 and 1969-70 seasons.
	Premiere of "Julia" series, the first to feature a black woman (Diahann Carroll) in a "serious" role other than a domestic or comedienne.
1969	Television pictures are transmitted from the moon, first by unmanned craft and then by astronauts of Apollo 11 mission, with the moon landing watched by 750 million viewers around the world, the most witnessed event in history.
1970	TV sets in use throughout the world are estimated at 231 million.
1971	Cigarette advertising is banned from television effective January 1.
	The three top-viewed series for 1970-71 season, according to Nielsen ratings, are Marcus Welby, M.D., The Flip Wilson Show, Here's Lucy.
	June 6 is the last telecast of "The Ed Sullivan Show," establishing a longest-running continuous prime time record of 24 years in the same format.
1972	More color sets than black-and-white are sold.
	Beginning with the 1971-1972 season, "All In The Family," starring Carroll O'Connor as Archie Bunker, enjoys an unprecedented consecutive five-year rating as the most-watched show, according to Nielsen ratings.
	Cable television on a pay basis has first commercial try.
1975	Home Box Office (HBO) begins national daily programming by satellite.
1976	Magnavox is the first maker to offer a home television video game, "Odyssey," followed shortly by Atari games.
1980	"Who Shot J.R.?" episode of "Dallas" serial is seen by more U.S. viewers than any other television program in history with 41.5 million households tuned in.
1983	Final episode of "M*A*S*H," the Korean War medical show, has largest non-sports viewing audience ever – 125 million people or 50.2 million households.

TV FAN CLUBS AND PUBLICATIONS

The following clubs and publications requested inclusion in this book. Some have broad interests in television history while others are devoted to specific shows, personalities, characters or types of collectibles. Be sure to include a self-addressed, stamped envelope when writing for additional information.

THE ANDY GRIFFITH SHOW APPRECIATION SOCIETY Interested in "The Andy Griffith Show" TV program. Publishes "The Mayberry Gazette." Contact: John Meroney, P.O.Box 330, Clemmons, NC 27012. Phone (919) 998-2860.

BARBARA EDEN INTERNATIONAL FAN CLUB Fan club reports on current and future activities of actress Barbara Eden. Publishes "Barbara Eden International Fan Club" newsletter. Contact: Kenneth A. Bealer, 1332 North Ulster Street, Allentown, PA 18103. Phone (215) 434-2977.

BATTLESTAR ONE INTERNATIONAL (B-1) Multi-genre, including any and all fan interests. Major interest areas include science fiction, fantasy, horror, comics, action and adventure movies and TV shows. Publishes "B-Bulletin/B-1 Mini-catalog." Contact: Charlie M. Clint, President, 7716 North Fessenden St., Portland, OR 97203-1615. Phone (503) 286-5455 (before 9:30 pm PT).

DARK SHADOWS FESTIVAL Interested in "Dark Shadows" TV series. Publishes "Shadow Gram" and holds an annual convention. Contact: Jim Pierson, P. O. Box 92, Maplewood, NJ 07040. Phone (201) 433-0948.

DAVID BIRNEY INTERNATIONAL FAN CLUB Interests include all aspects of his career, personal family events, contests and advance appearances. Publishes "The Birney Bulletin." Contact: Ruth Becht, 168 N. Lehigh Ave., Cranford, NJ 07016. Phone (201) 276-6889.

THE DOCTOR'S Club members interested in Dr. Who, Star Trek, general science fiction. Publishes "The Dalekenium Compound." Contact: Joe Imholte, 506 E. 3rd St., Morris, MN 56267. Phone (612) 589-1753.

DOCTOR WHO INFORMATION NETWORK Doctor Who fan club. Publishes "Enlightenment" (bimonthly) and "Myth Makers" (Fanzine). Contact: Goeffrey Toop, Doctor Who Information Network, P.O. Box 912, Station F, Toronto, Ontario, Canada M4Y 2N9.

FANDOM DIRECTORY A comprehensive reference to fans of TV, science fiction, Star Trek, comics, films and related areas. Lists over 20,000 fans including 2,000 international. 500+ pages. Published annually. Contact: Harry A. Hopkins, Fandata Publications, 7761 Asterella Court, Springfield, VA 22152-3133. Phone (703) 644-7354.

FLAKES Interested in cereal box collecting. Publishes "FLAKE." Contact: Scott Bruce, Box 481, Cambridge, MA 02140. Phone (617) 492-5004.

GALACTIC SCHOOL-BARGE "Battlestar Galactica" club for all ages with projects geared toward children. A member of B-1. Publishes "GS-B Report." Contact: Krystina Robinson, 6451 Cowles Mt. Blvd., San Diego, CA 92119.

GOLD SQUADRON "Battlestar Galactica" squadron-format club — assume persona and do written missions. A member of B-1. Publishes "Hieroglypics." Contact: Captain Darkiri (c/o Debra A. Stansbury), 1026 W. 7th #10, Eugene, OR 97402.

HOT BOXERS Interested in lunch box collecting. Publishes "Hot Boxing." Contact: Scott Bruce, P.O. Box 481, Cambridge, MA 02140. Phone (617) 492-5004.

HOWDY DOODY MEMORABILIA COLLECTORS CLUB Interested in anything related to Howdy Doody — old or new. Publishes "The Howdy Doody Times" and holds an annual convention. Contact: Jeff Judson, 12 Everitts Hill Road, Flemington, NJ 08822. Phone (201) 782-1159.

JACK SCALIA OFFICIAL FAN CLUB Club supports Mr. Scalia in all public functions. Publishes Scalia fan letter. Contact: Tommy Lightfoot Garrett, Jr., P.O. Box 215, New Canton, VA 23123.

LARAMIE REVISITED Publication containing stories, sketches, synopsis, reviews, interviews, etc. dealing with the TV show "Laramie" and its stars John Smith and Robert Fuller. Issued quarterly, premiere issue July 1990. Contact: Marcia A. Studley, 2108 Lorenzo Lane, Sacramento, CA 95864. Phone (916) 489-1406.

LOST IN SPACE FANNISH ALLIANCE Interested in all aspects of the TV show "Lost In Space." Publishes "LISFAN," and holds semi-annual meeting. Contact: Flint Mitchell, 7331 Terri Robyn Dr., St. Louis, MO 63129-5233. Phone (314) 846-2846.

MOMENTS WITH MEREDITH Club to keep fans up to date on activities of Meredith Baxter-Birney. Publishes "Moments With Meredith." Contact: Ruth Becht, 168 N. Lehigh Ave., Cranford, NJ 07016. Phone (201) 276-6889.

THE MOUSE CLUB Interested in all aspects of Disneyana. Publishes "The Mouse Club Newsletter" and holds annual convention. Contact: Kim & Julie McEuen, 2056 Cirone Way, San Jose, CA 95124. Phone (408) 377-2590.

THE NATIONAL ASSOCIATION OF FAN CLUBS A national association of celebrity fan clubs. Publishes "The Fan Club Monitor." (Quarterly as part of membership) and "The Fan Club Directory" (Annual $7.00 charge). Contact: Blanche Trinajstick, 2730 Baltimore Avenue, Pueblo, CO 81003. Phone (719) 543-6708.

NATIONAL FANTASY FAN CLUB Interested in all aspects of Disneyana. Publishes "Fantasyline." Holds national convention annually in July. Ten local chapters nationwide meeting regularly. Contact: Nicolasa C. Nevarez, P.O. Box 19212, Irvine, CA 92713. Phone (818) 509-1687.

THE "OFFICIAL" McCALLUM OBSERVER Fan club interested in David McCallum's present and past career. Publishes "The Observer." Contact: Lynda Mendoza, P.O. Box 165, Downers Grove, IL 60515-0165. Phone (708) 852-6518.

ONCE UPON A TIME (THE PRISONER) FAN CLUB Fans interested in the TV series "The Prisoner." Publishes "Once Upon A Time." Contact: David Lawrence, 515 Ravenel Circle, Seneca, SC 29678. Phone (803) 654-6187.

OUR LITTLE SECRET PRESS Interested in the TV series "Alias Smith and Jones." Also, actors Pete Duel and Ben Murphy and producer Roy Huggins. Publishes "Just You, Me and The Governor." Contact: Cinda Gillilan, P.O. Box 40247, Tucson, AZ 85717.

PEANUTS COLLECTOR CLUB Club for fans of the "Peanuts" comic strip and collectors of memorabilia. Publishes "Peanuts Collector" and holds a convention every four years. Contact: Andrea Podley, P.O. Box 94, N. Hollywood, CA 91603. Phone (818) 766-7954.

PETER BRECK FAN CLUB Interested in Peter Breck's current work with his acting academy and in movies. Also in Peter's TV series ("The Big Valley" and "Black Saddle"), movies and his work in the theater. Contact: Marilyn Bieler, Box 70, Mecklenburg, NY 14863.

PETE DUEL COMMEMORATIVE FAN CLUB Club devoted to actor Peter Duel. Publishes "Duel Memories." Contact: Cinda Gillilan, P.O. Box 40247, Tucson, AZ 85717.

PETER DUEL REMEMBRANCE CLUB Club devoted to actor Peter Duel. Object is to learn about his career, help fans add to their collections and make contact with other fans through pen pal listings. Contact: Melody Cecko, 2091 Duluth Street, Maplewood, MN 55109. Phone (612) 483-9180.

PINK SQUADRON "Battlestar Galactica" squadron-format club featuring missions, games, other "assignments." Member of B-1. Publishes "Pink Squadron Newsletter." Contact: Captain Tamara (c/o Krystina Robinson), 6451 Cowles Mt. Blvd., San Diego, CA 92119.

THE PRISONER APPRECIATION SOCIETY The Prisoner Appreciation Society (known also as "Six of One") is the oldest and largest officially recognized fan organization for the 1967 British cult television program "The Prisoner" starring Patrick McGoohan. The society is based in England but has members worldwide. Publishes "Number Six Magazine," (quarterly) and holds annual member convention in Portmeirion Wales, UK. Contact: Bruce Clark, American Coordinator, The Prisoner Appreciation Society, 871 Clover Drive, North Wales, PA 19454.

RECON SQUADRON "Battlestar Galactica" squadron-format club – specialists mission club. A member of B-1. Contact: Captain Crystalrose (c/o Heather Hobson), 5324 Manila Ave., Oakland, CA 94618.

"SIGHT SOUND STYLE" MAGAZINE Quarterly magazine devoted to vintage TV's and "Deco" radios. Contact: SSS, P.O. Box 2224, So. Hackensack, NJ 07606.

SILVER SQUADRON "Battlestar Galactica" squadron-format club – 11-year-old club focusing on BG. A member of B-1. Publishes "Silver Squadron Report." Contact: Captain Starlight (c/o Ellie Claassen), 1740-47 Avenue SW, Calgary, Alberta, Canada T2T 2S2.

SMURF COLLECTORS CLUB INTERNATIONAL Members are collectors of Smurf memorabilia 1957 to present. Publishes "Smurf Collectors Newsletter." Contact: Suzanne Lipschitz, S.C.C.I., 24 Cabot Road West Dept. H, Massapequa, NY 11758. Phone (516) 799-4294.

SPOTLIGHT – LEONARD NIMOY INTN'L FAN CLUB Fan club interested in Leonard Nimoy. Publishes "Spotlight" newsletter and issues occasional fanzines. Holds annual Leonard Nimoy convention. Contact: Carol Davies, 77 The Ridings, Ealing, London, England W5 3DP. Phone 081-997-7755.

SQUADRON CONTROL Interested in stories & artwork based on Battlestar Galactica genre. Publishes "Squadron Control Fanzine." Contact: (Miss) Louise Smith, R.R. #5 Read Road, Niagara-On-The-Lake, Ontario, Canada L0S 1J0. Phone (416) 934-3988.

STAR TREK: THE OFFICIAL FAN CLUB Interested in all aspects of Star Trek – past, present and future. Publishes "Star Trek: The Official Fan Club Magazine." Contact: Dan Madsen, P.O. Box 111000, Aurora, CO 80011. Phone (303) 341-1813.

STAR TREKKERS/ALL CHANNELS OPEN Club interested in the universe of "Star Trek," space, and the science of today. Publishes "Star Trekkers/All Channels Open." Contact: Vicky Walters, c/o J.A. Siefert, P.O. Box 286, Wildwood, FL 34785.

STAR TREK WELCOMMITTEE STAR TREK information service that will provide details on over 300 clubs, 400 fanzines, 100 books, conventions, etc. Publishes the STW Directory. Contact: Star Trek Welcommittee, Box 12, Saranac, MI 48881.

THE TV COLLECTOR Magazine that publishes articles about TV shows and stars of the past. Sample issue, $3.00. Contact: TVC Enterprises/Diane Albert, P.O. Box 188, Needham, MA 02192. Phone (508) 238-1179.

TELEVISION HISTORY MAGAZINE Bi-monthly magazine devoted to TV history. Sample copy $3.00 (or $5.00 overseas). Contact: William J. Felchner, 700 E. Macoupin St., Staunton, IL 62088. Phone (618) 635-2712.

WESTERNS & SERIALS FAN CLUB The club consists of a publication where members can share their views on old western and serial films, and find a source for material related to those fields. Publishes "Westerns & Serials" magazine (quarterly). Contact: Norman Kietzer, Route One, Box 103, Vernon Center, MN 56090. Phone (507) 549-3677.

YELLOW SQUADRON "Battlestar Galactica" squadron-format club – all female squad, with written missions. A member of B-1. Contact: Captain Eilona (c/o Irene Senkoff), P.O. Box 2223, Portland, OR 97208-2223.

BIBLIOGRAPHY

Brooks, Tim & Marsh, Earle. *The Complete Directory to Prime Time Network TV Shows 1946-Present.* (Revised Edition) New York: Ballantine Books, 1981.

Brown, Les. *Les Brown's Encyclopedia of Television.* New York: New York Zoetrope, 1982.

Fireman, Judy. ed. *TV BOOK – The ultimate Television Book.* New York: Workman Publishing Company, 1977.

Greenfield, Jeff. *Television – The First Fifty Years.* New York: Harry N. Abrams, 1977.

Grossman, Gary H. *Saturday Morning TV.* New York: Arlington House, 1987.

Hake, Ted. *Hake's Americana & Collectibles Auction Catalogues Nos. 68-108.* York, Pa: 1982-1990.

Hake, Ted and King, Russ. *Price Guide To Collectible Pin-Back Buttons 1896-1986.* York, Pa: Americana & Collectibles Press, 1986.

Hake, Theodore L. and Cauler, Robert D. *Sixgun Heroes – A Price Guide To Movie Cowboy Collectibles.* Des Moines, Iowa: Wallace-Homestead Book Co., 1976.

Harris, Jay S. ed. *TV Guide – The First 25 Years.* New York: Simon and Schuster, 1978.

Lenburg, Jeff. *The Encyclopedia of Animated Cartoon Series.* Westport, Connecticut: Arlington House Publishers, 1981.

McNeil, Alex. *Total Television – A Comprehensive Guide to Programming from 1948 to the Present.* Second Edition. New York: Penguin Books, 1984.

Mitz, Rick. *The Great TV Sitcom Book.* Expanded Edition. New York: Perigee Books, 1988.

Overstreet, Robert M. *The Official Overstreet Comic Book Price Guide, No. 20.* New York: The House of Collectibles, 1990.

Rovin, Jeff. *The Great Television Series.* New York: A.S. Barnes and Company, 1977.

NAME INDEX

Actual names of persons are listed alphabetically by last name. Names of characters are listed alphabetically by first name. Show titles are listed alphabetically in the Table of Contents.

179

Grant, Kirby 136
Grassle, Karen 97
Graves, Peter 63, 109
Gray Ghost 69
Gray, Erin 30
Green Hornet 37, 69-70
Greenbush, Lindsay 97
Greenbush, Sidney 97
Greene, Lorne 21, 27
Greene, Richard 9
Greg Brady 29
Greg Garrison, Lt. 65
Griffith, Andy 14
Grimes, Jack 152
Grizzly Adams 97
Gumby 71
Gunther Toody 38
Gwynne, Fred 38, 112

H

Hack, Shelly 40
Hackett, Buddy 164
Haggerty, Dan 97
Hagman, Larry 84
Hale, Alan 67-68
Hale, Barbara 117
Hall, Jon 122
Hamilton Burger 117
Hamilton, Bernie 142
Hamilton, John 10
Hanna, William (See Hanna-Barbera)
Hanna-Barbera 6, 16, 18, 38, 57, 59, 82-83, 88, 93, 97, 103, 121, 132, 151, 153, 157, 162
Hans Dietrich, Capt. 124
Hans Schultz, Sgt. 76
Hardin, Ty 40
Hardy Boys 72-73
Hardy Har Har 97
Hardy, Oliver 93
Harmon, Larry 29, 93-94
Harper, Ron 65, 119
Harriman Nelson, Admiral 156
Harris, Jonathan 101
Harrison, Noel 68
Hart, John 98
Hartline, Mary 143-144
Hashimoto 75
Hawkeye Pierce, Capt. B.F. 102
Hawkins, Jimmy 14
Hawn, Goldie 93
Hayes, George (Gabby) 63-64, 79
Heckle and Jeckle 74-75, 108
Hector Heathcote 75
Hedison, David 156
Helena Russell, Dr. 138

Henderson, Florence 29
Henry Blake, Lt. Col. 102
Herman Munster 112-114
Hickman, Darryl 105-106
Hickman, Dwayne 105
Hodge, Al 37
Hokey Wolf 82-83
Holland, Steve 58
Honey West 76
Honeymooners 86-87
Honor Blackman 17
Hopalong Cassidy 77-79
Hope, Bob 54
Hopper, William 117
Horton, Robert 156-157
Horwich, Dr. Frances 50
Hoss Cartwright 27-28
Hot Lips Houlihan, Maj. 102
Hovis, Larry 76
Howard, Ron 14, 72
Howdy Doody 36, 63, 71, 79-82
Huckleberry Hound 82-83, 162
Huggy Bear 142
Human Torch 57
Humble Tiger 148
Hunt, Alan 156
Hush Puppy 134-135
Hutch Hutchinson 142
Hutchins, Will 40

I

Illya Kuryakin 104-105
Imperious Leader 22
Incredible Hulk 86
Inspector Fenwick 34
Inspector Henderson 10
Invisible Girl 57

J

J. Fred Muggs 151
Jace Pearson 145
Jack Moffitt, Sgt. 124
Jackson, Kate 40
Jaime Sommers 27
James Kinchloe, Cpl. 76
James Kirk, Captain 140, 142
James West 160
Jan Brady 29
Jane Jetson 88
Jason, Rick 43
Jeannie 84
Jed Clampett 26
Jeff Miller 92
Jeff Spencer 134
Jess Harper 91
Jethro Bodine 26

Jetsons 88-89
Jill Munroe 40
Jim Bowie 7
Jim Hardie 145
Jim Newton 63
Jim Phelps 109
Jim Sinclair 44
Jimmy Olsen 10
Jingles 12
Jody 56
Joe Hardy 72
Joe Jitsu 49
Joey Newton 63
John Boy Walton 158
John Drake 132-133
John Koenig, Commander 138
John Mosby, Major 69
John Robinson 101
John Walton 158
Johnny Ringo 43-44
Johnny Yuma 125
Johnson, Arte 93
Johnson, Brad 14
Johnson, Russell 67
Jolo 63
Jonathan Steed 17
Jones, Anissa 56
Jones, Carolyn 6
Jones, Davy 111
Jones, Dick 31, 123
Jones, Shirley 116
Jonesy 91
Josh Randall 159
Judegast, Hans 124
Judge Henry Garth 156
Judy Jetson 88
Judy Robinson 101
Jughead Jones 15
Julia 89
Julia Baker 89
Julie Barnes 111
June Cleaver 95

K

K-9 52
Kaltor 20
Kane, Bob 18
Kaplan, Gabriel 160
Kate Bradley, 118
Kate McCoy 125
Kato 69-70
Kaye, Linda 118
Keeshan, Bob 36, 79
Keith Partridge 116
Keith, Brian 56
Kelley, DeForest 140

OTHER COLLECTIBLES PRICE GUIDES
BY
TED HAKE

The Button Book *(out of print)*

Buttons in Sets with Marshall N. Levin

Collectible Pin-Back Buttons 1896-1986: An Illustrated Price Guide with Russ King

The Encyclopedia of Political Buttons 1896-1972; Political Buttons Book II 1920-1976; Political Buttons Book III 1789-1916

The Encyclopedia of Political Buttons: 1990 Revised Prices for Books I, II, and III

Non-Paper Sports Collectibles: An Illustrated Price Guide with Roger Steckler

Sixgun Heroes: A Price Guide to Movie Cowboy Collectibles with Robert Cauler

A Treasury of Advertising Collectibles *(out of print)*